THE
COUNTRY
GOURMET
COOKBOOK

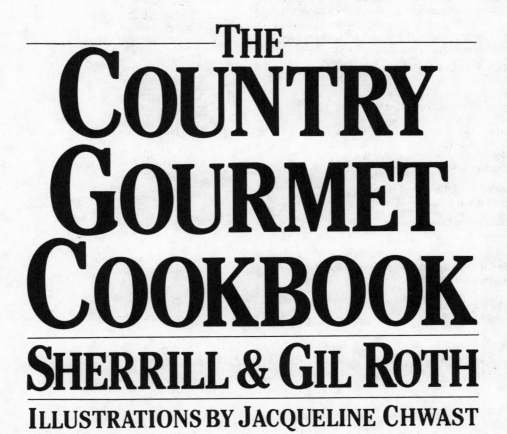

The
COUNTRY
GOURMET
COOKBOOK

SHERRILL & GIL ROTH

ILLUSTRATIONS BY JACQUELINE CHWAST

WORKMAN PUBLISHING, NEW YORK

Library of Congress Cataloging in Publication Data

Roth, Sherrill.
   The country gourmet cookbook.

   1.   Cookery.   I. Roth, Gil.   II. Title.
TX715.R846   641.5   81-40505
ISBN 0-89480-187-2   AACR2
ISBN o-89480-188-0 (pbk.)

Cover design and painting: Paul Hanson
Book design: Florence Cassen Mayers

Workman Publishing Company, Inc.
1 West 39 Street
New York, New York 10018

Manufactured in the United States of America
First printing November 1981

10 9 8 7 6 5 4 3 2 1

FOR RUSTY

ACKNOWLEDGMENTS

We wish to thank Lydie Pinoy Marshall for three inspiring years of classes in her extraordinary cooking school. If we were still in New York, we would be signed up as "lifers," just like most of her students who ask if they may study with her forever. Also, we remember the congenial series of classes with James Beard, who not only taught us the basic techniques of cooking, but impressed upon us the necessity for proper equipment and its care.

With very special feelings, we want to mention the late Moira Henry, a very close friend with whom we spent many, many years sharing recipes and thoughts about food. It was about 10 years ago that Moira called one day to say she had just prepared the most exciting sauce and must bring us some. It was pesto and we too, felt we had never savored such a sauce. This was only one of dozens of new foods Moira introduced us to.

To our editor, Suzanne Rafer, we owe so much for approaching us with the idea to write this book, for sticking with us throughout, and for always remaining cheerful. It is impossible to recount all the help she has given us.

And to Craig Claiborne, who is not only a brilliant food writer and chef de cuisine, but an extremely warm and gracious friend. We want to thank Craig for "coming to dinner."

A BOUNTIFUL LARDER

After living for many years in New York City's Greenwich Village, we moved to a small city in the South. At first we were dismayed that many of the foods we had come to take for granted were no longer available to us and that wonderful vegetable markets like the ones in which we had shopped daily did not exist. But with a little exploration and experimentation, we found that there are many foods that are better in our area than in New York, and that many others can either be made from scratch, grown, or ordered by mail.

The produce from our local farmers' market quickly replaced our longing for the city shops and inspired us to begin an extensive garden of our own. Now it is doing so well that we hardly need to shop at the farmers' market at all, but only visit to chat.

Living in an area known for its dairies, eggs, and chickens, we have the best ingredients for many recipes. But, although milk and buttermilk are superior, this is not true of all dairy products, so we have learned to make our own cottage cheese and yogurt and have developed recipes that use these two basics.

Breads and pastas proved to be more difficult, but mainly because we wanted to develop recipes that came close to the breads and pastas we missed. We think the recipes we have developed are even better.

As we continued creating our recipes and enlarging our garden, we gradually worked out a routine that made it possible to do all of this without an undue amount of work. The rewards have been such that we are eating better than ever and with a greater appreciation of our foods. We hope to encourage others to do the same, whether in a city with everything available or in an area where one must use some ingenuity to avoid the overprocessed convenience foods that are taking up far too much space in our markets.

The book is arranged by the month for several reasons. Each month features a new project or technique to be learned and many of the foods are seasonal to correspond with our garden or with what should be available in the markets. At the end of each chapter, we suggest items that may need to be purchased or ordered and finally, a few notes about our garden. They are more personal than professional, and we realize that what is flourishing in our garden in July may not be at the same time in other areas. The notes are included mainly because of our fondness for gardening and our earnest interest in creating recipes that are seasonal. If used in this manner, our book may be considered as a primer for becoming more self-sufficient. We hope that it will be enjoyed.

Sherrill & Gil Roth

CONTENTS

JULY

A MONTH OF SUMMER VEGETABLES . .255
As fresh vegetables become more plentiful, whether in the garden or in the market, prepare them in any of these delicious ways.

AUGUST

APPETIZING ONE-DISH MEALS 279
The garden eggplants are finally bearing fruits; spaghetti squash and Swiss chard are blooming. Use them in pizzas, gratins, and tians, all surprisingly easy one-dish summer suppers.

SEPTEMBER

PASTA 303
There is no substitute for homemade pasta, whether served simply with a sauce of fresh tomatoes or dressed with avocados and cream.

OCTOBER

GOOD OLD COUNTRY CORN 341
A favorite grain presented in standards like

Corn Pudding and more unique selections like Baked Polenta with Blue Cheese Sauce.

NOVEMBER

REAPING THE REWARDS 361
Time to relax your gardening efforts and enjoy some warming recipes, including a Portuguese Kale Soup from Provincetown, Martha Roth's Braised Cabbage with Noodles, and Hoppin' John.

DECEMBER

DESSERTS AND HOLIDAY GIFT IDEAS . .381
A few of our favorite sweets plus gift ideas that reflect our love of things homemade.

MAIL-ORDER SOURCES AND INDEX

If food or garden supplies and equipment aren't available locally, you can always send away for them.

JANUARY

OUR BASIC BREADS

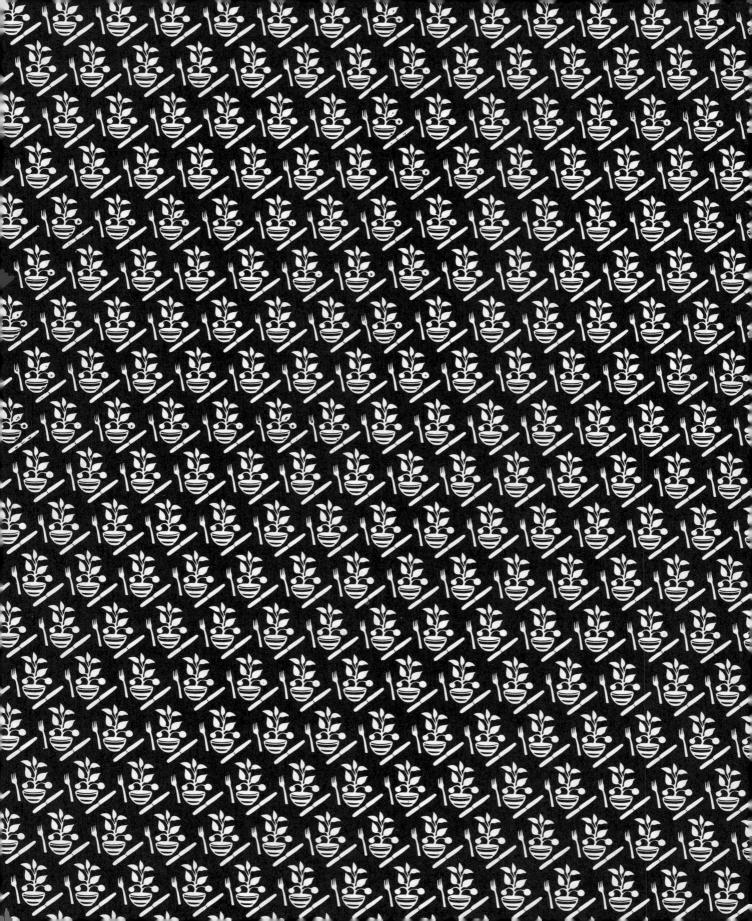

OUR BASIC BREADS

When we moved to North Carolina, our first culinary goal was to be able to bake the long, slender loaves of crusty bread which we could no longer buy fresh from a local bakery. It was our most difficult and, finally, our most rewarding venture. We experimented for over a year, trying every recipe we could find. Some were simple, but yielded breads with a crust that softened within hours. Others were difficult to prepare and unpredictable in their results.

In addition to innumerable recipes, we tried every type of baking pan and stone, dozens of flours, and a half-dozen brands of yeast.

Then one day, there they were — the loaves we had been striving for! To make sure that our success was not a fluke, we baked the bread the next day, stuffing ourselves (and friends) with the wonderful results.

Once we perfected the basic baguette loaf, we began to experiment with combinations of flours, additional ingredients such as cheese and herbs, and different shapes for the loaves. Essentially, the recipe remains the same, so if you master the basic baguette, you can prepare all of the variations. On some days, we begin the bread without having decided which type we will bake, and later, during the first or second rising, we determine whether we are in the mood for baguettes, one

big round loaf, or a loaf with sesame seeds.

When making the loaves for the first time, use a commercial, all-purpose, unbleached flour from the supermarket, as it will be easier to work with. Then progress to the more difficult flour combinations suggested in the recipes. As you experiment, you will find the combination of flours that you prefer (see Flour and Yeast, page 14).

We have become so accustomed to baking our bread two or three times a week, that it is done as part of the morning routine, requiring little time or headwork. If you plan to serve the bread for dinner, the initial mixing and kneading of the dough should be done before 11 A.M. With a little practice, this can be done in less than 15 minutes.

Long risings mean better bread

Never rush the bread. Except for one variation, the Dill Bread, all of our loaves have three slow risings. The three risings give the bread time to develop flavor and texture. Most of the variations included require that the dough triple in volume for the first two risings, rather than just doubling. This, too, develops the flavor and texture.

We like the long risings as it means we do not have to "hang around," but can go about other business for two to three hours, knowing that our bread dough is content. The first rising will take about 3 hours to triple at a temperature of 65°F to 80°F. The second rising will take from 2 to 2½ hours to triple, and the final rising about 1½ hours to double. Warmer or cooler weather can vary the times by approximately ½ hour. (We have successfully baked our bread on *very* humid, 90°F days and had loaves that retained their crusts after cooling. Closer attention was paid to the risings, though.)

Most of the time we use whey as the liquid in our breads. Because we make cottage cheese often, we always have some of this by-product on hand and have developed several delicious uses for it. In bread the whey seems to bring out the flavor of the flours without overwhelming the loaves with its own rather unique bouquet. Do not judge the flavor it will impart to breads by sampling it "straight." In breads, the taste is very subtle.

Getting it right

If, when you bake the bread for the first time, the loaves should not be as plump or good-looking as you would like, do not despair. They will still taste delicious. In experimenting with flours, we used one that just refused to triple and would hardly even double. Finally, the hour was so late and we were so aggravated because guests were expected for dinner, that we punched the dough down, formed the loaves, and gave them 2 hours for the third rising. They hardly budged. We baked them anyway, thinking all had been a waste. They were wonderful! Our guests missed them for dinner since the bread came out of the oven just as they were leaving, but we still managed to devour two loaves spread with the Strawberry Jam on page 135 before they left. In other words, keep working on your bread baking until you have mastered the art. Soon you will be able to recognize your mistakes as well as those of other bakers: "stretch marks," air

bubbles that have burst, poor slashing, to name a few. You will have become the "expert."

FLOUR AND YEAST

Finding good flours for our breads proved to be as much of a task as working out our recipes. Basically, we wanted a readily available, all-purpose, unbleached flour that would give our breads the proper texture and a superior flavor. After testing the flours from the larger mills that distribute nationally, we found the all-purpose, unbleached flour from General Mills to be the most reliable.

One brand that we tried from the supermarket that claimed to be unbleached was so full of chlorine that our bread tasted as if it had been made with a household cleanser. The first bite told us the bread only would be useful for scrubbing the sink. Now when we test a new flour, we mix a few tablespoons of it with water *and* give it a "sniff test" for an indication of what to expect. We suggest you do the same.

We were also disappointed in the so-called "bread flour." It did give our breads a good crust; however, the crusts fell apart and left the breads as they were sliced. Not only that, it seemed to lack any flavor.

For flavor, our favorite unbleached white flour is the one that we mail order from Walnut Acres. They grow and mill their own flour, as well as selling organic flours from other mills. Their bread flour contains a small amount of bran which gives the flour an excellent taste, plus a little bit of color. For our recipes, it is difficult to knead if used alone, so we combine it with the all-purpose, using 3 cups of all-purpose and 2½ cups of Walnut Acres.

Another outstanding flour is the unbleached white flour from El Molino Mills. The flour is made from hard wheat and need not be combined for use in our recipes. They do not ship and the flour can be difficult to obtain, but it is worth looking for. You may write or call them for the source nearest you. The address is 345 North Baldwin Park Boulevard, City of Industry, California 91746.

Other flours

For our other flours, such as whole-wheat, graham, and buckwheat, we mail order from Walnut Acres and the Vermont Country Store. Walnut Acres carries the flours from Arrowhead Mills, who perhaps have the best whole-wheat flour of all. It is often referred to as Deaf Smith County Whole-wheat. Arrowhead Mills no longer ships, but if you write, they will send you a wonderful free catalog filled with information about the growing and milling of their numerous products. Their address is P.O. Box 866, Hereford, Texas 79045.

Whatever flour you use for your breads, try to find one that is designated a hard-wheat flour, as opposed to a soft-wheat flour which is best for pastries. Hard wheat contains more gluten, a protein which helps bread to rise and hold its shape. Hard-wheat flour may be from either spring wheat or winter wheat. Spring wheat is planted in the spring and harvested in the fall. It is primarily grown in our most northern states. Winter wheat is planted in the fall and harvested in the spring. It is grown all over the United States.

In our recipes, we have given approximate sizes of the loaves after baking. This will vary, depending upon the flour you use. If you are using a flour from the supermarket, your loaves will probably be slightly larger and lighter in texture than they will be when your bread is a mixture of the supermarket flour and a "heavier" flour, such as Walnut Acres. To us, this is an advantage, as it gives us even more range for experimentation.

Ideally, all of your flours should be refrigerated or frozen, but this is impossible for us as we order in quantity. We do refrigerate our yeast, whole wheat, bran, cornmeal, and buckwheat, but for lack of space, we do not refrigerate the unbleached white flour. With any flour, there is always the possibility of insects developing from eggs that have escaped detection when the flour was packaged. Under refrigeration, the temperature is too cold for the eggs to hatch. Our solution is to keep the flours that cannot be refrigerated or frozen tightly closed, in the coolest, driest spot we can find. We check the flours periodically for any signs of "hatching." It has been rare (and never with Walnut Acres) that we have had a "hatching." If it does happen, the bugs can usually be sifted out and the flour still used. Flour should be discarded, though, if it shows signs of mold.

Purchasing yeast

For our active, dry yeast, we again order from Walnut Acres. It is incomparable for flavor and performance. It is more granular than other yeasts and will take a few more minutes to "proof" than ordinary yeast. The other yeast we recommend is from El Molino Mills, but again, it may be difficult to find. We do like fresh cake yeast (compressed), but we are unable to purchase it. All of our recipes call for 1 tablespoon of the active dry variety, but if you wish to use the fresh, use ½ ounce for the 1 tablespoon. Fresh yeast must be "proofed" at a lower temperature, so make sure that your warm water or whey is not over 90°F.

Although we have listed our preferences for flour and yeast, this does not mean that you should not experiment with ones that you are able to obtain. In our area, there are still a few small millers who produce only enough flour to sell locally. One stone grinds a remarkable coarse whole wheat and a white cornmeal. Another mills an unbleached white flour which makes exceptional pasta.

BAKING YOUR BREADS

For successful baking, you must be sure that your oven's temperature is accurate. Always use an oven thermometer and if the temperature does not fall within 10°F of the desired setting, have a qualified person repair the oven for you. Every place we have lived has been furnished with an inaccurate oven. One overheated to such an extent that a soufflé rose 10 inches, almost to the ceiling of the oven. It was a sight to see, but hardly edible, being nothing but a hollow crust with a bit of undone soufflé mixture at the bottom. Now we have made sure our oven is always correctly adjusted.

Except for the baguettes and for the times when we use loaf pans, we prefer to bake our breads on a baking stone. The breads can breathe through the porous stone as they bake, resulting in a more even baking and a better crust and flavor. However, if you do not have a baking stone, our recipes can be baked in baguette pans or on baking sheets.

If you use sheets or pans

Black steel conducts heat more evenly and will give your loaves a darker crust. Aluminum pans will not. Baking sheets, baguette pans, and loaf pans are all available in heavy black steel through mail-order sources.

Before using your pans for the first time, they will need some "seasoning." Instructions come with the pans. After the initial seasoning, any further seasoning is best accomplished by constant use. Our pans are so seasoned that they require no more cleaning than a brushing off of the crumbs after the loaves are baked.

When using sheets or pans for baking, they should be sprinkled liberally with cornmeal before the loaves are placed on them for their final rising. Do not oil the sheets or pans except for the loaf pan, which should be lightly oiled with corn oil and the cornmeal eliminated.

For breads baked on sheets or in pans, steam is necessary in the oven to create the proper crust and texture in the breads. The easiest way to create this steam is to half fill a shallow pan with water and place it in the lower third of the oven as it is preheated. We use the bottom of our roasting pan. The quantity of water should be such that it will have almost evaporated by the time the breads have baked.

If you use a baking stone

The final rising after shaping the loaves should take place on a wooden peel (paddle), liberally sprinkled with cornmeal. If no peel is available, you may use a heavy piece of cardboard sprinkled with cornmeal. Before sliding the breads from the peel into the oven, shake the peel back and forth several times to be sure that the breads will slide easily onto the stone. This way, no heat is lost from the oven when you open the door.

The baking stone should be placed in the lower third of the oven as you preheat the oven. This should be done 20 minutes prior to baking.

We find that with the baking stone, the pan of water is not necessary. The stone allows the bread to breathe as it bakes, and this is sufficient.

Never remove the baking stone from the oven until it has cooled completely. If you need the oven for additional cooking, just leave the stone in place. This will help season the stone and the more the stone is "seasoned," the stronger it will become.

If a stone becomes soiled, do not clean it with detergent as it will absorb the taste. Our bread stone needs only to be brushed free of crumbs when it has cooled. The pizza stone is occasionally scoured with hot water and a metal pad that contains no soap.

We strongly recommend that you purchase the baking stones. Ours have been in constant use for three years and we feel they are like members of the family.

Glazing your bread

Once our loaves are baked, whether on the baking stone, in or on pans, we, for the most part, do *not* glaze them, not even with water. We tried the various methods of glazing and found that none made a substantial difference in the color or crust. Brushing them with butter only changed the flavor, not for the better, and the butter became rancid very quickly. Sometimes we brush the round peasant loaves with olive oil. This, too, changes the flavor, but beneficially.

BAGUETTES

We call our long loaves Baguettes although ours are actually more like a bâtard, a shorter and wider loaf. The measurements for the ingredients remain the same for all of our variations, with the exception of the Braided Cottage Cheese Bread on page 34, which requires more flour. With these measurements memorized and after you've baked the bread a few times you will no longer have to refer to the recipe.

It is not necessary to use a food processor for mixing and kneading the dough; it is easily done in a large mixing bowl, which is then used for the dough as it rises. We bake our loaves on an extra-heavy black steel baking sheet, 19½ × 13 inches. (See Baking Your Breads, page 16.) If you are wary about this you may bake the loaves in baguette pans.

Makes 3 loaves, 18 inches long by 2½ to 3 inches in diameter; or 4 loaves, 18 inches long by 2 inches in diameter

> **1 tablespoon active, dry yeast (see Flour and Yeast, page 14)**
> **2 cups warm water or whey (105° F)**
> **5½ cups flour (see Flour and Yeast)**
> **1 tablespoon salt**
> **1 teaspoon corn oil**
> **Several tablespoons cornmeal for the baking sheet or pans**

1. In a large mixing bowl with a 3-quart capacity, dissolve the yeast in the warm water or whey. Give the yeast time to "proof" (foam). This will take from 5 to 10 minutes, depending upon the yeast. When the yeast has "proofed," add 1 cup of the flour and the tablespoon of salt. With a wooden spoon, mix thoroughly.

2. Continue adding flour, ½ cup or so at a time, until all but 1 cup of the flour has been used.

Mix thoroughly after each addition.

3. Begin kneading the dough in the bowl and as soon as you are able to gather up the dough, scrape it from the bowl onto your floured work surface. Continue to knead the dough, adding more flour as necessary. Reserve ¼ cup of the flour for later use.

Knead the dough vigorously for about 10 minutes until it is smooth. The kneaded dough should spring back into shape immediately after inserting and withdrawing two fingers ½ inch into the center of the dough.

Form the dough into a ball by cupping it with your hands and turning it on your work surface in a clockwise fashion.

4. Let the dough rest for about 3 minutes while you wash the mixing bowl. This small rest period will allow the gluten in the flour to relax so that the final 2 minutes of kneading will be easier.

After cleaning the mixing bowl, oil it with the corn oil.

5. Knead the dough vigorously for another 2 minutes. Form it into a ball and place it into the oiled mixing bowl.

Cover the bowl loosely with a cloth towel (*never* plastic wrap) and place it in a warm spot (65° F to 80°F). We use our oven with just the light turned on. A gas oven with the pilot light on is also a good spot or place the bowl on top of the refrigerator toward the back where it is warm.

6. Let the dough rise until it has tripled in volume, which will take from 2½ to 3 hours. Give the dough a good look before it begins to rise and remember that shape to determine when it has tripled. In our mixing bowl, the dough will have risen about 3 inches above the rim when it has tripled.

It is not imperative that the rising be exact. The range can be 2½ to 3 times in volume without jeopardizing the quality of the bread.

7. When the dough has approximately tripled in volume, punch it down and return it to your floured work surface. Knead again, adding some of the reserved flour as necessary, for 3 minutes. Return the dough to the mixing bowl, cover with the cloth towel, and let the dough rise a second time to triple in volume. This rising time will be about 2 hours.

If, during these risings, the dough develops something of a crust, do not worry. Once the dough is kneaded and rises again, the crust will disappear. It is much better to have this happen than to have the dough become soggy from being covered with plastic wrap. Also, the flour and yeast must breathe to develop their best flavor.

8. When the dough has tripled for the second time, punch it down and place it on your floured work surface. Do not knead the dough; it is now time to form the loaves, and you do not want to activate the gluten as it will make the dough more difficult to work with.

Flatten the ball of dough with your hands into a rectangle, approximately 10 × 5 inches. Depending upon whether you will be making 3 or 4 loaves, cut the dough crosswise into equal pieces.

If you are using a baking sheet (see Step 9), cut the dough into 3 pieces. If you are using the baguette pans (you will need two pans), cut the dough into 4 pieces.

Set the pieces aside on a floured section of your work surface as you prepare your baking sheet or pans. Again, this brief rest of several minutes will relax the dough.

9. We form our loaves of bread in such a way that the shaped baguette pans are not neces-

sary. This is done by folding and creating tension in the loaves as they are formed so that they retain their shapes as they rise for the third time.

Sprinkle your baking sheet or baguette pans liberally with cornmeal. Set aside as you form the loaves.

10. Lightly flour your work surface. Take the first piece of dough and flatten it with your hands into an oval shape approximately 6 inches long by 4 inches wide.

Bring one long edge of the dough over onto the opposite edge. Press the open edges together to form a seam. Turn the dough so that the seam faces up from your work surface.

11. Again, flatten the dough slightly by pressing down into the seam so that an indentation is made. Tuck the pointed ends of the oval into the body of the dough so that the dough now resembles an inflated raft.

Once more, bring one long edge of the dough onto the opposite side. Form a seam by pressing the open edges together. This time, turn the dough so that it is seam side down on your work surface.

12. Center your hands, one placed over the other, in the middle of the dough. With equal pressure from both hands, roll the dough back and forth, moving your hands apart from the center of the dough to the ends to form your long loaf.

With practice, you will be able to roll your dough to the desired length in this one motion. The first few times, you will probably have to do this three or four times in order to reach the desired 18-inch length (or the length of your bread pans).

At no point should the dough be pulled, as this will create "stretch marks," which will be evident after the loaves have baked. Pulling will also make the dough very tough.

13. Flour your work surface whenever it is necessary. If the weather is very humid, you may need more flour than that held in reserve.

If air bubbles should appear in the loaves as they are being rolled, pinch them firmly to release the air; they will only expand and eventually pop as the bread rises and bakes. The pinches will disappear as the bread rises.

14. As each loaf is formed, place it on your baking sheet or in the baguette pan. Continue until all of the loaves have been formed.

With a pastry brush, brush off any surface flour from the loaves; if it is not brushed off, it will remain, unbrowned, after the loaves are baked.

15. Cover the loaves with a cloth towel. Place them in a warm spot to double in bulk for the third and final rising. This will take from 1 to 1½ hours. Do not place them in your oven this time, as the oven must be preheated.

16. About 20 minutes before the loaves are ready to be baked, place a shallow pan, such as the bottom of your roasting pan, half-filled with water in the lower third of your oven. Place the other rack in the upper third of your oven. Preheat the oven to 450°F.

The pan of water will create steam in the oven, giving the bread the moisture needed for proper baking and the development of a rich crust that will not soften as the bread cools. The water will evaporate from the pan during the baking period.

17. When the loaves of bread have doubled in size, they must be slashed before baking. This will release pressure inside the loaves and allow them to rise even a little more as they are placed in the preheated oven.

A single-edge razor blade works best for slashing. The breads must be cut with three diagonal slashes, lengthwise along each loaf.

Begin by making the first slash at the end farthest away from you. The razor blade should be held at a very slight angle and not straight down.

Begin the slash about 2½ inches from the tip of the loaf and, cutting on a diagonal from right to left, make a slash about 3½ inches long and ⅓-inch deep. Make a second slash and finally a third, equally spaced along the loaf. Do not put any pressure on the risen loaves as you slash or you might deflate them.

18. Immediately, when all of the loaves have been slashed, place the baking sheet or baguette pans on the upper third rack of the preheated oven. Be prepared for a small burst of steam when you open the oven door.

19. Bake the loaves for 25 minutes. *Under no circumstances* open the oven door during the first 10 minutes of baking, as the loaves are making their final, small rising.

Since the loaves are baking at a high temperature, *do* check them after they have baked for about 18 minutes. If they are browning too quickly, cover them very loosely with aluminum foil for about 5 minutes, removing the foil for the last few minutes of baking.

During baking, the pans may buckle with the heat, but this is not a cause for alarm. The pans will regain their shapes later.

20. When the loaves have baked, take the baking sheet or pans from the oven. Remove the loaves and place them on a rack, in an airy spot, to cool.

21. Many purists will say the breads should cool for several hours before cutting and serving, but sometimes the temptation to sample is too great. We do as we please. Room temperature or hot, always cut at least 2-inch-thick slices, using a good bread knife.

22. The breads should cool completely if you wish to refrigerate or freeze them. For refrigerating or freezing, wrap the loaves tightly in aluminum foil.

When reheating, place the loaves, after they have come to room temperature, in the middle of a preheated 350°F oven for about 15 minutes. They should remain loosely wrapped in the foil as they reheat. Again, the bread may be served at room temperature or heated, but always cut generous slices, at least two inches thick.

BAGUETTES WITH SESAME SEEDS

Sesame seeds added to the crusts of the Baguettes give them a different flavor. The recipe remains almost the same except for the addition of the seeds.

Makes 3 loaves, 18 inches long by 2½ to 3 inches in diameter; or 4 loaves, 18 inches long by 2 inches in diameter

In addition to the ingredients on page 17 you need:
⅓ cup raw, hulled sesame seeds

1. Follow Steps 1 through 8 for Baguettes.

2. In Step 9 for baguettes, sprinkle your baking sheet or baguette pans with approximately ⅓ of the sesame seeds after they have been sprinkled with the cornmeal. Set aside.

3. Follow Steps 10 through 16 for baguettes.

4. When the loaves of bread have doubled in size, using a small pastry brush, carefully brush their surfaces with water. (Do not let the water dribble onto your baking sheet or pans as the breads will stick.) This will enable the sesame seeds to adhere to the loaves.

Place the remaining seeds in a small, shallow bowl. Using your fingers, pick up a teaspoon or so of the seeds at a time and sprinkle them on the loaves.

Once the surfaces are lightly coated, begin dipping your fingers, held together and straight out, first into the water and then into the remaining seeds. The seeds will stick to your fingers which you then pat onto the loaves of bread. This will take a little practice, but try to cover the loaves as evenly as possible. The more seeds, the tastier the breads.

5. When the loaves are coated with the sesame seeds, follow the instructions in Step

17 for slashing the baguettes.

6. Continue with Steps 18 through 21 for baguettes.

BAGUETTES WITH CRACKED WHEAT

The Baguettes become a different bread when cracked wheat is used as part of the flour. Do not confuse *cracked* wheat with bulgur (burghul), which is steamed before it is crushed. Cracked wheat is made from the dry, whole kernels of wheat, called red cereal wheat or hard red wheat berries. The whole kernels and the cracked wheat are available by mail.

We order the whole kernels and crack them in an antique coffee grinder. You may also use the Varco Coffee and Spice Grinder made by Moulinex (check the mail-order listings), but food processors and blenders do not work. Crack only a small amount at a time. Use 1 cup cracked wheat as part of the 5½ cups of flour being sure not to grind the kernels too fine so that the loaves will have more texture.

Makes 3 loaves, 18 inches long by 2½ to 3 inches in diameter; or 4 loaves, 18 inches long by 2 inches in diameter

1. In Step 1 for Baguettes, use the 1 cup of cracked wheat in place of the first cup of flour added to the yeast mixture. Mix thoroughly with a wooden spoon.

2. Continue with Steps 2 through 21 until the breads are completed.

ROUND LOAVES

After our success with Baguettes, we decided to experiment, using the same basic measurements to create other shapes with different combinations of flours. Round Loaves were the first that we tried. Using the same 5½ cups of flour, our recipe will make two round loaves. Because the loaves are larger, the baking time is different from the baguettes and within the variations of the round loaves, the time varies slightly. We bake the round loaves on our baking stone, but you may bake them on a heavy, black steel baking sheet. (See Baking Your Bread, page 16.)

Makes 2 loaves, 7 inches in diameter

> **1 tablespoon dry yeast (see Flour and Yeast, page 14)**
> **2 cups warm water or whey (105° F)**
> **5½ cups flour (see Flour and Yeast)**
> **1 tablespoon salt**
> **1 teaspoon corn oil**
> **Several tablespoons of cornmeal for the peel or baking sheet**
> **1 tablespoon olive oil (optional)**

1. Follow Steps 1 through 7 for Baguettes (see page 17).

2. When the dough has tripled in volume for the second time, punch it down and place it on your floured work surface. Cut the dough into 2 equal pieces. Do not work the dough any more than necessary so as not to activate the gluten.

   Fold and shape each piece of dough to form rounds. Pinch together the open edges of the dough and make them the undersides of the loaves.

   To further shape the loaves, cup under each loaf with your hands and turn it briskly in a clockwise fashion on your work surface to form a perfect round. Pinch any air bubbles that may appear.

3. As each loaf is formed, place it on your peel or baking sheet which has been liberally sprinkled with cornmeal. Position the loaves so that they will have ample space to *double* in volume for the third and final rising.

   If the breads are rising on a peel, arrange them so they will slide from the peel to the hot baking stone without interfering with each other. Side by side with space for rising is best.

4. Cover the loaves with the cloth towel. Place the peel or baking sheet in a warm spot, but not in the oven this time, as the oven must be preheated. This third rising will take from 1 to 1½ hours.

5. About 20 minutes before the loaves are ready to be baked, preheat the oven to 450°F.

   If you are using a baking stone, place it on the lower third rack of the oven at this time.

   If you are using a baking sheet, place a shallow pan, half filled with water, on the bottom rack of the oven and position another rack in the middle of the oven. The pan of water will create steam in the oven, giving the bread the moisture needed for proper baking and a rich crust. The pan of water is not necessary when using a baking stone.

6. When the loaves have doubled in size, they must be slashed before baking. This will release pressure inside the loaves and allow them to rise even a little more during the first 10 minutes of baking.

It is particularly important that the round loaves, made with an all-purpose, unbleached flour from the supermarket, be slashed accurately. If they are not, the loaves may become lopsided as they bake. Slashing the loaves to form a checkerboard pattern almost insures perfectly shaped breads. The slashing will take a little practice, but the checkerboard loaves are the most attractive.

7. To slash the loaves with a checkerboard pattern, use a clean, very sharp, single-edge razor blade. Begin by making a vertical slash, approximately 1½ inches from the outside of the loaf. Hold the razor blade at a slight angle, not straight down, and cut about ⅓ inch into the bread. This first slash will be the shortest.

Continue making parallel slashes working toward the center of the loaf. Each slash will become longer as you keep the 1½-inch outside margin. When you reach the center, the slashes become shorter until you reach the opposite side of the loaf. The distances between the slashes are determined by your expertise. If you are a beginner, space the slashes 1¼ to 1½ inches apart. With more practice, they can be spaced ½ inch apart.

8. When the loaf has been slashed vertically, turn the peel or baking sheet so you can cut across the vertical slashes. These slashes will be more difficult. Leaving a 1½-inch outside margin, begin the slashes from the side of the bread opposite you and cut toward yourself.

If the bread tries to pull out of shape as you cut across the slashes, reverse the razor blade and cut in the opposite direction. Try to put as little pressure on the bread as possible so as not to deflate it.

If the breads have formed a light crust during the final rising, do *not* brush them with water, as it will not help in slashing the bread. Just be patient. Even if a few cracks should appear, it will not matter. (Close examination of professional bakers's loaves sometimes show these cracks.)

9. If, when you make these loaves for the first time, you do not want to attempt the checkerboard pattern, you may slash the loaves with three to five long parallel slashes. You will still have fine-looking loaves of bread.

10. Before placing the loaves in the oven, you may brush them with olive oil. This is optional. The olive oil will give the loaves a depth of color and a little extra flavor.

Use a small pastry brush and be careful not to let the olive oil run onto the peel or baking sheet. Brush the entire exposed surface very lightly with the oil.

11. *If you are using a baking sheet*, simply place it in the preheated oven on the middle rack.

If you are using a baking stone, make sure that the loaves will slide from the peel before opening the oven door. Gently thrust the peel forward to see that the loaves will leave the peel.

Open the oven door and with a strong, forward thrust, slide the loaves onto the hot baking stone. If they refuse to leave the peel, use a wide spatula to aid you.

12. Bake the loaves for 10 minutes at 450°F. Do not open the oven door during this time, as the loaves will be making one small, final rising.

After 10 minutes, lower the oven temperature to 375°F and bake the loaves for an additional 25 minutes.

Check the loaves during the last 10 minutes of baking and if they are browning too quickly, cover them lightly with aluminum foil. Remove the foil for the last few minutes of baking.

To test the loaves for doneness, remove one from the oven after the baking period is up. Tap it on the bottom and if it sounds hollow, the loaves are done.

13. Remove the loaves from the baking sheet or stone and place them on a rack in an airy spot to cool. Do *not* slice the loaves for at least 1 hour as the texture of the loaves is still being formed as they cool. A cooling period of 2 to 3 hours is even better.

If you wish to serve the bread warm, reheat it after the cooling period. Cut the bread into generous slices, about ¾-inch thick.

14. If you wish to refrigerate or freeze the bread, wrap the loaves tightly in aluminum foil after they have completely cooled.

When serving, reheat the breads, loosely wrapped in the foil, after they have come to room temperature. Heat them for 15 to 20 minutes in a preheated 350°F oven.

ROUND LOAVES WITH CRACKED WHEAT AND WHOLE-WHEAT FLOUR

For the flour in this recipe, use ½ cup of cracked wheat, 2 cups of whole-wheat flour and 3 cups of an all-purpose, unbleached flour. These loaves will have a denser texture than the round loaves made entirely with an all-purpose, unbleached flour. For this reason, it is not necessary to slash them at all, as they will rise evenly without the slashing. For decorative purposes, we usually do slash them.

The type of whole-wheat flour you use will also determine the texture of the bread. With a very fine flour, the loaves will be firmer, making a bread that can be sliced thinly for sandwiches. The coarser flours will yield breads that are best cut into thick slices. The cracked wheat may be eliminated and, if it is, use 3½ cups of the all-purpose, unbleached flour.

Makes 2 loaves, 7 inches in diameter

1. Follow Steps 1 through 11 for the Round Loaves (see page 22). Add the ½ cup of cracked wheat and whole-wheat flour to the yeast mixture before you begin to add the all-purpose, unbleached flour. (If you are not slashing the breads, eliminate Steps 6-9.)

2. Continue with Steps 10 and 11.

3. In Step 12, the loaves should bake for an additional 30 minutes after the oven has been lowered to 375°F degrees, rather than 25 minutes, for a total baking time of 40 minutes.

4. Continue with Steps 13 and 14 until the loaves are completed.

ROUND LOAVES WITH BRAN FLAKES

We like to use the bran flakes with wheat germ from Walnut Acres. Their catalog describes the flakes as being coarse, but they are actually finer than most and give the round loaves an especially good flavor.

Use only 1 cup bran as part of the basic 5½ cups of flour. As it absorbs liquid bran grows, so if you use too much your loaves will grow before your eyes and be rather unmanageable. For the remaining 4½ cups of flour, use an all-purpose, unbleached flour, and be sure to slash the loaves. If you should wish to use a combination of 2½ cups of an all-purpose, unbleached flour, 2 cups of whole-wheat flour, and the 1 cup of bran, then the loaves do not require slashing.

Makes 2 loaves, 7 inches in diameter

1. Follow Steps 1 through 9 for the Round Loaves (see page 22). Add the 1 cup of bran to the yeast mixture first, followed by the whole-wheat flour, if you are using it. If the breads do not require slashing, eliminate Steps 6 through 9.

2. Omit Step 10. Olive oil is not good on these loaves. Continue with Step 11.

3. In Step 12, the loaves should bake for an additional 30 minutes after the oven has been lowered to 375°F, rather than 25 minutes, for a total baking time of 40 minutes.

4. Continue with Steps 13 and 14 until the loaves are completed.

ROUND LOAVES WITH CORNMEAL

It is imperative that these loaves cool completely before you attempt to slice them. Otherwise, they will crumble. When thoroughly cooled, they can be cut into thin, beautifully yellow slices.

Use 1 cup of yellow cornmeal as part of the basic 5½ cups of flour. The remaining 4½ cups of flour should be an all-purpose, unbleached flour. These loaves should not be slashed.

Makes 2 loaves, 7 inches in diameter

1. Refer to the recipe for Round Loaves on page 22. Place the 1 cup of cornmeal and the 1 tablespoon of salt in a small mixing bowl. Bring ½ cup of your water or whey to a boil and pour it over the cornmeal. Stir vigorously. Let the mixture cool to lukewarm.

2. In a large mixing bowl with a 3-quart capacity, dissolve the yeast in the remaining 1½ cups of *warm* water or whey. Give the yeast time to "proof" (foam). This will take 5 to 10 minutes, depending upon the yeast.

3. When the yeast has "proofed," add 1 cup of the all-purpose, unbleached flour. With a wooden spoon, mix thoroughly. Add the cornmeal mixture. Mix thoroughly. Continue adding flour, ½ cup or so at a time, until all but 1 cup of the flour has been used. Mix well after each addition.

4. Continue with the recipe for the round loaves through Step 5, eliminating Steps 6 through 10.

5. Follow Steps 11 through 14 until the loaves are completed.

ROUND LOAVES WITH SPROUTED WHEAT BERRIES

For these loaves, use sprouted whole kernels of wheat (see Growing Sprouts, page 39). These are the same kernels that are used for the cracked wheat bread. The sprouted wheat berries will give your breads an almost sweet flavor and a definite crunch.

Some sources list the kernels as red cereal wheat or hard red wheat berries. For the flour in this bread, use 2½ cups of whole-wheat flour and 3 cups of an all-purpose, unbleached flour.

Makes 2 loaves, 7 inches in diameter

1. Three days before you plan to make the bread, begin sprouting your wheat berries, using ½ cup of the whole kernels.

On the third day, the length of the sprouts should be about ¼ inch and the sprout yield will be about 1 cup. They should not be longer than about ¼ inch, but they must be sprouted, as during baking, unsprouted kernels will become hard.

2. Follow Steps 1 through 9 for the Round Loaves (see page 22). Add the sprouted wheat berries to the yeast mixture first, followed by the whole-wheat flour and then the all-purpose, unbleached flour.

Slashing is optional, so if you do not wish to slash the breads, Steps 6 through 9 can be eliminated.

3. Omit Step 10. Olive oil is not good on these loaves. Continue with Step 11.

4. In Step 12, the loaves should bake for an additional 30 minutes after the oven has been lowered to 375°F for a total baking time of 40 minutes.

5. Continue with Steps 13 and 14 until the loaves are completed.

ROUND LOAVES WITH HERBS

These loaves are so fragrant as the dough is rising that you will want to sample them even before they are baked. The aroma of the herbs should be the most prominent flavor, so use only an all-purpose, unbleached flour for your 5½ cups.

Dry the herbs very well before chopping them. If the herbs have not been dried thoroughly, it may be necessary to add additional flour. These loaves should not be slashed.

Makes 2 loaves, 7 inches in diameter

In addition to the ingredients on page 22 you need:
1 cup finely chopped parsley
2 tablespoons of a finely chopped fresh herb, such as dill, chives, or basil
½ cup finely chopped shallots
1 teaspoon finely minced garlic

1. Prepare your herb mixture.

2. In a large mixing bowl with a 3-quart capacity, dissolve the yeast in the warm water or whey. Give the yeast time to "proof" (foam). This will take 5 to 10 minutes, depending upon the yeast.

3. When the yeast has "proofed," add 1 cup of the all-purpose, unbleached flour. With a wooden spoon, mix thoroughly.

Add the herb mixture and the tablespoon of salt, blending them into the flour. Continue adding flour, ½ cup or so at a time, until all but 1 cup of the flour has been used. Mix well after each addition.

4. Continue with the recipe for the Round Loaves through Step 5, eliminating Steps 6 through 10.

5. Follow Steps 11 through 14 until the loaves are completed.

PEASANT LOAVES

The Peasant Loaves are the same as the Round Loaves (see page 22), except that instead of making 2 loaves, we make 1 huge round loaf, approximately 10 inches in diameter. Our favorite combination of flours is to use 3½ cups of an all-purpose, unbleached flour and 2 cups of unbleached white flour from Walnut Acres. Slashed with the checkerboard pattern, the bread is spectacular.

You may use any of the recipes for the round loaves, following the instructions for each particular recipe. Instead of forming 2 loaves as in Step 2 for round loaves, make only 1 large loaf.

In Step 12, the peasant loaf should bake for an additional 45 minutes after the oven has been lowered to 375°F for a total baking time of about 55 minutes. Test the loaf for a hollow sound before removing it from the oven to cool.

Check the bread during the last 15 minutes of baking and if it is browning too quickly, cover it with aluminum foil. Remove the foil for the last few minutes of baking. The peasant loaves *must* have a cooling period of *at least* 2 hours before you attempt to slice them.

OVAL LOAVES

Experimenting with oval shapes using our same basic recipe proved to be as successful as our other variations. Again, the basic 5½ cups of flour are used and you will have 2 plump, oval loaves that can be cut into thick slices to accompany soups and salads or thin slices for sandwiches and toast.

We give the basic instructions with a few variations, but actually, you can use all of the recipes for the Round Loaves and shape them as ovals. The baking times remain the same when the round loaves are shaped into ovals. In other words, the variations are endless once you have mastered the basic instructions.

Again, we bake our oval loaves on our baking stone, but you may bake them on a heavy, black steel baking sheet. (See Baking Your Bread, page 16.)

Makes 2 loaves, 9 inches long by 4 inches in diameter

1 tablespoon dry yeast (see Flour and Yeast, page 14)
2 cups warm water or whey (105°F)
5½ cups flour (see Flour and Yeast)
1 tablespoon salt
1 teaspoon corn oil
Several tablespoons cornmeal for the peel or baking sheet

1. Follow Steps 1 through 7 for Baguettes (see page 17).

2. When the dough has *tripled* in volume for the second time, punch it down and place it on your floured work surface. Cut the dough into 2 equal pieces. Do not work the dough any more than necessary so as not to activate the gluten.

Fold and cup each piece of the dough in your hands to form a plump, oval shape, approximately 7 inches long and 3 inches in diameter. Pinch together the open edges of the dough and make them the undersides of your loaves. Pinch any air bubbles that may appear.

3. As each loaf is formed, place it on your peel or baking sheet which has been liberally sprinkled with cornmeal. Make sure that the loaves are spaced far enough apart so that

they may *double* in volume for the third and final rising.

4. Cover the loaves with a cloth towel and place them in a warm spot for this third rising, which will take from 1 to 1½ hours. Do not use the oven, as it must be preheated.

5. About 20 minutes before the loaves are ready to be baked, preheat the oven to 450°F.

If you are using a baking stone, place it on the lower third rack of the oven at this time.

If you are using a baking sheet, place a shallow pan half filled with water on the bottom rack of the oven to create steam for proper baking. Position another rack in the middle of the oven. The pan of water is not necessary with the baking stone.

6. When the loaves have doubled in size, they must be slashed before baking. This will re-

lease pressure inside the loaves and allow them to rise even a little more during the first 10 minutes of baking.

With the oval loaves, there is a choice of slash designs. The simplest method is to make three long diagonal slashes as in Step 17 for baguettes. Or you may make 3 to 5 slashes crosswise along the loaves. Our preference for slashing the oval loaves is to make a lattice pattern. This is similar to the checkerboard pattern on the round loaves.

Using a very sharp, single-edge razor blade, begin making diagonal slashes across the loaf, working from the end farthest away from you. Continue until the loaf has been slashed in one direction, top to bottom. Again, the distances between the slashes are up to you. For an especially attractive loaf, the slashes should be ½-inch apart.

Working in the opposite direction, make a second set of slashes, cutting diagonally across the first set to form a diamondlike pattern.

7. *If you are using a baking sheet*, place it in the oven on the middle rack.

If you are using a baking stone, make sure that the loaves will slide from the peel before opening the oven door. Joggle the peel to see that the loaves will leave the peel.

Open the oven door and with a strong, forward thrust, slide the loaves onto the hot baking stone. If they refuse to leave the peel, use a wide spatula to prod them off.

8. Bake the loaves for 10 minutes at 450°F. Do *not* open the oven door during this time as the loaves will be making one small, final rising. After 10 minutes, lower the oven temperature to 375°F and bake the loaves for an additional 25 minutes.

Check the loaves during the last 10 minutes of baking and if they are browning too quickly, cover them lightly with aluminum foil. Remove the foil for the last few minutes of baking.

Test the loaves for doneness by tapping them on the bottom. If the sound is hollow, the loaves are done.

9. Remove the loaves from the baking sheet or stone and place them on a rack to cool. Do *not* slice the loaves for at least 1 hour as the texture and flavor are still developing.

10. If you wish to refrigerate or freeze the bread, wrap the loaves tightly in aluminum foil after they have completely cooled.

When serving, reheat the breads, loosely wrapped in the foil, after they have come to room temperature. Heat them for 15 to 20 minutes in a preheated 350°F oven.

OVAL LOAVES WITH RYE FLOUR

Rye flour can be most resistant to kneading, but used as only part of the 5½ cups of flour in our basic recipe, the dough is complaisant. The ingredients remain the same as for the Oval Loaves, but use 2½ cups of rye flour and 3 cups of an all-purpose, unbleached flour. Add 1½ tablespoons of black caraway seeds to the yeast mixture at the same time that you add the first cup of flour and the salt. We recommend that you use the black, rather than the regular dark-brown variety because they are smaller and have a subtle flavor the brown do not have.

Thinly sliced, these loaves make a choice bread for sandwiches. We like to fill our sandwiches with slices of Pressed Cottage Cheese, topped with a heaping handful of alfalfa sprouts.

Makes 2 loaves, 9 inches long by 4 inches in diameter

In addition to the ingredients on page 28 you need:
1½ tablespoons black caraway seeds

1. Follow Steps 1 through 5 for the Oval Loaves adding the 1½ tablespoons of black caraway seeds to the "proofed" yeast mixture along with the flour and salt.

Alternate the rye flour with the all-purpose flour, reserving 1 cup of the all-purpose flour for later kneading.

2. When the loaves have doubled in size after the third rising, make 3 to 5 slashes across the midsections of the loaves. This slash pattern most closely resembles a good delicatessen rye bread.

3. Continue with Steps 7 through 10, but when the oven temperature has been reduced to 375°F after the first 10 minutes of baking, bake the loaves for another 30 to 35 minutes for a total baking time of 40 to 45 minutes.

OVAL LOAVES WITH SESAME SEEDS

As with the Baguettes, the Oval Loaves become completely different breads with the addition of sesame seeds.

Makes 2 loaves, 9 inches long by 4 inches in diameter

In addition to the ingredients on page 28 you need:
⅓ cup raw, hulled sesame seeds

1. Follow Steps 1 through 5 for the Oval Loaves.

In Step 3, after sprinkling your peel or baking sheet with cornmeal, sprinkle approximately ⅓ of the sesame seeds on top of the cornmeal. Arrange the sesame seeds so that the formed loaves will cover them.

2. When the loaves of bread have doubled in size, using a small pastry brush, carefully brush their surfaces with water. (Do not let the water dribble onto your peel or baking sheet or the breads will stick.) Using your fingers, pick up a teaspoon or so of the remaining sesame seeds and lightly sprinkle on the loaves.

When the surfaces are coated, begin dipping your fingers, held together and straight out, first into water and then into the remaining seeds. The seeds will stick to your fingers. Pat the seeds onto the loaves. Cover the loaves evenly, pressing on as many seeds as possible.

3. When the loaves are coated with the seeds, slash them following Step 6 for the oval loaves. The lattice pattern is recommended.

4. Continue with Steps 7 through 10 until the loaves are completed.

ONE BIG OVAL LOAF WITH SESAME SEEDS

This loaf is quite showy for a buffet if slashed with a fine lattice pattern. Pack as many raw, hulled sesame seeds on the loaf as possible — at least ½ cup.

Makes 1 loaf, 12 inches long by 5½ inches in diameter

1. Prepare the loaf exactly as for the Oval Loaves with Sesame Seeds, except form only 1 loaf from the risen dough.

2. Bake the loaf in the same manner, but when the oven temperature has been reduced to 375°F after the first 10 minutes of baking, bake for another 40 to 45 minutes for a total baking time of 50 to 55 minutes.

BRAIDED LOAVES

Braided breads are always eye-catching, so we decided to attempt them, putting our basic recipe to the test. Again, the procedure is the same except for forming the braids. Most of our breads are good either at room temperature or hot, but braids seem to taste best hot.

You may slice the loaves as you would a regularly shaped bread, but we enjoy pulling the breads apart at the braids for very hefty pieces. The breads may be baked on a baking stone or on a heavy, black steel baking sheet. (See Baking Your Bread, page 16.)

Makes 2 loaves, 11 inches long by 4 inches in diameter

1 tablespoon dry yeast (see Flour and Yeast, page 14)
2 cups warm water or whey (105°F)
5½ cups flour (see Flour and Yeast)
1 tablespoon salt
1 teaspoon corn oil
Several tablespoons cornmeal for the peel or baking sheet

1. Follow Steps 1 through 7 for Baguettes (see page 17).

2. When the dough has tripled in volume for the second time, punch it down and place it on your floured work surface. Do not knead the dough. Instead, flatten it with your hands into a rectangle, approximately 10 × 5 inches.

Cut the dough crosswise into 6 equal pieces. Each loaf will use 3 of the pieces to form the braid. Set the pieces aside on a floured section of your work surface.

3. We form the braided loaves in a fashion similar to the baguettes, creating tension in the loaves so that they will hold their shapes as they rise for the third time.

Lightly flour your work surface. Take one piece of the dough and flatten it with your hands into an oval shape, approximately 6 inches long by 4 inches wide. Bring one long edge of the dough over onto the opposite edge. Press the open edges together to form a seam.

Turn the dough so that the seam faces up from your work surface. Again, flatten the dough slightly by pressing down into the seam so that an indentation is made. Tuck the pointed ends of the oval into the body of the dough so that the dough now resembles an inflated raft. Once more, bring one long edge of the dough onto the opposite side. Form a seam by pressing the open edges together.

Turn the dough seam side down onto your work surface. Center your hands, one placed over the other, in the middle of the dough. With equal pressure from both hands, roll the dough back and forth, moving your hands apart from the center of the dough to the ends to form a strand, 20 inches long by 1 inch in diameter. This movement may need to be repeated several times to reach the 20-inch length.

Set the strand aside and roll out 2 more of the pieces of dough to 20-inch lengths.

4. Arrange the 3 strands of dough on your floured work surface in a fan shape. The ends of the strands farthest from you should be placed side by side, with the 2 outside strands fanning out from the middle strand by about 2½ inches at the ends nearest you.

Begin the braid about 1 inch from the ends of the strands opposite you. Bring the strand on the right over the middle strand. Then, bring the strand on the left over it. Continue, braiding in this manner until

you have braided to within an inch of the end nearest you.

5. Firmly pinch the unbraided ends together. Tuck each end under the loaf and place the loaf on your peel or baking sheet which has been liberally sprinkled with cornmeal. Your loaf should be about 10 inches long.

Repeat this procedure with the remaining 3 pieces of dough to form your second loaf.

6. Cover the loaves with a cloth towel. Place them in a warm spot to double in bulk for the third and final rising. This will take from 1 to 1½ hours. Do not place them in the oven as it must be preheated.

7. About 20 minutes before the loaves are ready to be baked, preheat the oven to 450°F.

If you are using a baking stone, place it on the lower third rack of the oven at this time.

If you are using a baking sheet, place a shallow pan, half filled with water, on the bottom rack of the oven and position another rack in the middle of the oven. The pan of water will create steam for proper baking. It is not necessary with a baking stone.

8. When the loaves have doubled in size, simply place them in the oven, *if you are using a baking sheet*.

If you are using a baking stone, make sure that the loaves will move about on the peel so that they can be thrust from the peel onto the hot baking stone.

Open the oven door and with a strong, forward thrust, slide the loaves onto the stone. If they refuse to leave the peel, prod them off with a wide spatula.

9. Bake the loaves for 10 minutes at 450° F. Do not open the oven door during this time, as the loaves will make one small, final rising.

After 10 minutes, lower the oven temperature to 375° F and bake the loaves for an additional 25 minutes. Check the loaves during the last 10 minutes of baking and if they are browning too quickly, cover them lightly with aluminum foil. Remove the foil for the last few minutes of baking.

Tap the loaves on the bottoms to test for doneness. If the sound is hollow, the breads are done.

10. Remove the loaves from the baking sheet or stone and serve immediately or place them on a rack to cool. If you wish to refrigerate or freeze the bread, wrap the loaves tightly in foil after they have completely cooled.

When serving, reheat the breads, loosely wrapped in the foil, after they have come to room temperature. Heat them for 15 to 20 minutes in a preheated 350°F oven.

BRAIDED LOAVES WITH SESAME SEEDS

As always, each new shape is tested with sesame seeds and again, an entirely new bread is created.
Makes 2 loaves, 11 inches long by 4 inches in diameter

In addition to the ingredients on page 31 you need:
⅓ cup raw, hulled sesame seeds

1. Follow Steps 1 through 7 for the Braided Loaves. In Step 5, after sprinkling your peel or baking sheet with cornmeal, sprinkle approximately ⅓ of the sesame seeds on top of the cornmeal. Arrange the sesame seeds so that the formed loaves will cover them.

2. When the loaves of bread have doubled in size, using a small pastry brush, carefully brush their surfaces with water. (Do not let the water dribble onto your peel or baking sheet or the breads will stick.)

Using your fingers, pick up a teaspoon or so of the remaining sesame seeds and lightly sprinkle them on the loaves. When the surfaces are coated, begin dipping your fingers, held together and straight out, first into water and then into the remaining seeds. The seeds will stick to your fingers, which can then be patted onto the loaves. Cover the loaves evenly and as heavily as possible.

3. Continue with Steps 8 through 10 until the loaves are completed.

BRAIDED LOAVES WITH CHEESE AND PEPPER

These loaves are a perfect accompaniment for hot soups. Because the cheese contains salt, use only 1 teaspoon of salt in the basic dough, rather than 1 tablespoon.
Makes 2 loaves, 11 inches long by 4 inches in diameter

In addition to the ingredients on page 31 you need:
1 to 2 teaspoons freshly ground black pepper (to taste)
2 cups coarsely grated Cheddar cheese

1. Follow Steps 1 through 7 for Baguettes (see page 17 – 18), adding the black pepper at the same time that you add the 1 teaspoon of salt.

2. When the dough has tripled in volume for the second time, punch it down and place it on your floured work surface.

Flatten the dough with your hands into a large rectangle about 1¼ inches thick. Sprinkle the surface with 1 cup of the Cheddar cheese. Fold the dough, enclosing the cheese.

Knead briefly and flatten again into a rectangle about 2 inches thick. Sprinkle the surface with ½ cup of the cheese. Fold and knead again until the cheese is incorporated into the dough.

Flatten once again and sprinkle the dough with the remaining ½ cup of cheese. Fold and knead to incorporate the cheese. The dough will have a very rough appearance.

3. Again, flatten the dough into a rectangle about 10 × 5 inches. Cut the dough crosswise into 6 equal pieces. Each loaf will use 3 of the pieces to form the braid.

Set the pieces aside on a floured corner of your work surface. Since the dough was kneaded when the cheese was added, let the pieces rest for 5 minutes to relax the gluten.

4. When the pieces of dough have relaxed, proceed with Steps 3 through 9 for the Braided Loaves. The dough will be a little more difficult to handle when you form the braids as some pieces of the cheese may come out from the strands. Just push them back into the dough and use more flour on your work surface if necessary.

The loaves will not have a smooth appearance after shaping, but they will smooth out as they rise for the third time.

5. When the loaves have baked for the correct amount of time (Step 9), carefully remove them from the baking sheet or baking stone. It is quite possible that they will stick to the sheet or stone because of the cheese. Use a spatula to loosen them but do not pull on the loaves as you may tear them apart. Serve the bread right away. Otherwise, place the loaves on a rack to cool.

If you wish to refrigerate or freeze the bread, wrap the loaves tightly in aluminum foil after they have completely cooled.

When serving, reheat the breads, loosely wrapped in the foil, after they have come to room temperature. Heat them for 15 to 20 minutes in a preheated 350°F oven.

BRAIDED COTTAGE CHEESE BREAD

This loaf is gargantuan in size, but the lightest in texture of all of our breads. Because of this lightness, it must be made as one braided loaf in order to hold its shape. Even as you braid it, it will try to misbehave, so a little patience is required. Other than adding 2 cups of cottage cheese to the dough and increasing the flour to 6½ cups, the ingredients remain the same as for the Baguettes or Braided Loaves.

Makes 1 loaf, 14 inches long by 5 inches in diameter

In addition to the ingredients on page 31 you need:
1 *additional* cup flour
2 cups homemade Cottage Cheese (see page 88)

1. Follow Steps 1 through 7 for Baguettes (see page 17). In Step 1, when the first cup of flour and salt have been added to the yeast mixture, mix in the 2 cups of cottage cheese. The cottage cheese should be somewhat on the dry side and the curds should be small.

   If necessary, drain the cottage cheese in a sieve lined with cheesecloth. Large curds can then be pressed through the sieve after removing the cheesecloth. Add 5½ cups of flour, rather than 4½, to the dough and reserve 1 cup for further kneading.

2. When the dough has tripled in volume for the second time, punch it down and place it on your floured work surface. Do not knead the dough. Instead, flatten it with your hands into a rectangle, approximately 10 × 5 inches.

   Cut the dough crosswise into 3 equal pieces. Set the pieces aside on a floured section of your work surface.

3. Form your braided loaf by following Steps 3 through 8 for Braided Loaves, disregarding instructions for a second loaf.

4. Bake the braided loaf for 10 minutes at 450°F. Do not open the oven door during this time, as the loaf will be making one small, final rising. After 10 minutes, reduce the oven temperature to 375°F and bake the loaf for an additional 40 to 45 minutes.

   Check the loaf during the last 10 minutes of baking and if it is browning too quickly, cover it with aluminum foil. Remove the foil for the last few minutes of baking.

   Tap the bottom of the loaf for doneness. If it sounds hollow, it is done.

5. Remove the loaf from the baking sheet or stone and serve immediately, or place it on a rack to cool.

   If you wish to refrigerate or freeze the bread, wrap it tightly in aluminum foil after it has completely cooled. When serving, reheat the loaf, loosely wrapped in foil, after it has come to room temperature. Heat for about 15 minutes in a preheated 350°F oven.

DILL BREAD

For sandwiches or toast, Dill Bread is a fitting choice. And again, our basic ingredients work, yielding 2 loaves.

For the best possible crust, use black steel or tinned steel for baking. Baked in an aluminum pan a loaf will appear almost colorless, but baked in a black steel pan it will be golden brown. The steel loaf pans are available by mail, but there is some variation in size. You may use any in the range from 8½ × 4½ × 2¾ inches to 9½ × 5¾ × 3½ inches. The 2 loaves will just be a little smaller or larger. For extra interest, you may braid this bread.

Makes 2 loaves

1 tablespoon dry yeast (see Flour and Yeast, page 14)
2 cups warm water or whey (105° F)
2 cups homemade Cottage Cheese (see page 88)
1 tablespoon salt
2 tablespoons minced shallots
1 tablespoon dill seed
5½ cups flour (see Flour and Yeast)
Several teaspoons corn oil

1. In a large mixing bowl with a 3-quart capacity, dissolve the yeast in the warm water or whey. Give the yeast time to "proof" (foam). This will take from 5 to 10 minutes.

2. The cottage cheese should be on the dry side. If necessary, drain it in a sieve lined with cheesecloth. In a small bowl, cream the cottage cheese with the salt, shallots, and dill seed.

3. When the yeast has "proofed," add 1 cup of flour to the mixing bowl. Stir to blend and then add the cottage cheese mixture.

Mix and continue adding flour, ½ cup or so at a time, until all but 1 cup of the flour has been used. Mix thoroughly after each addition.

4. Continue with the bread, following the instructions in Steps 3, 4, and 5 for Baguettes (see page 18).

The Dill Bread differs from the other breads in that it will have *only two risings, doubling in volume*, rather than the three risings. The first will take approximately 2 hours.

5. When the dough has doubled in volume for the first rising, punch it down and place it on your floured work surface. Do not knead the dough as it is now time to form the loaves and you do not want to activate the gluten.

Cut the dough into 2 equal pieces. Let the pieces relax briefly while you lightly oil the loaf pans with the remaining corn oil.

6. *To form plain loaves*, fold and cup each piece of dough in your hands to form a plump oval shape that will fit your loaf pans. Pinch together the open edges of the dough and make them the undersides of your loaves. Place them in the oiled loaf pans.

To form the braided loaves, flatten each piece of dough into a rectangle and cut it crosswise into 3 equal pieces. Each loaf will use 3 of the pieces to form a braid. Set the pieces of dough aside on a floured section of your work surface.

Roll the first piece of dough into a strand 14 inches long by 1½ inches in diameter. This is easily accomplished by centering your hands, one placed over the other, in the middle of the dough. With equal pressure from both hands, roll the dough back and forth, moving your hanes apart from the center of the dough to the ends to form the strand.

This movement may need to be repeated several times to reach the desired length. Continue making strands with 2 more pieces of the dough.

To braid the 3 strands of dough, follow Step 4 for Braided Loaves (see page 32). Firmly pinch the unbraided ends together. Tuck each end under the loaf and place the loaf in your oiled loaf pan.

Repeat this procedure with the remaining 3 pieces of dough to form your second loaf.

7. Cover the loaves with a cloth towel and place them in a warm spot to double in volume

for the second time. This will take about 1½ hours. Do not place them in the oven as it must be preheated.

8. About 15 minutes before the loaves are ready to be baked, preheat the oven to 375°F.

9. When the loaves have doubled in size, bake them on the middle rack of the oven for 40 minutes. Do not open the oven door for the first 10 minutes of baking.

Check the loaves during the last 10 minutes of baking and if they are browning too quickly, cover them lightly with aluminum foil. Remove the foil for the last few minutes of baking. Remove a loaf from its pan and tap it on the bottom to test for doneness. If the loaf sounds hollow, the breads are done.

10. Remove the loaves from their pans and place them on a rack to cool for at least an hour before slicing.

If you wish to make very thin slices, the bread must cool completely. Refrigerate or freeze, following the instructions for the other breads.

BREAD STICKS

You can use our basic bread recipe to make delicious Bread Sticks. For plain sticks, the ingredients are exactly the same as for the Baguettes. If you wish, you may sprinkle them with raw, hulled sesame seeds, poppy seeds, or with coarse salt. If you are using sesame seeds, sprinkle some on the baking sheets after they have been sprinkled with the cornmeal. The sticks should be coated just before they go into the oven. Using a small pastry brush, brush them lightly with water and then sprinkle and pat on the seeds or salt. For plain bread sticks, do not use the water.

The size and number of bread sticks you make depends upon the sizes of your baking sheets or your mood. For snacking or parties, you may prefer to make them no longer than 9 inches, in which case you would have 32 bread sticks. We use two black steel baking sheets which each measure 19½ × 13 inches. Forming the sticks the length of the two pans, we are able to make 16 sticks, approximately 18 inches in length and 1 inch in diameter. Make adjustments for your pans, according to their sizes.

Makes about 16 bread sticks (see above)

In addition to the ingredients on page 17 you need:
⅓ cup raw, hulled sesame seeds, several tablespoons poppy seeds or several tablespoons coarse salt (optional)

1. Using the same ingredients, follow Steps 1 through 7 for Baguettes.

2. When the dough has tripled in volume for the second time, punch it down and place it on your floured work surface. Do not knead the dough. Instead, flatten it with your hands into a rectangle 12 × 6 inches.

Cut the dough crosswise into 16 equal strips. Set the strips aside on a floured section of your work surface to relax for about 5 minutes while you sprinkle your baking sheets with the cornmeal (and sesame seeds, if you are using them).

3. To form each bread stick, place your hands, one on top of the other, in the center of the strip. With equal pressure from both hands, roll the strip back and forth, moving your hands apart from the center of the dough to the ends to form a stick the length of your baking sheets (or the desired length you want).

Place each stick as it is formed on one of the baking sheets and continue until all of the bread sticks have been formed.

Flour your work surface as necessary. Leave about a ½ inch of space between each stick. The diameter of the sticks should be about ½ inch after rolling.

4. Cover the baking sheets with cloth towels and place them in a warm spot for the third rising. The third rising should be for 1 hour, in which time the bread sticks will almost double in size. Do not place them in the oven for this rising, as the oven must be preheated.

5. About 15 minutes before the bread sticks are ready to be baked, preheat the oven to 375°F.

6. When the bread sticks have completed their third rising, brush them with the water and sprinkle with the sesame seeds, poppy seeds, or salt, if you are using them. (Be careful that the water does not drip onto your baking sheets or the bread sticks will stick.) Bake the bread sticks, either plain or sprinkled, on a rack placed in the upper third of the oven for 30 minutes.

If your oven will not hold both baking sheets on the rack at the same time, bake each sheet of bread sticks separately. If the second sheet must wait, no harm will be done.

7. When the bread sticks are done, remove the baking sheets from the oven and let the bread sticks rest for just 2 minutes before removing them. During this short rest, the bread sticks will begin to cool and harden enough so that it will be easier to remove them from the baking sheets. Use a wide spatula to loosen the sticks and place them on a rack to cool and crisp.

If the bread sticks are to be eaten within a couple of days, we do not even refrigerate them but just place them, standing, in a deep basket. Otherwise, after they have thoroughly cooled, they may be wrapped in aluminum foil and refrigerated or frozen.

When serving, reheat the sticks to crisp them in a preheated 350°F oven for about 10 minutes after they have come to room temperature.

GROWING SPROUTS

More than any other month, January may be the most rewarding time in which to grow sprouts. In most parts of the country the weather can be foul, but the garden catalogs are arriving and the desire to plant and see something green and edible growing is overwhelming. With sprouting, you can have a miniature garden in the kitchen. The work involved is minimal and with the recent popularity of sprouts, there are dozens of commercial sprouters available, all of which work satisfactorily.

Sprouters range in price from under $5 to $25.00. We use store-bought jar lids fitted with three sizes of screening. These are inexpensive and they have given us a continual crop of sprouts for many years. The lids will fit any standard wide-mouth jars. We use our quart canning jars.

Choosing your seeds

A huge variety of seeds can be sprouted, from the tiny chia seeds with their peppery taste, to large chickpeas and soybeans. Keep two things in mind, though. You must use garden seeds that have not been chemically treated. Also, some sprouts, such as tomato, rhubarb, and potato are poisonous. Most sprouters will come with a list of what you can sprout and directions for each particular seed.

After experimenting with a dozen or so seeds, we have narrowed our sprouting almost entirely to alfalfa seeds and mung beans. We like to include sprouts at one meal during the day, and these two are the easiest to grow. Occasionally we'll sprout the whole-wheat berries for our breads and sometimes spicy chia seeds. They are delicious sprinkled on a tossed salad.

How to grow sprouts

To follow our simple method of sprouting, soak the seeds overnight in a quart-size canning jar. The water should come to 2 inches above the seeds. The next day we cover the jar with a lid (the screening size depends on the bean or seed size), and drain off the water. (Save this and the water from the first rinsings to water your plants; it contains nutriments.)

Place the jar(s) close to the sink in a dimly lighted spot — the darker, the better. You may keep them in a cabinet, but make sure there is ventilation. From then on it is a matter of rinsing the seeds until they have sprouted to the desired length. We try to rinse them 3 to 4 times a day, draining well after rinsing. It is not necessary to use a large quantity of water. Just fill the jar with water, let the sprouts soak for a minute and pour off the water. Even if you only rinse twice a day, you will have sprouts. It will just take a little longer.

As the sprouts grow, change to a larger screen so that the hulls will be rinsed away. If you are doing several jars at a time, just switch the screens around when you are rinsing.

As the sprouts grow larger, the hulls will fall away and, for the most part, be rinsed away. It is not essential that they be rinsed away, as they are healthful, but do make sure that there are no unsprouted seeds left in your minicrop. Alfalfa or any of the small seeds won't hurt if you bite into them, but a mung bean is hard. If the green hulls do not rinse away from the mung-bean sprouts, they are easy to remove by hand. This is purely a matter of choice.

Sprouting time (generally from 3 to 5 days) varies depending upon the seed variety and the weather. A moderate temperature is preferred as a very cold temperature will slow down the sprouting process and a high temperature may result in mold. We just watch our sprouts more closely at these times.

When your sprouts have reached their proper length, you may store them in the refrigerator right away or put the jars in bright sunlight for an hour as we do. This will develop the chlorophyll, turning the small leaves of the sprouts an appealing green, plus increase the vitamin C content. The vitamin C content of a half cup of sprouts is about the same as six glasses of orange juice. Sprouts are from 25 percent to 40 percent protein plus they contain a significant percentage of other necessary vitamins and minerals. And these potent little morsels contain less than 50 calories per 1 cup serving—more reason to make sprouts a wintertime staple.

Sprouts will keep well under refrigeration for about 1 week, but we try to consume a batch within three or four days for maximum food value and crispness. They must be stored in airtight containers. To insure that there is no moisture, use glass jars with a folded paper towel placed over the opening and then a piece of plastic wrap held in place with a rubber band. The paper towel will draw any excess moisture from the sprouts and keep them crispier.

Chia or cress seeds must be sprouted by the paper-towel method. (Use only white paper towels as colored towels can "bleed.") This is done by placing a damp paper towel on a plate, spreading the seeds thinly on the towel, and covering with another damp paper towel. Sprinkle water to moisten the top towel several times a day. To hasten the sprouting, place the plate inside an airtight plastic bag overnight. The seeds will sprout almost immediately. Remove the plate from the plastic bag once the seeds show signs of sprouting and continue to let them grow between the dampened paper towels. The seeds will probably grow through the towels and have to be pulled out.

WHAT CAN BE SPROUTED

As long as they have not been chemically treated or sprayed with insecticides, you may sprout:

BEANS AND SEEDS	MAXIMUM LENGTH OF SPROUTS
Adzuki beans	1 inch
Alfalfa seeds	3 inches
Cabbage seeds	1½ inches
Chia seeds	2 inches
Chickpeas (garbanzos)	1 inch
Cress seeds	2 inches
Fenugreek seeds	½ inch
Lentils	½ inch
Mung beans	3 inches
Peas	½ inch
Radish seeds	1½ inches
Soybeans	1 inch
Squash seeds (winter varieties)	½ inch
Sunflower seeds	½ inch
Triticale	½ inch
Wheat berries	1 inch

Crop size

Through experience you will learn how many seeds to sprout at one time, how large to let them grow, and what quantity you will have after sprouting. For instance, 1½ tablespoons of alfalfa seeds will yield 1 quart of sprouts and ½ cup of mung beans will be needed for 1 quart. One of our early mistakes was not allowing the sprouts to grow to their optimum, harvesting length. We were eating both the alfalfa and mung-bean sprouts when they were only 1½ inches in length, until we realized they will grow to 3 inches.

When buying seeds for sprouting, be cautious about prices. Some sources are very reasonable and others are extremely expensive. Most of the garden companies offer seeds for sprouting. (This is another reason to order the garden catalogs.) We like to order from companies that sell seeds by the pound. Although alfalfa will appear to be the most expensive,

AND IN OUR GARDEN

Early in the year the garden exists only on paper, as we have made a drawing detailing the layout and sizes of the beds. From this, we can decide what will go where and when for successive plantings. Referring to last year's drawing, we make sure to alternate our crops. For three years we have kept garden diaries and each day write down what was done, harvested, the temperature and any general information that might be helpful the next year. Last year's garden catalogs were saved and even empty seed packets for reference. Not all of the new catalogs have arrived, but we begin our orders.

Not much can be done in the actual garden, but as there are often a few warm days in the middle of the month, we use them to prepare the beds for planting in February. The winter covering of leaves is tilled under and fertilizers are added to the beds that will be planted very early.

WHAT TO BUY OR ORDER NOW

Everything purchased and ordered this month has to do with the garden. Excellent stores in our area cater to large farms and home gardens, so we buy fertilizers, some seeds and tools that may need to be replaced. All through the month, we order seeds from the garden catalogs as they arrive. Along with all the vegetables, we make a notation to order annual herb seeds as sometimes we forget.

keep in mind that 1½ tablespoons will make 1 quart of sprouts. Also, these seeds keep well, so we order 1 pound of alfalfa seeds and 3 pounds of mung beans at a time. This keeps us in sprouts for about 4 months.

Throughout the book, you will find recipes into which we have incorporated sprouts, from salads to omelets. Never treat sprouts as an unimaginative health food, but give them a place with your most elegant fare. They are inexpensive, first-rate food.

FEBRUARY

SAUSAGES AND OTHER STUFFED PLEASURES

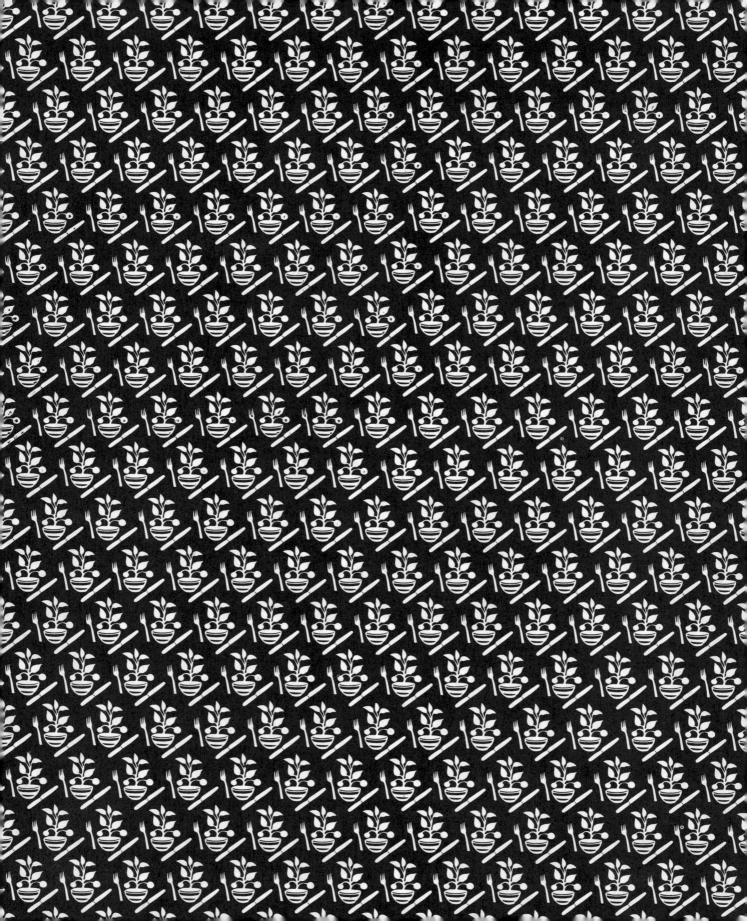

SAUSAGES AND OTHER STUFFED PLEASURES

Stuffed foods of all kinds are enticing whether served as hors d'oeuvres, appetizers or a main course. Just as a piñata is broken open to reveal wonderful surprises, stuffed foods are bitten into to reveal unexpected ingredients that make little gifts for the palate. With some ingenuity, otherwise bland foods can be transformed into mouth-watering fillips.

In February, we like to prepare plenty of two of our favorite stuffed foods—Hot Sausages and Empanadas—so that some can be frozen and enjoyed through the late winter and early spring. Then in April or during May, we will prepare more to be frozen for the summer months. It is a pleasant relief to find these treasures in the freezer after a long day of canning our summer vegetables.

Many stuffed foods call for an informality when being eaten, and fastidious table manners should be put aside, especially when eating the Stuffed Globe Artichokes or any of the Empanadas. Both definitely call for generous assistance from your fingers.

HOT SAUSAGE

On weekends in New York, we always had hot Italian sausages from Ottomanelli's on Bleecker Street. Usually, we would charcoal them, stuff them into Zito's excellent bread with lots of charcoaled peppers and onions, mustard, pesto, and whatever else would fit.

We missed those sausages when we moved to North Carolina, but were very hesitant to try making our own. Once we found the courage to attempt them, we found it was an extraordinarily easy and fast process. We list a mail-order source that carries a variety of equipment for sausage-making, from the very simple and inexpensive to the quite elaborate. The procedure is the same with any of the equipment whether you are using a hand-operated meat grinder, a food preparer, such as Kitchen Aid, with the grinder attachment, or a food processor. The meat grinders and food preparers can be fitted with a stuffing horn for filling the casings, or a very inexpensive, hand-held horn may be used.

Use small, natural hog casings, 32—35 mm, for the sausages. We also list a source for ordering them by mail. The casings are packed in salt in convenient storage containers, so they will keep almost indefinitely under refrigeration.

Make your first sausage when the weather is cool so as to prevent any spoilage. Once you become an "expert," you will be able to work so swiftly that the weather will not be a factor. Use your sausage within 2 or 3 days or freeze it. It will keep in the freezer for 3 months.

Makes 24 sausages, each 4 inches

2½ pounds fresh, boneless pork shoulder (about 25 percent fat for flavor and texture)
1 tablespoon fennel seeds
1 tablespoon caraway seeds
1 tablespoon freshly and coarsely ground dried hot red pepper
1 tablespoon sweet paprika
1 tablespoon minced garlic
1 tablespoon coarse salt
½ teaspoon freshly ground black pepper
3¼ yards natural hog casings (see above)
A little vegetable oil (for greasing the stuffing horn)

1. Cut the pork shoulder with its fat into ½-inch cubes. Place the cubes in a large mixing bowl. Mix the seasonings together and add them to the meat cubes. Toss to blend thoroughly.

If you should wish to taste the sausage for seasoning, fry a tablespoon in a skillet. Do not test the meat uncooked.

Cover the bowl with plastic wrap and refrigerate the meat for several hours or overnight, or place it in the freezer for ½ hour. The meat must be cold for proper grinding.

2. About 45 minutes before you are ready to stuff the sausages, prepare the casings. Cut the 3¼-yard length into 3 pieces. This amount of casing will give you an allowance for any holes or for practicing stuffing.

Soak the casings in a bowl of tepid water for ½ hour to remove the salt and soften them.

After ½ hour, open up one end of each casing and fit it over the mouth of the faucet. Keep the other end still in the bowl (they have a way of trying to slip down the drain, if you don't), while slowly running cold water through the casing. This will remove salt from inside the casings and show any holes. If there are holes, just cut the casings off at those spots.

As each casing is rinsed, let it drape over the edge of the sink to drain as you rinse the remaining ones.

When all of the casings have been rinsed, fill the bowl with fresh water and return them to the bowl until you are ready to use them.

3. Grind your sausage meat either with a hand meat grinder, with a food preparer fitted with the grinder attachment, or in a food processor.

If using a grinder, fit it with the coarse ³/₁₆-inch plate. Follow any special instructions that might apply to your type of grinder. Remove the plate after grinding the meat and fit the grinder with the stuffing horn.

If you are using a food processor, fit it with the metal blade and grind the meat in four batches. Be *very* careful not to grind the meat too fine. It should be coarsely ground, which will take 15 seconds or less in a processor.

4. Whatever type of stuffing horn you are using, lightly oil it with vegetable oil so that the casings will slip on and off easily.

Remove each individual casing from the water as you are ready to use it. Let it drain.

Slip the casing onto the horn, leaving a 1-inch overhang. Tie the end with a bit of kitchen twine. Place a plate under the stuffer, to catch the sausages as they are made.

5. Feed the sausage meat into the casing, forcing it through the hopper if you are using a grinder, or use your fingers or a wooden spoon if you are using a hand stuffing horn.

6. As soon as the tied end of the casing has 1 inch or so of sausage meat in place, prick the end of the casing with a threaded (so as not to lose it) needle. This will expel any air.

Continue to fill the casing with the sausage meat. Be very careful not to fill the casings too tightly or they will burst later.

If you are making sausage for the first time, you may want to give the first few sausages a brief rest to test them. Cut them from the horn and tie the other end with twine. Let them hang for about 10 minutes.

If they are filled too tightly, the meat will begin to work its way out of the casings or the casings will burst. Just remove the meat for use in restuffing and discard the casing.

7. For making the individual sausages, we have found it easiest to twist them as the casing is filled. This not only dispenses with the little lengths of twine, but expels air from the sausages as they are made.

Each time you have a 4-inch length of the casing filled, give it a double twist and go on to

the next sausage. If air bubbles should appear, just pierce the spot with the needle.

8. As each of the 3 casings is filled, remove it from the horn, leaving 1 inch unfilled. Tie the open end with another piece of twine and pierce the end with the needle.

Hang the sausages to dry as you fill the remaining casings. We use our pasta drying rack.

9. When all of the casings are filled, let them continue to dry for ½ hour or until the casings are no longer wet, but are not dried out.

Refrigerate and use within 3 days or freeze them for use within 3 months.

10. To cook the sausages, cut the lengths across where they were twisted and prick each sausage with a needle or the point of a knife in five or six places.

Fry the sausages over medium-low heat in a skillet with a tablespoon of oil added. You may also add ¼ inch of water to the skillet for moisture. Cook for 20 minutes, turning the sausages frequently so that they brown evenly.

If you wish, charcoal the pricked sausages over hot coals until they are well browned. Place sliced onions and quarters of bell peppers, seasoned with salt and black pepper, in aluminum foil bundles over the coals at the same time.

Note: The casings can be filled very quickly, particularly if you are using a Kitchen Aid as we do. However, this is not the point. The instructions with our Kitchen Aid suggest operating at Speed 4, but we find we have much more control at a lower speed. At a lower speed, we use one hand to hold the casing, smoothing it as it is filled, and with the other hand, we feed the meat into the hopper.

As each 4-inch section is filled, turn the motor off and give the sausage a double twist. Even with our method, the casings will be filled within minutes.

EMPANADAS

Whenever time allows, we make up a batch of Empanadas and freeze them. These little enclosed, quarter-moon-shaped pies are so versatile that we like to have them ready for hors d'oeuvres, first courses, or for last-minute suppers to accompany soups, thus making a full meal with perhaps a light salad to follow. If you are making them for the first time, give yourself a few relaxed hours to experiment and learn the stuffing technique. The second time will be easy and shortly you will be able to create your own fillings.

We are offering three fillings which we have devised. The first recipe is an adaptation of the traditional Argentinian specialty using beef. Our second recipe uses our Hot Sausage recipe on page 45, and the third recipe is meatless, combining our Cottage Cheese (page 88) with spinach and mushrooms.

You may make the empanadas any size that you wish. The baking time remains the same. We like to serve them with pots of chutney, the Coriander Sauce on page 271, the Tomato and Yogurt Sauce on page 296 or even a bit of mustard, depending upon the filling.

BASIC PASTRY DOUGH

For the 2 cups of flour in this recipe, we like to use 1 cup of all-purpose, unbleached flour and 1 cup of either the unbleached white flour from Walnut Acres or whole-wheat flour. The Walnut Acres or whole-wheat flours are a little difficult to work with if used straight, but when cut with all-purpose flour, the exceptional flavors they impart to the pastry dough are evident. However, you may use a regular all-purpose flour and still have a proper pastry dough. Use the pastry dough for empanadas, unsweetened pastry shells, or for a quiche.

For 24 empanadas, two 9-inch pastry shells, or one 11-inch quiche shell

> **2 cups flour**
> **½ teaspoon salt**
> **½ cup (1 stick) cold, unsalted butter (if you are making the dough in a food processor, use frozen butter)**
> **4 to 5 tablespoons iced water**

1. Prepare the pastry dough either on your work surface or in a food processor.

If making the dough by hand, measure the flour onto your work surface and sprinkle it with salt. Cut the *cold* butter into ¼-inch cubes and add to the flour mixture.

Using one hand, rub the butter and flour together until the mixture resembles coarse meal. Work rapidly and, if possible, keep a metal scraper in your other hand to gather up the dough to further facilitate the mixing.

Pour 4 tablespoons of the iced water over

the dough and quickly mix to incorporate the water. If the dough is crumbly, add the remaining tablespoon of water. Gather the dough into a ball, wrap it in a piece of waxed paper and then in a piece of plastic wrap. Refrigerate the dough for about 1 hour before rolling it out.

If making the pastry dough in a food processor, add the flour, salt, *frozen* butter (cut into ¼-inch pieces) and 4 tablespoons of the iced water to the work bowl, fitted with the metal blade.

Process with several On/Off motions for a few seconds to mix the ingredients and then continue to process until the dough forms a ball. This entire process should take no longer than 10 to 12 seconds.

Wrap the ball of dough in waxed paper and then in plastic wrap. Refrigerate for about 1 hour before rolling out the dough.

2. When you are ready to roll out the dough, if it has become hard from chilling in the refrigerator, let it sit at room temperature for about 10 minutes to soften.

3. *If you are using the dough for empanadas*, roll it out as described in the recipe for Argentinian Empanadas which follows.

If you are using the dough for unsweetened pastry shells, cut the dough in half and follow Steps 5, 6, and 7 for a Basic Pie Shell (see page 389). For two 9-inch shells roll the dough to less than ⅛-inch thick.

If you are using the dough for one 11-inch quiche, roll the dough to a ⅛-inch thickness.

ARGENTINIAN EMPANADAS

Makes about 24 empanadas

> **1 recipe Basic Pastry Dough**
> **¼ cup raisins, preferably Monnuka**
> **¼ cup dry white wine or vermouth**
> **2 tablespoons olive oil**
> **1 medium onion, chopped fine**
> **4 large cloves garlic, minced**
> **1 pound lean ground beef**
> **½ teaspoon salt**
> **1 teaspoon coriander seeds**
> **1 teaspoon cumin seeds**
> **1 teaspoon dried hot red pepper**
> **½ teaspoon black peppercorns**
> **1 imported bay leaf**
> **1 tablespoon sweet paprika**
> **2 fresh jalapeño peppers, chopped fine but not seeded, or any hot peppers packed in brine**
> **1 egg yolk for glazing**

1. Prepare the Basic Pastry Dough. Wrap it in waxed paper and then in plastic wrap. Refrigerate the dough while you make the filling.

2. Chop the raisins coarsely and combine them with the wine to soften.

3. Heat the olive oil in a 10-inch skillet and sauté the onion and garlic over medium-low heat until they have wilted. Add the ground beef, sprinkle it with the salt, and cook, stirring with a wooden spoon to break up any lumps, until the meat is no longer pink. Add the wine and raisin mixture. Continue to cook until the wine and meat juices have evaporated.

4. Toast the coriander and cumin seeds in a small skillet over low heat for about 5 minutes to bring out their flavor. Grind them along with the dried hot red pepper, black pepper, and bay leaf.

5. Add the freshly ground spices, sweet paprika, and chopped jalapeño peppers to the skillet. Combine the ingredients thoroughly, then remove the skillet from the heat to cool.

6. Preheat the oven to 400°F.

7. Lightly flour your work surface. Before rolling out the dough, cut it into several pieces. Keep the pieces that are not being rolled covered with the plastic wrap so they will not dry out.

Roll each piece into a ⅛-inch-thick circle. Add flour to the work surface if the dough is sticking.

8. Using a circular object of some sort, such as a bowl, tin can, or professional cutter with a 4½-inch diameter, cut as many circles of dough as the rolled dough allows. Gather up the scraps and set them aside to use later.

9. With a spoon, place about 3 tablespoons of the cooled filling in the center of each circle of dough, leaving a ¾-inch edge of dough around the outside. With a small pastry brush, brush the edges with water.

Fold the circle in half. Pinch the outside edges of dough firmly together, making sure that the filling is enclosed, then crimp them as you would a pie shell, pinching the dough between your thumb and index finger to form a ridged pattern.

Holding the filled dough cupped in one hand, give the stuffed side a little push with the thumb of your other hand to form a quarter-moon.

10. As each empanada is completed, place it on an unoiled baking sheet. Depending upon the size of your baking sheet, you may have to use two sheets. The empanadas should be ½ inch apart.

If you are making the empanadas for the first time and are working slowly, refrigerate the baking sheet and place the empanadas onto the sheet as they are filled. The butter in the pastry dough must not soften.

11. Continue with the other pieces of dough, rolling them out, cutting and filling them. Gather the scraps of dough together and roll them out, until all of the dough and filling are used.

12. When all of the empanadas are completed, brush them with the egg yolk which has been beaten with a tablespoon of water. If they are not glazed with the egg yolk, they will not brown properly.

13. Bake the empanadas on the middle rack of the preheated oven for 25 to 30 minutes until they are golden brown. If your oven will not hold two sheets on a single rack, bake each sheet of empanadas separately.

Remove them from the oven and after a 5-minute rest on the baking sheet, loosen them with a wide spatula if any are sticking.

14. Serve the empanadas in a basket lined with a cloth napkin. The filling will be very hot if served immediately, so another 5-minute rest is advised. Not only is there danger of heat from the filling, but the flavor is compromised when the empanadas are too hot.

15. If you wish to freeze the empanadas, cool them completely. Then carefully place them in an airtight plastic bag or aluminum foil.

Let them defrost before reheating. Reheat, wrapped in foil, in a 375°F oven for about 15 to 20 minutes.

EMPANADAS WITH HOT SAUSAGE AND MUSHROOMS

Makes about 24 empanadas

1 recipe Basic Pastry Dough (see page 48)
¼ cup shallots
1 pound fresh mushrooms
4 tablespoons unsalted butter
½ teaspoon salt
¼ teaspoon freshly ground black pepper
1 pound Hot Sausage (see page 45)
2 cups homemade Cottage Cheese (see page 88), at room temperature
1 egg yolk for glazing

1. Prepare the Basic Pastry Dough. Wrap it in waxed paper and then in plastic wrap. Refrigerate the dough while you make the filling.

2. Peel and mince the shallots. Remove the ends from the mushroom stems. Wipe the mushrooms with damp paper towels and chop them fine, preferably using a chef's knife.

Melt the butter in a 10-inch skillet and add the shallots. Sauté over medium-low heat until they have wilted.

Add the mushrooms, sprinkle with the salt and black pepper and sauté the ingredients over medium-low heat until the mushrooms have given up their moisture and it evaporates. Remove from the heat to cool.

3. Remove the casing from the sausages and chop the sausage meat fine. In a second skillet, cook the sausage meat over medium heat until the fat is rendered and the meat has lightly browned. Break up the meat as it cooks so that the pieces are no larger than ¼ inch.

Drain and cool the sausage before adding it to the other ingredients.

4. In a mixing bowl, cream the cottage cheese with the back of a wooden spoon until it is smooth. Add the cooled mixtures from the two skillets. Blend the ingredients thoroughly.

5. Preheat the oven to 400°F.

6. Proceed with Steps 7 through 15 for Argentinian Empanadas (see page 49).

EMPANADAS WITH COTTAGE CHEESE, SPINACH AND MUSHROOMS

Makes about 24 empanadas

1 recipe Basic Pastry Dough (see page 48)
½ pound fresh spinach leaves (weight without stems)
3 tablespoons shallots
1 pound fresh mushrooms
3 tablespoons unsalted butter
½ teaspoon salt
¼ teaspoon freshly ground black pepper
¼ cup dry white wine or vermouth
2 egg yolks, at room temperature
1 cup homemade Cottage Cheese (see page 88), at room temperature
½ cup freshly grated Parmesan cheese

1. Prepare the Basic Pastry Dough. Wrap it in waxed paper and then in plastic wrap. Refrigerate the dough while you make the filling.

2. Wash the spinach leaves. Place them in a large pot with just the water clinging to the leaves. Cover and cook over low heat, stirring several times, until the leaves have wilted.

Place the spinach in a colander and run cold water over the leaves to stop the cooking process and to preserve the color. In small handfuls, firmly squeeze the liquid from the spinach.

Chop the spinach fine using a chef's knife or in a food processor. Set aside.

3. Peel and mince the shallots. Remove the ends from the mushroom stems. Wipe the mushrooms with damp paper towels, then chop them fine, preferably using a chef's knife.

4. Melt the butter in a 10-inch skillet, add the shallots and sauté over medium-low heat until they have wilted.

Add the mushrooms and sprinkle with the salt and black pepper. Sauté over medium-low heat until the mushrooms have given up their moisture and it evaporates.

Add the wine. Increase the heat to medium and cook until the wine has evaporated. Set the skillet aside to cool.

5. In a mixing bowl, lightly beat the egg yolks. (The whites may be frozen for later use.) Set aside 1 tablespoon of the yolks for glazing the empanadas.

Add the cottage cheese and Parmesan cheese to the mixing bowl and cream the mixture with the back of a wooden spoon until it is smooth.

Add the reserved spinach and the mushrooms and shallots. Blend all of the ingredients thoroughly.

6. Preheat the oven to 400°F.

7. Proceed with Steps 7 through 15 for Argentinian Empanadas (see page 49).

STUFFED GLOBE ARTICHOKES

The peak season for globe artichokes is spring, although you can find them in the markets at other times of the year. Our climate is not suited for growing them ourselves, so we must rely on the supermarket.

The artichokes in this recipe are truly "stuffed" and look enormous when they are filled. Just use a little patience to stuff them fully. Do not add any salt, for the pancetta (Italian bacon), cheese, and anchovies provide perhaps more than necessary; however, at the same time they create a pungent and delectable contrast to the sweetness of the artichokes.

Serves 4

4 large globe artichokes
½ lemon
1 imported bay leaf
1 tablespoon olive oil
3 ounces pancetta, diced fine
½ cup pignolia (pine) nuts
2 tablespoons finely minced garlic
4 cups freshly made dry bread crumbs
2 cups finely chopped parsley
2 teaspoons dried oregano
½ teaspoon freshly ground black pepper
1 teaspoon freshly ground dried hot red pepper
1 cup freshly grated Parmesan cheese
2 cups cooking liquid from the artichokes
½ cup dry white wine or vermouth
2 -ounce tin flat filets of anchovies

1. Rinse the artichokes under a strong stream of water to remove any dirt. Cut or break off the stems. Check to make sure the artichokes remain level when placed on a flat surface.

With a large, sharp knife, cut 1 inch or so from the tops of the artichokes. Using a pair of kitchen shears, trim the sharp tips from the leaves, removing about ½ inch. Do this in a circular fashion, working from the bottom leaves to the top leaves.

Artichokes will discolor quickly when cut, so rub the surfaces with the lemon as you cut them. They will discolor anyway as they cook, so this is optional.

2. Bring 2 quarts of water to a boil in a large, heavy-bottomed pot into which the artichokes will fit. Add the trimmed artichokes along with the lemon half and the bay leaf.

Cover and simmer the artichokes over

medium heat until the bottoms are barely tender. Pierce the bottoms with a knife to test. This preliminary cooking (about 30 minutes) will make it easier to stuff the artichokes.

3. While the artichokes are simmering, prepare the stuffing. Place the olive oil in a skillet and sauté the pancetta over low heat until the dice are browned.

Add the pignolia nuts and sauté them until they take on some color. Toss frequently and be very careful that they do not burn. Add the garlic and sauté it briefly.

Remove the skillet from the heat and add the bread crumbs, parsley, oregano, black pepper, hot red pepper, and Parmesan cheese. Mix thoroughly. Set aside.

4. When the artichokes are barely tender, remove them from the pot and place them with their tops down on paper towels to drain. Reserve 2 cups of the cooking liquid.

5. To prepare the artichokes for stuffing, set them right side up on your work surface. Very carefully open them by pulling the leaves outward until the feathery choke is exposed. Pull this out with either your fingers or a small spoon, removing the chokes completely.

6. Begin stuffing the artichokes in their centers, which will hold a considerable amount of the stuffing.

Continue with the stuffing, placing some between all of the leaves and pushing it down in order to use all of the stuffing. Divide the stuffing equally among the artichokes.

If the stuffed artichokes seem unwieldy, tie them around their middles with twine.

7. In the original cooking pot, bring the 2 cups of reserved cooking liquid to a simmer. Add the wine and the anchovies with their oil and continue simmering until the anchovies dissolve.

When the anchovies have dissolved,

place the stuffed artichokes into the pot. They should fit snugly against each other without being crowded. Cover and simmer over low heat for 45 minutes, basting every 15 minutes.

If the liquid should evaporate while the artichokes are simmering, add a small amount of water. The liquid should have evaporated when the cooking time is up.

8. Carefully lift the artichokes from the pot and place them on individual serving dishes. They will be extremely hot inside, so give them a 10-minute rest before serving as a first course at dinner.

Note: This is optional, but if you wish, you may remove the artichokes from the pot to a gratin dish, sprinkle them with a little more Parmesan cheese, dribble olive oil over the tops and pass them briefly under the broiler to gratiné them. Watch them closely so that they do not burn.

PANCETTA

Many of our recipes include pancetta, Italian bacon, as one of the ingredients. We prefer it to smoked bacon for the zip it gives to dishes. Pancetta is not smoked, but seasoned with spices and salt, then rolled and cured. If you are not familiar with it, we encourage you to try it.

We order our pancetta whole from Manganaro's in New York (see the mail-order listings). The size can vary in weight from 3 to 5 pounds and smaller amounts may be ordered. Upon arrival, we cut the pancetta into slices weighing between 2 and 4 ounces. Each slice is wrapped in waxed paper, then packaged in a plastic bag and frozen to be used as needed. The frozen pancetta will be good for 6 months.

If you must substitute for the pancetta, use slab bacon or spicy ham. After it is diced, slab bacon should be blanched in simmering water for 3 to 5 minutes to remove the smoky flavor. Drain and dry the dice on paper towels before sautéing them.

STUFFED MUSHROOMS

Serve these spicy little morsels as hors d'oeuvres, as part of a buffet, as a first course, or as an accompaniment to your meat course. They are best served hot from the oven, but they may be prepared ahead and warmed up for serving. In that case, cover them with aluminum foil so they will not dry out when they are reheated.

Serves 6 to 8

½ pound Hot Sausage (see page 45)
3 tablespoons olive oil
1 medium onion
2 large cloves garlic
1 pound very firm mushrooms, preferably 1½ to 2 inches in
      diameter, all of a uniform size
½ cup freshly made dry bread crumbs
1 cup parsley, chopped fine
¾ cup freshly grated Parmesan or Romano cheese
1 tablespoon dried oregano
2 eggs, slightly beaten

1. Remove the casings from the sausage if they are encased. Chop the sausage meat fine. If the sausages were prepared ahead and have been frozen, chop them before they are completely defrosted as it will be easier.

2. Heat 1 tablespoon of the olive oil in a 10-inch skillet. Add the sausage meat and sauté over medium heat until it is rendered of its fat and the pieces begin to brown.

3. While the sausage is sautéing, peel the onion and garlic and chop them fine. Remove the ends from the mushroom stems. Wipe the mushrooms with damp paper towels.

    Remove the stems and chop them fine. Arrange the mushroom caps in a single layer, tops down, in a gratin dish that has been oiled with 1 tablespoon of the olive oil.

4. When the sausage meat begins to brown, add the chopped onion and garlic to the skillet. Sauté just until they are wilted.

    Add the chopped mushroom stems and continue to sauté until the mushrooms give up their liquid and it evaporates. Remove the skillet from the heat to cool briefly.

5. Add the bread crumbs, ¾ cup of the parsley, the oregano, and ½ cup of the cheese to the ingredients in the skillet.

    Mix and add the slightly beaten eggs. Mix again so that the eggs are absorbed into the stuffing mixture.

6. Preheat the oven to 400°F.

7. With a teaspoon, stuff the mushroom caps with the mixture from the skillet, heaping and mounding the stuffing until it is all used.

Sprinkle the mushrooms with the remaining ¼ cup of cheese and divide the remaining 1 tablespoon of olive oil, dribbling it a few drops at a time over the cheese.

8. Add ¼ cup of water to the bottom of the gratin dish. This will keep the mushrooms from drying out as they bake. Place the gratin dish on the middle level of the oven and bake the mushrooms, uncovered, for 20 to 25 minutes or until they are very hot and the cheese has lightly browned.

Transfer to a serving platter or individual plates. Sprinkle with the remaining ¼ cup of chopped parsley. Serve immediately.

EGGS STUFFED WITH TUNA

This recipe is a staple for us when we need to make hors d'oeuvres for unexpected (or expected) guests or when we do not feel like preparing an elaborate meal. The stuffed eggs make a fitting accompaniment to other cold foods for a light lunch or supper. As often as we have served them, they never fail to please.

Follow our instructions exactly for hard-cooking the eggs. If the eggs are not perfectly cooked, there is no point in stuffing them.

For a very unexpected garnish, decorate each egg with 3 Fresh Green Coriander Seeds.
Serves 6

6 large eggs, at room temperature
1 small onion, minced
¼ cup finely chopped canned Colorado Peppers, or other mildly hot
    pepper in brine
2 tablespoons liquid from the peppers
7-ounce can tuna, packed in olive oil
3 tablespoons finely snipped fresh dill
½ teaspoon freshly ground black pepper
⅓ cup homemade Mayonnaise (see pages 195 and 196)
Fresh Green Coriander Seeds (see below), capers, or small sprigs of
    fresh dill for garnish

1. Place the eggs in a 2-quart saucepan with water to cover. Cover the saucepan and cook the eggs over medium-low heat until the water is just ready to boil. This will take about 20 minutes.

Check the eggs occasionally, as the water must *not* boil or the yolks will become oxidized and the whites tough.

2. When the water approaches boiling, imme-

diately remove the saucepan from the heat and let the eggs stand, still covered, for exactly 8 minutes. Then run cold water over the eggs to stop the cooking process. Do not drain.

Peel each egg by first cracking the large end of the egg, with the air pocket, against the sink. Then gently crack the rest of the shell. Hold the egg under the water in the saucepan as you remove the shell. Place the shelled eggs on a paper towel to drain.

3. Halve each egg lengthwise, remove the yolks, and place them in a small mixing bowl.

Cut a small, thin slice from the bottom of each half of the white so that it will remain steady on your serving platter. Place the thin slice back into the cup of the egg for reinforcement.

4. Mash the yolks with the back of a fork until they are smooth. Mix in the onion, Colorado peppers, and the liquid or brine from the peppers. (We do not seed the peppers as we like the additional hotness the seeds contain.)

Add the tuna with its oil, crumbling the flakes as you do so. Sprinkle the stuffing mixture with the dill and black pepper. Blend in the mayonnaise. Do not overmix the ingredients as a little texture is desirable.

5. Divide the stuffing among the whites, creating little mounds that cover the surface of the whites. Garnish the eggs with the garniture of your choice. You may serve the eggs right away or they may be refrigerated for up to 24 hours before serving.

If they have been refrigerated, let the stuffed eggs come to room temperature for optimum flavor, then serve them on a bed of fluffed alfalfa sprouts.

FRESH GREEN CORIANDER SEEDS

We find green coriander seeds as tasty as both the coriander leaves and the mature dried seeds, and for an unusual, new flavor, they certainly surpass the green and pink peppercorns that are currently in vogue.

If you have a garden, grow them, and if not, look for them in shops that sell fresh coriander. Often, you'll find coriander that has passed its prime for leaves so that the small, green seeds will have formed. Use the green seeds just as they are, or we have found that they will keep indefinitely in the brine solution that follows.

The green seeds have a particular affinity to eggs or may be used as a garnish for any dish that would ordinarily use capers. Even the brine takes on a very special flavor and a teaspoon or so can be added to salads. One evening, with a table set with leftovers, we spread a small amount of the Mayonnaise and Tomato Sauce on page 117 over halved, hard-cooked eggs and topped the sauce with 3 or 4 of the green coriander seeds. What a wonderful combination! We are just beginning to experiment with the possibilities.

Our recipe is for a small amount of seeds, but if you are lucky enough to have a large crop, just double or triple the brine solution. The seeds must be covered with the brine and loosely packed.

¼ cup fresh green coriander seeds
½ teaspoon salt
¼ cup white vinegar
¼ cup water

1. Use only unblemished seeds that have matured in size, but are still a very deep green color. The hulls should show no signs of drying and the texture should be crisp, very much like a caper. Rinse and drain the seeds you have selected.

2. In a small *glass* jar or bottle with a tightly fitting lid, dissolve the salt in the vinegar and water. (We like to use little apothecary jars with ground-glass stoppers, or old caper jars will do nicely.)

3. Add the coriander seeds to the brine solution. Cap and refrigerate. Use the seeds and brine as desired. They will keep indefinitely.

STUFFED CHINESE CABBAGE

In this recipe, the head of cabbage is left whole and the stuffing is placed between the individual leaves. When selecting your cabbage, try to find one that is squat rather than elongated. We grow Burpee's Hybrid which is usually no taller than 12 inches, but is 8 inches in diameter. The leaves are curled and blanch almost white inside. We like to serve this dish as our main course with Spinach Fettuccine, dressed only with unsalted butter and salt, and pots of Jalapeño Relish and homemade Yogurt (see the recipe index). The yogurt tempers the relish!

Serves 4 to 6

1½- to 2-pound Chinese cabbage
1 cup raw brown rice
1 teaspoon salt
1 medium onion
4 large cloves garlic
1 pound small, fresh mushrooms
2 tablespoons unsalted butter
1 tablespoon olive oil
¼ teaspoon freshly ground black pepper
½ cup canned tomatoes, after draining (reserve 1 cup juice — see below)
⅓ cup chopped canned Colorado peppers or any hot green peppers, in brine

½ teaspoon freshly ground dried hot red pepper
1 cup Chicken Stock (see page 109)
1 cup juice from the drained tomatoes
¼ cup dry white wine

1. Wash and drain the cabbage, discarding any outer leaves that are blemished. Keep the head intact and trim the stem so that it is flush with the leaves. Do not core.

2. Tie the cabbage around the middle with a piece of kitchen twine so the leaves will not come apart while steaming. Steam the cabbage for 10 minutes, just so that it wilts. We use the Graniteware Blancher for this, but you may fashion your own steamer by inserting a colander into a larger pot. Have at least 2 inches of water in the bottom of the pot and place the cabbage upright in the colander above the water level. Cover while steaming.

3. While the cabbage is steaming, lay a cotton dish towel on an area of your work surface. Cut two lengths of twine that will fit around the cabbage and lay them crosswise on the towel. Lift the colander with the steamed cabbage from the pot and immediately refresh the cabbage under cold, running water. This will stop the cooking process and retain the color of the cabbage. Very carefully spread the cabbage out on the towel with the center core of the cabbage placed where the twines cross. One by one, open up the leaves of the cabbage until they are fanned out from the center. Let the cabbage remain on the towel as you prepare the stuffing.

4. In a small saucepan, bring the brown rice to a boil in 2 cups of water and ½ teaspoon of the salt. Cover and reduce the heat to low. Simmer until the water has evaporated, occasionally tossing with a fork to separate the grains. This will take 20 minutes. Set aside, still covered.

5. Peel and chop the onion fine. Peel and mince the garlic. Cut away the ends of the mushroom stems. Wipe the mushrooms with damp paper towels to clean and then cut them into thin slices.

6. In a skillet, heat the butter and olive oil. Add the onions and garlic. Sauté over medium heat until the onions have wilted. Add the mushrooms and turn the heat to medium-high. Sprinkle with the remaining ½ teaspoon of salt and the ¼ teaspoon of black pepper. Toss and sauté quickly until the mushrooms have given up their liquid and have begun to brown. Add the tomatoes, Colorado peppers, and the ½ teaspoon of hot red pepper. Toss just to mix. Remove from the heat and add the reserved rice. Toss again.

7. To stuff the cabbage, work from the inside leaves to the outside. Using a tablespoon, place some of the stuffing under each leaf of the cabbage, close to the core. As you add the stuffing, fold the leaves over toward the center so that when all the stuffing has been used, you will have a compact ball of cabbage. This is much easier to do than you would perhaps think, as the leaves are quite resilient. Bring the strings to the center of the cabbage and tie loosely. The strings not only will hold the cabbage together while it is braising, but they are useful for lifting the cabbage.

8. In a deep casserole large enough to hold the cabbage, bring the chicken stock, the leftover juice from the tomatoes, and the dry white wine to a boil. Lower the cabbage into the liquid and reduce the heat so the liquid re-

mains at a simmer. Cover and braise the cabbage for 30 minutes, basting frequently with the liquid.

During this time begin warming your serving platter.

9. To serve the cabbage, lift it by the strings to a heated serving platter. Cut the twine and remove it. Surround the cabbage with the buttered fettuccine. Quickly reduce the braising liquid to 1 cup by bringing it to a rapid boil. Pour over the cabbage and fettuccine. Cut the cabbage into wedges as you would a cake, giving each guest a generous portion with the fettuccine placed alongside. Pass the jalapeño relish and yogurt separately.

STUFFED BUTTERNUT SQUASH

The stuffing for the squash contains cooked brown rice as a binder and mung-bean sprouts for texture. Sausage is optional and the dried herb is up to you. Wild thyme, rosemary, winter savory, or sage are our choices.

The squash are so heavily stuffed that they could be the main course, but any fowl, plainly prepared, will harmonize commendably. Serve the stuffed squash with one of the Tomato and Apple Chutneys (see pages 146 and 147).

Serves 4

2 butternut squash, each 1½ pounds
1 teaspoon corn oil
4 cups cooked Basic Brown Rice (see page 74)
½ pound Hot Sausage (optional; see page 45)
4 tablespoons olive oil
2 medium onions, chopped fine
4 large cloves garlic, minced
1 pound fresh mushrooms, chopped coarsely
2 cups mung-bean sprouts (for growing instructions, see page 39)
1 cup freshly grated Parmesan or Romano cheese
1 cup finely chopped parsley
2 teaspoons of a dried herb of your choice (see above)
1 teaspoon freshly ground dried hot red pepper (use *only* if the sausage is omitted)
2 eggs, slightly beaten

1. Preheat the oven to 450°F.

2. Cut the squash in half lengthwise. Remove the seeds and the fiber clinging to the seeds. (You may save the seeds and roast them. See Roasting Fresh Pumpkin Seeds, page 377).

Line a baking sheet that has sides with aluminum foil and lightly oil with the corn oil. Place the squash, cut side down, on the foil and bake for 20 to 30 minutes in the upper third of the oven. Test them after 20 minutes to see if they are tender.

To test, loosen one squash with a spatula, turn it cut side up and pierce the flesh with a fork. When the squash are tender, remove the baking sheet from the oven and turn all of the halves cut side up. Set aside until the stuffing is ready.

Lower the oven temperature to 375° F and place the oven rack in the middle of the oven.

3. Prepare the brown rice and set it aside, covered.

4. *If you are using the hot sausage*, remove the casings and chop the meat coarsely. Heat 2 tablespoons of the olive oil in a 10-inch skillet and sauté the sausage meat over medium heat until it is rendered of its fat and begins to brown.

Add the onions and garlic and sauté them just until they wilt. Then add the chopped mushrooms.

Continue sautéing until the mushrooms have given up their liquid and it has evaporated. Remove the skillet from the heat to cool briefly.

If you are not-using the hot sausage, heat the 2 tablespoons of olive oil in the skillet and sauté the onions and garlic until they wilt.

Add the chopped mushrooms and continue to sauté until they give up their liquid and it evaporates. Remove the skillet from the heat.

5. Add the brown rice, mung-bean sprouts, ½ cup of the grated cheese, ½ cup of the chopped parsley, the dried herb of your choice, and the hot red pepper (if you are using it) to the ingredients in the skillet.

Toss to mix and add the slightly beaten eggs. Toss again until the eggs are absorbed into the stuffing mixture.

6. Divide the stuffing mixture among the 4 halves of squash, filling the bowl of the squash first and working down to the neck so that all of the flesh is covered. The stuffing will be high, so make sure that it is well packed.

Divide and sprinkle the remaining ½ cup of cheese over the stuffing. Dribble the remaining 2 tablespoons of olive oil over the cheese.

7. Return the squash to the 375° F oven and bake them on the middle rack for another 20 minutes. Carefully remove them from the baking sheet with a wide spatula and a large spoon.

Sprinkle each squash with some of the remaining chopped parsley before serving.

Note: When the squash are removed from the oven in Step 2, they can be served at that point as baked squash. Dot the flesh with a little unsalted butter and add salt and pepper to taste. When served this way or stuffed, we find the skins are often tender enough so that the entire squash may be consumed.

STUFFED ESCAROLE

We received a verbal description of this recipe from an Italian woman on Bleecker Street about ten years ago. It was our first experience with stuffing a whole "green" and we approached it cautiously, not knowing what to expect. It is a superlative recipe and to date, we have encountered nothing similar to it. Serve the escarole as a first course or as an accompaniment to a simply prepared meat or fish dish.

Serves 4 to 6

1½-pound perfect head of escarole
1 cup raw brown rice
3 ounces pancetta (Italian bacon, see page 54)
2 tablespoons plus 1 teaspoon olive oil
⅓ cup pignolia (pine) nuts
1 medium onion, chopped fine
1 tablespoon finely chopped garlic
½ cup freshly grated Parmesan or Romano cheese
¼ cup finely chopped parsley
2 teaspoons fresh or dried rosemary
¼ teaspoon freshly ground black pepper
½ teaspoon freshly ground dried hot red pepper
2-ounce tin flat filets of anchovies
3 large cloves garlic, peeled and crushed
1 imported bay leaf
¼ cup dry white wine or vermouth
½ cup water
1 cup Tomato Sauce (see pages 310 and 311)
½ cup Yogurt (see page 67), at room temperature
½ cup liquid, reserved from the braising

1. Carefully trim the base of the escarole so that it is flat against the leaves. Do not core it. Discard any outer leaves that are blemished. Wash and drain the escarole.

2. Tie the head of escarole around its midsection with a piece of kitchen twine so that the leaves will stay intact while the head is being steamed.

   Place the escarole in a colander over a large pot of simmering water and steam it, covered, for 15 minutes. The water should be to a depth of 2 inches and the colander above the water level.

3. While the escarole is steaming, begin the preparation of the stuffing. Prepare the brown rice. In a small saucepan, bring the brown rice and 2 cups of water to a boil. Cover the saucepan and reduce the heat to low. Simmer until

the water has evaporated, occasionally tossing the rice with a fork to separate the grains. This will take about 20 minutes. Set aside, still covered.

4. Cut the pancetta into ¼-inch dice. Place 1 tablespoon of the olive oil in a 10-inch skillet over low heat. Add the pancetta dice and sauté them until they have given up their fat and have lightly browned. This will take about 15 minutes. Do not drain.

5. In another, small skillet, toast the pignolia nuts over low heat until they color lightly. This will bring out their flavor. Stir frequently as they can quickly burn. Set aside.

6. Spread a cotton dish towel on an area of your work surface. Cut two 24-inch lengths of kitchen twine and place them crosswise on the towel. When the escarole has wilted, lift the colander from the pot and immediately run cold water over the escarole to refresh it and to avoid darkening of the leaves.

Very carefully lift the escarole by the tied twine and place it on the dish towel, centering it where the lengths of twine cross. Cut the tied twine and slip it from the escarole. One by one, open up the leaves of escarole until they are fanned out from the center. Let the escarole remain on the towel as you finish the preparation of the stuffing.

7. When the pancetta has lightly browned, add the chopped onion and finely chopped garlic to the skillet. Increase the heat to medium and sauté until the onion wilts, stirring several times with a wooden spoon.

8. Remove the skillet from the heat and add the brown rice. With a fork, toss the rice until it is mixed with the other ingredients. Add the pignolia nuts, grated cheese, and parsley. Sprinkle with the rosemary, and black and red peppers. Gently toss until the ingredients are well blended.

9. To stuff the escarole, work from the center to the outside leaves. Using a tablespoon, place some of the stuffing under each leaf. As the stuffing is added, fold the leaves over toward the center, so that when all of the stuffing has been used, the escarole will form a compact ball. Bring the pieces of twine to the center of the stuffed escarole and tie them loosely. The twine will hold the escarole together as it braises, as well as being useful for lifting.

10. In a deep saucepan or casserole, large enough to hold the escarole, heat the other tablespoon of olive oil over medium-low heat. Add the tin of anchovies with its oil. Mash the anchovies with a fork until they disintegrate. Add the crushed cloves of garlic, bay leaf, wine, and water. Bring to a simmer.

Using the twine as a handle, lower the stuffed escarole into the braising liquid. Adjust the heat so that the liquid remains at a low simmer. Cover and braise the escarole for 30 minutes. Baste it frequently with the liquid in the pan.

11. About 20 minutes before you are ready to serve, begin warming your serving platter.

Ten minutes before serving bring the tomato sauce to a simmer over medium-low heat. (We use the same saucepan that was used for cooking the rice.) Turn the heat to low and whisk in the yogurt. Let the sauce remain at a low simmer as you prepare the escarole for serving.

12. Oil the heated platter with the remaining 1 teaspoon of olive oil. Using the twine, lift the braised escarole from the braising pan and place it on the platter. Cut the twine and slip it away. Keep the platter warm.

13. Quickly add the remaining braising liquid to the saucepan with the tomato sauce and yogurt. You should have about ½ cup. If not,

use what does remain. If there is more than ½ cup, quickly reduce it over high heat before adding it to the tomato sauce and yogurt.

Bring the sauce to a simmer over medium-low heat, whisking constantly. Pour the simmering sauce around but not over the stuffed escarole.

14. Serve immediately, cutting the escarole into wedges as you would a cake. Give each guest some of the sauce, placing it alongside the escarole.

WHAT TO BUY OR ORDER NOW

In February, we restock our larder with perishable items. Although we ordered heavily in October and November to avoid delays during the holidays, our supplies by now have become low. Cheeses are ordered from all of our sources. Upon arrival, they are examined and repackaged if necessary. As with Parmesan and Romano cheeses, never store your cheese wrapped in aluminum foil, unless you first wrap it in plastic wrap or waxed paper.

Flours are ordered and some of them will be refrigerated if there is space. We always refrigerate cornmeal, chickpea flour, buckwheat flour, and bulgur wheat if they will not be used within a few weeks. Other items we refrigerate for a longer storage are paprika, sesame seeds, all nuts, ginger root, rices, and all whole grains. The pancetta we order is cut into 3- and 4-ounce slices. Each slice is wrapped in waxed paper and then the slices are arranged in a plastic bag and frozen. We do not refrigerate olive oil, but decant it as needed.

At the supermarkets we check for specials on sugar and stock up before the canning season begins. The savings can be substantial.

AND IN OUR GARDEN

After a restive January, it is time to begin planting our garden. Indoors, we plant all of our pepper seeds in Jiffy-7 Peat Pellets. The pellets expand when soaked in water and plants grow in them until it is time to set them out in the garden, eliminating the chore of transplanting. Peppers are slow to germinate, so a February sowing indoors is not too early. They will be just the right size for planting outdoors in May. We have no special equipment for indoor gardening—just a sunny window and a long table. We did have to build what we call "plant cages," as our cats eat the seedlings. We built 2-feet square by 1-foot high, wooden frames which we covered with wire to place over the seedlings. The cats sun on top of the cages, but cannot nibble on the plants. After building them we found they are also useful in the garden for curing (drying) our onions before storing them. In the fall and winter months, we use the cages, open-ends up, for storing our harvest.

We traditionally make Susan B. Anthony Day (February 15) our first day for outdoor planting with lettuce, peas, Swiss chard, spinach, onions, and fava beans being sown. Beginning next year, we will also plant our corn as our friend, Mr. Weston, has advised us to do.

MARCH

RECIPES FROM A
KITCHEN DAIRY

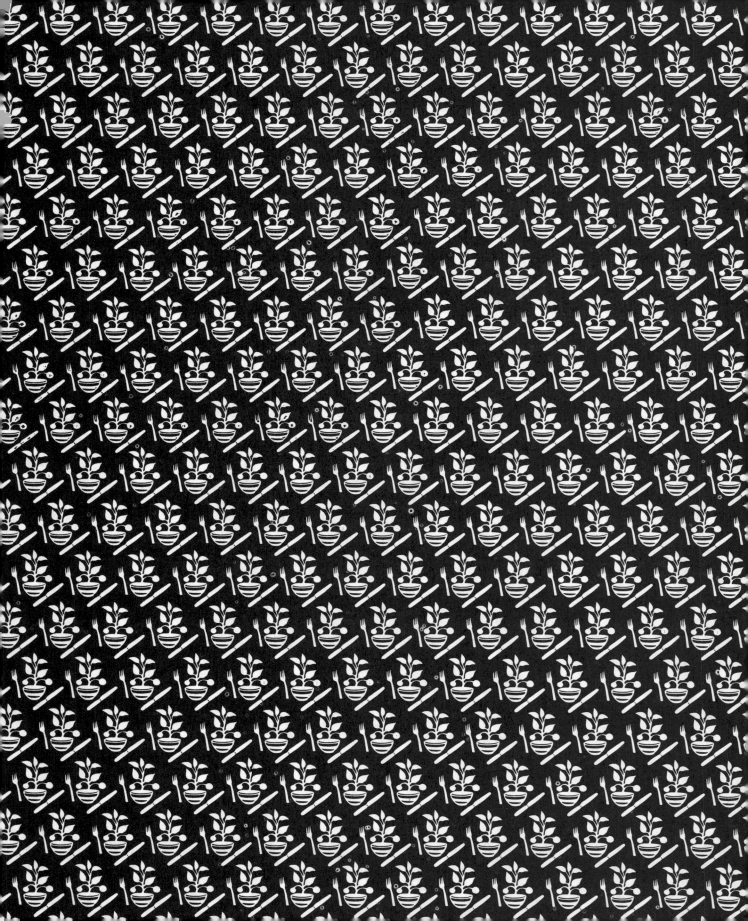

RECIPES FROM A KITCHEN DAIRY

Examining the dairy products on supermarket shelves today is a disheartening process. Almost every one of them seems to have been tampered with. Some butter is so salty it no longer tastes like butter. Store-bought cottage cheese can have as many as 14 nonessential ingredients. It is possible to buy a buttermilk that contains no real milk, and only in a few places is it still possible to buy cream that has not been sterilized or ultrapasteurized.

Alarmed by all of these unappetizing dairy products, we began making some of our own, and have developed a smooth, light-tasting yogurt, a refreshing buttermilk, and a pure basic cottage cheese with a delicious assortment of variations. Because other cheeses that we like are not always available, we have accumulated good sources for mail order. Butter and heavy cream are still a problem since it is illegal for the dairy farmers to sell their milk to individuals. Maybe we'll get a cow or two!

March seems a good time to experiment with homemade dairy products. The temperature is still cool in most areas and you will learn what to expect from your cheese before the hot weather arrives. We have no problems with the cheeses in the summer months, but a little closer attention should be paid to the clabbering time.

The yogurt-base soups we developed can be enjoyed anytime, but of course, the cold varieties taste better in the warmer months.

YOGURT

You do not need a commercial yogurt-maker to easily produce a delicious homemade batch. The only chore in making yogurt is scalding the milk, which must be done in order to kill any harmful bacteria, and the yogurt-makers don't do this for you. The yogurt will keep for about 1 week to 10 days under refrigeration.

Makes 2 quarts

½ gallon milk (whole or skimmed)
4 tablespoons plain yogurt

1. If you are making yogurt for the first time, you will need to buy a container of commercial plain yogurt to use as a starter, but from then on reserve several tablespoons of your own for the next batch. Find a brand that contains active cultures.

2. Run cold water around the inside of an enameled or stainless steel saucepan that is large enough to hold ½ gallon of milk. The cold water reacts with the metal of the saucepan to form a film and thus makes it easier to scald the milk without burning the pan.

Pour in the milk and, over medium heat, heat the milk almost to boiling. Let it cool to lukewarm and remove the skin that forms. If the milk is too hot when adding the yogurt, it will kill the culture.

3. In each of two very clean quart canning jars, put 2 tablespoons of yogurt. Pour equal amounts of milk in each and stir gently. It is not necessary to mix thoroughly.

Place the jars in a warm place (we use our oven with just the light on). The temperature should be at least 80°F but not over 110°F. The incubation time will vary. Our oven stays around 80° F, so we leave the yogurt in for about 16 to 18 hours. If your temperature is higher, check the yogurt after 8 hours.

To see if the yogurt is ready, tilt the jar slightly. If the yogurt comes away from the sides of the jar in a thickened mass, it is ready.

4. Cover and refrigerate. To cover, place a folded paper towel on the mouth of each jar, then cover with a piece of plastic wrap and a rubber band. The paper towel will absorb moisture from the yogurt and make it thicker.

Note: If after many months, your yogurt seems to be thinning, make 1 batch using ½ cup of yogurt to ¾ quart of scalded milk. This will renew it to its former thickness. Then proceed as before with future batches.

COOKING WITH YOGURT

Many of our recipes require that the yogurt be heated and simmered. For some, this may present a problem, as on rare occasions the yogurt will curdle if not handled properly. We use our yogurt so often in cooking that by now we don't even consider the possibility of that happening to us. At some point we must have developed a special "touch." However, if you think you may not have that touch, we offer a few suggestions for preventing curdling. Our recipes were tested using both our homemade yogurt and all of the available commercial brands of plain yogurt. None curdled for us, but these guidelines for prevention may be used for all yogurts.

1. The yogurt *must* be at room temperature. (We follow this step without exception.)

2. To stabilize the yogurt after it has come to room temperature, add 1 teaspoon of either an all-purpose flour, chickpea flour, or cornstarch for every cup of yogurt. Dissolve the flour or cornstarch in a small amount of water, just enough to make a paste, before adding to the yogurt. Mix well.

3. Before adding the yogurt to the simmering ingredients in a saucepan, warm the yogurt gradually by adding some of the hot ingredients to it, mixing thoroughly as you do so. When the yogurt has warmed, add it gradually to the saucepan.

4. Once you begin adding the yogurt to the saucepan, whisk or stir constantly until it has all been added. Continue to whisk or stir until the yogurt is well heated.

5. Some of our recipes say to simmer the ingredients, after the yogurt has been added, for 10 minutes or longer. Watch the yogurt carefully during this time and whisk as often as possible, keeping the ingredients at the very lowest simmer.

6. It is unlikely, but what if after all these precautions the yogurt still curdles? Unfortunately, it cannot be rectified, but the delicious taste of your dish will not be affected. Serve it anyway and, certainly, do not despair about cooking with yogurt. Yogurt gives an uncustomary dimension of flavor in cooking that cannot be duplicated.

COLD CUCUMBER SOUP WITH GARLIC AND DILL

For summer, Cold Cucumber Soup is incomparable. Even though this recipe has been a staple in our summer cooking for many years, it never fails to invigorate us. Under refrigeration the soup keeps well for about a week, so we try to keep some on hand during hot weather.

Serves 4

8 unwaxed, pickling type cucumbers, about 3½ inches long
½ teaspoon salt
2 cups Yogurt (see page 67)
1 teaspoon finely minced garlic
1 cup Chicken Stock, chilled (see page 109)
¼ teaspoon freshly ground white pepper
4 tablespoons cucumber dice reserved for garnish
2 tablespoons minced dill, coriander, or chives for garnish

1. Wash the cucumbers. Remove the ends, but do not peel them. Quarter the cucumbers lengthwise and remove the seeds if they are large; if the seeds are very tiny, there is no need to remove them. Chop the strips of cucumber into dice no larger than ¼ inch.

Place the dice in a colander or sieve, sprinkle with the salt, and toss. Let the cucumbers drain for ½ hour, tossing occasionally. This will draw excess moisture and any bitterness from the cucumbers.

2. Combine the yogurt, garlic, and chicken stock in a medium-sized bowl. Whisk so that the yogurt and stock are thoroughly blended.

3. When the cucumbers have drained, squeeze them gently between paper towels to dry. Fold them, along with the white pepper, into the liquid mixture, reserving 4 tablespoons for garnishing the soup.

Cover the soup and the reserved dice,

separately, with plastic wrap and chill for several hours or overnight before serving.

4. You may serve the soup from a tureen, in individual soup plates, or for an elegant touch, in stemmed wine glasses. Garnish the servings with the reserved cucumber dice and the minced herb of your choice. Dill, coriander, or chives will each give the soup a different character.

COLD TOMATO SOUP WITH FRESH BASIL

This soup is basically the same as the Cold Cucumber Soup, substituting fresh tomatoes for the cucumbers and using fresh basil as the herb. In both recipes, we tried making the soups into ices, but too much flavor was lost. Serving them well chilled is best.

Serves 4

1 pound fresh, ripe tomatoes
½ teaspoon salt
2 cups Yogurt (see page 67)
1 teaspoon finely minced garlic
1 cup Chicken Stock (see page 109), chilled
¼ teaspoon freshly ground white pepper
1 tablespoon finely minced fresh basil
2 tablespoons chopped tomatoes, reserved for garnish
4 thin slices of lemon for garnish
4 small sprigs of fresh basil for garnish

1. Core and seed but do not peel the tomatoes. Chop them into pieces no larger than ⅓ inch and then place them into a colander or sieve. Add the salt and toss to mix. Let them drain for ½ hour to remove excess liquid.

2. Combine the yogurt, garlic, chicken stock, white pepper, and minced basil. Whisk to thoroughly blend the ingredients.

3. Add the tomatoes to the yogurt mixture, reserving 2 tablespoons of the tomatoes for garnish. (If you like, you may purée the soup at this point, but we prefer not to, as we feel the tomatoes retain more of their fresh flavor if chopped.)

Cover the soup and the reserved chopped tomatoes, separately, with plastic wrap and chill for several hours or overnight in the refrigerator before serving.

4. Serve the soup from a tureen into individual soup plates or in stemmed glasses. Garnish the tureen by placing the lemon slices in the center of the soup and topping the slices with the reserved chopped tomatoes and the sprigs of fresh basil.

If you are serving the soup in stemmed glasses, place a slice of lemon on the rim of each glass and sprinkle the reserved tomatoes over the servings, placing the basil sprigs on top.

COLD BEET SOUP WITH DILL

This is the easiest of the yogurt-base soups to prepare and possibly the most colorful. We like to continue the deep-purple color scheme and serve the soup in white or clear soup bowls, centered on dinner plates that have been lined with Ruby lettuce, purple-tinged spring onions, sliced thin, and Early Purple Vienna kohlrabi that has been picked so young that it does not require peeling. You might even add a sprinkling of mung-bean sprouts that have grown long enough to sprout their own little purple leaves. The "salad" should be dressed with a simple vinaigrette sauce and eaten with the soup or after the soup bowls are removed.

Serves 4

1 pound (without their tops) fresh, raw beets
1 tablespoon olive oil
1 medium onion, coarsely chopped
1 teaspoon minced garlic
½ teaspoon salt
¼ teaspoon freshly ground white pepper
1 tablespoon red wine vinegar, or more to taste
¼ cup water
2½ cups Yogurt (see page 67)
2 tablespoons minced fresh dill
4 small sprigs of fresh dill for garnish

1. Wash the beets and remove tops and root ends. Save the tops for Braised Beet Tops (see page 267). Peel the beets and grate them coarsely on the medium cutting edge of a hand grater. You will have about 3 cups. Set aside.

2. Heat the olive oil in a 2-quart saucepan. Add the onion and garlic. Sprinkle them with the salt and white pepper. Sauté over medium-low heat until the onion has wilted.

3. Add the shredded beets, vinegar, and water to the saucepan. Stir to mix the ingredients. Cover and simmer over low heat for about 15 minutes or until the beets are tender.

4. Remove the saucepan from the heat and allow the beets to cool for another 15 minutes.

5. Place the ingredients from the saucepan in a food processor fitted with the metal blade. Add 2 cups of the yogurt and the minced dill. Purée the mixture.

If you do not have a food processor, this may be done in batches, using a blender. Transfer the soup to a bowl. Cover it with plastic wrap and refrigerate the soup until it is chilled. The soup will keep for 3 or 4 days.

6. When you are ready to serve the soup, divide it among individual soup bowls. With the remaining ½ cup of yogurt, place a dollop (2 tablespoons) in the center of each serving. Place a sprig of fresh dill on the yogurt for garnish.

CARROT SOUP WITH LEMON AND SPROUTS

We first envisioned this refreshing soup served hot in the winter months, but when trying it chilled the second day, we found it just as flavorful cold. The puréed carrots are added only at the end of the cooking time, so they retain their fresh, raw taste. The lemon juice adds a complementary tang.

Serves 4 to 6

3 tablespoons unsalted butter
2 medium onions, coarsely chopped
2 medium stalks celery, trimmed and coarsely chopped
½ teaspoon salt
¼ teaspoon freshly ground black pepper
2 tablespoons lemon juice (about ½ lemon)
2 cups Yogurt (see page 67), at room temperature
½ cup heavy cream, at room temperature
1 pound raw carrots, puréed (see Note)
½ to ¾ cup alfalfa sprouts (for growing instructions, see page 39)
½ cup parsley or fresh dill (if available), chopped fine
Thin slice of lemon for each serving (use the other ½ lemon)

1. Melt the butter in a 2-quart saucepan over low heat and add the onions and celery. Sprinkle with salt and black pepper and braise, covered, for 20 minutes. The vegetables should be cooked only enough to remove the sharpness from the onions. Begin warming your soup plates.

2. Add the lemon juice to the onions and celery and purée the mixture in a processor, blender, or food mill.

Return the purée to the saucepan. Whisk in the yogurt (see page 68) and heavy cream and bring the ingredients to a full simmer over medium heat.

Just before you are ready to serve, add the puréed carrots and cook just until the soup is hot—this will be only a matter of minutes.

3. To serve, ladle the soup into individual heated soup plates. Sprinkle each serving with 2 tablespoons of alfalfa sprouts, fluffing them as you go. Then sprinkle with a small amount of the chopped parsley or dill. Place a slice of lemon in the center of each serving.

If you plan to serve the soup chilled, refrigerate it for several hours or overnight. Ladle the soup into soup plates and garnish as for the hot soup. Or, if you wish, serve the soup in wine goblets, placing the lemon slice on the rim of the goblet.

Note: To purée the carrots in a food processor, first cut the carrots into 1½-inch lengths before adding them to the container. Use the metal blade of the processor.

If you are using a blender, also cut the carrots into 1½-inch lengths.

If you are preparing them by hand, do not cut them into lengths. Use the smallest cutting edge on your grater.

Although there will be a difference in the quantity of purée with the methods, the difference will not alter the outcome of the soup. With the processor, you will have about 3½ cups of purée; less with the blender; and with a hand grater, only about 2 cups, as the purée is more concentrated. Set the puréed carrots aside, covered with plastic wrap.

GARDEN PEA SOUP WITH A PARSLEY-LEMON GREMOLADA

This soup should be served as soon as it is done while the color is a vivid green. It pales after standing or being refrigerated. When served with a garnish combination of Parmesan cheese, gremolada (usually a combination of parsley, lemon peel, and garlic, but here it is made without garlic), and alfalfa sprouts, the soup is exceptional.

Serves 4 to 6

1 recipe Basic Brown Rice (see below)
¼ cup finely chopped parsley
1 tablespoon finely chopped lemon peel
2 tablespoons unsalted butter
1 medium onion, coarsely chopped
1½ cups coarsely chopped celery
2 cloves garlic, minced
¼ teaspoon freshly ground white pepper
2 cups Chicken Stock (see page 109)
4 cups fresh peas (about 4 pounds, unshelled) or two 10-ounce packages frozen
2 cups Yogurt (see page 67), at room temperature
1 cup freshly grated Parmesan cheese
1 cup alfalfa sprouts (for growing instructions, see page 39)

1. Cook the brown rice while you prepare the soup. If it is ready before the soup is done, it can sit, covered, for up to ½ hour.

2. Make the gremolada by mixing the parsley and lemon peel together in a small bowl. Set aside.

3. In a 3-quart saucepan, melt the butter over medium-low heat. Add the onion, celery, and garlic along with the white pepper.

   Sauté the vegetables until limp, but not browned.

4. Add the chicken stock, raise the heat to medium, and bring to a simmer. Add 3 cups of peas and return to a simmer. Begin warming your soup plates.

5. Purée the mixture in batches either in a food processor or blender, or through a food mill. Return the ingredients to the saucepan. Bring once again to a simmer over medium heat and add the yogurt (see page 68) and the remaining cup of peas.

6. When the soup is very hot, divide the brown rice among individual, heated soup plates. Ladle the soup onto the rice.

   Sprinkle each serving with several tablespoons of the Parmesan cheese, a little of the gremolada, and top with several tablespoons of the alfalfa sprouts. Pull the sprouts apart as you place them on the soup. Serve immediately.

BASIC BROWN RICE

Brown rice has so much more flavor than white rice that we use it almost exclusively. We use a little less water than most recipes call for and cook the rice for a shorter time so that the grains remain *al dente*. Whey, when used as part of the liquid, adds even more flavor and an unusual tang to the rice. However, the rice will resemble a risotto with its creamy texture.

Serves 4 to 6 (about 5 cups cooked rice)

2 cups raw short- or long-grain brown rice
1 teaspoon salt
4 cups water (or 2 cups water and 2 cups whey, see page 91)

1. Place the rice and salt in a heavy, 2-quart saucepan and add the water. Cover the saucepan and bring the water to a boil over medium-high heat.

   If you are using water and whey, do not add the whey until the water has come to a boil. The rice must absorb some of the water before the whey is added. Otherwise, the rice will not cook properly.

2. When the water comes to a boil, immediately turn the heat to very low. If you are using whey, add it at this time.

   Cook the rice, covered, over very low heat for about 30 minutes until all of the liquid has been absorbed. Do not stir, but check occasionally to make sure the liquid is not evaporating too quickly. If it is, reduce the heat.

Taste the rice after 30 minutes. If the grains are too firm for your taste, continue to cook a little longer.

Serve immediately or remove the saucepan from the heat and let it sit, still covered, until you are ready to serve.

TOMATO SOUP WITH PESTO AND PARMESAN

This soup tastes so rich it is as if it had been made with only heavy cream. Serve it in warmed, shallow soup plates for a colorful presentation. The addition of pasta makes the soup a satisfying main course when served with crusty chunks of freshly baked bread, followed by a large salad and cheese. You may follow it with a meat course, but if you do, serve small portions unless you omit the pasta.

Serves 4 to 6

1 recipe Basic Egg Dough (see page 305)
5 tablespoons unsalted butter
2 medium onions, coarsely chopped
4 large cloves garlic, minced
2 cups drained canned tomatoes
2 cups liquid from the drained tomatoes
2 cups Yogurt (see page 67), at room temperature
½ cup heavy cream, at room temperature
¼ teaspoon freshly ground black pepper
1 tablespoon salt (for cooking the pasta), plus additional if needed
1 cup freshly grated Parmesan cheese
1 cup Pesto (see page 309)

1. Roll out the pasta dough. Instead of cutting the dough into strips, cut it into squares no larger than ½ inch. The cutting goes very quickly with a good pair of kitchen shears.

Spread the squares on a cloth towel until you are ready to cook them.

2. Melt 3 tablespoons of the butter in a heavy 1½-quart saucepan over low heat. Add the onions and garlic, raise the heat to medium, and sauté until the onions wilt and begin to take on some color.

3. Add the drained tomatoes to the saucepan,

bring just to a simmer then remove the saucepan from the heat.

Using a food processor, blender, or food mill, purée the mixture. Return the purée to the saucepan and add the 2 cups of tomato liquid. Bring to a simmer.

Whisk in the yogurt (see page 68) and, when it is well incorporated, whisk in the heavy cream. Add the black pepper and taste for salt. Keep in mind that you will be serving the soup with cheese and pesto, so no salt may be needed, particularly if the canned tomatoes contain salt.

Simmer the soup, covered, over medium-low heat for 15 minutes. Whisk occasionally during this time.

4. While the soup is simmering, bring 4 quarts of water to a boil in a large pot. Also begin warming your soup tureen and plates.

Add 1 tablespoon of salt and when the water returns to a boil, add the pasta squares. Cook just until *al dente*, which could take only 2 minutes if the pasta has not dried too long.

Drain the pasta onto the heated platter and quickly toss it with the remaining 2 tablespoons of butter.

5. Divide the pasta among your heated soup plates. Spoon the soup over the pasta. The size of the servings depends upon what courses will follow the soup.

Sprinkle a tablespoon or so of the Parmesan cheese over each serving and place a tablespoon of pesto in the center of the soup.

Serve immediately, passing the remaining cheese and pesto at the table for those guests who would like more.

CORN SOUP WITH RED PEPPERS AND PARMESAN

This soup is basically the same as Tomato Soup with Pesto and Parmesan, but without pasta. The flavor of the yogurt is more pronounced, but is counterbalanced nicely by the sweetness of the corn.

Serves 4 to 6

5 cups corn kernels, fresh (6 large ears) or frozen
2 medium onions
4 large cloves garlic
4 tablespoons unsalted butter
1 tablespoon olive oil
1 large red bell pepper, fresh or frozen
2 cups Yogurt (see page 67), at room temperature

½ cup heavy cream, at room temperature
½ teaspoon salt
¼ teaspoon freshly ground black pepper
½ teaspoon freshly ground dried hot red pepper
¾ cup freshly grated Parmesan cheese
¼ cup minced parsley

1. To prepare the fresh corn, shuck the ears, remove the silk, and cut the kernels from the cob. If you are using frozen corn, let it defrost enough so that you can measure the cups.

2. Peel and chop the onions and the garlic coarsely. In a 2-quart saucepan, melt 3 tablespoons of the butter with the tablespoon of olive oil. Add the chopped onions and garlic and sauté over medium heat until the onions have wilted.

3. While the onions and garlic are cooking, seed and core the bell pepper and cut into ¼-inch dice. (If you are using frozen peppers that have been seeded, cored, and quartered, let them defrost slightly before dicing them.)

In a small saucepan, heat the remaining tablespoon of butter and sauté the diced pepper with 2 cups of the corn, just long enough to cook them slightly.

4. When the onions have wilted, add the remaining 3 cups of corn to the 2-quart saucepan. Toss with the onions and garlic and sauté briefly just to heat through.

Purée the mixture in a food processor, blender or food mill. Return the purée to the saucepan and add the yogurt (see page 68) and cream. Stir with a wooden spoon, just to blend, and add the sautéed pepper and corn. Season with the salt, black pepper, and red pepper.

Bring the soup to a simmer over medium heat and cook, covered, for about 15 minutes until bubbling and very hot. Stir occasionally during this time. Warm your soup plates.

5. Ladle the soup into the heated soup plates and sprinkle each serving with 2 tablespoons of the Parmesan cheese and a small amount of the minced parsley. Serve immediately.

MUSHROOM SOUP WITH SHERRY AND CREAM

For a superb soup be sure to use only very fresh, white mushrooms, chopped very fine. Fresh tarragon imparts a lovely color as well as flavor but if it isn't available, frozen or dried of a fine quality will do.

Serves 4

1½ pounds fresh mushrooms
2 tablespoons unsalted butter
3 tablespoons minced shallots
½ teaspoon salt
¼ teaspoon freshly ground white pepper
½ cup dry sherry
1 tablespoon finely snipped fresh or frozen tarragon or ½ teaspoon dried
3 cups Yogurt (see page 67), at room temperature
1 cup heavy cream, at room temperature
Additional tablespoon *fresh* tarragon, snipped, for garnish (optional)

1. Prepare the mushrooms. Trim and discard the ends from the stems. Wipe the mushrooms clean with damp paper towels, then chop them very fine, reserving 4 whole ones for garnish. Slice the reserved mushrooms thin, and set aside.

2. In a heavy 2-quart saucepan, melt the butter over medium-low heat, and add the shallots. Sauté until they are wilted. Add the chopped mushrooms, salt, and pepper.

Stir and continue sautéing until the mushrooms have given up most of their liquid and the mixture begins to dry. This will take about 20 minutes.

3. Add the sherry and tarragon. Increase the heat to medium. Simmer until the sherry is reduced to ¼ cup then lower the heat and whisk in the yogurt (see page 68).

Let the ingredients simmer for about 15 minutes before adding the cream. During this time, begin warming your soup tureen and plates.

4. Add the cream, bring the soup back to a simmer and serve immediately, either from a heated soup tureen or ladled into individual, heated soup plates.

Garnish the tureen or the plates with the thinly sliced reserved mushrooms and the fresh tarragon, if available. Do not use frozen or dried tarragon as garnish.

SPINACH SOUP WITH SHALLOTS AND LEMON

This delicious soup deserves to be made with only the freshest, greenest spinach. It is difficult to give a precise amount to use as sometimes fresh spinach has very short stems and other times, the stems will account for a large amount of the weight. If the stems are very short, buy 1½ pounds and if long, buy 2 pounds.

Serves 4

1½ to 2 pounds fresh spinach
2 tablespoons unsalted butter
3 tablespoons minced shallots
1 large clove garlic, minced
1 tablespoon fresh lemon juice
3 cups Yogurt (see page 67), at room temperature
¼ teaspoon salt
¼ teaspoon freshly ground black pepper
1 cup heavy cream, at room temperature
½ cup freshly grated Parmesan cheese
4 lemon slices for garnish

1. Thoroughly wash the spinach to get rid of any sand, then remove the stems.

Place the spinach leaves in a large pot, cover, and over low heat steam in the water clinging to the leaves, until they are wilted.

Immediately drain the spinach in a colander and refresh it with cold, running water. Squeeze the spinach, in small handfuls, to remove the liquid.

2. Melt the butter in a 2-quart saucepan over medium-low heat and sauté the shallots and garlic until they become soft.

In a food processor, blender, or food mill purée the shallots and garlic combined with the spinach, lemon juice, and 1 cup of the yogurt. Begin warming your soup plates.

3. Place the ingredients back in the 2-quart saucepan and add the salt and black pepper. Bring to a simmer over medium-low heat and whisk in the remaining yogurt (see page 68) and heavy cream.

When it returns to a full simmer, serve the soup immediately. (Longer cooking will cause the spinach to darken, although it does not affect the flavor.)

4. Serve the soup in individual, heated soup plates. Sprinkle each serving with 2 tablespoons of the Parmesan cheese and garnish with a slice of lemon in the center.

POTATO SOUP WITH BAY LEAVES AND CHIVES

Each time we create a new yogurt-base soup, we think it the best of them all. This soup ranks high on our list. It is thicker than the others and seems to taste richer, although it contains no heavy cream. The secret to the superb flavor is in the quality of the fine, imported bay leaves. See our mail-order listings if none is available where you live.

Serves 4

1¾ pounds very fresh boiling potatoes (about 5 or 6 medium size)
3 tablespoons unsalted butter
2 medium onions, coarsely chopped
2 imported bay leaves (each about 1½ inches long)
½ teaspoon salt
¼ teaspoon freshly ground white pepper
2 cups Yogurt (see page 67), at room temperature
4 tablespoons of a fresh, minced herb for garnish, such as chives,
    parsley, or dill

1. Wash and scrub the potatoes, but do not peel them. Steam them whole until they are tender.

2. Meanwhile, melt the butter in a heavy 2-quart saucepan or casserole over medium-low heat. Add the onions and the bay leaves. Sprinkle with the salt and white pepper.
    Cover, lower the heat slightly, and braise the onions for ½ hour. Check to make sure that they do not brown. They should only be soft and infused with the aroma of the bay leaves.

3. When the potatoes are tender and cool enough to handle, remove the skins. In a food processor, blender, or food mill, purée the potatoes with the braised onions, removing the bay leaves first. The mixture will be very thick.

4. Return the purée to the saucepan and whisk in the yogurt (see page 68). Simmer, covered, over medium-low heat for about 15 minutes. Whisk occasionally during this time. Begin warming your soup tureen and plates.

5. Serve the soup from the heated soup tureen or ladle it into heated, individual soup plates. Sprinkle each serving with a tablespoon of the fresh herb you have chosen.

WINTER CABBAGE SOUP WITH TOMATOES

This cabbage and yogurt soup, which we gratiné, is rich and luscious with the slow cooking of the vegetables and the addition of the cheeses. The tartness of the yogurt balances the sweetness of the braised cabbage and onions.

Serves 4

4 tablespoons plus approximately 4 teaspoons olive oil
2 medium onions, coarsely chopped
4 large cloves garlic, chopped fine
2-pound winter cabbage

1 teaspoon dried winter savory or 1 teaspoon wild thyme, crumbled
½ teaspoon freshly ground black pepper
1 cup well-drained, canned tomatoes
1 cup liquid from the drained tomatoes
8 slices of a very dry baguette, ½-inch thick
2 cups Yogurt (see page 67), at room temperature
1 cup coarsely grated Swiss Gruyère cheese (3 ounces)
¼ cup freshly grated Romano or Parmesan cheese

1. Heat 3 tablespoons of the olive oil in a 3-quart pot. Add the onions and garlic and sauté over medium-low heat until wilted.

2. Discard the outer leaves of the cabbage. Core and shred the cabbage fine. A food processor, fitted with the medium shredding disk, works best for this. If you do not have a food processor, shred the cabbage by hand or with a cabbage cutter, but it must be shredded fine.

3. Add the shredded cabbage along with the winter savory or wild thyme and the black pepper to the pot. Stir to mix. Cover and braise over low heat for 20 minutes.

4. After 20 minutes, add the drained tomatoes and the 1 cup of liquid from the tomatoes. Braise, covered, for 45 minutes over low heat. Stir occasionally.

5. Meanwhile, prepare the slices of bread, which will be placed on top of the soup before gratinéing. Preheat the oven to 350°F. Remove the crusts from the bread, saving them for crumbs at some later date. Arrange the bread slices on a baking sheet and brush the tops with ½ tablespoon of the olive oil. Bake on the middle level of the oven until the tops are golden brown.

Turn the slices over and brush with another ½ tablespoon of olive oil. Return to the oven until the slices are very dry and nicely browned on both sides. This will take about 10 minutes per side. Set aside. Reheat the oven to 400°F.

6. When the vegetables have braised for 45 minutes, stir in the yogurt (see page 68) and bring to a simmer. Add the grated Gruyère cheese and stir until it has melted.

7. You may either gratiné the soup in individual bowls with a 2-cup capacity (preferred) or in the pot itself, if it can withstand oven temperatures. If you are using individual bowls, place them on a baking sheet. This makes it easier to get them into and out of the oven and is a safeguard against spills or breakage.

8. For individual servings, ladle the soup into the bowls and top each with 2 slices of the toasted bread. The bread should cover the soup. Sprinkle each with 1 tablespoon of the Romano or Parmesan cheese and dribble 1 teaspoon of olive oil over the cheese.

9. If you are gratinéing the soup in the pot, cover the top with the toasted bread, sprinkle with the Romano or Parmesan cheese and dribble about 1 tablespoon of olive oil over the surface.

10. Place the soup on a rack in the middle of the oven and bake for 15 to 20 minutes until the soup is bubbling and the top is browned.

The soup will be extremely hot, so you may wish to let it sit for about 10 minutes before serving.

RED LENTIL SOUP WITH GARAM MASALA AND CROUTONS

Lentils suggest soups and red lentils suggest Indian foods, so we created this curried soup using our ubiquitous yogurt and Garam Masala, a hot mixture of Indian spices. You may wish to serve it with the other selections for an Indian meal (see June chapter).

Red lentils lose most of their coral hue when cooked, but by adding sweet paprika and dried hot red pepper, not only is the flavor augmented but we have a soup that is as colorful as the name implies.

Serves 4 to 6

1 pound split red lentils (2½ cups)
2 tablespoons unsalted butter
1 tablespoon olive oil
2 medium onions, coarsely chopped
4 large cloves garlic, minced
1 teaspoon freshly ground dried hot red pepper
2 teaspoons sweet paprika
2 cups water (approximately)
2 teaspoons Garam Masala (see page 190)
½ teaspoon salt
¼ teaspoon freshly ground black pepper
2 cups well-drained, canned tomatoes
2 cups liquid from the drained tomatoes
Croutons for the soup (see below)
2 tablespoons lemon juice
2 cups Yogurt (see page 67), at room temperature

1. Rinse the lentils in a sieve and discard any little bits of grit.

2. Over medium heat, melt the butter with the olive oil in a 3-quart pot. Add the onions and garlic and sauté them until they begin to color lightly.

3. Dissolve the hot red pepper and the paprika in 1 cup of the water.

4. When the onions and garlic have begun to color, add the garam masala. Stir and sauté for only a moment. Add the lentils to the pot along with the water with the dissolved spices, the salt, and the black pepper. Stir to mix and add

the tomatoes and the tomato liquid. Stir again and bring to a simmer.

Cover and reduce the heat to medium-low and cook for 45 minutes, stirring occasionally. Add the remaining cup of water as the soup thickens.

5. While the soup is simmering, prepare the croutons (see recipe) and set aside.

6. After 45 minutes, add the lemon juice to the pot. Also begin warming the soup plates.

Purée the soup in batches in a food processor, a blender, or pass it through a food mill.

7. Return the soup to the pot as it is puréed. Stir in the yogurt (see page 68) and bring the soup to a full simmer.

8. Serve the soup in individual, heated soup plates. Sprinkle each serving with some of the croutons.

CROUTONS FOR SOUPS

Take the same care making your croutons as you do in making your soups. Clarifying the butter then adding the olive oil helps prevent the butter from burning—hastily made croutons can ruin an otherwise wonderful soup.

Makes about 1½ cups, or enough croutons for 4 to 6

6 slices of a very dry baguette, ½-inch thick
4 tablespoons unsalted butter
1 tablespoon olive oil
3 large cloves garlic

1. Remove the crusts from the slices of bread. (Save them to use at some later date for bread crumbs.) Cut the slices of bread into ½-inch cubes.

2. Clarify the butter by melting it in a small skillet over low heat or in a 200°F oven. Let it cool and remove the white foam and milky solids either by carefully skimming with a spoon or by straining the butter through cheesecloth placed in a sieve over a bowl.

3. Heat the clarified butter with the olive oil in a skillet over medium-low heat. Peel and crush the garlic. Do not mince it.

Add the garlic to the skillet and sauté until it is golden brown. Discard the garlic. The butter will be richly flavored with the aroma of the garlic.

4. Add the bread cubes to the skillet and brown them evenly, tossing often. When the croutons are a golden brown and very crisp, remove them with a slotted spoon onto paper towels to drain.

Keep the croutons warm until you are ready to serve.

CHICKPEA SOUP WITH PASTA AND PANCETTA

This is the most robust of our yogurt-base soups and any course served after it should be light. We prefer dried chickpeas to canned for a better texture. They are also more economical, although chickpeas are the most expensive of the dried beans because there is generally only one bean to a pod. We think this soup tastes best made with pancetta (Italian bacon, see page 54), and because it is not available in our area we mail order ours in quantity from Manganaro's (see the mail-order listings).

Serves 4 to 6

1½ cups dried chickpeas
½ teaspoon salt, plus 1 tablespoon (for cooking the pasta)
1 recipe Basic Egg Dough (see page 305)
1 tablespoon olive oil
2 ounces pancetta, cut into ¼-inch dice
1 medium onion, chopped into ¼-inch pieces
4 large cloves garlic, chopped fine
2 medium stalks celery, chopped fine
1 cup coarsely chopped, well-drained, canned tomatoes
1 cup liquid from the drained tomatoes
½ teaspoon crumbled fresh or dried rosemary
½ teaspoon freshly ground dried hot red pepper
¼ teaspoon freshly ground black pepper
2 medium, imported bay leaves
Liquid from the cooked chickpeas
2 cups Yogurt (see page 67), at room temperature
1 cup freshly grated Romano or Parmesan cheese,
   or 1 cup Pesto (see page 309)

1. Rinse and pick over the dried chickpeas, discarding any that are blemished. Place the chickpeas in a heavy 3-quart pot. Add water to cover by 1 inch, cover the pot, and bring to a boil over medium heat.

   Immediately remove the pot from the heat and let it sit, still covered, for 1 hour or longer. This eliminates an overnight soaking.

2. Return the pot to the stove and add ½ teaspoon salt. Simmer the chickpeas over medium-low heat until they are tender, but not mushy. This will take about 45 minutes.

   Drain the chickpeas in a colander or

sieve placed over a bowl to reserve the liquid. (You will have about 4 cups of cooked chickpeas.) Set aside.

3. While the chickpeas are simmering, prepare the pasta dough. Roll it out and, with a pair of kitchen shears, cut it into squares no larger than ½ inch. This goes very quickly if you first cut the pasta into long, ½-inch strips and then across into the ½-inch squares. Spread the squares on a cloth towel until it is time to cook them.

4. Place the olive oil over medium-low heat in the same 3-quart pot in which the chickpeas were cooked. Add the pancetta and sauté until it is lightly browned.

Add the onion and garlic, along with the chopped celery, to the pot and continue sautéing until the vegetables are limp and beginning to color.

5. Add the drained tomatoes, the 1 cup of liquid from the tomatoes, and the rosemary, red and black peppers, and bay leaves. Simmer, covered, for 10 minutes.

6. While the soup is simmering, in a large pot bring 4 quarts of water for cooking the pasta to a boil. Also begin warming your soup plates.

7. In a food processor, blender, or food mill, purée ½ the chickpeas with 1 cup of the reserved chickpea cooking liquid. Add the purée to the pot along with the yogurt (see page 68) and the remaining chickpeas.

Simmer, partially covered, over medium-low heat for 15 minutes. Stir occasionally. If the soup is too thick for your taste, add more of the reserved liquid from the cooked chickpeas.

8. About 5 minutes before the soup is ready, add the tablespoon of salt to the boiling water. Return to a boil and add the squares of pasta. Cook until *al dente*, which will take only about 2 minutes if the pasta has not dried too long. Allow the pasta to drain in a colander.

9. To serve the soup, divide the pasta among individual, heated soup plates and, removing the bay leaves first, ladle the soup over the pasta. Sprinkle each serving with several tablespoons of the grated cheese, or if you prefer, a dollop of pesto in the center.

FISH SOUP WITH POTATOES AND CREAM

We specify filets of flounder for the fish soup as they seem to be the most readily available and the freshest fish in any area. However, you may use another saltwater fish if you wish, but choose one that is not oily.

You may also use the heads, tails, and bones in the poaching liquid. Since our garden is of prime importance, we compost the raw trimmings to enrich the soil. On "Fish Night," everyone gets a treat — the cats, the garden, and finally ourselves. Accompany your fish soup with Linney's Mill Biscuits (see below).

Serves 4 to 6

Poaching Liquid:
¼ cup dry white wine or vermouth
2 cups water
¼-inch slice of lemon
1 imported bay leaf
1 teaspoon wild thyme

1½ pounds filet of flounder (about 3 pounds before filleting)
2½ cups reserved poaching liquid, strained
1 pound boiling potatoes
2 ounces pancetta (Italian bacon, see page 54)
1 medium onion, chopped fine
1 cup celery, chopped into ¼-inch dice
½ teaspoon freshly ground white pepper
½ teaspoon dried hot red pepper (optional)
1 cup reserved liquid from the drained tomatoes
1 cup well-drained, canned tomatoes
2 cups Yogurt (see page 67), at room temperature
1 cup heavy cream, at room temperature
1½ cups Croutons (optional; see page 83)
2 tablespoons of minced dill, basil, or parsley for garnish (optional)

1. Prepare the poaching liquid for the fish. In a 2-quart saucepan, combine the wine and water with a slice of lemon, bay leaf, and wild thyme. (You may wish to tie the aromatics in a small piece of cheesecloth.)

Bring the ingredients to a boil and add the fish filets. Cut them in half if they are too large for the saucepan. Cover and gently poach the fish over medium-low heat for 10 minutes.

2. Remove the fish to a fine sieve placed over a bowl to catch the liquid. Flake the fish into chunks, discarding any skin or small bones. Place the chunks in a bowl and set aside. You should have about 2½ cups of fish.

Pour the poaching liquid through the sieve and reserve it. Again, there should be about 2½ cups.

3. Peel the potatoes and place them, still whole, in a bowl of cold water until you are ready to cook them. Kept in water, they will not discolor and some of the starch will be removed.

4. Mince the pancetta as fine as possible. Sauté the pancetta in a 3-quart pot over low heat until it has lightly browned. Add the chopped onion and celery along with the white pepper and the optional red pepper.

Sauté the vegetables just until they wilt, but do not brown. Add the poaching liquid and the liquid from the drained tomatoes. Bring the ingredients to a simmer.

5. Dry the potatoes and cut them into ½-inch cubes. Add them to the pot and cook, covered, over medium heat for about 20 minutes. The potatoes should be tender, but not soft.

Begin to heat your soup plates.

6. Reduce the heat to medium-low and add the fish chunks and the drained tomatoes. Bring just to a simmer and stir in the yogurt (see page 68) and the heavy cream. Simmer, uncovered, for 10 minutes.

7. Serve the soup in individual, heated soup plates or bowls. If you are garnishing, first sprinkle each bowl with several croutons and then with the herb of your choice.

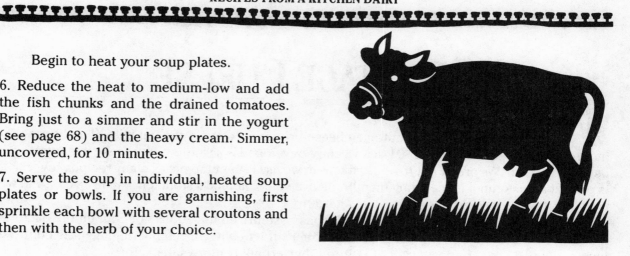

LINNEY'S MILL WHOLE-WHEAT DROP BISCUITS

Often, handwritten recipes are tacked on the wall at Linney's Mill located in Union Grove, N.C., not far from our home. This is one of our favorites.

If your whole-wheat flour is very fine, substitute ¼ cup of bran flakes for ¼ cup of the whole-wheat flour to add texture.

Makes 30 biscuits

2 cups whole-wheat flour
1 teaspoon salt
1 teaspoon baking powder
½ cup corn oil
½ cup milk
1 egg, beaten

1. Preheat the oven to 425° F.

2. In a large mixing bowl, combine the whole-wheat flour, salt, and baking powder. In another small bowl, mix the corn oil, milk, and the beaten egg.

3. Add the liquids to the dry ingredients and incorporate with a wooden spoon. Remove the dough from the bowl onto your work surface and knead briefly. The dough will be as moist as it should be for drop biscuits.

4. To form the biscuits, drop a heaping tablespoon of the dough onto an ungreased aluminum baking sheet.

Continue dropping by the tablespoon, leaving 1 inch of space between each biscuit, until all the dough is used. Do not worry about the shapes. They should be irregular.

5. Bake on the middle rack of the preheated oven for 25 minutes until the biscuits are golden brown. Serve hot in a basket lined with a cloth napkin for any meal.

COTTAGE CHEESE

We started making our own cottage cheese primarily to avoid the long list of additives that most commercial brands contain. What we have developed is a whole-milk cheese remarkable for its creamy flavor. We prefer not to add salt nor do we use rennet tablets as many recipes suggest. It is perfect as is. Rennet is the lining membrane of a young animal's stomach, usually a calf, and we would just as soon keep our cheeses vegetarian.

Some sort of clabbering agent is needed, as pasteurized milk does not contain the bacteria found in raw milk that allows the milk to clabber on its own. Our clabbering agent is cultured buttermilk. We have tried yogurt, but cultured buttermilk is more satisfactory.

No special equipment is required, but you will need a large stainless-steel pot or bowl with a ½-gallon capacity to hold the milk during the clabbering and cooking processes and a pan to hold the heated water for cooking the curds. We use the bottom of our steam canner. The bottom of a roasting pan will do, but if the metal is aluminum, add a few drops of vinegar to the water to prevent the pan from discoloring.

To drain the curds, using an ordinary colander lined with cheesecloth and placed over a bowl with a ½-gallon capacity to catch the whey.

For a very rich cottage cheese, heavy cream may be added after the curds have drained, but do this only if you have pure cream. Never use the sterilized or ultra-pasteurized cream, as it would defeat the whole purpose of making honest cheese. If you prefer, you may use skimmed rather than whole milk.

Makes 12 ounces of cheese

½ gallon whole milk, at room temperature
½ cup cultured buttermilk

1. Pour the milk into a stainless-steel bowl with a ½-gallon capacity. Stir in the cultured buttermilk. Cover with cheesecloth or a thin towel loosely taped to the bowl. Do not use plastic wrap, as the mixture must breathe.

Place the milk mixture in a warm spot, such as an oven with just the light on (for gas stoves, the pilot light is sufficient). The top of the refrigerator is another warm spot. The temperature should be at least 80°F, but not over 100°F.

2. Let the milk mixture sit in this warm spot for 16 to 18 hours. When it has clabbered, it will resemble yogurt.

3. With a spatula or long knife, cut the curds. Do this by cutting through the cheese to the bottom of the bowl, making strips about ½ inch wide. Do this again, cutting crosswise.

Loosen the cheese from the sides of the bowl with the spatula or knife. Gently jostle the bowl to separate the curds ever so slightly.

4. Fill a shallow pan with water to a depth of 1½ inches. Bring the water not quite to a simmer and place the bowl with the curds in the pan. It is important that the water does not simmer or boil as it would overcook the curds.

Keeping the heat low, cook the curds for 15 to 20 minutes. Every 5 minutes or so gently move the curds about, using a rubber spatula, being careful not to break up the curds. During this time the curds will completely separate from the whey, a thin, yellowish liquid.

Since the cottage cheese contains no rennet, or artificial agent such as gum, the curds may vary in size.

5. After the cheese has separated from the whey and cooked for 15 to 20 minutes, remove the bowl from the water bath.

Line a colander with a single layer of cheesecloth and place it over another bowl which will hold the whey as it drains from the curds. It must be large enough to hold ½ gal-

lon of liquid, for there will be 7 cups of whey from the original ½ gallon of milk.

Gently ladle the curds and whey into the colander and let the whey drain from the curds for ½ hour before storing the cheese. Do not rinse the curds as some recipes suggest, for you will be removing vitamins as well as flavor.

6. Store the cottage cheese, covered, in any type of container you wish. We prefer glass or little pots of porcelain for individual servings. The cottage cheese will keep for a week. The whey will also keep for a week in the refrigerator or may be frozen for months.

COTTAGE CHEESE CREAMED WITH PESTO AND CELERY

This refreshing mixture can be used as a dip for crisp, raw vegetables or as a spread on thinly sliced bread. If it is moist, the cottage cheese should be drained. Try to find Pascal celery with its deep-green stalks and distinctively nutty flavor, as it will heighten the savoriness of the Pesto.

Makes 2 cups

1 cup homemade Cottage Cheese
¼ cup Pesto (see page 309)
1 teaspoon lemon juice
1 cup *very* finely chopped celery (about 3 medium stalks)

1. In a small mixing bowl, cream the cottage cheese with the pesto and lemon juice. When the mixture is smooth, fold in the chopped celery.

2. Cover the bowl with plastic wrap and refrigerate the mixture for several hours before

serving. It will be thicker after cooling and of a proper consistency for dipping or spreading.

If you are serving it as a dip, garnish your serving bowl with fresh basil or celery leaves chopped fine. Thin slices of lemon which have been cut in half may also be arranged in an attractive pattern around the serving bowl.

A SERVING SUGGESTION

We like to use Cottage Cheese Creamed with Pesto and Celery as a stuffing for ripe tomatoes, serving it as a light lunch or salad on a bed of leaf lettuce.

Before stuffing the tomatoes, cut a small slice from the top of each one to create an opening for scooping out the interiors. Cut around the opening, leaving an outside wall about ¼-inch thick.

Scoop out the flesh and seeds, reserving the flesh for another purpose. A serrated grapefruit spoon makes this an easy job. Sprinkle the insides of the tomato cups with a small amount of salt. Let them drain, cut side down, on paper towels for ½ hour to draw out excess water.

Stuff the drained tomatoes with the cottage cheese mixture. Cover and refrigerate the tomatoes for several hours before serving so that the stuffing will solidify.

Arrange the stuffed tomatoes on a bed of leaf lettuce. If they do not stand upright, cut a thin sliver from the bottoms so that they will. With a very sharp knife, cut midway through the tomatoes, creating equal-sized wedges so that knives will not be necessary. Smooth the surface of the stuffing if it is disturbed. Garnish each tomato with a little fresh basil or celery leaves chopped fine and a thin slice of lemon.

There will be enough of the cottage-cheese mixture to stuff 4 medium-size ripe tomatoes (about 5 ounces each).

COTTAGE CHEESE WITH CRACKED WHITE PEPPERCORNS

There is almost no limit to the ingredients that may be added to freshly prepared cottage cheese. We particularly like the addition of cracked white peppercorns—and even here, there are variations.

Makes one 12-ounce cheese or four individual 3-ounce cheeses

1 recipe homemade Cottage Cheese (see page 88)
2 teaspoons freshly cracked white peppercorns
½ teaspoon salt
4 small imported bay leaves

1. Prepare the cottage cheese.

2. While the cottage cheese is draining in the cheesecloth, crack the peppercorns coarsely, either in a mortar with pestle or in the Varco grinder made by Moulinex (check the mail-order listings).

3. With the cheese still in the cheesecloth, blend in the cracked peppercorns and salt, using a rubber spatula.

4. *If you wish to make 1 large cheese*, use a 1-pint plastic container, round or square, that has a lid. Punch tiny holes into the sides and

bottom of the container, about 1 inch apart. Cut the edges from the lid so that it fits down into the container 1 inch deep.

Arrange the bay leaves in an attractive manner in the bottom of the container. Firmly pack in the cheese, making sure that there are no spaces.

Place the cut-down lid on top so that it fits down onto the cheese. Place a weight of some sort on the lid. Place the container on a plate to catch the extra whey that will drain through the holes. Refrigerate the weighted cheese overnight.

The next day, remove the weight and lid from the container. Place a plate over the container and invert to unmold the cheese. Rearrange the bay leaves if they have shifted or do not unmold. The cheese may be served at this point or will keep for a week under refrigeration. When serving, cut the cheese into thin wedges.

5. *If you wish to make 4 individual cheeses*, select 4 small dishes or containers with ½-cup capacities. (We use porcelain ramekins.) Cut four, 9-inch-square pieces of cheesecloth. (If your cheesecloth is thin, cut at least a double thickness.) Dampen them slightly and fit them into your molds with the edges of the cheesecloth lapping over the sides.

Place a bay leaf in the bottom of each mold and divide and pack in the cottage cheese. Pull on the edges of the cheesecloth to eliminate any folds. When the cheese is densely packed in, bring up the edges of the cheesecloth and fold over the tops of the molds.

Again, devise weights of some sort. (The ramekins stack on top of each other, thereby creating the weights. We shift them once to distribute the weights.) Place the molds on a plate and refrigerate them overnight. The next day, open up the cheesecloth and unmold each cheese, removing the cheesecloth. The

WHAT TO DO WITH THE WHEY

With about 7 cups of whey left from the drained cottage cheese, it was most important for us to find ways to use it. By no means could we discard it, knowing that it is about 13 percent protein, and has more calcium than milk itself, plus riboflavin and iron. Unfortunately, whey has gotten a bad name by being introduced into products that the public has found unpalatable. After experimenting, using whey as our liquid ingredient, we found that it enhances many dishes, plus breads, and pasta. Here are a few suggestions.

1. Use whey as part or all of your liquid for cooking pasta or rice. In order for rice to become tender, it must be started in a little water, before the whey is added. Once the rice has absorbed the water, begin adding the whey and cook the rice either using your own method or ours (see Basic Brown Rice, page 74). Whey froths as it boils so keep close tabs on your pot.

2. Prepare Cottage Cheese (see page 88) and a recipe of freshly made Fettuccine (see page 305). As soon as the whey has drained from the cheese, place it in a large pot and bring to a boil. Cook the fettuccine in the whey just until it is *al dente*. Drain the fettuccine and quickly toss it with the warm cottage cheese, salt, and freshly ground white pepper, 1 tablespoon of butter, and ¼ cup of chopped parsley or basil. In many eastern European countries, cinnamon is sprinkled on top. In this case, omit the fresh herb.

3. Use whey instead of water in your homemade breads. We find it makes our breads more flavorful.

4. Feed it to your pets. Several of our cats are very fond of it and the whey is excellent for moistening dry dog food. See our recipe for Dog Biscuits (page 395).

5. Dilute the whey with water and feed it to your houseplants. If it is not diluted, half and half, you may eventually have a build-up of dried whey powder. Diluted with water, it is also an excellent cleanser for your plant leaves. They will glisten after a sponging with whey. If we have more than we can use, we use the whey undiluted in the herb garden.

cheesecloth will have absorbed the excess whey. Individually wrap the cheeses in plastic wrap and keep them refrigerated until you are ready to serve them.

The cheeses may be served at any time during the week. Serve the cheeses as a first course with raw vegetables, ripe olives, and thin slices of freshly baked bread, giving each guest one cheese. Or serve them with the salad course. As an hors d'oeuvre, serve the cheeses with crackers.

Note: Vary this cheese by omitting the bay leaves and, instead of mixing in the crushed peppercorns, patting them on the top and sides of the cheese after it is unmolded.

COTTAGE CHEESE WITH FRESH HERBS

Fragrant with fresh spring herbs, this cheese is more enjoyable than the expensive herbed cream cheeses that are commercially produced. The amounts given for the herbs are only suggestions; you may increase or substitute as you please. Sometimes we add 1 teaspoon of finely minced garlic or use a small spring onion instead of the shallots.

Makes one 12-ounce cheese or four individual 3-ounce cheeses

1 recipe homemade Cottage Cheese (see page 88)
½ teaspoon salt
¼ teaspoon white pepper
2 tablespoons finely chopped parsley
1 tablespoon finely snipped chives
1 tablespoon finely snipped dill
1 tablespoon finely minced shallots
4 small, imported bay leaves (optional)
4 small sprigs of dill (optional)
8 lengths of chive, 2 inches each (optional)

1. Prepare the cottage cheese.

2. When the cottage cheese is well drained, place it in a mixing bowl. Add the salt and pepper and blend thoroughly. Add the parsley, chives, dill, and shallots. Fold the herbs into the cheese, using a rubber spatula, until they are evenly distributed.

3. *For 1 large, molded cheese*, follow Step 4 in the recipe for Cottage Cheese with Cracked White Peppercorns (see page 90). Before adding the cheese, arrange the bay leaves in the bottom of your container along with the sprigs of dill and chive leaves, creating an attractive pattern.

4. *For 4 individual cheeses*, follow Step 5 of Cottage Cheese with Cracked White Peppercorns, again making attractive arrangements of the herbs in the bottom of the molds before adding the cheese.

Note: This cheese may be served as an enticing dip accompanied by a platter of cucumber sticks and sugar snap peas. Follow the recipe through Step 2 then thin the cheese with yogurt and 1 tablespoon of white wine vinegar.

COTTAGE CHEESE CREAMED WITH BLUE CHEESE

This cheese may be molded as in the previous recipes or served as a dip. If after refrigeration the cheese is too solid for dipping, thin it by blending in yogurt until the desired consistency is obtained.

Makes 1 pound of cheese

1 recipe homemade Cottage Cheese (see page 88)
4 ounces blue cheese
½ teaspoon salt
¼ teaspoon freshly ground white pepper

1. Prepare the cottage cheese.

2. While the cottage cheese is draining in the cheesecloth, cream the blue cheese in a mixing bowl, using the back of a wooden spoon.

3. When the cottage cheese is well drained, add it to the mixing bowl along with the salt and white pepper. Cream the ingredients until they are thoroughly blended.

4. The cheese may be served as a spread or a dip (see above) or, if you wish, it may be molded into 1 large cheese or several smaller ones.

For 1 large cheese, follow Step 4 in the recipe for Cottage Cheese with Cracked White Peppercorns on page 90, omitting the bay leaves.

5. *If you wish to make smaller, individual cheeses*, follow Step 5 of the recipe, again omitting the bay leaves. The serving suggestions are appropriate for this cheese, too.

LIPTAUER CHEESE

Liptauer made with homemade Cottage Cheese is especially sublime. Martha Roth tells us that as a child, spending summers on a farm in Czechoslovakia, Liptauer was made only with fresh cottage cheese and not with cream cheese as many recipes specify. Ours does not need a cream enrichment, either.

Makes ¾ - pound cheese

1 teaspoon whole caraway seeds
1 teaspoon whole cumin seeds
3 tablespoons sweet paprika
3 tablespoons minced shallots or onion
3 tablespoons minced, fresh chives (omit, if not available)
¼ teaspoon freshly ground dried hot red pepper
½ teaspoon salt
¼ teaspoon freshly ground black pepper
2 teaspoons Dijon mustard
1 teaspoon capers
1 recipe homemade Cottage Cheese (see page 88)
Additional capers and minced chives for garnish (optional)

1. Toast the caraway and cumin seeds in a small skillet over low heat for about 5 minutes to bring out their flavor. Stir so that they do not burn.

Remove from the heat and stir in the paprika. The saucepan will still be hot enough to bring out the flavor of the paprika without burning it.

2. Add the toasted spices along with the remaining ingredients (except for the garnish) to the cottage cheese and blend thoroughly.

3. Spoon the Liptauer into an attractive crock, cover with plastic wrap and refrigerate several hours before serving.

Just before you are ready to serve, sprinkle additional capers and minced chives around the edge of the cheese. Let the guests serve themselves, spreading the cheese onto plain crackers. The cheese will keep for at least 1 week.

Note: Kohlrabi and Liptauer Cheese make good companions. We often hollow out small, peeled, raw kohlrabi (no more than 1½ inches in diameter) and fill them with the cheese. Top each kohlrabi with a caper. If you are unable to find small kohlrabi, peel and slice larger ones so that guests may use them instead of plain crackers.

PRESSED COTTAGE CHEESE

Needing a drier and crumbly cheese to replace feta cheese, which is difficult to find where we live, we decided to age our cottage cheese. It makes a good substitute for feta in our Shrimp with Feta Cheese on page 119, as well as being an attractive cheese to serve.

Makes one 12-ounce cheese

1 recipe homemade Cottage Cheese (see page 88)
Salt and pepper to taste

1. Make the cottage cheese through Step 4. Begin Step 5 but do not remove the cheese from the cheesecloth. Instead, season it with salt and pepper, blending them into the cheese with a spatula. We use ½ teaspoon of salt and ¼ to ½ teaspoon of freshly ground white pepper. Bring the corners of the cheesecloth together and tie them. Hang the cheese over a bowl and let it drain for 24 hours.

2. After 24 hours, press the cheesecloth gently to extract any additional whey. The cheese is now ready to be molded and weighted.

For the mold, use a 1-pint plastic container, round or square, that has a lid. Punch tiny holes into the sides and bottom of the container, about 1 inch apart. Cut the edges from the lid so that it fits down into the container to the depth of 1 inch.

3. Using a tablespoon, pack the cheese densely into the container. Hold the container up as you pack it to see that there are no spaces in the cheese. Continue packing until all the cheese is used. Place the cut-down lid on top, adjusting its shape if necessary so that it fits firmly upon the cheese.

Place a weight of some sort on the lid—we use a glass jar filled with pebbles. Set the weighted container on a plate for another 24 hours. Small amounts of whey will still come out from the cheese through the holes.

4. After 24 hours, remove the weight and lid. Unmold the cheese onto the plate (wipe off the accumulated whey) and let the cheese age, uncovered, at room temperature for another 4 to 5 days.

5. You may serve the cheese at any point after unmolding it, depending upon what you wish to use it for. Generally, at around 4 days, the cheese will begin to form a rind and will, of course, be drier than at 2 or 3 days. For the Shrimp with Feta Cheese, we let the cheese age the full 5 days, as we want it to remain crumbly while cooking.

Variation: For a very peppery cheese, press coarsely cracked white or black pepper into the sides and onto the top of the cheese just after unmolding it. Use ¼ cup or more of the cracked pepper and serve it very thinly sliced.

WHAT TO BUY OR ORDER NOW

Having ordered heavily for foodstuffs in February, we need only think of the garden in March. A check is made of the garden catalogs for any last minute items and we place our orders for all perennial herb plants. The perennial herbs will be peeping up during the first weeks of March, if they have survived the winter. If not, we must order them. By this time, the herb farms will know what they have available.

BUTTERMILK

Buttermilk is the easiest of all dairy products to produce at home. You may make it from a cultured buttermilk purchased at the supermarket or from a powdered buttermilk culture which can be mail ordered. The powdered cultures can be frozen and used only as needed.

The savings in making your own are substantial, but you must remember that buttermilk culture, unlike yogurt, has a limited life span. The process is the same as yogurt — saving a little from each quart to make the next quart or quarts. We have found a culture will last for 6 to 8 quarts before it begins to thin.

Buttermilk, made with purchased cultured buttermilk, is generally tarter than that made with a powdered culture. If you use the powdered culture, follow the instructions it comes with. Our recipe uses a purchased cultured buttermilk.

Makes 1 quart

1 quart whole milk, at room temperature
2 tablespoons cultured buttermilk

1. Mix the milk and cultured buttermilk together in a quart jar. Cover with cheesecloth or a thin towel and place in a warm spot, as for yogurt.

Check the milk after 12 hours and if it has thickened, cover and refrigerate. It will resemble yogurt and may have to be stirred slightly in order to pour. Do not let the milk stand too long as it might clabber.

2. Always reserve 2 tablespoons for your next batch, but after 5 batches, watch that it is not thinning. If so, start with a newly purchased buttermilk.

AND IN OUR GARDEN

Many of the vegetable seeds planted in February will have sprouted by now and grown several inches tall so we begin to mulch thickly with our fall leaves. If the plants are very tiny, we keep the mulch four inches or so from the rows, pushing the leaves closer as the seedlings grow taller. Beginning to mulch this early will save hours of weeding later and will keep the soil moist. As soon as we see that the perennial herbs have not been winterkilled, we divide them if the plants are large. What a treat to find tarragon plants so large that they can be dug up and divided into a half dozen or so new plants. However, it is just as likely that there will be no tarragon at all. Chives, oregano, lemon balm and mint *always* need to be divided, if not dug up and discarded.

We continue to plant more seeds with first sowings of radishes, garden cress, kohlrabi, cabbage, beets and leeks and second sowings of lettuce and peas. Early in the month, we plant parsley seed and later, dill seed. Both must be kept moist in order to germinate. Garlic is also planted.

Indoors, we start our Supersteak tomatoes in Jiffy-7 Peat Pellets. With limited space, unusual peppers and Supersteak tomatoes are about the only seeds that we start indoors, for if we can not sow seeds directly in the garden, our area has many garden shops with huge arrays of inexpensive plants.

APRIL

IN PRAISE OF CHICKEN, FISH, AND EGGS

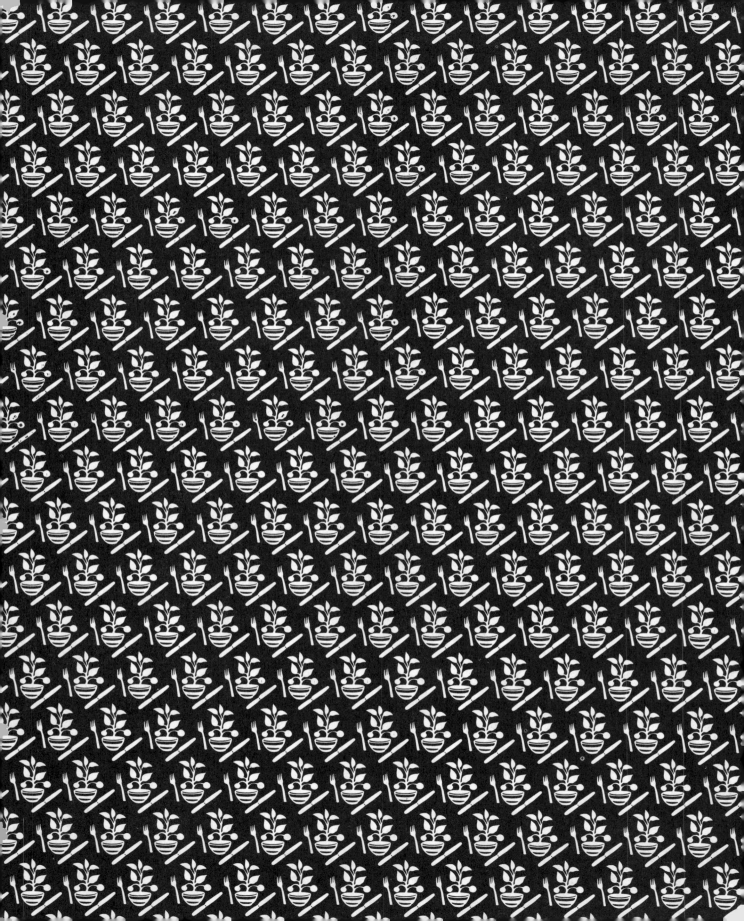

In Praise of Chicken, Fish, and Eggs

North Carolina is a state unsurpassed for its excellent chicken, seafood, and eggs, and our entrées will usually include one or another of these versatile foods. We are surrounded by poultry farms which makes for very fresh chicken on our table, and the seafood we buy, caught off the coast of the Carolinas, tastes as if it came straight from the sea to our pan.

Eggs began to have a prominent place in our cooking once we left the city. The yolks of the ones we buy locally are so yellow that when we scramble eggs, it looks as though the whites were omitted. One farm, which produces the best, has such a limited quantity that the eggs can only be bought from two small family-owned grocery stores. But even if they run out, we are not left high and dry because those bought at the local farmers' market are brought in fresh three times a week, sometimes not even in containers. What a refreshing sight after seeing eggs nestled in plastic compartments for so many years!

An Omelet with Cottage Cheese and Alfalfa Sprouts

This is our favorite omelet. To us, it is what an omelet should be—light, simple to prepare, and filled with ingredients that complement the eggs without overpowering their flavor.

The essentials for preparing a perfect omelet are having all of the ingredients ready before beginning, the proper pan to cook them in, and high heat to cook them over. The total cooking time for this omelet should be less than 2 minutes.

Omelet pans are inexpensive, so if you are serious about good omelets, the investment should be made and the pan used only for omelets. There are a variety of sizes available from 8- or 9-inch pans for individual omelets, 10-inch for larger omelets containing 4 to 6 eggs, or the 12-inch, which we use for frittatas (Italian-style omelets). For an electric stove, the aluminum pan seems to work best, and the black steel pan works best for a gas stove.

Never scour your omelet pan, but use a soft brush to clean it if it is necessary. Once your pan is well seasoned, just a quick wipe and rinse will be sufficient for cleaning. Black steel pans must be dried thoroughly or they will rust.

For this dish, we recommend that you use homemade Cottage Cheese or a commercial brand that is free of additives, particularly gum. Homemade cottage cheese is a creamy delight; a commercial brand with a half dozen additives, a disappointment.

Makes 1 omelet for 1 serving

> **2 eggs, at room temperature**
> **¼ teaspoon salt**
> **¼ teaspoon freshly ground white pepper**
> **⅓ cup homemade Cottage Cheese (see page 88), at room temperature**
> **¾ cup alfalfa sprouts, lightly packed (for growing instructions, see page 39)**
> **1 tablespoon unsalted butter**

1. In a small bowl, beat the eggs with the salt and white pepper. Have the egg mixture placed close to the stove along with the cottage cheese and alfalfa sprouts in their individual bowls.

Begin warming your serving dish.

2. Place an 8- or 9-inch omelet pan over medium to medium-high heat until it is hot. Add the butter. The butter should instantly melt and begin to sizzle. Tilt the pan so that the butter evenly coats the sides and bottom of the pan.

3. Immediately add the eggs so that the butter does not burn. With the back of a fork, give the eggs a quick stir. Shake the omelet pan with rapid back and forth motions, keeping the pan firmly on the burner. This step should take less than 30 seconds.

4. Quickly add the cottage cheese by placing it over the omelet half farthest from the handle. Place ½ cup of the alfalfa sprouts over the cottage cheese.

Fold the omelet over and slide it from the pan onto a heated serving dish. To accomplish this in the easiest manner, reverse the position of your hand on the handle. Grasp the handle with your palm up and tilt the pan so that the side of the omelet without the filling falls over onto the filling. Use your fork as an aid in lifting the omelet. With the pan still held in this position, the omelet should slide out with ease onto your serving dish.

5. Sprinkle the remaining ¼ cup of alfalfa sprouts over the top of the omelet and serve immediately. A tablespoon or so of the Tomato and Apple Chutneys (see pages 146 and 147), alongside, add another dimension of flavor.

GRATINÉED OMELETS WITH A MORNAY SAUCE

For this more elaborate version of the preceding recipe, we cover the omelets with a Mornay Sauce and gratiné them briefly under the broiler. Serve the gratin as an entrée for lunch or as a light supper.

Serves 4

5 tablespoons unsalted butter, plus 1 teaspoon
1 heaping tablespoon flour
2 cups milk, heated
8 eggs, at room temperature
1⅓ cups homemade Cottage Cheese (see page 88), at room
    temperature
2½ cups alfalfa sprouts, lightly packed (for growing instructions,
    see page 39)
1 teaspoon freshly ground white pepper
1 cup coarsely grated aged Colby cheese
½ cup freshly grated Parmesan cheese

1. Begin the Mornay Sauce. Melt 1 tablespoon of the butter over medium heat in a 1½-quart saucepan. Add the heaping tablespoon of flour and whisk until the mixture bubbles. Add the heated milk in a steady stream, whisking constantly, so that no lumps form.

Continue whisking until the mixture begins to thicken. Reduce the heat to low so that the sauce remains at a slow simmer. Whisk occasionally. The sauce will continue to thicken and become somewhat reduced as you prepare the omelets.

2. Have all of your ingredients (the eggs, the remaining 4 tablespoons of butter, cottage cheese, and sprouts) ready to use and by the stove. Break the eggs into 4 small bowls and beat them with the white pepper. (Each bowl should have 2 eggs and ¼ teaspoon of white pepper.) Salt is not necessary because of the cheeses.

3. Butter a gratin dish with the 1 teaspoon of butter. The gratin dish should be of a size to hold the folded omelets side by side. A 16-inch oval gratin dish is perfect.

4. Preheat the broiler. Also begin warming your serving plates.

5. Just before you cook the omelets, add the grated Colby cheese to the simmering sauce.

Whisk until the cheese melts. Continue to simmer the sauce on very low heat.

6. Prepare the omelets individually, following Steps 2, 3, and 4 in the preceding recipe. Reserve ½ cup of the alfalfa sprouts for garnish after gratinéing. As each omelet is completed, slide it into the gratin dish. If necessary, wipe the omelet pan out with a paper towel between omelets.

7. When all of the omelets have been prepared, cover them with the mornay sauce. Sprinkle the surface with the Parmesan cheese and place 6 inches under the broiler for about 3 minutes. The surface should be nicely browned and the sauce bubbling.

8. Sprinkle the gratin with the reserved ½ cup of alfalfa sprouts and serve immediately on heated plates.

AN OMELET WITH CHARD OR ESCAROLE

This is another favorite omelet. From spring until frost, we make it with Swiss chard and fresh herbs from the garden; during the coldest months, we use purchased escarole. Like many of our recipes, it is very flexible.

Depending upon the cheese or the green we use, it is a little different each time we prepare it. Generally, we use a small piece of leftover cheese that is not large enough for other dishes. Any of the Cheddars, Gruyères, or cheeses with a good melting quality are perfect or you can use your homemade cottage cheese in this one, too.

Serves 2

¼ **pound fresh mushrooms**
½ **pound Swiss chard or escarole**
3 **tablespoons unsalted butter, plus 1 teaspoon**
½ **teaspoon salt**
5 **eggs, at room temperature**
¼ **teaspoon freshly ground black pepper**
1 **cup coarsely grated cheese (see above)**
¼ **cup freshly grated Parmesan or Romano cheese**
¼ **cup finely chopped fresh basil, dill, or parsley**

1. Cut the ends from the mushroom stems. Wipe the mushrooms with damp paper towels to clean them. Slice them thin.

2. Wash the Swiss chard or escarole. If you are using Swiss chard, cut the ribs from the leaves. Chop the ribs fine and chop the leaves coarse.

If you are using escarole, trim the tough ends from the leaves. Chop the leaves coarse.

3. In a 10-inch skillet (not your omelet pan), melt 1 tablespoon of the butter over medium heat. Add the sliced mushrooms and ¼ teaspoon of the salt. Sauté until the mushrooms give up their liquid and it evaporates. Add the chopped greens with the moisture still clinging to the leaves and toss with the mushrooms.

Continue to sauté on medium heat, uncovered, until the greens have wilted and the moisture evaporates from the pan. Set aside over very low heat.

4. In a small bowl, beat the eggs with the remaining ¼ teaspoon of salt and the black pepper.

5. Preheat the broiler. Also begin warming your serving platter and plates.

6. Place a 10-inch omelet pan over medium to medium-high heat until it is hot. Add the remaining 2 tablespoons of butter. The butter should begin to sizzle right away. Tilt the pan so that the butter coats the pan evenly, including the sides.

7. Pour in the eggs and, with the back of a wooden spoon, quickly stir the eggs. Shake the omelet pan with rapid back and forth motions, keeping the pan firmly on the burner.

As soon as you see that the omelet is not sticking, spread the sautéed mushrooms and greens over the eggs and cover them with 1 cup of coarsely grated cheese. Turn the heat to medium low.

Cook for another minute or so until the underside of the omelet is golden and the cheese has begun to melt. Do not overcook. The center of the eggs should still be a little runny.

8. Sprinkle the surface of the omelet with the grated Parmesan or Romano cheese. Place the omelet pan 6 inches under the broiler. Broil for 2 minutes. The omelet will puff slightly.

9. Slide the omelet onto the heated serving platter, folding it in half as you do so. The best method for sliding an omelet from the pan is to grasp the handle with your palm up, tilting the pan so that the omelet slides onto the serving dish, simultaneously falling over on itself.

Spread the 1 teaspoon of butter over the surface and sprinkle with the chopped herb. Serve immediately, dividing the omelet in half for 2 servings. Sautéed New Potatoes (see page 261) go well with the omelet. Use the same herb with the potatoes and the omelet.

SAVORY CHICKEN LIVERS WITH PANCETTA

Chicken livers prepared with pancetta (Italian bacon, see page 54) instead of the usual bacon cook up into a dish so rich that it is best served in small portions as a first course with thin slices of buttered toast. It might be followed by a pasta course, lightly dressed, and then a simple salad. Portions should be small.

Serves 4 to 6

1 pound chicken livers
3 ounces pancetta
2 tablespoons olive oil
1 teaspoon dry mustard
½ teaspoon freshly ground dried hot red pepper
2 teaspoons sweet paprika
½ cup dry white wine
1 medium onion
4 cloves garlic
1 teaspoon wild thyme
¼ teaspoon salt
Parsley for garnish

1. Prepare the chicken livers by removing the white membrane and cutting them in half if they are very large. Rinse and drain on paper towels until it is time to sauté them.

2. Cut the pancetta into ¼-inch dice. Heat 1 tablespoon of the olive oil in a heavy skillet. Add the pancetta and cook over low heat, tossing often, until the dice are nicely browned. This will take about 15 minutes.

3. In a small bowl, whisk together the dry mustard, hot red pepper, paprika, and wine. Set aside.

4. Chop the onion coarse and mince the garlic. When the pancetta has browned, add the onion and garlic to the skillet. Sauté until the onion has wilted and taken on some color. Add the remaining tablespoon of olive oil and turn the heat to medium-high.

Place the chicken livers in the skillet and sprinkle with the wild thyme and salt. Using a spatula, quickly toss the ingredients until the livers have browned. Shake the pan, if necessary, to separate the livers. The cooking time should be no more than 5 minutes. Otherwise, the livers will be overcooked.

5. With the heat still at medium high, add the wine mixture and toss again until the liquid has almost evaporated. Serve on individual plates, garnished with parsley and several pieces of buttered toast for each plate.

FOR THE BUTTERED TOAST

1. Slice a day-old (so that it will be slightly dry) baguette into pieces ¼-inch thick. Removal of the crust is optional.

2. Arrange the slices on a baking sheet and place them under the broiler for several min-utes until nicely browned.

3. Remove the bread from the broiler, turn the slices over, and spread unsalted butter over the surface. Return them to the broiler and brown the buttered side.

CHICKEN TARRAGON LOKI

If our French tarragon survives the winter, by April it is abundant in the garden. Its fragrance infused into a small spring chicken affirms that winter has ended.

Serves 4

3 medium onions, cut into ¼-inch-thick slices
1 tablespoon olive oil, plus 1 teaspoon
½ teaspoon salt
¼ teaspoon freshly ground black pepper
2 tablespoons minced fresh tarragon, or 1 teaspoon dried
¼ cup dry white wine or vermouth
2½-pound chicken
2 tablespoons plus 1 teaspoon Dijon mustard
Additional black pepper for the surface of the chicken

1. Preheat the oven to 375° F.

2. Separate the onion slices into rings. Toss them in a 14-inch oval gratin dish with 1 tablespoon of the olive oil, the salt, black pepper, and tarragon. Pour the wine over the onions.

3. To clean the chicken, rinse the cavity in cold water, removing any excess fat. Pat dry inside and out with paper towels.

   Cut out the backbone with a pair of poultry shears. Open up the chicken and, with the skin side up, press down firmly on the breastbone until it cracks and the chicken remains flat.

   Turn the chicken over and spread the 2 tablespoons of mustard over the inside area. Place the chicken, flattened and skin side up, over the onions in the gratin dish. Tuck the wing tips under and arrange the legs so that they point out from the body of the chicken.

   Rub the remaining teaspoon of both the olive oil and mustard into the skin of the chicken. Add a few grindings of black pepper on top.

4. Bake the chicken on the middle rack of the oven for about 1 hour and 15 minutes. After the first ½ hour, baste the chicken every 15 minutes with the liquids in the gratin dish.

   The chicken may appear to be dry at first, but both the chicken and the onions will later release their liquids and the chicken will become moist and tender. As you baste, move the onions about so that they do not burn.

   About 15 minutes before the chicken is done, begin warming a serving platter.

5. When the chicken is tender and nicely browned on the surface, remove it to the heated serving platter. Surround the chicken with the onions. Present the chicken at the table before cutting it into serving pieces.

FRIED CHICKEN

After devouring the most exceptional southern fried chicken we had ever tasted, we asked the notable cook if she would give us a demonstration. Her instructions were very much to the point and, if followed, result in a truly crisp chicken, second to none. Perhaps we have a slight advantage over some, as the chickens raised in our area are incomparable for flavor. Do take the time to seek out a quality chicken, for even frying will not disguise a poor bird.

This recipe is easily doubled or tripled for a large party. If we are frying 2 or 3 chickens, we begin frying them about an hour before the guests arrive and let the pieces remain at room temperature. This gives us time to clean up the kitchen and the chicken is not harmed by this brief wait. It can be reheated in a preheated, 350°F oven for about 15 minutes just before serving. This fried chicken is still excellent served cold the next day.

Serves 4

3-pound chicken, cut into serving pieces
1 cup all-purpose, unbleached flour
1 teaspoon salt
1 teaspoon freshly ground black pepper
½ teaspoon freshly ground dried hot red pepper (optional)
1 cup milk
Corn oil for frying

1. Wash the chicken pieces in cold water and pat dry with paper towels. Cut away any excess fat. Arrange the pieces close by the burner you will be using.

2. In a large, shallow mixing bowl, combine the flour, salt, black pepper, and red pepper, if you are using it. (The red pepper will add a spicy note to the chicken.) Place the bowl, plus another bowl containing the cup of milk, close by the chicken.

3. Pour corn oil to a depth of 1 inch into a heavy, 10-inch skillet. (A cast-iron skillet is definitely recommended.) The skillet should not be more than half filled with the oil. Heat the oil over medium-high heat until it is about 365°F A cube of bread should take about 20 seconds to brown. The temperature must not be quite as high as one generally uses for frying.

4. The chicken pieces must *not* be coated with the flour until you are ready to add them to the skillet. Otherwise the flour coating will become moist and absorb the cooking oil and the chicken will be greasy and lack crispness. Just as important, the skillet must never be crowded. When you are ready to fry, begin warming your serving platter.

Dip the chicken wings, with their tips folded in, first into the milk and then into the flour mixture, coating them evenly. With tongs, a spatula, or your hand, lower the wings into the hot oil, skin side down. Proceed in the same manner with the thighs and add them to the skillet.

5. Fry the wings and thighs for 12 minutes or until the edges are golden brown. If they are browning too quickly, lower the temperature. If your skillet will comfortably hold more pieces, add them. When each piece has fried for 12 minutes, turn and fry for another 12 minutes on the other side. Turn the pieces only once as they fry.

6. As each piece of chicken is fried and becomes a golden brown, remove it to a heated serving platter.

If the chicken is to be kept until later, place the pieces in a roasting pan for reheating. Do *not* drain the pieces on paper towels, as they will stick to the towels.

7. Continue with the legs and breast halves until all of the chicken pieces have been fried. If it seems illogical that all of the chicken pieces, although different in size, are still fried for the same amount of time, remember: if pieces are left over, they tend to be the smaller ones (wings and legs), and the next day they taste better when they have been very crisply cooked.

MOCK VITELLO TONNATO

Mock Vitello Tonnato *is* our favorite recipe for the warmer months. For years we prepared the traditional Vitello Tonnato using a boned loin of veal, and when that became prohibitively expensive, we experimented with turkey breast. It works beautifully. Frozen turkey breasts are available all year and often at a very reasonable price. Do not buy one that is self-basting.

Besides being an extraordinarily delicious dish, Mock Vitello Tonnato can be prepared in advance. None of the steps is difficult, but the recipe as a whole is time consuming. However, with planning you can begin it even a week in advance by first making your stock and freezing it. The mayonnaise can be made several days ahead, and the turkey breast, after defrosting, can be cooked 2 days ahead.

The dish must be completed 1 day in advance for the thinly sliced turkey to absorb the flavor of the tuna sauce but it will keep for a week under refrigeration. Served on a large platter and colorfully garnished, the presentation is beautiful. Even slaked appetites will be stimulated.

Serves 8 as a main course, or 10 to 12 as part of a buffet

5-pound frozen turkey breast (or slightly larger)
3 tablespoons olive oil
1 medium onion, coarsely chopped
2 medium stalks celery, coarsely chopped
2 medium carrots, peeled and coarsely chopped
3 cloves garlic, peeled and crushed
1½ quarts turkey or Chicken Stock (see below)
1 cup dry white wine or vermouth
1 imported bay leaf
5 or 6 large sprigs of parsley
1 teaspoon wild thyme
12 whole peppercorns
3 cups stock, reserved from the cooked turkey breast
7-ounce can tuna, packed in olive oil
2 tablespoons lemon juice (about ½ lemon)
½ cup heavy cream
½ teaspoon freshly ground white pepper
1½ cups homemade Mayonnaise (see pages 195 and 196)
1 cup Roasted or Sautéed Red Peppers (see pages 264 and 265)
1 dozen ripe olives
12 very thin slices of lemon
2 tablespoons capers
¼ cup minced fresh basil or parsley

1. One day before you plan to cook the turkey breast, let it defrost in the refrigerator. After it has defrosted, rinse it under cold water and wipe it dry with paper towels.

2. Select a deep, heavy casserole that will hold the turkey breast covered with almost 2 quarts of liquid. Heat the olive oil in the casserole. Add the onion, celery, carrots, and garlic. Sauté over medium heat until the vegetables begin to color.

3. Add the stock and wine. Tie the bay leaf, parsley sprigs, wild thyme, and peppercorns in a piece of cheesecloth. Add them to the casserole and bring the ingredients to a simmer. Do not add salt as the stock contains salt

and the sauce will also be salty from the tuna and capers.

Lower the turkey breast, skin side up, into the simmering liquid. (The liquid should come halfway up the sides of the breast — if it does not, add some water.) Cover the casserole tightly, using aluminum foil if your cover is not snug.

4. Simmer the turkey breast over medium-low heat until it is tender. This will take about 2½ hours. Baste the breast with the liquid every 20 minutes or so.

After the breast has simmered for 1 hour, turn it over to simmer for the next hour. Then, ½ hour before it is tender, turn it again, skin side up.

5. When the turkey breast is tender, remove the casserole from the heat and let it cool for 1 hour, uncovered. Continue to baste during this time.

When the turkey breast is cool enough to handle, lift it from the casserole onto a platter. Refrigerate the breast, covered with plastic wrap, until it is thoroughly chilled, preferably overnight.

6. Strain the cooking stock through a colander lined with cheesecloth and placed over a bowl. Press down on the vegetables to extract as much liquid as possible. Cover and chill the stock.

7. An hour before you are ready to prepare the tuna sauce, place 3 cups of the reserved stock in a small saucepan and bring to a boil over high heat. Reduce the stock to 1½ cups. Cool the reduced stock in the refrigerator.

8. In a blender or food processor, combine the reduced stock with the tuna fish (do *not* drain it of its oil), lemon juice, heavy cream, and white pepper. Purée until the mixture is very smooth. Scrape the mixture into a bowl and blend in the mayonnaise. Refrigerate while you slice the turkey breast.

9. To slice the turkey breast, first remove the skin. With a very sharp knife, cut the slices on a bias about ⅛ inch thick. Try to make the slices as thin and as uniform as possible. If some of the meat falls off into small pieces, they can still be used.

10. Select a large serving platter which will also fit in your refrigerator. Spoon a thin layer of the tuna sauce over the bottom of the platter. Arrange the turkey slices in an overlapping fashion over the sauce. For this first layer, use the less attractive pieces.

Spoon another very thin layer of sauce over the turkey. Save ½ of the sauce for the second and final layer of turkey. Arrange the remaining half of the turkey slices on the platter in the same manner as the first. Cover the surface of the turkey with the rest of the sauce.

11. Stand colorless toothpicks partway into the turkey slices in about a half-dozen places. Cover the platter with plastic wrap. The toothpicks will keep the plastic wrap from falling into the sauce. Refrigerate overnight.

12. About ½ hour before you are ready to serve, decorate the platter. Rim the edge of the Mock Vitello Tonnato with the red pepper cut into julienne strips 2-inches long by ¼-inch wide. Place the olives evenly around and just to the inside of the red peppers. Arrange the lemon slices over the surface of the dish and sprinkle with the capers and minced basil or parsley.

Serve this dish at room temperature or just slightly cooled. It should not be cold.

CHICKEN STOCK

To make a wholesome chicken stock, long cooking is a fundamental requirement. For this reason, we prepare stock in large quantities when time is available. This recipe is for the minimum amount we would make.

For the chicken parts, we usually use raw scrap pieces we have kept frozen over several months and, if we do not have enough, chicken backs are inexpensive to purchase. You may use the gizzards and hearts, but not the livers, as they will give an "off" taste.

Makes 3½ quarts

> **3 pounds raw chicken parts such as backs, necks, and gizzards**
> **4 quarts cold water**
> **¾ pound carrots**
> **½ pound leeks or ½ pound onions**
> **3 large celery stalks**
> **1 large, imported bay leaf**
> **1 teaspoon wild thyme**
> **½ teaspoon whole black peppercorns**
> **3 or 4 large sprigs parsley with their stems**
> **1 teaspoon salt**
> **3 cloves garlic, unpeeled**
> **½ cup dry white wine or vermouth**

1. In a large pot with a 1-gallon capacity, place the chicken parts. Cover with the cold water and bring just to a simmer. Only partially cover, so that the scum and fats will rise to the surface. Do not allow the stock to boil at any time and never stir during the entire cooking time. Boiling or stirring will cause the fats to break down, resulting in a cloudy stock. Using cold water to begin the stock also works as an aid against clouding.

2. When the water comes to a simmer, begin skimming all the unpleasant-looking scum from the surface. Watch the heat so that the liquid does not boil.

Continue doing this until no scum appears on the surface. This will take about 15 minutes. As you remove the scum, replace it with the same amount of cold water.

3. Meanwhile, prepare the vegetables and aromatics. With a vegetable peeler, scrape the carrots and cut them into 1-inch pieces. Cut the leeks in half lengthwise and wash thoroughly. Cut them into 1-inch pieces. If using onions, peel and quarter them. Wash the cel-

ery stalks and cut them into 1-inch pieces.

Tie the bay leaf, wild thyme, peppercorns, and parsley in a small piece of cheesecloth.

4. When the simmering liquid has been completely cleansed of scum, add the vegetables, the aromatics tied in cheesecloth, the salt, the unpeeled garlic, and the wine.

Be cautious about the amount of salt. Since the stock reduces while cooking, it could become too salty. Again, do not stir, but press the solids down into the simmering liquid.

5. Watch the heat and bring the ingredients back to a simmer. Partially cover and simmer for 4 hours. Extend the cooking time if you are making a larger amount.

During this time, periodically check the stock and skim any scum from the surface. Press down on the solids from time to time to release their flavors.

6. When the stock has cooked for 4 hours, strain it through a colander lined with cheesecloth into a large bowl. Press down on

the solids so they will give up their liquids.

Cool as quickly as possible and either refrigerate or freeze. The stock will keep for 3 or 4 days refrigerated and for 3 or 4 months frozen. If freezing, leave 1½-inch headspace in the container for expansion.

7. Do not throw away the vegetables or the meat from the chicken. If you do not wish to eat them, carefully go over them, removing all bones, and give the vegetables and meat to a favorite dog or cat. Mixed with their regular food, the leftovers are a treat.

Note: When making our stock, we use the Graniteware Blancher, sometimes called the Everything Pot, as it is handy for straining the stock. Just remove the fitted colander from the pot and set it over a large bowl to drain. All the solids remain in the colander. For a clearer stock, you may wish to strain the liquid through cheesecloth later.

CHICKEN STUFFED UNDER THE SKIN WITH PESTO

This recipe can be prepared quickly if the Pesto has been made ahead of time. Stuffing the chicken between the skin and the flesh, rather than in the cavity, makes a superbly moist and flavorful bird, and for those unfamiliar with the technique, a pleasant surprise. Do not salt the chicken, as the pesto with its salt and cheese is sufficient. Before you carve it, present the chicken on a serving platter surrounded with fettuccine tossed with 2 tablespoons of butter and ¼ cup finely chopped fresh basil or parsley.

Serves 4

3-pound chicken
1 cup very dry, fine bread crumbs made from a day old baguette
½ cup Pesto (see page 309)
1 lemon, cut into eight ¼-inch-thick slices
2 teaspoons olive oil
1 tablespoon lemon juice (use the ends of the lemon for the juice)
½ teaspoon freshly ground white pepper

1. When purchasing your chicken, look it over carefully to make sure the skin is intact and not torn. With shears or a knife, cut out the backbone of the chicken and remove any excess fat. (Save the backbone, minus the tail, and the fat for a future stock.)

Spread the chicken open, skin side up. Press down firmly on the breastbone until it cracks and the chicken remains flat. Rinse the chicken under cold water and dry with paper towels.

2. With the breast nearest you, loosen the skin from the flesh of the chicken. This is much easier than it would seem; the only area that might present a problem is the center of the breastbone where the skin is more firmly attached. Loosen it first by carefully snipping the skin away from the flesh with a small pair of scissors or a knife.

Once this is accomplished, you should be able to loosen the rest by inserting one hand under the skin and, working slowly, raising the skin from the flesh.

Work all the way down, almost to the tips of the legs, and then just to the outside edge of the thighs and into the largest joints of the wings. Be extremely cautious not to tear the skin. Leave the skin intact on the outer edges of the chicken.

3. Place the bread crumbs in a small bowl and thoroughly blend in the pesto.

4. Preheat the oven to 350°F.

5. To stuff the chicken, again work with the breast closest to you. Use a teaspoon and insert the pesto mixture first onto the legs under the skin. Each leg should hold about 2 tablespoons.

With your free hand on the skin of the chicken, smooth and distribute the stuffing on the legs. Place a slice of lemon under the skin and on top of the stuffing in each leg.

Insert about 3 tablespoons of stuffing onto each thigh and cover with a slice of lemon.

Each wing should be stuffed with a teaspoon of the mixture and, finally, the remaining stuffing should be smoothed over the breast. Place the other 4 slices of lemon over the stuffing on the breast.

6. Oil a 14-inch oval gratin dish with 1 teaspoon of the olive oil. (The flattened chicken will fit exactly.) Place the chicken in the dish, arranging it with the legs and wings pointing out horizontally from the body. Tuck the wing tips under. Pull and smooth the skin into place.

To close the neck opening, fold the edges of the skin underneath.

Some stuffing may come out during baking, but not enough to worry about.

Rub the tablespoon of lemon juice into the skin and then rub in the remaining teaspoon of olive oil. Sprinkle with the white pepper.

7. Bake the chicken on the middle rack of the preheated oven for 1½ hours. After ½ hour of baking, begin to baste the chicken with the juices that accumulate in the pan. Continue to baste every 15 minutes. The chicken will become golden brown, tender, and fragrant with the pesto stuffing.

LEMON CHICKEN BAKED ON A BED OF SAUERKRAUT

One of the most pleasing ways to enjoy sauerkraut is to prepare it with chicken. In our recipe, the sauerkraut is baked under the chicken so it absorbs the flavor of the chicken and, in turn, bestows some of its aroma to the fowl. The preparation is simple and takes little time.

Serves 4

3-pound chicken
1 quart Sauerkraut (see page 137)
½ teaspoon freshly ground dried hot red pepper
½ teaspoon dried rosemary, crumbled
Juice of 1 lemon
2 teaspoons olive oil
¼ teaspoon salt
¼ teaspoon freshly ground white pepper

1. Preheat the oven to 375° F.

2. With a pair of kitchen shears, remove the backbone of the chicken. Flatten the chicken by spreading it open, skin side up, and pressing on the breastbone until it cracks and the chicken remains flat. Rinse the chicken under cold water removing any excess fat. Wipe it dry with paper towels. Tuck the tips of the wings under and arrange the legs so they point out horizontally from the body.

3. Place the sauerkraut in a colander and rinse it with cold water to remove some of the salt. Drain and squeeze dry (use your hands or wrap the kraut in a thin dishtowel and twist). Place the sauerkraut in an oval gratin dish brushed with 1 teaspoon of the olive oil. The dish should be just large enough to hold the chicken. Toss the sauerkraut with the red pepper and rosemary.

4. Arrange the flattened chicken, skin side up, on top of the sauerkraut, making sure all of the kraut is covered by the chicken. Rub ½ of the lemon juice into and over the surface of the chicken. Brush the chicken with the remaining olive oil and sprinkle with the salt and pepper.

5. Bake on the middle rack of the oven for 1 hour and 20 minutes to 1½ hours until the chicken is well browned, but still moist. During the first ½ hour or so of cooking, the chicken may appear to be dry but soon it will begin to exude its juices and brown.

About halfway into the baking time, remove the chicken from the oven and rub the rest of the lemon juice over the surface. If the sauerkraut appears to be browning too quickly, mix it slightly and rearrange it under the chicken. As soon as the juices begin to flow from the chicken, the sauerkraut will have sufficient moisture.

BAKED CHICKEN WITH VEGETABLES

This dish is an excellent choice for an informal dinner. It is always a favorite with guests, and the ingredients can be assembled ahead of time. The chicken, baked with a large melange of vegetables, remains very moist and cooked at a relatively high temperature, the vegetables retain their crispness and do not lose their individuality.

You may use just chicken breasts instead of a whole chicken, if you wish. Serve the dish with pasta, tossed with olive oil, salt, and pepper; or steamed potatoes, or brown rice. With brown rice, have a dish of one of the Tomato and Apple Chutneys (see pages 146 and 147) on the table.

Serves 4

> **3-pound chicken**
> **1 tablespoon olive oil**
> **2 tablespoons Dijon mustard**
> **1 teaspoon salt**
> **½ teaspoon freshly ground black pepper**
> **1 teaspoon wild thyme**
> **1 pound onions**
> **4 large cloves garlic**
> **1 pound fresh bell peppers (a combination of red and green, if**
>   **possible)**
> **1 pound ripe tomatoes**
> **1 pound mushrooms**
> **5 canned Colorado peppers or mildly hot peppers, packed in brine, or**
>   **1 teaspoon freshly ground dried hot red pepper**
> **¼ cup dry white wine or vermouth**
> **1 dozen ripe olives (optional)**
> **¼ cup chopped fresh basil or parsley**

1. Preheat the oven to 400°F.

2. Cut the chicken into serving pieces, then rinse the pieces in cold water removing any excess fat. Wipe them dry with paper towels.

3. Rub a large gratin dish with olive oil. (A 17-inch-long oval gratin dish is perfect.) In it, arrange the pieces of chicken, skin side down.

Brush the pieces with the mustard and sprinkle them with ½ teaspoon of the salt, ¼ teaspoon of the black pepper, and the thyme.

4. Bake the chicken in the upper third of the oven for ½ hour. The chicken will not brown during this baking period and may appear to be dry, but the juices will be released later in the baking.

5. Meanwhile, prepare the vegetables. Peel and quarter the onions, lengthwise. Cut the quarters into coarse slices. Peel and mince the garlic. Core and seed the bell peppers. Cut them into chunks about 1½ inches in diameter. Peel, core, and seed the tomatoes and chop them coarse.

Trim off the ends of the mushroom stems. Wipe the mushrooms with damp paper towels, then slice them thin. If you are using the Colorado peppers, chop coarse, but do not seed them.

6. After ½ hour of baking, remove the chicken from the oven. Deglaze the pan with the wine, scraping any bits clinging to the dish.

Turn the pieces skin side up. Cover the chicken with the prepared vegetables, mixing them as you do so. The chicken will be almost hidden. Sprinkle with the remaining ½ teaspoon of salt and ¼ teaspoon of black pepper.

If you are using the dried hot red pepper, sprinkle it on at this time.

7. Return the gratin dish to the oven and bake for another ½ hour.

8. Remove the gratin dish from the oven. Turn the temperature to "broil." Arrange the chicken pieces on top of the vegetables. At this time, the ripe olives should be added if you are using them. Mix them into the vegetables.

9. Place the gratin dish 6 inches under the broiler and cook the chicken for another 10 to 15 minutes, until the pieces are a deep golden brown. Watch them so that they do not burn. Just before serving, sprinkle the chicken with the chopped basil or parsley.

FRIED FISH

Many people are unaware that when they buy filets of sole, unless the sole has been imported, they are actually buying flounder. The preference for one name or the other seems to be regional. Here in the South, with the excellent fish from the coast, there is great pride in calling a flounder a flounder.

If you are buying flounder that has already been filleted, you will need ½ pound per person. If the fish has not been filleted, you will need 1 pound per person. As is customary in our area, our fish market does not remove the skin when the flounders are filleted, but we do remove the darker skin later at home. The thinner white skin tends to fry away, so we leave it. Select filets that will be between ½- and ¾-inch thick.

Since all cooking oil is at a premium, we find we can use less oil by frying our fish in a 10-inch iron skillet rather than in a deep fryer. Although we save some of our cooking oils and use them a second time, the oil from fried fish cannot be kept. So as not to feel terribly extravagant, we always fry something before using the oil for our fish. Hush Puppies (see page 343) of course, are perfect. Full-leaved stems of parsley are also very tasty, but make sure that they are completely dry before dropping them into the hot oil. Even dry, they will sputter as they instantly fry. Drain the parsley on paper towels; they are a deliciously crisp treat.

Serves 4

2 lemons, cut into wedges
2 pounds flounder filets
1 cup yellow cornmeal
1 teaspoon salt
½ teaspoon freshly ground black pepper
Corn oil for frying
½ cup finely chopped parsley or fresh dill

1. Prepare the lemon wedges by cutting the lemons lengthwise into quarters. Then with a serrated knife remove the white running along the center. Make 2 or 3 small crosswise slashes into the lemon wedges. This not only makes it easy to remove the seeds, but the wedges will not squirt as they are squeezed. And for presentation, the lemons will look more attractive than in those strange cheesecloth wrappings one occasionally encounters. Set aside.

2. Go over the fish filets, carefully removing any small bones that may remain. If the filets are very large, cut them so that they will fit into your skillet.

3. In a large, shallow mixing bowl, combine the cornmeal, salt, and black pepper.

4. Pour corn oil into a heavy, 10-inch skillet (preferably cast iron) to a depth of 1 inch. The skillet must not be more than half filled with oil. Heat the oil over medium-high heat to 375° F or until a cube of bread browns instantly. As frying fish can cause a bit of splatter, we cover the other burners on the stove with aluminum foil to keep them clean.

Begin warming your serving platter.

5. Place each filet of flounder into the cornmeal mixture just as you are ready to fry it. If the pieces of fish are dredged in the mixture beforehand, the coating will become moist and will absorb the frying oil, resulting in a soggy fish. Turn each filet about in the cornmeal mixture until it is well coated.

Lower the filet, fleshlike side down, into the hot oil, using tongs or a spatula. Continue with more filets, being careful never to crowd the pan. In 3 or 4 minutes, you will notice the edges of each filet becoming golden brown. Turn the filet and fry on the other side for another 3 to 4 minutes. Try to turn the fish only once during the frying period.

6. As each filet becomes golden brown on both sides, remove it with a slotted spatula or tongs to the heated serving platter. If the fish has been fried properly, draining on paper towels will not be necessary. Watch the temperature of the oil and adjust it. If the fish fry at a lower temperature, they will absorb the oil.

As soon as you have one layer of fish on the serving platter, sprinkle it with some of the chopped parsley or dill. Continue in this manner, reserving some of the chopped herb for the top layer of fish. The total frying time for all of the fish should be less than 20 minutes.

7. Surround the fish with the lemon wedges and serve immediately. Have a pot of Mayonnaise and Tomato Sauce (see below) on the table.

MAYONNAISE AND TOMATO SAUCE

This sauce could not be easier to prepare — *if* you have your homemade Mayonnaise and Tomato Sauce on hand. It is absolutely essential that they be homemade using our recipes, otherwise we can not guarantee the results. We especially like this sauce with Fried Fish or on cooked shrimp surrounded with lemon wedges. If you are inclined to put ketchup on fried potatoes, try this sauce instead.

Makes 1½ cups

½ cup homemade Mayonnaise (see pages 195 and 196)
1 cup Tomato Sauce (see pages 310 and 311)

1. Place the mayonnaise in a small mixing bowl. Using a whisk, gradually whisk in the tomato sauce. The sauce must be very smooth.

2. You may serve the sauce right away, or if it is chilled for several hours, it will become thicker. The sauce will keep for a week in the refrigerator.

Note: These proportions are not absolute. At one time we had the amounts reversed, but finally decided we like more tomato sauce and less mayonnaise.

ESCABECHE

One of the most pleasing cold dishes to serve spring or summer is Escabeche. In its more authentic Portuguese version, vinegar is used to "pickle" the fish, but we prefer the flavor of lemon juice. You may substitute lime juice if it is more to your taste.

The choice of fish you use should be determined by what is available fresh. We are able to buy excellent flounder, but any other fish that can be filleted and fried may be used. If you do not have your own canned Colorado or jalapeño peppers, most supermarkets carry similar peppers packed in brine, or you may order them by mail. Escabeche can be served as a main course or as a very attractive dish for a cold buffet.

Serves 4 to 6 as a main course, or 6 to 8 for a buffet

Corn oil for deep frying
2 pounds flounder filets
½ cup yellow cornmeal, seasoned with salt
     and freshly ground black pepper
2 teaspoons dry mustard
1 teaspoon salt
¼ teaspoon freshly ground black pepper
¼ teaspoon freshly ground dried hot red pepper
4 large cloves garlic, minced
⅓ cup lemon juice (about 2 lemons)
Peel from the 2 lemons
½ cup olive oil
1 large green or red bell pepper
2 medium red or yellow onions
2 canned Colorado or 3 canned jalapeño peppers
     or mildly hot peppers packed in brine
2 tablespoons chopped fresh dill
2 tablespoons chopped fresh parsley
3 or 4 imported bay leaves
Thin slices of lemon, fresh coriander or additional fresh dill and
     parsley, cherry tomatoes, and ripe olives as garnish

1. Heat the corn oil for deep frying to about 375° F or until a cube of bread fries instantly. A heavy iron skillet is recommended. Whatever you use, the oil should be to a depth of 1 inch, but no more than half full.

2. If the fish filets are large, cut them in half. They should be uniformly about 4 inches long. When the oil is hot, dredge each filet in the seasoned cornmeal. Using a slotted spatula, carefully lower each filet, fleshlike side down, into the oil. Do not crowd the pan.

In about 3 minutes, you will notice the outside edges of the filets begin to brown. Turn the fish and continue to fry another 2 minutes until they are a light golden brown all over.

Remove the filets with the spatula and drain on paper towels. Continue until all the filets have been fried.

3. While the fish are draining, prepare the marinade. In a small bowl, combine the dry mustard, salt, black pepper, red pepper, garlic, and lemon juice (first remove the peel from the lemons and reserve it). Whisk briefly, until the mustard, salt, and peppers have dissolved. Begin adding the olive oil in a thin stream, whisking constantly, until the oil has been absorbed and you have a thick emulsion.

4. Cut the reserved peel from the lemons into fine julienne strips. Core and seed the bell pepper and also cut it into fine julienne strips. Peel and slice the onions about ⅛-inch thick. Break the slices into rings. Chop fine, but do not seed, the Colorado or jalapeño peppers.

5. Spread half of the marinade onto your serving platter. Arrange half of the fish in a single layer on top of the marinade. Distribute half of

the julienne strips of lemon and half of the strips of bell pepper evenly over the surface. Then scatter all of the chopped Colorado or jalapeño peppers and half of the onion rings on top.

6. Make another layer of the remaining fish filets and arrange the rest of the strips of lemon and bell pepper and onion rings over the fish. Sprinkle with the dill and parsley. Place 3 or 4 bay leaves on top.

Cover the platter tightly with plastic wrap and let the fish marinate overnight in the refrigerator. Escabeche is just as good 2 or 3 days later.

7. When you are ready to serve the Escabeche, remove the bay leaves and garnish the platter with lemon slices and additional dill and parsley. Border the fish with cherry tomatoes and ripe olives. If fresh coriander is available, a tablespoon of the leaves, finely chopped, adds an interestingly pungent touch. In that case, omit the additional dill and parsley. Serve the Escabeche with Billie's Jalapeño Pepper Relish (see page 144).

SHRIMP WITH FETA CHEESE

Although we use our Pressed Cottage Cheese instead of the traditional Greek feta, we still refer to this dish as Shrimp with Feta Cheese. It is delectable with either. Serve it with thick slices of freshly made bread.

Serves 4

2 cups drained, coarsely chopped tomatoes, canned or fresh (about 2½ pounds)
4 tablespoons olive oil
1 large onion, coarsely chopped
4 large cloves garlic, minced
1 teaspoon dried oregano
½ teaspoon freshly ground dried hot red pepper
½ teaspoon salt
¼ teaspoon freshly ground black pepper
½ cup red wine
1 pound fresh shrimp, unshelled
½ pound Pressed Cottage Cheese (see page 95) or feta cheese
¼ cup lemon juice
Lemon wedges for garnish
¼ cup chopped fresh basil (if available) or parsley for garnish

1. If you are using canned tomatoes, drain them in a sieve placed over a bowl, reserving the liquid for another use.

   If you are using fresh tomatoes, drop them into boiling water for 30 seconds to loosen the skins. Peel, core, and seed the tomatoes, then chop them coarse. Place them in a sieve over a bowl to drain. This is particularly important if you are using fresh tomatoes, as otherwise they would have too much liquid.

2. Heat 2 tablespoons of the olive oil in a 1½-quart saucepan. Add the onion and garlic and sauté over medium heat until the onion begins to take on color.

3. Add the tomatoes to the saucepan along with the oregano, hot red pepper, salt, black pepper, and wine. Stir to blend. Reduce the heat to medium-low, cover, and simmer for 30 minutes. Stir occasionally.

4. Preheat the oven to 400°F.

5. While the sauce is simmering, shell and clean the shrimp (see Box). Heat the remaining 2 tablespoons of olive oil in a 1-quart casserole and quickly sauté the shrimp while stirring frequently. This should take only a minute or so—just until the shrimp are pink.

6. Add the simmering sauce to the shrimp.

HOW TO SHELL AND CLEAN SHRIMP

It is worth the extra effort to shell and clean shrimp properly. This means removing the tail shell, but not the tail itself. With a little practice, it goes very quickly and the shrimp are more appealing when served. Use this method for raw or cooked shrimp.

1. Using a small, very sharp knife, or your thumb, crack the underside shell of the shrimp just above the tail. The crack should be about ⅓-inch long. Gently tug the tail shell until it pulls off, leaving the tail intact.

2. Again, using the knife or your thumb, crack the remaining shell underneath and pull around the shrimp to remove.

3. If there are any signs of the black intestinal vein on the top of the shrimp, remove it by running your knife down the back of the shrimp and pulling out the vein. This is almost always necessary on large shrimp and it is a good practice on all shrimp.

Crumble the cheese over the top and sprinkle with the lemon juice. Do not stir.

7. Bake on the middle rack of the preheated oven for 20 minutes until bubbling. The cheese should not brown. Serve garnished with lemon wedges and chopped fresh basil or parsley.

SHRIMP IN PIMIENTO SAUCE

Each time we serve this entrée at a dinner party, we are asked by our guests for the recipe. The sauce is outstanding and goes especially well with a brown rice accompaniment.

Serves 4 to 6

2 pounds fresh, unshelled shrimp
2 eggs
½ cup all-purpose flour, plus 2 tablespoons
½ teaspoon salt
¼ teaspoon freshly ground black pepper
3 tablespoons olive oil
1 cup finely chopped onions
1 teaspoon minced garlic
1 cup dry white wine or vermouth
2½ cups Chicken Stock (see page 109), heated
1 cup Roasted Red Peppers (see page 265)
¾ cup chopped parsley
1 teaspoon dried oregano
Corn oil for frying

1. Shell and clean the shrimp (see Box). Set aside.

2. Prepare the batter. Beat the eggs well in a medium-size bowl. Add the ½ cup of flour, salt, and pepper and continue beating until the batter is smooth. Cover with plastic wrap and set aside.

3. Heat the olive oil in a 2-quart saucepan and add the onions and garlic. Sauté over medium heat until the onions have wilted, but not browned. Add the remaining 2 tablespoons of flour. Whisk to mix the ingredients and when the flour begins to bubble, add the white wine or vermouth.

Continue to whisk until the mixture begins to thicken. Add the heated chicken stock, ½ cup or so at a time, whisking constantly, so that the sauce is smooth.

4. Cut the roasted peppers in julienne strips 2-inches long by ¼-inch wide.

When all of the chicken stock has been incorporated into the sauce, add the roasted peppers, ½ cup of the chopped parsley, and the oregano. Stir to mix. Cover the saucepan and simmer over very low heat while you fry the shrimp.

Begin warming your serving platter.

5. Pour corn oil to a depth of 1 inch in a heavy skillet. Heat the oil to 375° F or until a bread cube browns instantly.

Using a large spoon, dip each shrimp into the batter, coating it heavily, and with the aid of another spoon, slip the shrimp into the heated oil. As each shrimp begins to brown around the edges, turn it over and brown the other side. The total cooking time for each shrimp will be only about 3 minutes.

Continue until all of the shrimp have been fried, being careful not to crowd the pan. Place the shrimp on paper towels to remove excess oil.

6. Add the fried shrimp to the sauce and bring back to a simmer. Ladle the shrimp with the sauce onto a heated serving platter and circle the entrée with brown rice. Garnish the platter with the remaining ¼ cup of chopped parsley. Serve immediately.

BAKED FLOUNDER WITH VEGETABLES

This recipe was adapted from Baked Chicken with Vegetables on page 114, and it is every bit as succulent. Do not be alarmed at what seems a long cooking time for fish. The filets are blanketed in the vegetables and therefore can take the longer period in the oven without drying or being overcooked. Serve potatoes or brown rice to accompany the fish and vegetables. If you have leftovers, the dish is very good cold.

Serves 4 to 6

1 pound onions
4 large cloves garlic
1 pound fresh bell peppers (a combination of red and green, if
    possible)
1 pound ripe tomatoes
1 pound mushrooms
5 canned Colorado peppers, or mildly hot peppers, packed in brine,
    or 1 teaspoon freshly ground dried hot red pepper
1 teaspoon wild thyme
3 tablespoons unsalted butter
2 pounds flounder filets
¼ cup lemon juice
½ teaspoon salt
¼ teaspoon freshly ground black pepper
1 tablespoon olive oil
1 dozen ripe olives (optional)
3 tablespoons very dry bread crumbs
¼ cup chopped parsley
¼ cup chopped fresh basil (if available)
1 lemon, sliced thin

1. Prepare the vegetables. Peel and quarter the onions lengthwise. Cut the quarters into coarse slices. Peel and mince the garlic. Core and seed the bell peppers, cutting them into pieces about 1½ inches in diameter. Peel, core, and seed the tomatoes and chop them coarse. Cut the ends from the mushroom stems. Wipe the mushrooms with damp paper towels and slice them thin. If you are using the Colorado peppers, do not seed them, just chop them coarse.

Combine the prepared vegetables in a

large bowl and toss with the wild thyme and, if you are using it, the dried hot red pepper, just to mix the ingredients.

2. Preheat the oven to 450°F.

3. Lavishly butter a gratin dish with 2 tablespoons of the butter. The gratin dish should be of a size to hold the filets snugly in a single layer. A 17-inch oval gratin dish is an approximate size.

4. Make a layer of ½ of the vegetable mixture in the gratin dish. Cover the vegetables with the fish filets. If the filets are very large, cut them in half. Place the filets close together, tucking under the smaller tail ends of the fish, if necessary, to form a single layer. Sprinkle the filets with the lemon juice, salt, and black pepper.

5. Cover the filets with the remaining half of the vegetables. Dribble the olive oil over the vegetables.

6. Place the gratin dish in the upper third of the oven and bake for 45 minutes.

7. After 45 minutes, remove the gratin dish from the oven and raise the oven temperature to "broil."

8. Add the ripe olives, if you are using them, to the top layer of vegetables and gently mix them in. Combine the dry bread crumbs with the chopped parsley and basil. Sprinkle over the surface of the dish. Arrange the thin slices of lemon on top. Cut the remaining 1 tablespoon of butter into small bits and evenly distribute them.

9. Place the gratin dish 6 inches under the broiler and cook for another 5 minutes or so until the surface lightly browns.

10. When serving, be careful that the filets do not break apart as you lift them from the dish. A spatula is useful for this. Give each guest several filets and a generous amount of the vegetables.

BAKED FLOUNDER ON A BED OF SWISS CHARD GREENS

The chard greens combined with the pignolia nuts, raisins, and aromatics make a very distinctive bed for baking the fish filets. (Save the ribs for another meal. See the recipe for Gratin of Swiss Chard Ribs on page 366.) For the baking use a large gratin dish that can be brought to the table when serving. We use a 17-inch oval earthenware dish. Serve the fish with brown rice to which you have added chopped parsley.

Serves 4 to 6

1½ pounds flounder filets (about 12 small filets)
3 pounds Swiss chard
¼ cup pignolia (pine) nuts, toasted (see Step 3)
¼ cup dark raisins, preferably Monnuka
¼ cup dry white wine
6 tablespoons unsalted butter
1 tablespoon olive oil
3 tablespoons minced shallots
1 tablespoon minced garlic
1 teaspoon salt
½ teaspoon freshly ground black pepper
¼ cup lemon juice
An additional lemon, cut into ⅛-inch slices
¼ cup chopped fresh parsley or basil for garnish

1. Rinse the flounder filets under cold water then wipe them dry with paper towels. If they are large, cut them in half so none is more than 6 inches in length.

2. Wash and drain the Swiss chard. To remove the ribs, place each one face down on your work surface and, using a small knife, cut out the rib. (Save the ribs for another meal.) You should have about 1⅓ pounds of chard greens.

Stack the leaves in manageable amounts and shred them with a large chef's knife. Gather up the shreds and coarsely chop them into 1-inch to 1½-inch squares.

3. Toast the pine nuts in a 225°F oven for about 20 minutes. This will bring out their flavor. Watch them so they do not burn. Soak the raisins in the wine for ½ hour to plump them.

4. Melt 3 tablespoons of the butter with the tablespoon of oil in a large skillet. Add the shallots and garlic and sauté over medium-low heat until they just begin to take on some color. Add the raisins with the wine and sauté for a moment just to take the edge off the wine. Add the shredded chard greens. Sprinkle with ½ teaspoon of the salt and ¼ teaspoon of the pepper. Toss to mix.

WHAT TO BUY OR ORDER NOW

Last call before summer for all perishable items! In particular, we order the soft cheeses, such as Brie, blue, Italian Fontina and feta. It is impossible to keep most of them through the summer months so we enjoy them now. Some of the hard cheeses, we have been successful in ordering in June and the blue cheese from Maytag arrives in excellent shape, even in warm weather. A wheel of cheddar from The Vermont Country Store arrived once when the temperature was over 100 degrees and it, too, was unscathed. In the spring, we serve the soft cheeses with our salads and sometimes a braided string cheese which we order from Cheese Junction. Unbraided, cut into 6-inch lengths, then pulled apart into very thin shreds it is fun to eat. This is easily done if the cheese is very cold. We serve the shreds piled on a platter, to be scooped up with one's fingers.

All of the pancetta that we will need until fall is ordered now and frozen. Also, we check our flour and rice supplies. In an emergency, they can be ordered later, but if there are any insect eggs lurking in the bags, they could take the warm traveling time as an opportunity to hatch. The same problem applies to spices so we stock up on them.

Cover the skillet and cook over medium heat until the greens have wilted—about 15 minutes. Toss several times as they cook. Remove from the heat and add the pine nuts, tossing again to distribute them throughout the greens.

5. Preheat the oven to 450°F.

6. Rub the inside of the gratin dish with another tablespoon of the butter. Add the greens mixture and spread it evenly over the surface. Arrange the fish filets in a single layer to cover the greens entirely.

Sprinkle the filets with the lemon juice and the remaining ½ teaspoon of salt and ¼ teaspoon of pepper. Cut the remaining 2 tablespoons of butter into ¼-inch bits and distribute them evenly over the fish.

7. Place the gratin dish in the upper third of the oven and bake for 15 minutes. Remove the dish from the oven and turn the temperature to "broil." Arrange the lemon slices over the fish.

Place the dish 6 inches under the broiler for 5 minutes until the lemon slices have browned slightly. Sprinkle with the chopped parsley or basil and serve from the gratin dish.

AND IN OUR GARDEN

The first two weeks of April are mostly spent tidying, thinning and mulching the garden, but as the weather warms, we begin to plant cucumber, squash and carrot seeds, beans and more beets, lettuce and peas to extend our harvesting period, and at the very end of the month, the tomato and pepper plants from the house. We do not take a chance by planting all of them at once for a late frost could occur. Eggplants are the last things to go into our summer garden for they must have a warm soil.

In our first year of gardening, we ordered earthworms from Burpee Seed Company and in the three years that have passed, our original 500 worms have increased enormously in population. Not only do they loosen the soil, but their castings are a free organic fertilizer. UPS delivered our "family" late in the day, so we just left the box on the floor until morning. During those hours, many managed to escape to the delight of our cats, so we advise you to introduce worms to their soil upon arrival.

Another organic aid for the garden is composting. We use the simplest methods for our composting and to date, have not started a compost bin. Almost all uncooked and unseasoned vegetables, egg shells and spent flowers from the house go into our soil. We merely dig a hole about a foot deep, empty in the kitchen scraps and cover them with soil. Fish trimmings and bones are especially valuable in the soil, but we bury them a little deeper for we have field mice on the fringes of the garden waiting to dig them up. For this same reason, we do not compost cooked or seasoned foods.

In the warmer months, the materials will decompose in a matter of days. In the winter, they may remain somewhat in their original state, but will decompose quickly once spring arrives. We do not compost potato peelings as they may sprout and could be diseased. Nor do we compost squash seeds as they will definitely sprout, sometimes for years, and not necessarily produce squash the same as the original variety. Even so, a few seeds manage to get into our garden and out of curiosity, we usually leave them. By the end of the summer, we will have a collection of "mystery" squash. Jerusalem artichoke peelings should be composted only if you want the plants. They are so proliferous that we have had them grow while stored in the refrigerator.

MAY

TIME TO THINK ABOUT CANNING

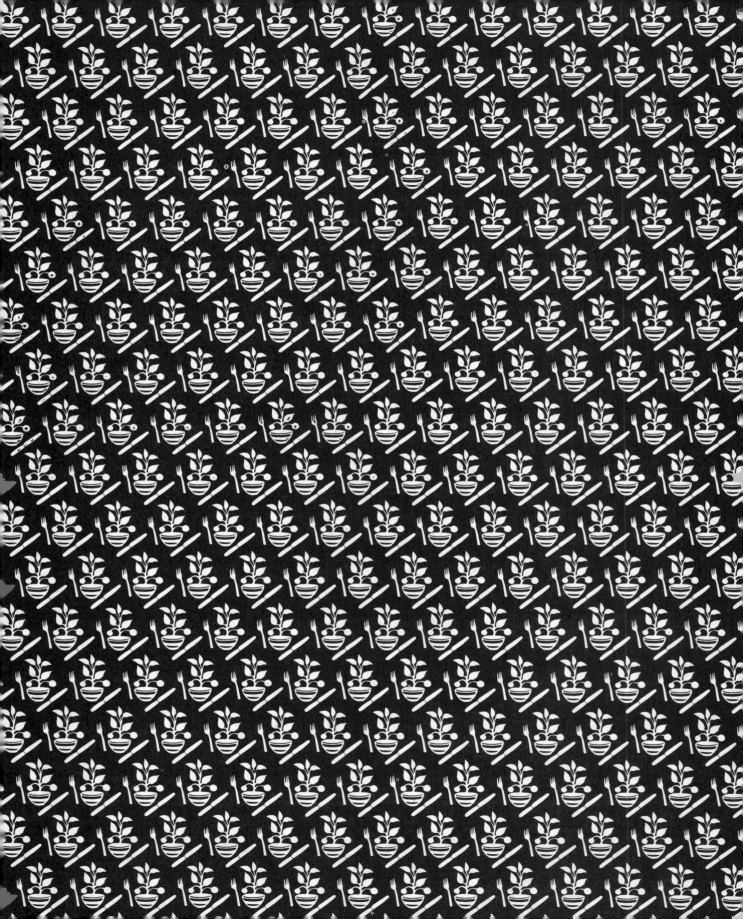

TIME TO THINK ABOUT CANNING

May is perhaps the most joyful month for a gardener. With perfect weather and sufficient rains, you are filled with optimism for the best garden ever. One wishes the sun would never go down and it is a letdown to have to come into the house in the evening. One of the hardest things we had to accept is that these perfect conditions for gardening do not always exist; that there will be some plants that die, and that vicious storms can wreck a plentiful crop. The first summer we gardened, two terrifying storms swept through within weeks of each other. Our first reaction was to abandon the garden, but too much effort had gone into it. After both storms, we cleaned up the debris and salvaged what we could and, in the end, we had a good, if not perfect, garden. Now we are a little more accepting of losses.

May is also one of our busiest months. The bulk of the garden is planted at this time and we begin to harvest the first of our salad greens, spring onions, radishes, kohlrabi, beets, and peas. The produce to can or freeze in early May is scant, but it is essential to be prepared for the actual work which will begin in earnest in another month. This preparation must be done early in the month before it is too hot to order oils, cheeses, and garlic by mail. Also, we check our canning jars from the previous year to see if we need to buy more.

CANNING

Even if we did not grow our own vegetables, we would still can. When we lived in New York we did not can as much, but we did always put up a large supply of tomatoes, tomato sauce, and jams. Before learning how, we thought of canning as a long, difficult process which would only bore us. However, when our friend, Virginia Busby, offered to give us a lesson, we found we loved it. We were fortunate to have Virginia teach us, as in one afternoon we received a remarkable lesson that was so thorough we felt confident to proceed on our own. The main things she stressed were freshness of produce, strict adherence to processing times, and absolute cleanliness.

We will not attempt to give complete instructions for canning procedures here, as there are many booklets available which do this. We will give you a few basic suggestions and hope to convince doubters that canning is a simple and rewarding activity. For us, almost nothing in cooking compares with opening a closet and finding it full of a colorful array of delicious canned goods.

Where to write

Here are four addresses to write for detailed booklets. They are all quite reasonable in price. Write for the prices, as with publication costs, they go up slightly every year or so. You should also check your local Agricultural Extension Service, as they offer many booklets which are free. Ask their home economists and specialists in food conservation and preparation about specific questions.

1. Superintendent of Documents, U. S. Government Printing Office, Washington, D.C. 20402. Ask for Agriculture Information Bulletin #410, *Canning, Freezing, Storing Garden Produce*. This is an excellent guide that covers every phase of preserving food.

2. Consumer Information Center, Pueblo, Colorado 81009. Ask for the free *Consumer Information Catalog* which lists about a dozen free or very inexpensive booklets.

3. Ball Corporation, Box 2005, Dept. PK 6A, Muncie, Indiana 47302. This manufacturer of canning jars has a very detailed booklet of over 100 pages in color. Ask for *The Ball Blue Book*.

4. *Kerr Home Canning Book*, P. O. Box 97, Sand Springs, Oklahoma 74063. Kerr, another manufacturer of canning jars, has an estimable booklet in full color.

ABOUT CANNERS

Until a few years ago, there were two general methods for canning: the boiling water bath and the pressure canner. The boiling water bath is used for acid foods such as pickles and tomatoes or for recipes like jams and jellies that contain a large amount of sugar. In the boiling water bath, the jars reach a sufficient internal temperature to preserve the high-acid foods.

The pressure canner is used for low-acid foods such as corn, peas, and beans, plus some meats. With the pressure canner, the jars reach a much higher internal temperature in processing than in the water-bath canner. Mainly because of lack of time, we have not used a pressure canner, as our freezer works very well for low-acid vegetables. We do plan to use the pressure canner in the future as it will save valuable freezer space and it is more economical.

The new method of canning that we started using in 1978 is the steam canner and it has revolutionized the ease with which we can and the amount of canning that we are able to do. Before then, we had used the water-bath canner which requires the heating and boiling of gallons and gallons of water. This not only heated up the kitchen and cost more for fuel, but it took time and strength to move the canner from the sink to the stove and back again to empty it.

The steam canner uses only 2 quarts of water and, as is implied, works on the principle of steam. Some tests have shown it reaches a higher internal temperature than the water-bath canner. It eliminates a tedious cleanup after the canning is completed, as it can be washed and tucked away within 5 minutes. The water-bath canner can take an hour or so just to cool off enough to be cleaned.

There are two steam canners on the market. The original one is from Ideal Harvest, Inc., P. O. Box 15481, 3272 South West Temple, Salt Lake City, Utah 84115. It is made of aluminum.

The second is made by General Housewares Corp., P. O. Box 4066, Terre Haute, Indiana 47804. It is made of graniteware. We have both and find they perform equally well. They cost only a few dollars more than the water-bath canner. In theory, you are able to can anything in the steam canner that you can in the water bath. We have done all of the following recipes for the last few years in the steam bath, but if you are unsure of recipes other than these, contact your Agricultural Extension Service. They can be helpful with any canning problems and often give free demonstrations.

SOME GENERAL SUGGESTIONS FOR CANNING

1. Decide what and how much you want to can. Our goal is a minimum of 200 jars each season. We are not exactly generous with our canned goods, but we do give some away, so that must be considered.

Our recipes are of a basic sort that can be utilized in numerous recipes rather than the sweet and pretty jellies and pickles containing packaged pectin or artificial coloring.

2. At the same time, decide how much time you have for canning. Even if you do only 25 jars in a season, it is worth it.

We have arranged our recipes in order of their garden appearance, with July and August being our busiest canning months.

3. Follow all canning instructions precisely and do not change recipes unless you are an expert. The ratio of vinegar or sugar determines whether your product will keep or spoil.

4. In some of our recipes, you will notice that we have not given the precise amount of headspace to leave in each jar. This is because the steam canner requires slightly more headspace than the water-bath canner. Your canner will come with detailed instructions about this. When we have indicated the amount, it is safe for both canners. Since all of our recipes are hot pack, leaving ½-inch headspace is always safe.

5. Before storing your jars, label each one as to what it is and the date it was canned. In addition, keep a list of each item canned with the date (we keep our list in the back of our gardening diary). This can be of great value. You will not only have a record, but in case a jar should not be good, you can refer to your list to see what others might have been canned that same day.

Each time a jar is used, make a notation on your list so you will have a general idea of what is left.

6. Use only jars, lids, and bands that are manufactured specifically for canning. Examine them thoroughly before using. We have had only one jar break during processing and this was when we forgot to check for cracks or nicks. The bands, if not rusted, may be used again, but not the lids.

To prevent the lids and bands from rusting, wash the outsides of the jars after they have cooled and dry under the bands as well as you can. Rusting is usually caused by salt or vinegar under the bands which has leaked out during processing.

7. Some instructions for canning will say to remove the bands after the jars have cooled. There are valid reasons for doing this. One is that you may reuse the bands throughout the season and secondly, in case the jars should develop pressure inside, the lids would pop off rather than the jars exploding. However, we leave our bands intact and we have had no explosions, as we store our goods in a cool, dark closet and check them periodically.

8. Floating is a problem. This happens when the jars are not packed as tightly as they should be and after processing and cooling, the contents float to the top, leaving several inches of liquid at the bottom. This will take practice, so if you are a beginner, can only a few jars to start with. If they float, pack them tighter next time. It will not affect the flavor.

9. You will notice that some of our recipes say to sterilize the canning jars and others do not. If anything is to be processed under 15 minutes, sterilize the jars. If they will be processed 15 minutes or longer, it is not necessary.

To sterilize your jars, wash them in hot, soapy water, rinse, and immerse in a boiling water bath for 15 minutes or place them upright in a steam canner for the same amount of time. A dishwasher will not sterilize the jars.

10. After completing the canning process place your jars on several layers of toweling with 3 inches of space between the jars. Make very sure there is no draft and leave them undisturbed until completely cooled (we leave them overnight). Then test for a seal.

Press down on the center of the lid. If it does not pop back, you may assume the jar is sealed. If it does pop back, reprocess the jar. The contents must be removed, reheated, and placed back into a clean jar and processed again for the specified time. This rarely happens and if it does, we usually just use up the jar as quickly as possible rather than reprocessing.

11. Before tasting any of your canning, check the jars and contents very carefully. If the seal on a jar has broken, if there is a bad odor or any mold or discoloration, discard it. If you should be unsure about the Tomatoes, Tomato Sauce, or Sauerkraut, boil them in an open saucepan for 15 minutes before tasting. Although your canned goods will keep for years, try to use them within the year for best flavor and color.

12. Our recipes specify the use of canning salt. Sometimes the salt will be labeled "plain salt" on the bag. Do not use regular table salt, which contains iodine or other additives which might cause your canned goods to cloud. Do not use kosher salt either, as it is lighter in weight than canning or plain salt.

13. Vinegars must have an acidity of at least 5 percent. All vinegars will have the acidic strength on the labels. We generally use a plain white vinegar, but there is no reason you cannot use a fine French wine vinegar, as long as it has an acidity of 5 percent.

14. When sterilizing the jars, lids, and bands, it is a good idea to sterilize an extra of each in the next smallest size. That is to say, if you are canning quarts, sterilize an extra pint jar with its lid and band. Although our recipes are very close to the amount indicated, it is possible to have some left over.

If there is less than a half pint, we use it right away. If you have some of your boiling pickle brine left, let it cool and refrigerate it for the next batch, but label it. Do not reuse overnight salt solutions.

15. Do not boil the lids when sterilizing, as it could damage the sealing composition. Merely place them in water that is just under a boil along with the bands and canning tools. Turn the heat off and leave them under the water until ready to use. Place the canning tools back into the water after use. Never place them on your work surface.

Ideally, once you begin the canning process, you should never touch the jars, lids, and bands with your hands, but always use the sterilized tools for filling the jars and the jar lifter for moving the jars and adjusting the lids. This can be difficult and sometimes impossible, but at least make sure not to touch the tops of the jars or the lids with your hands.

Basic Canning Equipment

Canning equipment is inexpensive and after the initial outlay of money, it can be used year after year—even for generations. If your area does not have a good source for canning equipment, almost everything can be bought by mail.

The canner

If you do not have a canner, we encourage you to purchase the steam canner rather than the water-bath canner (see page 130).

Jars, lids, and bands

Until recently in large cities canning jars were hard to find, but we understand they are more available now and at a good price. If not, some of the fancier styles are available by mail as well as the lids and bands for standard jars.

Saucepans

Chances are you will have these in your kitchen. Use only enameled or stainless steel, as other metals such as aluminum can become stained, in addition to discoloring the item you are canning. You will need a 2-quart saucepan for sterilizing your canning tools, another for boiling your brine, and, if you are making large quantities of, say Tomato Sauce, you will need a 1-gallon-capacity saucepan or several smaller ones.

We like Le Creuset saucepans as they are very heavy enameled iron and, although expensive, last forever. Many stainless steel pans of high quality are available, but since we have Le Creuset, we have not purchased them.

Canning tools

A jar lifter is most important for lifting your jars into and out of your canner. Various spoons and ladles are quite handy to have. We have a 1-cup-capacity ladle and several slotted spoons, all stainless. A funnel is also a big help. There are plastic and metal ones. We prefer the metal as it seems more sanitary. It is aluminum, so we are careful to wash it immediately after use so that it does not discolor.

Dish towels

Have a supply of at least a half dozen which you use for canning only. We prefer a white, 100 percent cotton terry cloth.

Paper towels

Again, use only white as the dyes from some colored towels bleed. We use the paper towels for wiping the jars clean before sealing. Dip them into hot water before wiping the jars.

Measuring cups and spoons

Have a variety of different sizes. We have a glass measuring cup with a ½ gallon capacity which is most helpful for measuring liquids for brines.

STRAWBERRY PRESERVES

Strawberries are the first fruit of the season to can. In our area, they appear at the farmers' market during the first two weeks of May. South of us and on the West Coast, it is earlier. Elsewhere, it is a little later. Not only is the picking time short, but they disappear from the farmers's trucks instantly. During the strawberry season, we try to be at the market to meet the farmers no later than 6:00 A.M. We are growing our own strawberries, but have not been able to harvest as many as we need for canning.

When buying strawberries, try to buy them when it has not rained for several days. One day we bought several gallons that were perfect and a few days later, bought more after a heavy rain. These berries were very watery and had to be drained before canning so there was a loss in the number of jars we were able to make.

Most recipes for strawberry preserves call for either lemon juice or vinegar, so it occurred to us that raspberry vinegar might add a very special touch. It does and is worth the effort and cost to obtain it. We like the Paul Corcellet brand from France, which contains only wine vinegar and raspberries. Some contain sugar or other unnecessary ingredients.

If you plan to give some of the preserves as gifts, they will look even prettier canned in the French-style canning jars. Check the mail-order listings to find out where to buy them.

Do not double this recipe, but make separate batches if you wish to make more than 4 pints. Otherwise, the berries will fall apart and later float in the jars.

Makes 8 half-pints or 4 pints

2 quarts ripe strawberries, rinsed and hulled
6 cups sugar
3 tablespoons raspberry vinegar

1. Over very low heat, cook the whole strawberries, uncovered, in an enameled or stainless steel pot with a 1-gallon capacity until the juices begin to flow. Do not stir.

Add the sugar and the raspberry vinegar. Cover and bring to a rolling boil, again not stirring.

Uncover and boil the ingredients for 15 minutes, shaking the pot occasionally rather than stirring. This allows the strawberries to absorb the sugar, but does not break them up. Skim the thick, pink foam from the surface as it appears. It is extremely important to remove all of the foam for clear preserves.

2. Remove the pot from the heat and let stand at room temperature for 24 hours so that the berries can absorb more of the sugar. Cover with cheesecloth to keep out insects. Continue to shake the pot occasionally and skim during this time.

3. After 24 hours, ladle the preserves into sterilized jars to within ½ inch of the tops. Use

a slotted, stainless steel spoon to drain the berries. The preserves will be thick with berries and will not float.

4. Seal and process in a steam or water bath container for 10 minutes for either ½ pints or pints.

Note: If you have leftover syrup, can it just as you did the preserves by pouring it into sterilized jars, sealing and processing for 10 minutes. The syrup is excellent mixed with fruit and yogurt, or use it to make a delightful Strawberry Ice (see page 157).

STRAWBERRY JAM

As with the Strawberry Preserves, the special difference in this recipe is the raspberry vinegar. We cannot decide which we enjoy the most, so we make lots of both. Use the jam when making Belle Sherrill's Jam Cake (see page 391).

Makes 7 half-pints

3 quarts strawberries, rinsed and hulled
6½ cups sugar
3 tablespoons raspberry vinegar

1. Coarsely cut the strawberries into small pieces and place them in a heavy enameled saucepan with a 1-gallon capacity. Add the sugar and the raspberry vinegar. Stir briskly, mashing the berries somewhat as you do so. Cover and bring to a boil over medium heat.

2. Uncover and continue to cook at a low boil until thick. This will take about 45 minutes. To test the thickness, remove a spoonful and let it cool. Jams are thicker after cooling.

3. While the jam is cooking, stir often to make sure it does not stick to the bottom of the saucepan and burn. Also, skim off any foam that forms on the surface as it will show up later in the jars.

4. When thick, pour into sterilized half-pint canning jars. Seal and process in a steam or water-bath canner for 10 minutes.

DILL PICKLES

Dill pickles are the most popular item we can so we make enough for ourselves and for gifts throughout the year—around 60 quarts. Since our dill may be ready in the garden before the cucumbers, we cut the sprigs and flower heads and freeze them in small bundles. There is no loss in flavor and once in the brine, they will look as pretty as fresh dill.

Our hot peppers often do not turn red until we are well into pickle canning, so we freeze and dry the whole peppers in the late summer for use the next year. Again, the flavor and color are not affected. We grow Long Red Cayenne peppers as our hot peppers, but the dried peppers from Aphrodisia, listed in their catalog as "Peppers, Chili, whole," approximate ours in hotness. They are shorter, so use 2 per quart of pickles.

You will need a little practice in packing the cucumbers into the jars. Your first quarts may "float," but you will quickly find that you can pack the jars very tightly. Our brine will exactly fill 4 tightly packed jars, so if you are a beginner, make a little extra brine.

You may pickle any size cucumber that you wish. We have specified cucumbers 3 to 4 inches long, but you may use either larger ones or very tiny ones. When your cucumbers are too large for whole pickles, slice them ¼ inch thick and proceed with the recipe, packing them in tight layers.

Our favorite cucumber for pickling *was* Salty, but to our great disappointment, it is no longer being produced by its developer. It was a fitting name for a pickling cuke, but we have been assured by two seed companies that we will be happy with their suggested substitutions. Comstock, Ferre and Company has recommended Liberty as the variety to replace Salty, and Stokes Seeds feels we will like Pioneer. We will grow both varieties next season and see if "old Salty" can be replaced.

Makes 4 quarts

60 to 80 hard pickling cucumbers, 3 to 4 inches long (see above)
3 cups white vinegar
3 cups water
6 tablespoons canning salt
8 large cloves garlic, peeled
4 tablespoons yellow mustard seeds
16 small sprigs fresh dill
4 small flower heads fresh dill (if available)
4 fresh, frozen, or dried hot red peppers (approximately 5 inches long) or 8, if small (see above)

1. Trim the stems of the cucumbers to ¼ inch. Wash the cucumbers, making sure that the blossom end is well cleaned.

2. In a 2½-quart saucepan, bring to a boil a brine made of the vinegar, water, and salt. Stir to make sure that the salt is completely dissolved. Watch the boiling brine, so that it does not reduce.

3. Place 2 of the garlic cloves and 1 tablespoon of the mustard seeds in each jar. Make 4 bouquets of the dill sprigs and flower heads. Add 1 bouquet and 1 red pepper to each jar.

4. Begin packing in the cucumbers, making the jars as attractive as you can. Try to keep the contents standing upright, and pack the cucumbers as tightly as you can without bruis-ing them. When the jars are filled, pour in the boiling brine to within ½ inch of the tops of the jars. Seal and process 20 minutes in a steam or water-bath canner.

5. Often, as the jars are being processed, the brine will overflow, leaving a residue of salt under the bands after the jars have cooled. For this reason, we rinse the jars before storing them. After rinsing dry them completely underneath the bands so that rust will not form. If rust should form, it will not affect the pickles.

6. The pickles may shrivel after processing, but they will plump again as they cure. You may sample the pickles right away, but it is best to wait 2 months, as they will taste best then or in the months to follow. Some "pickle people" suggest that they cure for a year.

PICKLED BEETS

This is the only canned item we have had difficulty with. Pickled beets can be unappetizing if the beets are overcooked, but if they are not cooked enough before processing, the jars will not seal. Just watch them closely as they cook. A fork should pierce them easily. Small beets, about 1½ inches in diameter, will take about 15 minutes to cook, and larger beets ½ hour or more. Can the small beets whole and cut the large ones into ⅜-inch slices. We can both red and yellow beets. The yellow beets take on a deep orange hue after canning.

Makes 2 quarts

> **4 pounds beets (red or yellow)**
> **2 cups white vinegar**
> **1 cup sugar**
> **2 teaspoons canning salt**
> **2 tablespoons pickling spices, tied in cheesecloth**
> **½ pound onions, sliced thin**

1. Trim the tops of the beets to 2 inches. Leave the roots intact. Drop the beets into rapidly boiling water and cook until just tender. Drain and peel. Leave whole if small and slice into ⅜-inch slices if large.

2. While the beets are cooking, prepare the brine by bringing to a boil the vinegar, sugar, salt, and pickling spices. Turn off the heat and let the mixture steep until the beets are ready.

3. Pack the beets, alternating with the onion slices, into quart canning jars to within ½ inch of the top. Remove the cheesecloth with the pickling spices from the brine. Bring the brine back to a boil and pour over the beets to within ½ inch of the top of the jars.

4. Seal and process in a steam or water-bath canner for 30 minutes.

SAUERKRAUT MADE IN JARS

Although many purists will disagree, we find our sauerkraut made right in the canning jars just as good as that made in a crock. And it has the advantages of being almost foolproof and more sanitary. It is certainly easier.

We can our first sauerkraut in June, using Early Jersey Wakefield cabbage which has a small, pointy head and a more delicate flavor than later varieties. In late September, we can more, using Surehead or Flat Dutch, both of which are flat in shape. If you are unable to grow these as we do, look for them in the markets, as they are easy to recognize.

Before using the canned sauerkraut, we wash it in several changes of cold water. This is to remove some of the salt that was necessary in the canning. It is a matter of taste and you may prefer not to.

Makes 2 quarts

5 pounds cabbage
3½ tablespoons canning salt
Cold water

1. Remove the dirty outside leaves from the cabbage, then quarter, core, and finely shred it. Place the cabbage in a very large bowl and, with your hands, gently but thoroughly toss in the salt. Pack solidly into 2 wide-mouth quart canning jars. Use a wooden spoon or your fist to pack down. Fill to within 1 inch of the top of the jars.

If the cabbage has not released enough liquid to come within 1 inch of the top, add cold water to do so. Put on lids and bands and screw the jars firmly tight, using only your hand strength.

2. Place the jars on a platter and keep in a cool area. A temperature around 60°F is preferred.

Fermentation will now begin to take place and liquid will run from the jars onto the platter. You will notice bubbles inside the jars.

In 4 to 5 days, when no more liquid is running out and the bubbling has subsided, fermentation will have ceased. Wash the outside of the jars and tighten the bands. It may happen that the lids will have become misshapen. If so, replace with new lids.

3. Process jars in a steam or water-bath canner for 15 minutes.

Note: If you have fresh hot red peppers (cayenne, in particular), add 1 to each jar when you are packing the cabbage into the jars.

TOMATOES

The most valuable items we can during the summer are our tomatoes. Nothing is more welcome in the winter months, and the flavor is actually improved upon canning. We try to can at least 50 quarts and could use more. We are fortunate that we are able to grow our own, but most stores will sell tomatoes at a good price if you buy in quantity.

Select either a very firm, uniform variety of regular tomatoes or very ripe plum tomatoes. We grow Supersteak, Fantastic, Yellow Sunray, and two varieties of plum tomatoes, Roma and San Marzano. Altogether, we have about 60 plants, which will yield over 20 bushels of tomatoes.

Our recipe is for 24 pounds of tomatoes (about ½ bushel). It is difficult to be precise about the amount this will make, as some tomatoes contain more water than others. To be safe, we figure 6 pounds of tomatoes per quart.

We are very careful that our tomatoes do not float in the jars but are tightly packed after processing. This explains the 6-pound allowance for each quart. Consider it a bonus if you are able to can more. We compared our drained, canned tomatoes with several commercial brands and we had double the amount of tomatoes after draining, not to mention a superior taste. We also sampled the drained liquid from both: we poured the commercial brands down the sink, whereas we could chill and drink ours as tomato juice.

When you are ready to use your tomatoes, examine the jars and contents carefully. Certainly, if there is a bad odor, dark discoloration, mold, or the jars are no longer sealed, discard them. Sometimes, because of the high acid content of the tomatoes, the insides of the lids will rust or even become black. This is no cause for alarm. To be absolutely sure, you may cook the tomatoes in an open pot for 10 to 15 minutes before tasting.

Makes 4 to 5 quarts

24 pounds very ripe, perfect tomatoes
Canning salt
Sprig of fresh basil for each jar

1. Wash the tomatoes and discard any that show signs of spoilage. Peel the tomatoes by first immersing them in boiling water for about 30 seconds to loosen the skins. After peeling, core and seed the tomatoes, then depending upon their size cut them into chunks by either halving or quartering.

If you are using plum tomatoes, cut them in half lengthwise to remove the seeds and can them as halves.

2. Place the tomatoes in a large pot (or pots), cover, and over medium heat, cook until they lose some of their water and come to a boil.

This is known as hot-pack preparation, as opposed to raw pack. The tomatoes are less likely to float with the hot-pack preparation, but they invariably do with raw pack. Turn the heat to very low as you pack the jars.

3. With two slotted metal spoons, lift the tomatoes from the pot, a few tablespoons at a time, draining and pressing gently to remove more liquid. Pack into quart or pint canning jars. A stainless steel funnel is useful for this.

When the jars are about three-quarters full, drain the accumulated liquid in the jars back into the pot. You will use this liquid later for Tomato Juice (see below). At this time, add a sprig of basil to each jar.

Continue packing the tomatoes until the jars are filled to within ½ inch of the tops. Do *not* drain off any more of the liquid.

Add 1 teaspoon of canning salt to each quart jar. It is not necessary to stir, as the salt will dissolve during processing. Salt and basil are optional, but the tomatoes will lack in flavor with the omission of either.

4. Seal and process in a steam or water-bath canner. Process quarts for 45 minutes.

Note: Yellow tomatoes are beautiful when canned, but we take the precaution of adding 1 teaspoon of fresh lemon juice to each quart and ½ teaspoon to each pint before processing. Many articles say the acid content of yellow tomatoes is as high as that of red, but we prefer to be safe and the addition does not affect the taste.

TOMATO JUICE

Many recipes for Tomato Juice use peeled tomatoes that are simmered and sieved to obtain the juice. We find this is a needless task. The liquid left from our canned tomatoes is a thick juice in itself and requires only a minimum of effort to process.

Figure that for every 4 quarts of tomatoes that you can, you will have enough liquid left for 2 quarts of juice. Since the juice has no emulsifier, it will separate in the jars after processing, but do not worry. Just chill and shake it before serving.

Leftover liquid from canned tomatoes
Canning salt

1. Pour leftover liquid from the canned tomatoes through a sieve. Measure and add 1 teaspoon of canning salt for every quart of liquid. Bring to a boil and pour immediately into quart or pint canning jars.
2. Seal and process in a steam or water-bath canner for 15 minutes for both quarts and pints.

TOMATO SAUCE

If we are unable to do without canned Tomatoes during the winter, the same can be said for Tomato Sauce. Again, can as many jars as you think you will need, and then some. There is a tremendous feeling of security in having them stowed away in anticipation of enjoying them later.

We did can the tomato sauce for several years using a food mill, but a food processor makes it possible to make larger amounts in less time. You may use either regular or plum tomatoes, but we prefer a combination of the two. Plum tomatoes will make a thicker sauce but the flavor of the tomatoes is more pronounced using both.

As with canned tomatoes, we work with about 24 pounds of tomatoes at a time as that is about the amount we can handle in one day. The yield will vary depending upon the choice of tomatoes and the thickness of the sauce. We make our sauce very thick, so that sometimes there is just over 4 quarts of sauce from 24 pounds of tomatoes. If there is more, we usually will eat it that evening, being too exhausted to cook anything else.

Makes 4 to 5 quarts

24 pounds very ripe, perfect tomatoes
1½ pounds onions
1 cup olive oil

15 to 18 large cloves garlic, peeled
4 teaspoons canning salt
1 teaspoon freshly ground black pepper
Sprigs of fresh basil for each jar

1. Wash, core, and seed the tomatoes, but do not peel them. After it is puréed, the peel adds flavor and thickness to the sauce. Cut the tomatoes into chunks about 1½ inches in diameter. If using plum tomatoes, cut in half lengthwise to remove the seeds. Set aside.

2. Peel and chop the onions coarse. Heat the olive oil in a heavy enameled saucepan with at least a 1-gallon capacity. Add the onions and the peeled garlic. Sauté over medium heat until the onions have wilted and are beginning to turn a light golden color. This will take about 20 minutes.

3. While the onions and garlic are cooking, purée the tomatoes in a food processor or in a food mill. Set aside. When the onions and garlic are cooked, purée and return them to the saucepan. Add the puréed tomatoes, salt, and black pepper. Stir and bring to a simmer.

At this point, you may want to transfer some of the sauce to another saucepan. By dividing the sauce, it will cook down and thicken faster.

Continue to simmer over medium heat until the sauce is as thick as you like it. Stir often enough so that it does not stick or burn. With this amount of sauce, the cooking time can be as much as 4 hours to obtain a really thick sauce, such as we prefer. There should be no visible liquid floating on top of the sauce nor should it appear when you stir the sauce. The long cooking time insures a safer sauce after canning.

4. When the sauce has thickened, ladle it into quart or pint canning jars to within ½ inch of the tops of the jars. A metal funnel is useful for this. Place a sprig of fresh basil in each jar. (Remove the basil before using the sauce.)

5. Seal and process in a steam or water-bath canner. Process quarts for 35 minutes. If you are using pint jars, process for 25 minutes. If you are worried that your tomatoes are not as acidic as they should be, add 1 teaspoon of fresh lemon juice to each quart jar and ½ teaspoon to each pint and increase the processing time by 10 minutes for both quarts and pints.

TOMATO MARMALADE

You may use either red or yellow tomatoes in this recipe. The red are easier to come by, but if you grow or are able to buy yellow tomatoes, the marmalade is especially pretty, as the color is a deep shade of orange. We like to serve tomato marmalade at breakfast or brunch with freshly made cottage cheese that is still warm.

Makes 5 half-pints

3 pounds very ripe tomatoes
3½ cups sugar
2 lemons
¾ cup finely chopped crystallized ginger

1. Immerse the tomatoes in boiling water for about 30 seconds to loosen the skin. Peel, core and remove the seeds. Chop into small cubes about ½ inch in diameter. Place the tomatoes in the pot you will be using for cooking. A heavy enameled iron pot is preferable.

Cover with the sugar and allow to stand for an hour or so.

2. Remove the peel from the lemons and cut into very fine julienne strips. Squeeze the juice. Combine the strips, the juice, and the chopped ginger with the tomatoes and sugar.

3. Bring to a simmer, then cook uncovered over low to medium heat, stirring often, until the mixture thickens. This will take about 20 to 25 minutes.

4. When the marmalade has thickened to your taste, pour it into sterilized half-pint canning jars.

Seal and process in a steam or water-bath canner for 5 minutes.

PICKLED COLORADO PEPPERS

The Pickled Colorados are enjoyable eaten just as they are, but we usually chop and add them to other dishes, such as our pizzas or in various starchy preparations. Any cold salads such as potato, rice, or cracked wheat benefit from the addition. Coleslaw is particularly enhanced by it. We use this recipe for Hot Banana peppers as well, but prefer the Colorados as they are not quite as hot. We can around 15 quarts each season, growing our plants from seed.

Makes 2 quarts

1 cup canning salt, for the first brine, plus an additional ¼ cup
    for the second brine
2 pounds Colorado peppers, 4 to 6 inches long
4 large cloves garlic, peeled but left whole
4 medium onions, sliced thin
2 fresh or 4 dried hot red peppers
Several sprigs of fresh dill (if available)
¼ cup white vinegar

1. Using a crock or glass container with a 1-gallon capacity, make a brine by dissolving 1 cup canning salt in ½ gallon water. Wash the peppers and cut the stems to ½ inch. Make 3 or

4 slits about ¼ inch long in each pepper.

When the salt has completely dissolved, add the peppers. Weight them down with either a heavy plate or a watertight plastic bag, half filled and sealed. Let stand 24 hours.

2. The next day, drain the peppers, discarding the brine. Place 2 cloves of garlic in each sterilized quart canning jar. Pack the Colorado peppers, the sliced onions, the hot red peppers (1 fresh or 2 dried per jar), and the sprigs of dill into the jars, making as attractive an arrangement as possible.

Pack the vegetables tightly and if there are not enough hot peppers to fill the jars, slice more onions and add them. The onions are delicious on their own.

3. Make a second brine of 1 quart of water, ¼ cup white vinegar, and ¼ cup canning salt. Bring to a boil and pour over the peppers.

Seal and process in a steam or water-bath canner for 5 minutes.

PICKLED JALAPEÑO PEPPERS

These peppers are going to look and smell so irresistible after canning that you may be tempted to sample them as they are. But be warned—they are fiery! We do have friends who are able to eat these plain with nary a tear, but we use ours chopped into other foods, or to perk up a potato, cabbage, or bean salad; and in our vinaigrette sauce when it seems appropriate. Always save the juices and onions for similar uses.

Many canned items will keep for several years, but use the Pickled Jalapeño Peppers within 1 year; the olive oil becomes a little stale in flavor after that time.

Makes 4 pints

**4 cups white vinegar
1 cup water
1 cup olive oil
4 teaspoons canning salt
4 tablespoons pickling spices, tied in cheesecloth
2 pounds jalapeño peppers
8 cloves of garlic, peeled but left whole
4 medium onions, sliced thin**

1. In an enameled or stainless-steel saucepan, combine the vinegar, water, olive oil, salt, and pickling spices. Bring to a boil and turn off the heat. Let steep, covered, while you prepare the other ingredients. This will give the liquid time to absorb the flavors from the pickling spices.

2. Wash and dry the peppers. Trim the stems to be no longer than ½ inch but do not remove entirely.

3. Place 2 cloves of garlic in each of 4 sterilized pint canning jars. On top, alternating, pack the

peppers and sliced onions. (If you should run short on jalapeños, just add more onions.)

Pack as tightly as possible so they will not float later in the jars. Fill jars to within 1 inch of the tops.

4. Discard the cheesecloth with the pickling spices, bring the liquid back to a boil, and pour over the peppers to within 1 inch of the tops.

Seal and process in a steam or water-bath canner for 10 minutes.

BILLIE'S JALAPEÑO PEPPER RELISH

This recipe came from our friend, Billie Hurmence. It is an old family recipe from Texas which Billie has never written down, but makes instinctively. When she gave us some of her relish, we *had* to know how to prepare it and were able to figure out proportions by what she told us. She tasted and approved! The relish is very hot but perfect with any Mexican dish, with pita combinations, and as an accompaniment to potato dishes. Actually, we try it on just about everything.

Later in the season, when the jalapeño peppers turn red, make some using red jalapeños and ripe red tomatoes (see box). Jalapeño peppers are becoming more available in the markets, but if you are unable to buy them and do have a garden, they are very prolific. Three or four plants will probably yield more than you can use. Seeds are available by mail and we start ours indoors about 8 weeks before the last spring frost date.

Makes 8 half-pints or 4 pints

1½ pounds jalapeño peppers
2 pounds green tomatoes
4 teaspoons canning salt
¼ cup white vinegar

1. Wash and dry the peppers and tomatoes. Remove the caps from the peppers. Cut the peppers into 3 or 4 chunks, but do not seed them. If your fingers are sensitive, wear rubber gloves while cutting the peppers. (Be careful not to get juice from the peppers near your eyes.)

Core the tomatoes, but do not peel or seed them. Cut them into chunks the same size as the peppers.

2. Grind the peppers and tomatoes together in a food processor or a blender, or put through the medium blade of a food mill. Do not grind too thoroughly as the mixture should be crunchy, not mushy.

3. Put the mixture into an enameled saucepan and add the salt and vinegar. Stir and bring the mixture just to a boil over medium heat. Spoon into hot, sterilized canning jars.

Seal and process in a steam or water-bath canner. Process 5 minutes for half-pints and 10 minutes for pints.

ALL RED RELISH

This relish is dazzling to look at and is as intensely hot in flavor as it is flaming in color. The taste is tantalizing.

The method for making it is the same as for the green peppers and tomatoes except for the handling of the tomatoes. Since the ripe tomatoes will contain more liquid than the green, wash, core, and seed them to get rid of as much of the liquid as you can. Cut them into chunks, then place them in a colander over a bowl, and let drain for ½ hour. If you do not do this, the relish will be too thin. After the tomatoes have drained for ½ hour, continue with the preceding recipe.

Because of the loss of liquid, the yield will not be the same as the green relish. Take this into consideration if you wish to make more. One-and-a-half pounds of red jalapeños and 2 pounds of red tomatoes will make 3 pints or 6 half-pints of relish.

MOTHER'S OKRA PICKLES

We always look forward to the first of October as that is when we open our first jar of Okra Pickles. We can them in August, but they must "cure" in the jars for 6 to 8 weeks.

Now that we have our own garden, we are able to pick the pods when they are only 1½ inches long. The okra plant in itself is beautiful, as it is a member of the hibiscus family with colorful yellow flowers with deep red centers. Our plants grow over 8 feet tall and produce until frost, making our fall garden more attractive.

You may can the okra when the pods are longer than 1½ inches, but gauge the size so they will fit your canning jars. These pickles retain their crispness and are deliciously hot from the red peppers.

Makes 4 pints

> 2 pounds small, fresh okra
> 3 cups white vinegar
> 1 cup water
> 6 tablespoons canning salt
> 4 teaspoons yellow mustard seeds
> 4 large cloves garlic, peeled but left whole
> 4 fresh cayenne peppers or 4 dried hot red peppers

1. Do not wash the okra, but wipe clean with damp paper towels. Cut the stems to ¼ inch, being careful not to cut into the pods.

2. In an enameled or stainless-steel saucepan, bring the vinegar, water, and salt to a boil, stirring to make sure the salt is completely dissolved.

3. While the brine is coming to a boil, place 1 teaspoon of mustard seeds in each sterilized jar along with a garlic clove and a hot pepper.

Pack the okra upright in the jars, fitting them in as tightly as possible. For the tightest fit, alternate the okra, placing a stem end down against a pointed end and so on.

4. Pour the boiling brine over the okra to within ½ inch of the tops of the jars.

5. Seal and process in a steam or water-bath canner for 5 minutes. Wait 6 to 8 weeks before serving, as they must "cure" in the jars.

TOMATO AND APPLE CHUTNEY

We enjoy this chutney not only with our Indian dinners, but with other foods as well. It is an unusual accompaniment to our Cottage Cheese and Alfalfa Sprout Omelet (see page 99) or meat entrées that are not too highly seasoned.

Makes 3 pints, or 6 half-pints

4 large, ripe tomatoes
3 hard, tart apples (we like Stayman Winesap)
3 medium onions
2 large, red bell peppers
2 large cloves garlic
1 cup raisins, preferably Monnuka
3 cups light brown sugar
2 cups white vinegar
2 tablespoons peeled and finely chopped fresh ginger root
1 tablespoon yellow mustard seeds
2 teaspoons Garam Masala (see page 190)
1 teaspoon freshly ground dried hot red pepper or 1 fresh cayenne pepper, chopped fine
1 teaspoon freshly ground coriander seed
1 tablespoon canning salt

1. Peel the tomatoes by first immersing them in boiling water for about 30 seconds to loosen the skins. After peeling, core and seed them.

Chop the tomatoes, apples, and onions coarse into ⅓-inch dice.

   Core, but do not peel the bell peppers

and chop them into ⅓-inch pieces. Mince the garlic fine.

2. Place all of these ingredients into a heavy saucepan with a ½-gallon capacity. Add the raisins. Cover with the brown sugar and pour the vinegar over all.

3. Turn the heat to medium and add the remaining ingredients.

4. Bring to a simmer and cook until thickened. This will take about 1 hour. Stir frequently during the cooking.

5. When the chutney is thick, ladle it into hot, sterilized canning jars. Seal and process in a steam or water-bath canner for 10 minutes for both pints and half-pints.

Let the chutney mature in the jars for a month or more before opening.

GREEN TOMATO AND APPLE CHUTNEY

Even with all the canning we do during the summer, it is hard to stop as winter approaches. We feel if we continue canning, we will hold off the cold months. Green Tomato and Apple Chutney is one recipe we can make late into November if we are not content to pack away the canning equipment. The recipe is essentially the same as Tomato and Apple Chutney with the few changes that follow.

Makes 4 pints, or 8 half-pints

1. For the red tomatoes, red bell peppers, and hot red pepper, substitute green. Do not peel or seed the green tomatoes. Just wash, core, and chop them.

For the hot green peppers, use fresh jalapeños, if possible. Two jalapeños will have about the same pungency as the teaspoon of dried hot red pepper.

2. Instead of the light brown sugar, use honey—but only 1 cup.

3. Proceed with the recipe for Tomato and Apple Chutney, keeping in mind that the chutney will thicken faster with green tomatoes. The cooking time will be only 30 minutes. The yield will also be larger—4 pints instead of 3.

The flavor of this chutney is entirely different from the other. We made it up on a whim and when we tasted it immediately after cooking, we were quite disappointed as it was slightly bitter. However, within a few days when it had mellowed a little, we found it delicious. Let it mature for a month and you will have an exceptional chutney.

VIRGINIA'S GREEN TOMATO PICKLES

This is one of the few pickle recipes that we like that contains sugar. The sweetness is not apparent. We eat this more as if it were a relish or chutney. Make this at the end of the summer with green tomatoes that are too small to have time to mature into ripe fruit. Our friend Virginia Busby gave us the recipe.

Makes 7 pints

5 pounds very hard, green tomatoes
1½ pounds onions
4 large, green bell peppers
2 green cayenne or jalapeño peppers
2 tablespoons yellow mustard seeds
1 tablespoon celery seeds
4 teaspoons canning salt
2 cups white vinegar
1¼ cups sugar

1. Core the tomatoes, but do not peel or seed them. Chop them into cubes about ½ inch in diameter. As you chop, place them in a heavy, enameled saucepan with a 1-gallon capacity. Peel and chop the onions coarse. Add them to the tomatoes.

Seed and core the bell peppers. Chop them into pieces about ⅜ inch in diameter. Add them to the saucepan. Chop the hot peppers fine, stirring them into the mixture along with the spices, salt, vinegar, and sugar.

2. Mix thoroughly, cover, and place over medium heat until the mixture comes to a boil. Uncover, lower the heat and cook, just at a simmer, for about 10 minutes.

3. Spoon into hot, sterilized canning jars. Seal and process in a steam or water-bath canner for 10 minutes.

ARTICHOKE PICKLES

This recipe is entering its third generation and has gone through many changes in that time. This latest version is ours; we have cut down on the sugar, but retained the unusual ingredients that are combined with the Jerusalem artichokes. Make the pickles after there have been several frosts, as their flavor will be improved. In fact, you can make the pickles all through the winter if you can dig up or buy the artichokes.

Jerusalem artichokes, which are related to sunflowers, are sold in most supermarkets and if purchased as soon as they are on display, are generally of a quality for canning. They are extremely easy to grow, but once planted, are almost impossible to get rid of and can take over a small garden.

If you do have the space to grow them, the plant is beautiful, resembling bamboo and bearing yellow flowers. The tubers (which is the part of the plant one eats) are planted like potatoes and multiply profusely.

Makes 6 pints

2 cups canning salt, for the salt solutions
3 pounds Jerusalem artichokes, unpeeled

3 medium onions
5 large stalks celery
1 medium cauliflower
4 cups white vinegar
1 cup sugar
2 tablespoons canning salt
1 tablespoon yellow mustard seeds
1 teaspoon turmeric
1 teaspoon celery seeds
6 fresh cayenne peppers
or 2 teaspoons freshly ground dried hot red pepper

1. In two large bowls, prepare individual salt solutions for soaking the vegetables overnight. Do this by dissolving 1 cup of canning salt in ½ gallon of tepid water in each bowl.

The artichokes will soak separately from the other vegetables; it is necessary to prepare the salt solutions first so that the vegetables may be plunged immediately into the salted water to avoid discoloration.

2. Scrub the artichokes. Peel and cut each artichoke individually, dropping it into one of the salt solutions.

When cutting the artichokes, do not try to make them uniform, but leave them with the irregular shape of the tuber. The pieces should be no larger than 1 inch in diameter. After peeling, you will have about 2 quarts of artichokes.

3. Peel and slice the onions thin and drop them into the other bowl containing the salt solution. Wash and trim the celery. Cut it into ½-inch slices and add to the onions.

Wash and core the cauliflower. Break it into flowerets no larger than ½ inch. Trim the stems if they are long or tough. Add the flowerets to the onions and celery.

Weight down the vegetables in each bowl with a leakproof, gallon-capacity plastic bag, half filled with water. Let them soak overnight.

4. The next day, using an enameled or stainless saucepan with a ½-gallon capacity, bring to a boil the vinegar, sugar, canning salt, mustard seeds, turmeric, celery seeds, and dried hot red pepper, if using it. (If you are using fresh cayenne peppers, they will be added whole to each jar.)

5. When the ingredients have come to a boil, quickly drain the onions, celery, and cauliflower. Add them to the saucepan and cook for 5 minutes at a brisk simmer. Drain the artichokes, add them to the saucepan, and briskly simmer for another 5 minutes.

6. Remove from the heat to prevent further cooking and pack the vegetables into sterilized pint canning jars, adding a cayenne pepper to each jar, if you are using them. Pack the vegetables to within ½ inch of the tops of the jars.

7. Bring the liquid in the saucepan back to a boil and ladle it along with the spices over the vegetables, again to within a ½ inch of the tops of the jars.

Seal and process in a steam or water-bath canner for 10 minutes. Let the artichoke pickles cure in the jars for at least a month before serving. They will be crisp and agreeably spicy.

PICKLED BUT NOT PROCESSED

MARTHA ROTH'S PICKLES

During the summer months, we make Martha's pickles. Unfortunately, we have not been able to figure out a way to can them safely without adding vinegar, which would result in a different pickle altogether.

Basically, they are a naturally fermented pickle in a salt brine. Martha never measures the amount of salt she uses, but goes by the taste of the salted water. For us, she did measure and we feel we have a close approximation of her fresh pickles. They are not long keepers even with refrigeration, so plan to eat them within 3 weeks.

The reason these do not keep as long as some brine pickles is that the salt solution is weaker than the standard 10 percent solution. The 10 percent solution contains as much as 2 cups of salt to every gallon of water. Theoretically, pickles brined in a 10 percent solution will keep indefinitely without refrigeration, but you will have a very salty pickle, even after soaking in plain water overnight.

Martha prefers her pickles when they have become full-sour, but we start eating them after 1 day of brining. You will have to decide which you prefer. Generally, half-sour pickles will be ready in 2 to 3 days and full-sour in a week. Refrigerate them when they are to your liking.

For a 1-gallon container

> 2½ to 3 pounds pickling cucumbers
> 4 large cloves garlic, peeled and crushed
> A small bunch of fresh dill with flower heads attached, if possible
> 1 fresh cayenne pepper (optional)
> ½ gallon water
> 6 tablespoons kosher or canning salt (kosher is more traditional)

1. Use only unwaxed, pickling cucumbers that are very firm. The size is up to you. Wash very carefully and cut the stems to ¼ inch.

In a crock or glass container with a

1-gallon capacity, arrange the cucumbers in several layers. Add the garlic, dill, and the cayenne pepper, if using one.

2. In a separate container, prepare the salt solution by measuring first your water and then adding the salt. Stir until the salt is completely dissolved.

This step is very important. If the salt is not completely dissolved, it will sink to the bottom of the crock and the pickles on the bottom will be too salty.

3. Pour the salt solution over the cucumbers and fashion a weight to hold the cucumbers under the brine. You may use a plate with a weight or stone on top. We use a leakproof plastic bag half filled with water.

Cover with cheesecloth and let stand at room temperature until the pickles have fermented to the stage you like. Check them every day and remove any gray film that might develop on the surface.

4. When ready to refrigerate, remove the cheesecloth and replace it with plastic wrap. You can transfer the pickles to smaller jars, but use only glass or ceramic containers. Metals will impart a bad flavor and may corrode.

Check the pickles from time to time, removing any film that may again appear. They will keep for 3 weeks and maybe longer. If they become soft or show any signs of mold, discard them.

PICKLED SUGAR SNAP PEAS

Although the sugar snap peas are not processed, they will keep indefinitely in the refrigerator and their crispy flavor will be most welcome in the winter as part of an hors d'oeuvres platter.

We make our Pickled Sugar Snap Peas in quart canning jars, but you may use a crock. Just do not use metal or plastic. If you have no cover, fashion one of the cheesecloth covered with plastic wrap and secured with a rubber band.

Makes 1 quart

12 ounces sugar snap peas
2 cloves garlic
2 teaspoons yellow mustard seeds
Several sprigs of fresh dill
1 medium onion, sliced thin
1 fresh or 2 dried hot red peppers
1 cup white vinegar
½ cup water
1 teaspoon canning salt

1. String the sugar snap peas by cutting the stem end off with a small, sharp knife and continuing around the sides, pulling the string off in one motion. This goes very quickly.

2. In the bottom of your jar or crock, place the garlic and mustard seeds. Begin adding the peas, the dill, and the onion alternately. At some point, add the hot red pepper so that it will look attractive in the arrangement.

Continue until all the peas have been used and the container is firmly packed.

3. Mix the vinegar, water, and salt together. Stir until the salt is completely dissolved. Pour over the sugar snap peas. If you need more liquid to cover the peas, add more vinegar.

4. Cover and refrigerate for at least 2 months before using. If you sample before this time, you will probably be disappointed, as they will not have had time to develop the desired flavor or crispness.

AUNT ROBIN'S PICKLED SHRIMP

Pickled Shrimp have been a specialty of Aunt Robin's for many years. They were always a gift to be hoped for during the holiday season. She was very accommodating when we asked for the recipe, and gave us her stamp of approval when we tested it. We made only one small change — since we rarely use ketchup, we substituted our Tomato Sauce.

Makes 1 quart

1 pound fresh, unshelled shrimp
2 medium onions, sliced thin
3 imported bay leaves
1 large fresh cayenne pepper
    or ½ teaspoon freshly ground dried hot red pepper
2 teaspoons sugar
1 teaspoon dry mustard
1 teaspoon salt
½ teaspoon freshly ground black pepper
1 tablespoon Worcestershire sauce
¼ cup Tomato Sauce (see pages 310 and 311) or ketchup
¼ cup white wine vinegar
½ cup olive oil
½ cup corn oil

1. Cook the unshelled shrimp in boiling, salted water just until pink. This will take only 3 or 4 minutes. Drain immediately and run cold water over them to stop the cooking process. When they are cool enough to handle, shell and devein the shrimp (see How to Shell and Clean Shrimp, page 120).

2. Using a quart canning jar or any glass jar with a 1-quart capacity, arrange the shrimp, onions, and bay leaves in alternating layers. Add the cayenne pepper if you are using it.

3. In a small bowl, combine the sugar, dry mustard, salt, black pepper, and dried hot red pepper, if using it.

Whisk in the Worcestershire sauce, the Tomato Sauce (or ketchup), and the vinegar. Combine the olive oil and the corn oil.

Whisking constantly, add the combined oils in a steady stream to the other ingre-

dients. When the oils are thoroughly incorporated and the marinade is of a homogenemus consistency, pour it over the shrimp. Cover and refrigerate.

4. Let the shrimp marinate for 3 days before serving. During the time, turn the shrimp occasionally to make sure they marinate evenly. The shrimp will keep for 3 weeks under refrigeration.

5. Offer the shrimp as hors d'oeuvres or as a first course at dinner, and serve with lemon wedges.

PICKLED EGGS

An extra bonus from our pickles is the leftover juice, and one of our favorite ways to use it is for Pickled Eggs. Save all the juice from the Dill Pickles and the Pickled Colorado Peppers. You may even mix them together if you wish.

The refrigerated eggs will keep for a month and can be very convenient when preparing a last-minute cold supper. We always have a quart on hand. You can use the same batch of juice twice, but after that, it begins to lose its zest.

Makes 1 quart

8 large raw eggs, at room temperature
½ quart leftover pickle juice (do not remove the spices and garlic)

1. Place the eggs in a 2-quart saucepan. Cover with tepid water. Place over medium-low heat and cook, covered, just until the water is ready to boil. Do not let the water boil as this will oxidize the yolks. This will take about 20 minutes.

2. Immediately remove the saucepan from the heat and let the eggs stand, still covered, for exactly 8 minutes. Then, moving the saucepan to the sink, run cold water over the eggs to

stop the cooking process. Do not drain.

One by one, peel each egg by first cracking the large end, which has an air pocket, against the sink and then gently cracking the rest of the shell. Hold the egg under the water in the saucepan to remove the shell.

3. After draining the eggs on a paper towel, place them in the pickle juice. Cover and refrigerate for a week before serving.

FREEZING

Freezing is the easiest way to preserve food, but the most expensive. We concentrate on freezing items that are costly or hard to find in the winter or that cannot be canned at home.

We also freeze herbs that will not be in season at the time we will need them the next year for canning. Specifically, dill and cayenne peppers are not ready to harvest when we begin canning our first dill pickles. Until the fresh are available, we make our first jars of pickles using dill and cayenne peppers that we have frozen the previous season. Rarely do we freeze prepared dishes as there is some loss in flavor.

The two most important factors to be aware of in freezing are enzyme action and air, both of which can cause frozen food to spoil. Enzyme action, which is desirable when fruits and vegetables are ripening, must be halted before foods are frozen. This is accomplished by blanching or steaming your produce, cooling it promptly, packaging and freezing it.

The blanching or steaming time varies for each individual fruit or vegetable. For example, peppers need no cooking before freezing and beets must be fully cooked.

Air, the second destructive factor, must be eliminated from your frozen goods. This can be achieved in several ways. Always use moisture-proof packaging, fill containers properly, and if using wrappings, mold them around the item you are freezing.

There are many helpful freezing aids on the market that are available by mail. The most important one to us is the Graniteware Blancher, sometimes called the Everything Pot. This pot allows you to blanch or steam large quantities of a particular vegetable without having to reboil fresh water. The strainer lifts out from the pot so that one batch of vegetables can be quickly drained, the strainer refilled with another batch, returned to the pot, and so on.

HELPFUL BOOKLETS

For detailed booklets on freezing write to the four sources mentioned under "Canning" (see page 130). Two additions are:

1. *Handbook for Freezing Foods,* Cornell Extension Bulletin 1179. Write to Publications Mailing Room, Cornell University, Research Park, Ithaca, New York 14853. This 59-page booklet covers all aspects of freezing.

2. *Freezing Foods At Home.* Write to Shirley Rolfs Meidinger, 733 Fifth Street Northeast, Jamestown, North Dakota 58401. This 80-page booklet has had over 12 printings and is the original one we used.

And again, check your Agricultural Extension Service for free booklets and advice.

SOME GENERAL SUGGESTIONS FOR FREEZING

1. Before freezing large quantities of foods make sure that your freezer is operating properly. Some freezers (usually old) have an On/Off type of defrosting arrangement that can be very sneaky. The temperature can fluctuate as much as 40° F as things freeze, defrost, and freeze again without one knowing it. Put a thermometer in the freezer and check it every few hours for 3 or 4 days before stocking up. Fill containers with water to see if they remain frozen while making your check.

2. Our freezer space is relatively limited so we use it judiciously. Since we enjoy and always seem to need pesto, we allow space for 50 or more pints for the winter months.

Peppers of all varieties are our second choice for space. Often, during the winter, we are able to buy good bell peppers at a reasonable price, but there are times when the price is exorbitant. Whether you grow your own or purchase them in the summer, they are the easiest vegetable to freeze as they require no blanching. Merely wash, core, seed, and cut them into the desired size. We quarter ours and, if required, cut them smaller later.

Red peppers are almost never available during the winter, so try to freeze them as a priority. Sautéed and served with pasta, they are a warming sight on a freezing evening.

We freeze many shelled beans such as lima for bean salads. Corn is another favorite and through experience, we have decided it is much better frozen off the cob. Even with allowing frozen corn on the cob to defrost somewhat before cooking, the flavor is wrong and the kernels are soft.

The only other prepared item we freeze in addition to pesto is Eggplant Sauté (see page 279) for Pizza or Caponata. During the winter, we rarely find eggplant that is not rubbery, so we prepare a half-dozen containers of the Sauté and freeze them.

3. It is just as important in freezing as in canning to strictly label your goods and keep a separate list. Always mark off on your list when you use something from your freezer. It is much harder to see things in a freezer than on the canned-goods shelves. Obviously, use the frozen goods with the oldest dates first.

4. Always allow headspace for expansion in your freezing containers. Generally, ½ inch is sufficient for dry pack and 1 inch for liquid, but to be safe, we allow 1½ inches for liquids. We started doing this after 2 quarts of chicken stock burst in the freezer with a 1-inch headspace.

PESTO IN QUANTITY FOR FREEZING

As we mentioned, we adore Pesto and fortunately, basil is the easiest of all herbs to grow. Even in an apartment with a sunny window, one can harvest a decent crop. With a small terrace such as we had in New York, we had 60 thriving plants and enough basil to give to our pesto-loving friends.

If you are growing your own basil, keep pinching it back as each new set of leaves appear. It will then double and be retarded in going to seed. Try to make your pesto when the plants are young, for as they age and finally go to seed, the flavor is unpleasantly pungent.

As pesto is time-consuming whichever method one uses, we have worked out a system by which we can make and freeze 6 pints in an afternoon using a food processor. It can be done in a blender, but this doubles your time, as certain things, such as grating the cheese, must still be done by hand. Our pesto is rather thick, which we like for freezing. Later, one can add more olive oil.

The pesto must be eaten at room temperature to have full flavor. We prefer pesto made with pignolia nuts and parmigiano-reggiano, but with the high cost of both, it is rather prohibitive for large quantities. We also like the addition of lemon juice as it helps to retain the color of the basil and gives a slight, but pleasant tartness.

Makes 6 pints

3 cups pignolia (pine) nuts, pecans, or walnuts
1 pound fresh, young basil, leaves *only* (about 16 cups, tightly packed)
12 large cloves of garlic, peeled
½ cup of lemon juice
4 cups olive oil
4 cups freshly grated Parmesan or Romano cheese
Salt and freshly ground black pepper to taste

Method for a Food Processor

1. Preheat the oven to 225° F.

2. Toast the nuts on a baking sheet in the oven for about 15 minutes to bring out their flavor. Stir occasionally to make sure they don't burn.

Allow the nuts to cool, then chop them fine in a food processor fitted with the metal blade. Put the nuts aside.

3. Rinse the basil, then dry it with paper towels, or in a salad spinner.

4. Put 3 or 4 cloves of garlic into the processor and chop. With the garlic still in the bowl, pack in about one-quarter of the basil. Sprinkle with a little lemon juice and add a cup or so of the oil. Blend into a purée.

Remove to a large bowl and continue with another batch until all the garlic, basil, lemon juice, and oil have been used.

5. Add the grated cheese and chopped nuts to the mixture. Add salt and pepper to taste and blend thoroughly. Pack into pint freezer containers, leaving ½-inch headspace for expansion, and freeze.

Method for a Blender

1. Follow Steps 1 to 3 of the processor method chopping the nuts in several batches; do not try doing them all at once. With a little practice, you will find out how much your blender can purée at one time. Put the nuts aside.

2. Put 1 or 2 of the garlic cloves into the blender and chop. Add 2 cups or so of the basil. Sprinkle with a little of the lemon juice and

add ⅓ to ½ cup of oil. Blend into a purée. If there is any difficulty, add a bit more oil.

Remove to a large bowl and continue with another batch until all the garlic, basil, lemon juice, and oil have been used and the entire mixture is in the large bowl.

3. Add the grated cheese and chopped nuts to the mixture. Add salt and pepper to taste and blend thoroughly using a wooden spoon. Pack into pint freezer containers, leaving ½-inch headspace for expansion. Freeze.

STRAWBERRY ICE

In experimenting with the syrup left over from the preserves recipe on page 133, we developed this recipe for an ice. It could hardly be easier and, with the syrup canned, an elegant dessert can be prepared on short notice.

Serves 4 to 6

Peel and juice of 1 lemon
1 cup strawberry syrup (see Note, page 134)
1½ cups water
Sprigs of fresh mint or strawberries (fresh or preserved)

1. Grate the peel of the lemon fine. Squeeze and strain the juice through a sieve into a medium-size bowl. Add the strawberry syrup and the water, stirring continuously.

Place the mixture in a quart-size freezer container and freeze for several hours. During this time, scrape down the sides several times to be sure all the ingredients are well mixed. (This step can be done days in advance.)

2. When it is frozen, break up the mixture with a spoon and purée it in a food processor or blender until smooth. The ice may be served immediately or returned to the freezer.

We freeze the ice in tall wine glasses or sometimes in scooped-out lemon shells. To do this, cut the top third from 4 to 6 lemons and scoop out the pulp and juice, saving them for another use. Cut a small sliver from the bottom of each shell so it will not topple over, and freeze the shells on a plate until ready to fill.

3. When ready to serve, decorate with sprigs of mint or a few strawberries.

TOMATO MARMALADE ICE

After our success with the Strawberry Ice, we decided to try an ice using our Tomato Marmalade. It, too, is delectable, especially with the nip of the crystallized ginger. If using marmalade made with yellow tomatoes, serve in frozen orange shells, following the instructions for lemon shells in the Strawberry Ice recipe.

Serves 4 to 6

1 cup Tomato Marmalade (see page 141)
1½ cups water
Julienne strips of lemon peel and crystallized ginger as garnish

1. Mix the marmalade and water together in a freezer container. Freeze for several hours, scraping down the sides and stirring several times to insure an even mixture.

2. When frozen, break up the mixture with a spoon and purée it in a food processor or blender until smooth. The ice may be served immediately or returned to the freezer.

3. When ready to serve, decorate with julienne strips of lemon peel and a piece of crystallized ginger for each serving.

WHAT TO BUY OR ORDER NOW

1. Check all canning and freezing equipment to make sure it is in good shape. This includes canning jars, bands, lids, plastic bags, and containers. All plastic bags must be purchased and an examination made of the containers to see if they are in a condition to be reused. Have a small surplus of everything, as you may find that each year you can and freeze a bit more than before. Make a note to order a new freezer marking pen.

2. Carefully go over your recipes for canning and freezing and figure the approximate amounts of ingredients used.

3. Check items you may have previously purchased that have been on special, such as sugar, or that you have ordered in season, such as pecans. Buy or order more if needed.

4. If you are not growing your own dill and basil, find someone who is or make arrangements with a fresh produce market to order it for you. Dill will keep well in the refrigerator for about a week. Basil will keep for only 3 or 4 days. For our Pesto, we use close to 10 pounds in a season.

AND IN OUR GARDEN

In our area, it is rare to have a killing frost in May, so we continue our planting with alacrity—more cucumber seeds, more tomato plants, another planting of radishes, lima and October beans, peppers, okra seed between the lettuces to fill the space when the lettuce is finished, and another long row of basil seed.

It is time to thin and transplant (or give away) the small cabbage, leek, squash, and Swiss chard plants. We cannot, with a good conscience, pull up and throw away healthy seedlings or small plants, even if it means we end up with 100 cabbages when we can only use two dozen. If there is no space, pass the plants onto a gardening neighbor and give him or her the responsibility of a good or bad conscience!

Around now, our eggplants begin to look terrible due to flea beetles. For two seasons, we dusted with carbaryl regularly, but it did no good. Now, we do nothing except plant marigolds close by. They are a natural protection against insects and plant disease. Eventually, as the eggplants become large, they recover.

As the month ends and the garden is filled with young plants, too much lettuce, kohlrabi, and radishes, the first peas and strawberries and maybe even a cucumber before June (we usually pick our first sugar snap peas on Mother's Day and the first cucumber on Memorial Day), do not close the gardening catalogs—it is time to plan your fall garden.

Consider what space will be vacant the middle of August and what you would like to plant. It is imperative that if you have not ordered your seeds, you do so now. Either the companies will be out of the seeds or local stores will have sent the remainder of their seeds back to the seed companies.

JUNE

A MIDDLE EASTERN OR
INDIAN DINNER

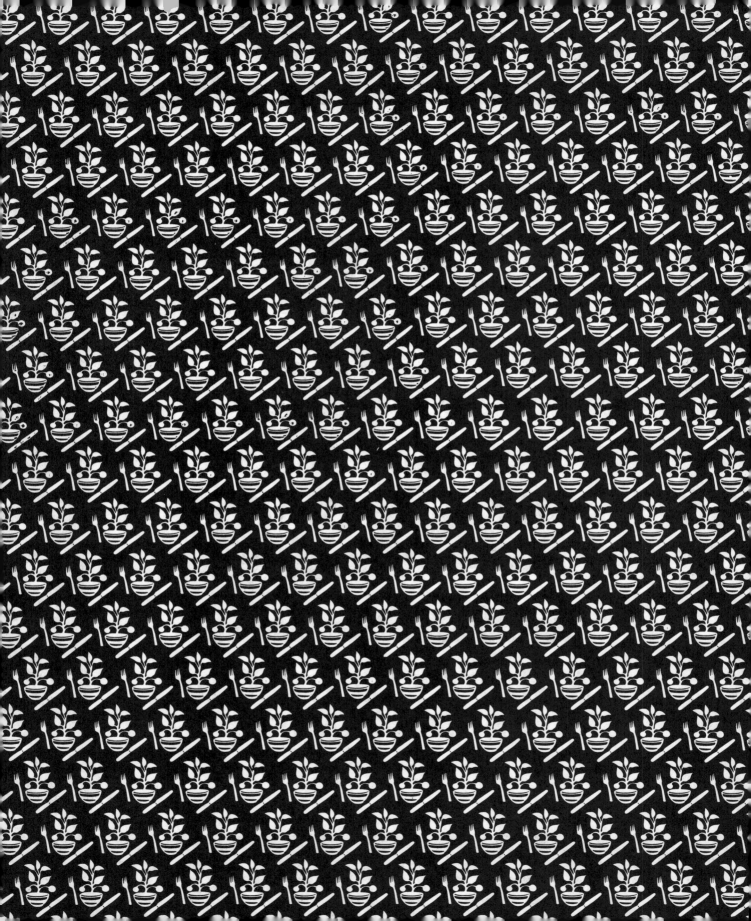

A Middle Eastern or Indian Dinner

In June we begin thinking about and preparing foods to be enjoyed throughout the summer. Middle Eastern and Indian foods are two favorites for the warmer months. The recipes make use of our garden vegetables and they are fitting alternatives to our simply prepared dishes. Although there are times during the summer when the temperature and humidity are so high that neither of us wants to cook, one sniff of some of the spices used in these recipes and our waning appetites are once again whetted.

We have included menus for both a Middle Eastern and an Indian dinner. The Middle Eastern menu is a complete meal and all of the recipes should be prepared. Except for frying the falafel, everything can be prepared in advance. As the pita bread requires a high oven temperature, we often set aside a day early in June to prepare and freeze enough for the entire summer.

For the Indian dinner, there is a selection of curries to choose from. If you plan a very elaborate dinner, all of the other dishes may be served. Many can be prepared ahead and the cooking time for most is short, if the ingredients are assembled ahead of time. You'll find that the assembled ingredients will be inviting to the eye as well as to the nostrils.

As an aside, we are including two favorite meal starters this month because they can be prepared with the fresh herbs from our garden—Baked Whole Heads of Garlic and Poached Marrow Bones. Also, June is the time when those superbly fresh heads of purple-tinged garlic can be found. As they mature they will blanch to white and the cloves will not have that clear crispness.

Baked Whole Heads of Garlic

If you have not been initiated into eating such large amounts of garlic, at first glance you may be wary of this dish. We, however, are addicted to these luscious, softened cloves. Be assured that they become mellowed (almost sweet) when properly prepared. Each guest is served a whole head with the garlic cloves still in their skins. These are easily slipped off and the cloves spread on slices of bread. (Paper napkins, discreetly placed about the table, are in order.)

The choice of the herb with which the heads of garlic are baked is yours, but use only one herb, as its flavor alone should be prominent. We like to use rosemary, either fresh or dried, more often than any other, but other suggestions are imported bay leaves, winter savory, tarragon, wild thyme or, when they are available, fresh sprigs of dill.

If you are using a dried herb, 1 tablespoon will be sufficient for this recipe. If you are using fresh rosemary, you will need one 4-inch sprig. With fresh tarragon, use two 4-inch sprigs. With fresh dill, four 4-inch sprigs.

Buy the largest heads of garlic you can find. We like to use heads weighing 2½ ounces apiece. Although it is not listed in their catalog, Manganaro's in New York has the large heads from time to time and will mail them. Check the mail-order listings for the telephone number and address.

Garlic will keep very well at room temperature in an open basket, so when we are able to buy the large heads, we order several dozen at a time.

Serves 4

4 very large, perfect whole heads of garlic
½ teaspoon salt (approximately)
1 tablespoon unsalted butter
½ cup Chicken Stock (see page 109) or water may be used
¼ cup dry, white wine or vermouth
4 teaspoons olive oil
½ teaspoon freshly ground black pepper (approximately)
An herb of your choice (see above)

1. Prepare the heads of garlic by peeling off some of the dry outer skin to expose the individual cloves. Be very careful that you do not break off the cloves. Trim any root growth.

2. Place the heads of garlic in a 1½-quart saucepan and pour in water to a depth of 1 inch. Add ¼ teaspoon of the salt.

Simmer the garlic, covered, over medium heat for 10 minutes. This preliminary cooking will aid in ridding the garlic of any harshness and will expedite the cooking.

3. Preheat the oven to 300°F.

4. Rub a gratin dish, that will just hold the garlic, with the butter. Transfer the heads of garlic to the gratin dish.

5. Add the chicken stock and wine to the gratin dish. Dribble 1 teaspoon of olive oil over each head of garlic. Sprinkle each head with a pinch of salt and a generous grinding of pepper.

Add the herb of your choice. If you are using a dried herb, crumble and distribute it over the garlic heads. If you are using sprigs of a fresh herb, place them alongside the heads.

6. Cover the gratin dish tightly with aluminum foil and bake on the middle rack of the oven for 1 to 1½ hours.

Baste the heads every 20 minutes, adding more liquid if it should evaporate. The cooking time will depend upon the size of the garlic heads. The cloves should be very soft.

GARLIC

In the last few years, many varieties of garlic have become available, either at specialty food shops or from seed companies to be grown in the home garden. In all of our recipes using garlic (and they are numerous), we are referring to ordinary garlic (Allium sativum). However, we would like to mention the currently popular varieties—Garlic chives, Society garlic and Elephant garlic—as we also grow them.

Garlic chives (also known as Oriental garlic) and Society garlic are grown for their leaves and are used as you would regular chives. The Garlic chive leaves, as the name suggests, have a faint garlic flavor. Society garlic, with its variegated, flat leaves, is more pungent than regular chives.

We have not yet harvested the Elephant garlic, but the cloves we planted were enormous—over 3 inches in length and over an inch in girth. Once harvested, we are anxious to try Baked Whole Heads of Garlic and Fettuccine with a Garlic Sauce using them. The flavor is much milder than ordinary garlic, so we are curious to see how much we will need per person. Probably some ridiculous amount— maybe even ½ pound!

Many seed companies are offering Elephant garlic. Our cloves were ordered from Shumway's. The Garlic chives were started from Burpee seeds, and also from plants ordered from Taylor's Herb Gardens. Taylor's sells five varieties of garlic plants, including the Society garlic. For the seed companies' addresses, check the mail-order listings.

7. Serve the heads of garlic as a first course, giving each guest 1 whole head. Have a basket of thick slices of freshly made bread to spread the cloves onto.

For an exceptionally creamy delight, serve thin slices of Pressed Cottage Cheese (see page 95) with the garlic and bread. Spread the bread with the cheese first and then the garlic. A bowl of ripe olives would not be amiss for total euphoria.

POACHED MARROW BONES

One day in our supermarket, we noticed a package labeled "Bones for Pets." They were perfectly cut and uniformly sized beef marrow bones—a pound for 20 cents. They looked too good to pass up, and since then we have had the butcher save them for us. Feeling a little guilty for depriving someone's pet of bones, we save them, minus the marrow, for a neighbor's miniature dachshund.

Serve the marrow bones as a first course arranged in heated, individual gratin dishes and garnished with the herb you have used in poaching. For a very informal gathering, you may serve each guest a pound apiece of the bones piled in a heated soup plate. However you serve the bones, accompany them with thick slices of crusty bread which can be buttered and then dipped into the poaching liquid.

Serves 4

2 pounds marrow bones, 2 inches in diameter and sliced ½-inch thick
3 tablespoons olive oil
½ cup dry white wine or vermouth
½ teaspoon salt
½ teaspoon freshly ground black pepper
4 sprigs of a fresh herb, such as tarragon (our choice), dill, or
  rosemary, each 4 inches long

1. Trim the marrow bones of any excess fat.

2. Place the olive oil over medium-low heat in a 10-inch skillet. Add the marrow bones and sauté them on both sides until they color slightly and any fat on them browns. This will take only a few minutes.

Begin warming your serving dishes.

3. Add the wine to the skillet. Sprinkle the marrow bones with the salt and pepper. Place the sprigs of the herb you are using among the marrow bones. Cover the skillet tightly and poach the bones for 5 minutes. Baste once during this time, using the liquid in the skillet. Do not overcook the marrow as it will diminish in size.

4. Divide the bones and any remaining liquid among heated individual dishes and garnish each with one of the herb sprigs. Each guest will have about 6 small marrow bones. Let your guests know that it is permissible to pick up the bones for nibbling after the marrow has been eaten.

A MIDDLE EASTERN DINNER

BABA GHANOUJ

The ways in which this Middle Eastern eggplant purée called Baba Ghanouj can be served are numerous, as are the variations one can make. For hors d'oeuvres, it can be served in a bowl as a dip, using toasted triangles of pita bread as scoops.

One can serve it as a chilled appetizer or salad arranged on a platter and surrounded with sliced fresh vegetables, olives, and chopped fresh herbs.

We often serve it as a side dish when we are having Falafel, sesame seed sauce, and a raw salad stuffed into pita bread. It should be made one day ahead for the flavors to mellow, particularly the raw garlic. Double the recipe for a large crowd.

Makes 2½ cups

1½-pound eggplant
½ teaspoon salt
2 large cloves garlic
1 medium onion
¼ cup lemon juice
¼ teaspoon freshly ground black pepper
½ teaspoon freshly ground dried hot red pepper
3 tablespoons plain Tahini (see page 167)
¼ cup olive oil
¼ cup chopped fresh herb of your choice, such as parsley, basil, or coriander for garnish

1. For the eggplant to achieve the desired charcoal flavor, it must be roasted over coals, a gas flame, or broiled. Before peeling, the skin of the eggplant must be totally charred and blackened and the flesh inside soft.

For coals or a gas flame, simply pierce the eggplant in a dozen places and cook directly over the flame, turning with two forks as the skin chars. Do not remove the stem, as it can be used to hold the eggplant.

For the broiling method, first preheat the broiler. Pierce the eggplant with a fork in a dozen places. Place the eggplant on a foil-lined baking sheet with sides, then place the baking sheet on a rack 6 inches under the broiler. Broil, turning three or four times, until the skin is black and blistered. This will take about 45 minutes.

2. Once the eggplant is charred, let it cool on the baking sheet until you can handle it. Peel back some of the charred skin and discard it.

With a tablespoon, scoop out the pulp and place it in a sieve. If there are a large amount of seeds, discard them—a few small ones will not matter. Sprinkle the pulp with the ½ teaspoon salt and gently stir, just to distribute the salt.

Let the pulp drain for 15 minutes. The salt will help rid the eggplant of some of its liquid and bitterness.

3. A food processor works extremely well for the completion of the eggplant appetizer or you may finish it by hand.

If you are using a food processor, first peel the garlic and chop coarsely, using the metal blade. Add the peeled onion, cut into chunks, and chop it coarse. (When chopping garlic in a processor with other ingredients, it is always best to do the garlic first. When all the ingredients are added at the same time, the garlic is not chopped properly.)

BABA GHANOUJ VARIATIONS

The above recipe for Baba Ghanouj, although the most traditional, is not absolute and we have made a few interesting variations.

1. Prepare the recipe, but do not chop the onion as fine, so that it will have texture. Omit the tahini paste and use 3 tablespoons of Pesto instead (see page 309). Fresh basil should be your chopped garnish.

2. For a thinner and milder purée, fold ½ cup yogurt into the mixture before chilling. Or serve a pot of yogurt on the side.

3. Blend ½ teaspoon of Garam Masala (see page 190) into the mixture for a very unusual combination of flavors. With this addition, it is most important to allow the appetizer to chill overnight so the sharpness of the garam masala will be tempered by the eggplant.

Add the drained eggplant along with the lemon juice, black pepper, red pepper, and tahini paste. Purée the mixture and add the olive oil in a steady stream through the feed tube. When the mixture is smooth, scrape the contents into a small bowl. Cover with plastic wrap and refrigerate overnight.

If you are completing the purée by hand, peel and mince the garlic and onion. Place them in a small bowl and add the drained eggplant, lemon juice, black pepper, red pepper, and tahini paste. Mash to a purée, either with the back of a fork or a wooden spoon. Beat in the olive oil.

When the mixture is smooth and the olive oil incorporated, cover with plastic wrap and refrigerate overnight.

4. When you are ready to serve, arrange the purée on a serving dish and surround it with ¼ cup of a chopped fresh herb of your choice.

TAHINI (SESAME SEED SAUCE)

Learning to make our own Tahini, a very special sesame seed sauce, from scratch has been one of our most rewarding ventures. After savoring the sauce made from freshly roasted sesame seeds, it would be hard to use the purchased brands again, although they are quite good.

A food processor is necessary to grind the seeds into a paste, as a blender does not work. It is conceivable that you could pound the seeds in a mortar, but the job would be laborious. If you do not have a food processor, buy the unseasoned sesame tahini (ground sesame seed paste) and blend it with our remaining ingredients, using 1 cup of the prepared paste. When using purchased tahini, it will occasionally become extraordinarily thick and appear to be separating as you add the other ingredients. Just keep beating with a wooden spoon, adding more water if necessary, and it will thin out.

Serve the tahini on Falafel (see page 169) which have been stuffed into one of the Pita Breads on pages 172 or 174 or as a dip by itself, using toasted triangles of pita or fresh vegetables as scoops.

Makes 1½ cups

> 1 cup raw, hulled sesame seeds or 1 cup prepared unseasoned sesame
>   tahini
> 6 large cloves garlic, minced
> ½ teaspoon salt
> ½ to 1 teaspoon freshly ground dried hot red pepper
> 1 tablespoon sweet paprika
> ½ cup lemon juice
> ⅓ cup water (approximately)

1. Preheat the oven to 225° F.

2. Spread the sesame seeds on a baking sheet and toast them in the oven for about 20 minutes until they turn pale golden brown. Stir several times so that the seeds brown evenly.

3. Fit the food processor with the metal blade. Peel the garlic and chop it first in the processor with several On/Off motions.

Add the toasted sesame seeds, salt, hot red pepper to your taste, and sweet paprika. With the motor running, add the lemon juice and then the water through the feed tube. The sauce should be smooth and thick. If you prefer a thinner sauce, add more water.

You may serve the sauce immediately or refrigerate. It will easily keep a week.

Note: Keep raw, hulled sesame seeds under refrigeration, as at room temperature they will become rancid. Our mail-order sources always supply very fresh seeds, but if you are purchasing them in a store, sniff them — the rancid odor will be detected right away.

HUMMUS BI TAHINI

Serve this appetizing purée of chickpeas and Tahini as a side dish with a Middle Eastern meal or as a dipping sauce at other times. If you will be serving Falafel and sesame seed sauce at the same time as the Hummus bi Tahini, prepare more of the cooked chickpeas and more of the sesame seed sauce and the time involved in making this recipe will be minimal.

Makes about 3 cups

¾ cup dried chickpeas (¼ pound)
½ teaspoon salt
¾ cup (½ recipe) Tahini (see page 167)
2 tablespoons olive oil
Several tablespoons of water and lemon juice, if needed for thinning
    the purée
½ tablespoon sweet paprika
¼ cup finely chopped fresh parsley or basil for garnish

1. Rinse and pick over the dried chickpeas, discarding any that are blemished. Place the chickpeas in a 2-quart saucepan and add water to cover by 1 inch. Cover the saucepan and bring the chickpeas to a boil over medium heat.

Remove the saucepan from the heat and let it sit, covered, for 1 hour. This step eliminates an overnight soaking.

2. After 1 hour, return the saucepan to the stove. Add the salt and simmer the chickpeas over medium-low heat, partially covered, for 45 minutes until they are tender but not mushy.

Drain the chickpeas in a colander. You will have about 2 cups of cooked chickpeas.

3. While the chickpeas are simmering, prepare the tahini, halving the ingredients listed in the recipe so that you have ¾ cup.

4. *If you have prepared the tahini in a food processor*, simply leave the sauce in the work bowl and add the cooked chickpeas and the olive oil. Blend to a purée.

If the purée seems too thick, add equal amounts of water and lemon juice by the tablespoonful until you have the desired consistency. This is up to you. We like a rather thick mixture that will remain on a spatula when suspended, but you may thin it so that it slowly runs from the spatula.

If you have used a purchased sesame tahini, purée the cooked chickpeas in small amounts in a blender or pass them through a food mill fitted with the medium blade. Add the chickpeas and olive oil to the sauce and blend thoroughly. Thin as described above.

5. Spoon the hummus bi tahini into a serving bowl and sprinkle with the paprika. Garnish the edges with the parsley or basil.

FALAFEL

Falafel, spicy deep-fried vegetable balls made from either chickpeas (garbanzos) or fava beans (English broadbeans), are extremely popular all over the Middle East and they are becoming much more so in this country. In the larger cities, falafel stands are giving hot dog vendors some stiff competition.

The only difficult step in making the falafel is the frying. After frying a dozen or so of the little balls, the oil becomes so filled with spicy residue that it tends to foam up. In order to eliminate this problem, we coat the falafel with chickpea flour just before they are lowered into the hot oil. By doing this, the entire recipe can be prepared without the danger of foaming oil. All-purpose flour may be used instead of chickpea flour, but we feel the chickpea flour is more in keeping with this Middle Eastern specialty.

The batter for falafel may be prepared several days ahead and refrigerated until you are ready to fry it. If the mixture should thicken too much during refrigeration, thin it with a little water or more lemon juice.

Makes about 40 falafel, each 1¼-inches; serves 6 to 8

1½ cups dried chickpeas (½ pound)
1½ teaspoons salt
2 teaspoons cumin seed
2 teaspoons coriander seed
1 medium onion
4 large cloves garlic
1½ cups parsley, tightly packed
1 teaspoon freshly ground dried hot red pepper
1 teaspoon freshly ground black pepper
½ cup lemon juice
Corn oil for frying
About 1 cup chickpea flour or an all-purpose flour

1. Rinse and pick over the dried chickpeas, discarding any that are blemished. Place the chickpeas in a heavy, 3-quart saucepan and add water to cover the chickpeas by 1 inch.

Cover and bring to a boil over medium heat. Remove the saucepan from the heat and let it sit, covered, for 1 hour. This step will eliminate an overnight soaking.

2. After 1 hour, return the saucepan to the stove. Add ½ teaspoon of the salt and simmer the chickpeas over medium-low heat, partially covered, for about 45 minutes. The chickpeas should remain crunchy and not be over-cooked.

Drain them in a colander. You will have about 4 cups of cooked chickpeas.

3. While the chickpeas are simmering, prepare the other ingredients for the falafel mixture.

Toast the cumin and coriander seeds in a small skillet over low heat for about 5 minutes to bring out their flavors. Grind the seeds.

4. *If you are using a food processor*, fit it with the metal blade. Remove the stems of the parsley, coarsely chop the onion and garlic, then add half of the onion and half of the garlic to the bowl. Chop them fine.

Add half of the chickpeas and half of each herb and spice: the parsley leaves, cumin seed, coriander seed, hot red pepper, black pepper, and ½ teaspoon of salt. Pour ¼ cup of the lemon juice over the ingredients and purée the mixture.

With a spatula, scrape the contents into a mixing bowl and proceed to purée the remaining half of these ingredients in the same manner. Combine this second batch with the first in the mixing bowl. The mixture should be moist, but not wet.

If you are using a food mill, finely chop the onion, garlic, and parsley leaves. Pass the chickpeas, in several batches, through the medium blade into a mixing bowl. Add the very finely chopped onion, garlic, herbs, spices, and lemon juice. Mix thoroughly.

If you are using a blender, finely chop the onion, garlic, and parsley leaves. Purée the chickpeas in small batches and place in a mix-ing bowl. Add the very finely chopped onion, garlic, herbs, spices, and lemon juice. Mix thoroughly.

5. You may fry the falafel in a 10-inch iron skillet (our preference) or in a deep fryer. In an iron skillet, the corn oil should be to the depth of about 1 inch, but less than half full. In a deep fryer, the oil depth may be increased, but still under half full. Heat the corn oil to 375° F or until a cube of bread browns instantly.

6. Pour the flour for coating the falafel onto a dinner-sized plate. Using two tablespoons, scoop up a small amount of the falafel batter. Turn and "cup" the batter in the bowls of the spoons until you have formed a small ball about 1 inch in diameter.

Drop the ball into the flour and turn it until it is lightly coated. Again using the spoons, pick up the falafel ball and slide it into the hot oil.

Continue forming and frying the balls until all of the batter has been used. Fry each falafel, turning only once, until it is lightly browned. This will take only about 2 minutes. Do *not* crowd the pan.

Remove each falafel with a slotted spoon as it browns. Drain on paper towels. If it is necessary to hold the falafel, keep them warm in a 200°F oven.

TABBOULEH

Our Middle Eastern meal would not be complete without Tabbouleh, a salad made with bulgur. Bulgur, sometimes known as burghul wheat, has been partially cooked before being cracked, as opposed to the cracked wheat used for pita bread.

Tabbouleh can be rather bland if it is not seasoned properly. When it stands for a time, the flavors seem to mellow as the seasoning is absorbed, so we make the salad at least several hours ahead and taste it again for additional seasoning before serving. The mint and lemon juice should be quite evident as ingredients and not overshadowed by the abundance of parsley.

You may add finely chopped cucumbers, tomatoes, and celery to the salad, if you wish. Use ½ cup of any or all of them, but after lightly salting them, drain the cucumbers and tomatoes in a sieve for a ½ hour before adding them to the salad. Otherwise they will add too much liquid.

Serves 6

1 ½ cups bulgur
2 teaspoons coriander seeds
1 medium onion, very finely chopped
1 tablespoon minced garlic
⅓ cup finely chopped fresh mint leaves or 3 tablespoons dried mint
2 cups finely chopped parsley, tightly packed
1 ½ cups alfalfa sprouts (for growing instructions, see page 39)
½ teaspoon salt
½ teaspoon freshly ground white pepper
½ cup olive oil
½ cup lemon juice

1. Place the bulgur in a large mixing bowl and pour in water to cover by 1 inch. Soak for about an hour. Depending upon the bulgur, the water may become very dirty. If so, drain it off and add fresh water several times as the bulgur soaks. It will expand considerably as it absorbs the water.

2. Meanwhile, prepare the other ingredients. Toast the coriander seeds in a small skillet over low heat for about 5 minutes to bring out their flavor. Grind the seeds.

3. After an hour, drain the bulgur in a sieve. To further dry it, gather it up, a small handful at a time, and squeeze it as dry as you can.

Place the dried bulgur back into the mixing bowl, which has been wiped clean.

4. Add the onion, garlic, mint, parsley, and alfalfa sprouts to the bulgur and mix the ingredients. (We use our hands.) Sprinkle the salad with the salt, white pepper, and coriander seed.

Pour on the olive oil and lemon juice and toss to mix the ingredients thoroughly. (For the tossing, we use wooden spoons.)

5. Let the tabbouleh sit at room temperature for about an hour. Taste again for seasoning, adding more if you feel a particular flavor is lacking. If the salad seems dry, add more olive oil and lemon juice, according to your taste.

If the salad is not to be served at this point, cover it with plastic wrap and refrigerate it. Let it come back to room temperature when you are ready to serve. The salad will keep for 4 or 5 days under refrigeration, but again, taste for seasoning before serving.

6. Traditionally, tabbouleh is served on a platter surrounded with crisp, whole lettuce leaves (such as Romaine), which are used as scoops for eating the salad. Garnish it with a combination of any of the following: sliced cucumbers or pickles, olives, radishes, tomato wedges, or avocado slices that have been sprinkled with lemon juice.

CRACKED WHEAT PITA

Pita is a Middle Eastern bread, round and somewhat puffy in shape, which when slit pulls open to reveal a pocket for stuffing a myriad of ingredients. Anything that would be used in a sandwich can be put into pita bread. Meats, meatballs, shish kebab, and the like are excellent choices, but for a Middle Eastern meal we suggest you try it with the Falafel on page 169, smothered with the Tahini on page 167.

For a tastier pita bread, we like a combination of cracked wheat with whole-wheat and all-purpose, unbleached flour. We buy the whole kernels of wheat, which are sometimes called red cereal wheat or hard red wheat berries, and grind them in an antique coffee grinder which gives a very even texture. You may also grind them in the small Varco Coffee and Spice Grinder made by Moulinex (check the mail-order listings), but do only a small amount at a time so the grinding will be uniform. Food processors and blenders do *not* work.

Or you may order the cracked wheat by mail if it is not sold nearby. Here again, it may be listed as cracked wheat or cracked-wheat cereal, not to be confused with crushed wheat (which is finer) or bulgur (burghul), which has been steamed before crushing.

And, finally, a baking stone of some sort is essential (baking sheets are not reliable). Any type will do, including baking tiles. Before we purchased our baking stone, we experimented with unglazed flagstones from a garden supply shop, and we even used broken flue bricks. They all worked perfectly, but a true baking stone has more "style."

Makes 12 individual pita breads

> 1 cup cracked wheat
> 1 cup whole-wheat flour
> 1½ cups all-purpose, unbleached, flour
> 1 teaspoon salt
> 1 tablespoon active dry yeast
> 1⅓ cups warm water (105° F)
> 1 tablespoon olive oil or corn oil

1. *If you are using a food processor*, fit it with the metal blade. In the processor bowl, using several On/Off motions, combine the cracked wheat, whole-wheat and all-purpose flours with the salt.

Using a 2-cup measuring cup, dissolve the yeast in the warm water. When it has dissolved, add the tablespoon of olive oil. With the processor on, pour the yeast mixture through the feed tube. Within 30 seconds the dough will form a ball and leave the sides of the processor bowl.

Remove the dough from the bowl onto a lightly floured work surface and knead briefly, just to form a compact ball. Place the dough in a 2-quart bowl, cover with a dish towel, and let the dough rise in a warm place (80°F) until it doubles in bulk (about 2½ hours).

If you are preparing the dough by hand, mix the cracked wheat, flours and salt together, either on your work surface or in a bowl. Make a well in the center of the flours and pour in the yeast and oil mixture.

Work the flours into the liquid until you have a soft dough. Knead the dough for 5 minutes and place in a bowl to rise, as described above.

2. When the dough has doubled in bulk, return it to your floured work surface and knead again for 2 minutes. Return the dough to the bowl, cover, and let it rise a second time until it has doubled (about 1½ hours).

3. When the dough has completed its second rising, turn it onto your floured work surface and flatten it with the palms of your hands into a pie shape 1-inch thick.

Cut the dough into 12 equal wedges. One by one, form the wedges into balls by first bringing the three edges of each wedge to the center and pinching them together. Between the palms of your hands, roll each piece of dough gently until you have a perfect ball.

Place the balls on a floured surface and cover them with floured plastic wrap so they will not dry out.

4. You are now ready to shape the pita bread. Spread cloth towels covering an area about 20 × 30 inches and lightly flour the towels. One at a time, place a ball of dough on your floured work surface. Flatten it a bit by patting it with one of your hands. Then roll the dough into a circle with your rolling pin.

The secret to rolling a perfect circle is to start in the middle of the dough and roll away from you (never back and forth). After each roll, turn the dough a quarter turn. At some point during the rolling, turn the dough over and roll on the other side for several turns — this will eliminate any tears in the dough, which would prevent the pita bread from puffing in the oven.

Continue rolling until you have formed a circle about 6 inches in diameter and ¼-inch thick. As each round is formed, place it on the floured towels and cover with floured plastic wrap. It is vital for the success of your pita bread that there be no tears and that the rounds are rolled evenly and exactly. ¼-inch thick.

5. After all of the rounds have been formed and covered with plastic wrap, let them rise for 30 minutes.

6. While the rounds are rising, place your baking stone on a rack in the lower third of your oven. Preheat the oven to 550°F. A preheating temperature of 550°F is imperative before baking the bread.

7. When your oven has reached 550°F and the breads have risen for 30 minutes, lightly flour your peel. (If you do not have a peel, a thin board or even a piece of cardboard will work just as well.) Place two of the pitas on your peel and slide them into the oven onto your hot baking stone. In about 1 minute, the breads will begin to form bubbles and then puff up. Immediately after they puff, they will deflate slightly. At this point, begin the timing. (See Note.) They will be done in 1 minute and should be removed from the oven promptly.

Use a wide spatula to bring them from the oven onto the peel. Place the breads on a rack to cool. Continue in this manner until all the breads have been baked. This will go very quickly with such a short baking period. The breads must remain soft and without more than a hint of color.

8. You may serve the breads immediately or they may be refrigerated or frozen after cooling completely. Use airtight plastic bags, such as Ziploc.

Our breads remain inflated, so we place them carefully in the plastic bags to retain this quality. However, you may deflate them by pressing them down if you wish. When reheating the breads in the oven, they must be tightly wrapped in foil or they will become dry and brittle.

Note: If your oven does not have a window, you will have to test the timing for the first few pitas that you bake. Bake them for a total of 2 minutes without opening the door, then check. The breads should be done; if not, adjust your timing for the remaining pitas. A few seconds more or less are not crucial.

CORNMEAL PITA BREAD

After perfecting our Cracked Wheat Pita Bread, we experimented with other flours. We tried rye flour as part of the flour mixture and used some caraway seeds. It worked, but was not what we had hoped for. Then we tried yellow cornmeal, which makes a wonderful pita bread.

Makes 12 individual pita breads

1 cup yellow cornmeal
2½ cups all-purpose, unbleached flour
1 teaspoon salt
1⅓ cups warm water (105° F)
1 tablespoon active dry yeast
1 tablespoon olive oil, or corn oil
4 tablespoons hulled sesame seeds or 2 tablespoons poppy seeds

1. Follow Steps 1 through 3 for Cracked Wheat Pita Bread (see page 172), using 1 cup of yellow cornmeal and 2½ cups of all-purpose, unbleached flour for your flour mixture.

2. If you are using sesame seeds for the tops of your pita breads, toast the seeds very lightly in a small skillet over low heat for about 5 minutes. The cooking time in the oven for the breads is so short that the sesame seeds will not have time to brown, so a prior toasting, just to give them a hint of color, is necessary.

3. Follow Step 4, but do not turn the circles of dough over as you roll them. With the addition of cornmeal, the flour mixture is softer and does not require rolling on the other side. Also, the tops of the breads must stay moist in order to hold the seeds.

If the circles stick as you are rolling them, lightly flour your work surface. As each circle is rolled to a diameter of 3½ inches, sprinkle it with some of the sesame seeds or poppy seeds.

Continue to roll the circle, pressing the seeds just into the surface of the dough, until you have a circle 6 inches in diameter.

4. Continue with Steps 5 through 8 to complete your breads.

AN INDIAN DINNER

FRESH MINT RAITA

A raita is an almost mandatory condiment with an Indian dinner to assuage the spiciness and/or hotness of the other dishes.

Young spearmint leaves make the best raita. Try it as a dressing on a salad of lettuce, as well as serving it at an Indian meal.

Makes 1 ½ cups

½ teaspoon cumin seeds
1 teaspoon coriander seeds
3 small spring onions or 1 small onion
1 cup fresh mint leaves, loosely packed
2 tablespoons lemon juice
½ teaspoon freshly ground dried hot red pepper
½ teaspoon salt
1 cup Yogurt (see page 67)
Additional fresh mint leaves for garnish

1. Toast the cumin and coriander seeds in a small skillet over low heat for about 5 minutes to bring out their flavors. Grind the seeds.

2. Trim the root ends from the spring onions and cut the onions into small pieces, using some of the green tops. If you use a regular onion, peel and cut it into several pieces.

3. Place the mint leaves in the work bowl of a food processor or blender. Pour the lemon juice over the leaves. This will prevent them from discoloring when they are chopped.

Add the onion, red pepper, cumin and coriander seeds, and salt. Chop the mixture fine.

4. If you prefer the raita to be somewhat thin in

consistency, add the yogurt to the mixture in the processor or blender and blend until smooth.

If you wish a thicker raita, transfer the mixture to another bowl and fold in the yogurt.

5. Cover the raita with plastic wrap and refrigerate it for several hours or overnight. The raita will keep for days under refrigeration.

Just before serving, garnish the raita with additional fresh mint leaves.

Note: If you do not have a food processor or blender, the raita may be made by hand. As soon as the mint leaves are chopped fine, place them in a small bowl and pour the lemon juice over to prevent them from discoloring. Chop the onions fine by hand and add them to the mint leaves along with the remaining ingredients. Chill and serve as in Step 5.

CUCUMBER RAITA

A raita can be made with a variety of fresh vegetables combined with yogurt. You may even add a small amount of finely minced onion and chopped tomatoes to this raita, if you wish. What we offer here is a very basic raita. You may vary your spices according to taste.

Makes about 2 cups for 4 to 6 servings

¾ **pound cucumbers (preferably the unwaxed pickling type)**
½ **teaspoon salt**
½ **teaspoon cumin seeds**
1 **teaspoon coriander seeds**
⅛ **teaspoon freshly ground white pepper**
½ **teaspoon freshly ground dried hot red pepper**
1 **cup Yogurt (see page 67)**
2 **tablespoons fresh coriander leaves, finely chopped, or if**
   unavailable, use parsley

1. If your cucumbers are unwaxed, scrub, but do not peel them. Cut the cucumbers in half lengthwise and then into quarters.

If the seeds are large, remove them. (Sometimes unwaxed cucumbers will have such small seeds that this is unnecessary.)

Shred the quarters of cucumber on the medium side of a hand grater. Place the shreds in a sieve. Sprinkle with the salt and toss, just to mix.

Let the cucumbers drain for ½ hour to draw out excess moisture. Otherwise, the raita will be too thin.

2. Toast the cumin and coriander seeds in a small skillet over low heat for 5 minutes to bring out their flavors. Grind the seeds.

3. Press down on the shredded cucumbers to extract more moisture. Combine them in a small bowl with the yogurt and ground spices. Stir to mix.

Cover the bowl with plastic wrap and chill thoroughly before serving.

4. When you are ready to serve, sprinkle with the chopped coriander leaves or parsley.

INDIAN BROILED SHRIMP

We have found these savory marinated and broiled shrimp to be extremely popular served hot or cold as hors d'oeuvres, or served hot as a main course with rice. If you plan to serve the shrimp as a main course, double this recipe to serve 4. As hors d'oeuvres, 1 pound of shrimp should serve 6 to 8, depending upon what else is being served.

> 1 teaspoon dry mustard
> 1 teaspoon turmeric
> 1 teaspoon Garam Masala (see page 190)
> 1 teaspoon freshly ground dried hot red pepper
> 3 tablespoons crumbled dried mint leaves
> ½ teaspoon salt
> ¼ teaspoon freshly ground black pepper
> 1 teaspoon finely minced garlic
> 2 tablespoons white or red wine vinegar
> ½ cup olive oil
> 1 pound unshelled, fresh shrimp

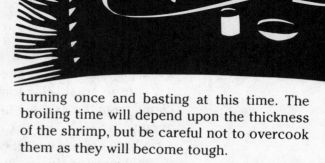

1. Combine all of the spices, dry herbs, and seasonings in a medium-size bowl. Add the garlic and wine vinegar. Whisk to mix.

   In a slow, steady stream, whisk in the olive oil until the mixture is smooth and thickened. Set the marinade aside.

2. Shell and clean the shrimp. (See How To Shell and Clean Shrimp, page 120.)

3. Add the cleaned shrimp to the marinade and stir to coat the shrimp evenly. Cover and let the shrimp marinate at room temperature for 3 to 4 hours or overnight in the refrigerator.

4. About 15 minutes before you are ready to broil the shrimp, preheat the broiler. Position your broiler rack about 4 inches from the heat.

5. Transfer the shrimp with its marinade to a shallow baking dish that will hold the shrimp comfortably in one layer.

   Broil the shrimp for about 5 minutes, turning once and basting at this time. The broiling time will depend upon the thickness of the shrimp, but be careful not to overcook them as they will become tough.

6. Serve immediately with the marinade, or if you wish to serve the shrimp cold, let them come to room temperature before refrigerating them. Under refrigeration, the shrimp will keep for a week.

KOFTAS

Do not be alarmed by the number of spices in these irresistible stuffed meatballs. After simmering in the sauce, they are decidedly captivating without being overpowering.

One year, as our contribution to a party menu, we made 150 of the meatballs. About 5 minutes after they were put out they had all been consumed! Keep this in mind when you make them and make more than you think you will need. If there should be leftovers, they freeze very well.

This recipe will serve 4 generously if the meatballs are to be the main course accompanied by rice. If they are to be served as part of a larger Indian meal, the recipe should serve 6 to 8. It is rare for us to find lamb, but lean ground lamb may be used instead of the ground beef.

Makes 24 koftas, 1 inch in diameter

Ingredients for the Meatballs:

1 pound lean ground beef
1 medium onion, chopped fine almost to a purée
2 tablespoons Garam Masala (see page 190)
½ teaspoon salt
½ teaspoon freshly ground black pepper
1 egg, lightly beaten
1 tablespoon peeled and finely chopped fresh ginger root
¼ cup finely chopped raisins
¼ cup finely chopped pecans
Corn oil for frying

Ingredients for the Sauce:

2 teaspoons cumin seeds
2 teaspoons coriander seeds
2½ pounds fresh, ripe tomatoes or 2 cups drained, canned tomatoes
Liquid from the drained tomatoes
⅓ cup olive oil
4 medium onions, coarsely chopped
1½ tablespoons finely minced garlic
1 teaspoon turmeric
1 tablespoon finely chopped fresh ginger root
1 teaspoon freshly ground dried hot red pepper
Water as needed

1. Prepare the meatballs before you make the sauce. Place the ground beef in a mixing bowl. Add the very finely chopped onion, Garam Masala, salt, black pepper, and lightly beaten egg to the ground beef.

Mix the ingredients thoroughly. This is best accomplished by using your hands.

2. To form the meatballs, you may either divide the mixture into 2 dozen equal pieces or pull off small amounts as each meatball is shaped. Place each small piece between the palms of your hands and roll it in a clockwise fashion to form a ball about 1 inch in diameter.

3. In another bowl, prepare the stuffing by combining the ginger root, raisins, and pecans.

4. Stuff each meatball by cupping it in the palm of one hand and, with the index finger of the other hand, make a small indentation in the center.

Using a very tiny spoon, fill the hollow with about ½ teaspoon of the stuffing. Bring the meat mixture back over the opening and pinch it closed. Place the meatballs on a large platter as they are formed.

5. Pour corn oil to the depth of ½ inch in a heavy, 10-inch skillet. Heat the oil over medium-high heat to 375° F or until a cube of bread fries almost instantly.

Using two spoons, pick up the meatballs and lower them into the hot oil. Do not crowd the pan. Fry the meatballs until they are browned all over, turning only once. The total frying time for each meatball should be 4 to 5 minutes.

As the meatballs brown, remove them from the skillet and return them to the platter. Continue until all have been fried. Set aside.

6. Before beginning the sauce, prepare all of the ingredients. Toast the cumin and corian- der seeds in a small skillet over low heat for about 5 minutes to bring out their flavors. Grind the seeds.

7. *If you are using fresh tomatoes*, first immerse them in boiling water for about 30 seconds to loosen the skins. Then peel, core, and seed the tomatoes. Chop them coarsely and allow them to drain for about 20 minutes in a sieve placed over a bowl. Reserve the liquid.

If you are using canned tomatoes, chop them coarsely and allow them to drain, reserving the liquid.

8. In a heavy, 2-quart saucepan, heat the olive oil. Add the onions and garlic and sauté over medium heat until they are wilted.

Add the turmeric and ginger root. Stir and sauté for about 1 minute, being very careful not to burn the turmeric. Add the hot red pepper, cumin, and coriander seeds. Again, stir and sauté for only a minute.

This brief sautéing brings out the flavor of the spices before the liquids are added.

9. Add the drained tomatoes to the saucepan. Stir and bring the ingredients to a simmer. Add 1 cup of the liquid from the drained tomatoes and, when the ingredients return to a simmer, carefully add the meatballs and any liquid that has accumulated on the platter.

10. Turn the heat to medium low and cover the saucepan. Simmer for 20 minutes.

Stir the ingredients several times. Do this by very gently moving the meatballs around, using the back of a wooden spoon. This way the meatballs will stay intact.

Add more liquid from the tomatoes (or water, if there is no tomato liquid), if necessary. The liquid should just cover the meatballs as they begin to simmer; then it should reduce and thicken somewhat as they cook.

A few minutes before serving, uncover and simmer the sauce to further thicken it.

PAKORA

As with many other Indian foods, the preparation of Pakora should not be restricted just to the times when a full Indian meal will be served. These savory little batter-fried vegetables can be relished as hors d'oeuvres or as a vegetable accompaniment with seafood or meats.

Two requisites for successful pakoras are a batter of a proper consistency and a well-dried assortment of perfect vegetables. As part of an Indian dinner, 2½ pounds of assorted vegetables will generously serve 4 to 6. As hors d'oeuvres, this amount will serve 6 to 8. Have several bowls of a Raita on hand for dipping or spooning over the Pakoras.

If you are serving the Puri on page 188, prepare it first in your hot oil and then the pakora.

> 2 cups chickpea flour
> 1 to 1½ cups water
> ½ teaspoon turmeric
> 1 teaspoon freshly ground dried hot red pepper
> 2 teaspoons Garam Masala (see page 190)
> 2½ pounds of assorted fresh vegetables (see below)
> Corn oil for frying

1. Prepare the pakora batter. Place the chickpea flour in a medium-size mixing bowl. Gradually whisk in 1 cup of the water, being careful that no lumps form in the batter. When the batter is smooth, whisk in the turmeric, red pepper, and garam masala.

Let the batter rest for about ½ hour for the ingredients to meld and thicken.

2. Meanwhile, prepare the vegetables for frying.

3. Pour corn oil to a depth of 1 inch into a heavy 10-inch skillet or wok. Heat the oil to 375°F or until a cube of bread browns instantly.

4. When the oil is hot, test the consistency of your pakora batter by dipping several pieces of the prepared vegetables into it, coating them well and then lowering them into the hot oil. (We use our fingers on one hand for the dipping and lowering, but you may use two wooden spoons.) The batter should adhere to the vegetable pieces throughout the frying.

If the batter is too thin, it will slide from the vegetables. More chickpea flour can be whisked in if this is the case. If the batter seems to coat the vegetables too thickly, add more of the remaining ½ cup of water until you have a proper consistency.

Fry each pakora for about 2 minutes on each side, turning only once, until it is golden brown. (Lighter, leafy vegetables will be ready in less time.) Do not crowd the pan as you fry.

5. As each pakora is fried, remove it from the hot oil with a slotted spatula and place it on a platter lined with paper towels to drain.

If the pakoras must wait for more than 10 minutes, place them in a warm oven (200°-225°F). Continue until all of the vegetables have been fried. Serve as soon as possible after frying. Pakoras do not keep well.

VEGETABLES FOR PAKORA

We are listing the vegetables that are suitable for Pakora in the order in which they should be fried. Always fry the denser vegetables that contain less moisture first and save the leafy vegetables for last.

All of the vegetables should be thoroughly dried and cut into pieces that can be eaten in one or two bites. Always have a selection of at least 5 vegetables for your pakora.

Eggplant
Do not peel, but cut the eggplant lengthwise into ¾-inch slices and the slices into ¾-inch strips. Cut the strips into ¾-inch cubes. Lightly sprinkle the cubes with sat and let them drain on paper towels for ½ hour to draw out excess moisture and any bitterness. Squeeze dry with additional paper towels.

Cauliflower
Break the cauliflower into flowerets and trim the ends if they are tough.

Bell Peppers
Core and seed the bell peppers and cut them lengthwise into quarters. If they are very large, halve the quarters.

Mushrooms
Try to use small mushrooms so that they will not have to be cut in half. Trim the ends from the stems and wipe the mushrooms with damp paper towels to clean them.

Okra
The okra pods must be no longer than 2½ inches. Trim the stem to within ⅛ inch of the pod, being careful not to cut into the pod. Wipe the pods with damp paper towels to clean them.

Zucchini
Do not peel the zucchini, but cut them crosswise, into ¾-inch slices. Lightly sprinkle the slices with salt and let them drain for ½ hour on paper towels to draw out excess moisture. Pat dry with additional paper towels.

Potatoes
Peel the potatoes and cut them into ⅛-inch slices.

Sugar Snap Peas
Remove the strings and leave the pods whole.

Onions
Peel the onions and cut them into slices about ¼ inch thick. Pull the slices apart to form rings.

Leaves of Spinach or Swiss Chard
Try to use small, young leaves so that they may be fried whole. If necessary, tear them in half.

CURRY SAUCE WITH YOGURT

This simple curry sauce may be served just as it is on rice or you may add cooked vegetables, seafood, or chicken during the last 10 or 15 minutes of simmering just to heat them through. Your kitchen will have a wondrous smell as the spices are sautéing.

We like to serve the sauce on unpeeled potatoes that have been steamed, then sautéed in butter and sprinkled with Garam Masala and freshly ground coriander seed, and a tablespoon of chopped, fresh coriander leaves when they are available. For this combination, you will need 1½ pounds of small "new" or red potatoes to serve 4.

If you are unfamiliar with simmering yogurt, you may wish to read Cooking with Yogurt (see page 68). In our curry sauces using yogurt, there is the advantage of having chickpea flour added to the yogurt and water mixture. The chickpea flour not only acts as a thickening agent, but also as a stabilizer, so the chances of the yogurt curdling are slim.

Serves 4

2 cups Yogurt (see page 67), at room temperature
1 tablespoon chickpea flour
1 cup cold water
1 teaspoon cumin seeds
1 teaspoon coriander seeds
3 tablespoons clarified butter (see Butter and Oils in Indian Cooking, page 186)
1 teaspoon freshly ground dried hot red pepper
½ teaspoon turmeric
1 tablespoon peeled and finely chopped fresh ginger root
1 medium onion, coarsely chopped
1½ tablespoons minced garlic
½ teaspoon salt

1. In a small mixing bowl, pour in a little of the yogurt. Sprinkle with the chickpea flour and whisk until there are no lumps. Add the remaining yogurt and whisk again. Slowly whisk in the water until the ingredients are smooth. Set aside for ½ hour.

2. Toast the cumin and coriander seeds in a small skillet over low heat for about 5 minutes to bring out their flavors. Grind the seeds.

3. In a 2½-quart saucepan, heat the clarified butter over medium heat. Add the cumin and coriander seeds and hot red pepper. Sauté for 1 minute.
   Add the turmeric and ginger root and sauté for another minute, being very careful not to burn the turmeric, as it will become bitter.

4. Add the onion and garlic to the saucepan. Sprinkle with the salt. Sauté, still over medium heat, until the onion has wilted and begun to color. Stir with a wooden spoon as it sautés.

5. When the onion has begun to color, gradually whisk in the yogurt mixture. Bring to a simmer and reduce the heat to medium low. Simmer the curry sauce for 15 to 20 minutes. The longer it simmers, the thicker the sauce will become with the aromatics more pronounced in flavor.

CURRY SAUCE WITH CHICKEN STOCK

With a few small changes in the ingredients, this curry sauce is essentially the same as the Curry Sauce with Yogurt. Serve the sauce as it is on rice or add pieces of cooked chicken, red meat, or seafood during the last 10 to 15 minutes of simmering to heat them through.

Serves 4

3 cups Chicken Stock (see page 109), at room temperature
2 tablespoons chickpea flour
1 teaspoon cumin seeds
1 teaspoon coriander seeds
3 tablespoons corn oil
1 teaspoon freshly ground dried hot red pepper
½ teaspoon turmeric
1 tablespoon peeled and finely chopped fresh ginger root
1 medium onion, coarsely chopped
1½ tablespoons minced garlic

1. Pour a little of the Chicken Stock into a small mixing bowl. Sprinkle it with the chickpea flour and whisk until there are no lumps.

Add the remaining stock and whisk until the mixture is smooth. Set aside for ½ hour for the ingredients to meld.

2. Toast the cumin and coriander seeds in a small skillet over low heat for about 5 minutes to bring out their flavors. Grind the seeds.

3. In a 2½-quart saucepan, heat the corn oil over medium heat. Add the cumin and coriander seeds and hot red pepper. Sauté for 1 minute.

Add the turmeric and ginger root and sauté for another minute, being careful not to burn the turmeric, as it will become bitter.

4. Add the onion and garlic to the saucepan. Sauté, still over medium heat, until the onion has wilted and begun to color. Stir with a wooden spoon as it sautés.

5. When the onion has colored, gradually whisk in the chicken stock. Bring to a simmer and reduce the heat to medium-low.

Simmer the curry sauce for 15 to 20 minutes. It will become thicker the longer it simmers and the flavors of the aromatics will become more pronounced.

SUGGESTIONS FOR CONDIMENTS

There are dozens and dozens of foods that suggest themselves for condiments at an Indian meal. We will always have at least a dozen little bowls filled and arranged on the buffet. With good company, your dinner may last for hours and these little bowls may be brought to the table to be nibbled from as the relaxed evening progresses.

Chutneys (see the recipe index)
Grated fresh ginger root
Crystallized ginger
Yogurt
Radishes
Cherry tomatoes
Spring onions
Onion rings
Sliced cucumbers
Sliced or diced avocados, sprinkled with lemon
    juice
Chopped parsley
Chopped coriander or parsley
Ripe and green olives
Sliced pickles
Hard cooked eggs, either quartered or chopped
Crumbled slices of crisp bacon
Raisins
Sliced bananas
Freshly grated coconut
Chopped apples
Fresh pineapple
Kumquats
Sliced mangoes
Nuts such as almonds, peanuts, cashews, pecans and macadamia

EGGPLANT AND OKRA CURRY

The method for making this curry is a little different from the preceding recipes. It is also flexible in that if one of the vegetables is not available, it may be eliminated. In that case, increase the amount of the vegetable you are using to 1 pound.

Serves 4 to 6 as a main course, or 6 to 8 as part of a larger dinner.

¾-pound eggplant
½ teaspoon salt
2 cups Yogurt (see page 67), at room temperature
1 tablespoon chickpea flour
1 cup water
¾ pound okra, the pods no longer than 2½ inches
1 teaspoon cumin seeds
1 teaspoon coriander seeds
3 tablespoons clarified butter (see Butter and Oils in Indian Cooking, page 186)
1 teaspoon whole black mustard seeds
½ teaspoon turmeric
1 tablespoon peeled and finely chopped fresh ginger root
1½ tablespoons finely chopped garlic
1 teaspoon freshly ground dried hot red pepper
1 medium onion, coarsely chopped

1. Cut off the "hat" from the eggplant. Do not peel. Cut the eggplant into lengthwise slices, ⅓-inch thick. Cut each slice into ⅓-inch strips and the strips into ⅓-inch dice.

Place the dice on paper towels and sprinkle them with the ½ teaspoon of salt. Let them drain on the paper towels for ½ hour to rid them of excess moisture and any bitterness.

After ½ hour, squeeze the dice between fresh paper towels to dry them even more.

2. Pour a little of the yogurt in a small mixing bowl. Add the chickpea flour and whisk until there are no lumps.

Add the remaining yogurt and whisk again. Then slowly whisk in the water. Set aside for ½ hour for the ingredients to meld.

3. Do not wash, but wipe the okra with damp paper towels. Trim their stems to within ⅛ inch of the pod, being careful not to cut into the pod. Set aside.

4. Prepare the remaining ingredients. Toast the cumin and coriander seeds in a small skillet over low heat for about 5 minutes to bring out their flavors. Grind the seeds.

5. Place the clarified butter in a 2½-quart saucepan, over medium heat. When it is hot,

add the cumin, coriander, and mustard seeds. Sauté briefly—just until the mustard seeds begin to "dance."

Stirring constantly with a wooden spoon, add the turmeric, ginger root, garlic, and red pepper. Again, sauté for only a minute or less, being careful that the turmeric does not burn, as it will become bitter.

6. Add the onion and eggplant to the saucepan. Toss and continue to sauté the ingredients over medium heat until the onion has wilted and begun to color. This should take about 5 minutes.

7. Add the okra and toss thoroughly with the other ingredients. Reduce the heat to medium low and immediately begin to add the yogurt mixture, carefully stirring it in. Bring the ingredients back to a simmer and cook the curry, uncovered, for 15 minutes.

Stir often with a wooden spoon, without damaging the okra. The okra should remain whole and somewhat firm in texture.

CARROT AND CHICKPEA CURRY

This curry is delightfully colorful with the orange of the carrots and the green of the fresh mint leaves. Make certain that your dried chickpeas are not stale. We order ours by mail from sources with a good turnover (see the mail-order listings).

Serves 4 to 6 as a main course, or 6 to 8 as part of a larger dinner.

> 1½ cups dried chickpeas (½ pound)
> 1¼ teaspoons salt
> 1 recipe Curry Sauce with Yogurt (see page 181)
> 1 pound carrots
> 1 teaspoon clarified butter (see Butter and Oils in Indian Cooking, page 186)
> ½ teaspoon Garam Masala (see page 190)
> ½ cup chopped fresh mint leaves

1. Begin the cooking of the chickpeas several hours ahead. Look over the chickpeas for any that are not perfect and discard them.

Rinse the chickpeas, place them in a 2½-quart saucepan and add water to cover by 1 inch. Cover the saucepan and bring the chickpeas to a boil over medium-high heat.

Remove the saucepan from the heat and let it sit, covered, for 1 hour. This eliminates an overnight soaking.

2. After 1 hour, return the covered saucepan to the heat. Add 1 teaspoon of the salt and bring the chickpeas back to a boil. Turn the heat to medium low and simmer for 20 minutes.

Drain and set the chickpeas aside. You

will have about 4 cups. The chickpeas will complete their cooking later in the curry sauce.

3. About 1½ hours before you plan to serve the curry, begin the preparation of the curry sauce. Complete Steps 1 and 2 for the Curry Sauce with Yogurt.

4. Cut and discard the ends from the carrots. Scrape the carrots with a vegetable peeler and cut them crosswise into 1-inch pieces.

Place the carrots in a 2-quart saucepan and add water to a depth of ½ inch. Sprinkle them with the remaining ¼ teaspoon of salt. Cover the saucepan and bring the carrots to a boil over medium-high heat. Turn the heat to medium-low and simmer for only 7 minutes (less, if the carrots are under ¾-inch in diameter). They must remain firm.

Drain the carrots immediately and toss them with the teaspoon of clarified butter. Sprinkle on the Garam Masala and toss again. Set aside, uncovered.

5. Continue with the preparation of the curry sauce, following Steps 3 through 5. In Step 5, when the curry sauce has simmered for 10 minutes, add the cooked chickpeas.

Bring the sauce back to a simmer and cook for another 10 minutes or until the chickpeas are done to your taste.

6. Add the carrots to the curry. Cook only long enough to bring the ingredients back to a simmer, so as not to soften the carrots. Serve at once over plain or Minted Rice (see Box), sprinkling the chopped fresh mint leaves on top of the curry.

BUTTER AND OILS IN INDIAN COOKING

Ghee is most often used as the cooking fat in India. Although it is similar to clarified butter, ghee has a nutty flavor. It is usually prepared from at least a pound of butter which is cooked for a long period of time to rid it completely of all milk solids and water.

After being strained through several thicknesses of cheesecloth to an absolutely pure, golden color, it can be kept at room temperature for months without spoiling. This is a definite advantage when refrigeration is limited. However, we find clarified butter to be satisfactory for our Indian cooking as it is faster when only a small amount is needed.

To make our clarified butter, we place several more tablespoons of butter than we will need for cooking in a small skillet and let it melt slowly in a 200 F oven. Once the butter has melted, we allow it to cool briefly and then carefully skim off and discard any white milk solids on the surface or edges of the skillet. This may also be done over low heat on top of the stove. For an even clearer clarified butter, you may strain it through cheesecloth.

Oil, when used in Indian cooking, is usually peanut oil. We find corn oil more to our liking for frying and occasionally olive oil for sautéing.

SWEET INDIAN RICE

If you wish to serve an elaborate rice with your Indian meal, this recipe is ideal. The ingredients that make it sweet will not overwhelm any of our curries. The sweet rice, in fact, will complement the Koftas on page 178.

Serves 4 to 6

½ cup raisins, preferably Monnuka
4 cups water (approximately)
2 tablespoons clarified butter (see Butter and Oils in Indian Cooking, page 186)
1 medium onion, coarsely chopped
1 cup coarsely chopped celery
½ teaspoon salt
20 whole, green cardamom seeds (about 5 pods)
1 teaspoon Garam Masala (see page 190)
¼ teaspoon turmeric
2 cups raw brown rice
2-inch stick cinnamon

1. Soak the raisins in 1 cup of the water for ½ hour to plump them.

2. Place the clarified butter in a 2½-quart saucepan, over medium-low heat. Add the chopped onion and celery. Sprinkle with the salt and sauté the vegetables, uncovered, until the onion wilts. Stir several times. This will take about 10 minutes.

3. Add the cardamom seeds, Garam Masala, and turmeric to the sautéed vegetables and sauté for only 1 minute. Immediately add the rice. Stir just to mix and add 3 cups of the water.

Cover the saucepan and bring the ingredients to a boil over medium high heat.

4. When the ingredients come to a boil, add the cinnamon stick and the raisins with their soaking water. Quickly mix them into the other ingredients.

Reduce the heat to medium low and cook, covered, until the rice is tender. This will take from 40 to 45 minutes. Check the rice every 15 minutes and add more water as needed.

Occasionally toss the ingredients with a fork to fluff the rice, being careful not to crush it. During the last 10 minutes of cooking, it may be necessary to reduce the heat to very low.

MINTED RICE

In India, there are a multitude of ways to prepare rice and an abundance of rices to choose from, with Basmati rice considered supreme. Brown rice is not often used, but we prefer its nutty flavor with our curries. For added interest, we mix in 3 tablespoons dried crumbled mint or ½ cup chopped fresh mint.

Serves 4 to 6 (about 5 cups cooked rice)

1. Prepare the brown rice, following the recipe for Basic Brown Rice (see page 74).

2. If you are using dried mint, gently mix it into the rice with a fork about 5 minutes before it is done.

If you are using fresh mint, add it just before serving the rice so that the leaves will retain their green color.

5. The rice may be served as soon as it is tender, but if you are not ready to serve, it can sit, covered and off the heat, for ½ hour. Remove the cinnamon stick before serving.

PURI

Of all of the Indian breads, the round, slightly puffed, fried Puris are our favorites. As with pita bread, success is determined by the way the breads are formed and by having the proper heat for cooking.

Puris do not keep and should be eaten immediately or within ½ hour after they have been fried. Later they will become limp and taste oily. The frying time is very quick and, once fried, the puris will stay hot long enough for you to use the hot cooking oil for another purpose. We fry the puris first, let them drain on paper towels and then fry our Pakora.

For a large crowd, the recipe may be doubled and there still will be ample time to fry the puris and pakora without the breads cooling. Puris are so delicious that you should allow 3 or 4 per person.

Makes 15 to 18 puris

½ cup whole-wheat flour
¾ cup all-purpose, unbleached flour
½ teaspoon salt
2 tablespoons clarified butter (see Butter and Oils in Indian Cooking, page 186)
½ cup Yogurt, (see page 67), at room temperature
Corn oil for frying

1. Sift the whole-wheat flour, unbleached flour, and salt together onto your work surface. Add the clarified butter and rub the flour and butter together until it resembles a coarse meal.

2. Make a well in the center of the flour mixture and pour in the yogurt. Gradually, bring in the sides of the well onto the yogurt and mix with your fingers until all of the yogurt has been incorporated into the flour.

3. Gather up the dough and form it into a ball. Knead the dough on your floured work surface for about 5 minutes until it is smooth and elastic.

Cover the dough with a piece of plastic wrap and let it rest for ½ hour.

4. After ½ hour, begin forming the puri by pinching off a small piece of dough—enough to form a ball 1¼ inches in diameter.

WHAT TO BUY OR ORDER NOW

By the end of June we have completed canning our strawberry preserves and jam and have started canning pickles. If the crops have been good and we can more than usual, we may need to reorder a few items.

We don't order perishable foods now, but we do study the summer catalogs for gift items. Since it is summer, many feature baskets, colorful table linens and inexpensive little utensils, crocks and jam pots that will combine nicely with our home-canned foods as gifts later in the year. Some catalogs offer tin and wooden canisters of various sizes, some just right for dried herbs.

In keeping with thinking ahead for future gift giving, we save the wooden boxes from our brie cheeses. With a little cleaning and sanding, they are handy for holding homemade gifts.

As a final note, wooden mushroom baskets make wonderful, individual picnic baskets.

Roll the dough in a clockwise fashion between the palms of your hands. Set it aside on a corner of your work surface. Continue until all of the dough has been used.

Cover the balls of dough with plastic wrap as they are formed so that they will not dry out.

5. Roll out each ball of dough by placing it on your floured work surface and flattening it slightly with your rolling pin.

Working from the center, roll the ball of dough into a circle 4 inches in diameter and just under ⅛-inch thick. After each roll, lift the dough and give it a quarter turn. Flour your work surface as necessary.

At some point, turn the dough over and roll on the opposite side to make sure that there are no tears. The circle *must* be even in thickness in order to puff evenly in the hot oil. Do not roll backward and forward, but always away from you.

As each puri is formed, place it aside on your work surface and again cover with the plastic wrap. Don't layer the puris. Continue until all of the puris have been formed.

6. In a heavy 10-inch skillet or wok, pour in corn oil to a depth of 1 inch. Heat the oil to 375°F or until a cube of bread browns instantly.

7. Lower each puri into the hot oil using a slotted spatula. Do not crowd the pan.

The puri will blister and puff up almost immediately, and the total cooking time will be only 1 minute. Since they cook so quickly, we fry only 2 at a time so that we can watch them closely. If they do not puff right away, press them down gently into the oil with the spatula.

Our puris are smaller than some so that they will become golden on both sides without requiring turning. As soon as each puri has browned, remove it with the slotted spatula to a large platter lined with paper towels to drain.

AND IN OUR GARDEN

June is the month when most of our herbs are at their best. When the hotter weather begins, many go to seed or lose their delicate flavors so we begin to freeze or dry them before this can happen.

We have found the best way to freeze herbs is to first spread the sprigs on a baking sheet. Place the baking sheet in the freezer for an hour or so and when the sprigs have frozen, place them in an airtight, plastic bag. Label it with the name of the herb and the date and return it to the freezer. The flavors will remain for at least a year.

Our method for drying herbs is simple. We just tie small bundles at the stem ends with twine and hang them from the ceiling in the kitchen. Any airy spot, out of direct sunlight, will do. The herbs take about one week to dry completely, depending upon the humidity. When the bundles have dried, place them in airtight containers away from direct light. You may strip the leaves from the stems before storing. We prefer not to store all our dried herbs and leave some hanging all year, for on a humid day they will scent the kitchen. Catnip is the only herb that is dried elsewhere. Since we have cats, it is necessary to hang it in the garage, where it dries safely and alone. The only herb seed that we dry and save is dill seed. These seeds will be used in cooking and for planting the next year. See the December chapter for suggestions on giving herbs as gifts.

Outdoors, an inspection is made of our basil crop and if it looks as though more will be needed for our pesto, we plant more seeds. If we have just received fresh ginger root, rather than refrigerating it, we cut the roots into 1½ to 2-inch pieces and plant them several inches deep in a large garden pot, filled with good potting soil. Left outdoors during the summer, the roots will grow, producing a beautiful plant resembling bamboo. When ginger root is needed in cooking, we dig a bit up. In the fall, the plants will die back, but with the garden pot brought indoors and kept in a cool spot, the roots may be dug as needed. We do not water the plant but when the weather warms the following year, we place the pot outside, then water it, and with a little luck, the roots will grow for another season.

GARAM MASALA

This spice blend from India is beautiful even as it is being made — the spices arranged on the baking sheet resemble a palette filled with warm earth colors. The flavor is very different from a commercial curry powder, but it can be used instead of curry powder in many recipes.

In addition to the recipes we give, sprinkle a small amount on various sautéed vegetables, baked potatoes that have been split and filled with yogurt, or just plain yogurt itself. The proportions of the spices can be changed to your taste.

Keep the garam masala in a tightly closed spice jar and it will stay fresh for 6 months.

Makes ½ cup

4 tablespoons green cardamom seeds in their pods
3 sticks of cinnamon, each 2 inches long
4 tablespoons whole black peppercorns
4 tablespoons black caraway seeds
4 tablespoons coriander seeds
4 tablespoons cumin seeds
2 tablespoons whole cloves

1. Preheat the oven to 225° F.

2. Arrange the spices individually on a baking sheet with sides, keeping the cardamom pods and sticks of cinnamon separate from the other groups.

3. Toast the spices in the preheated oven for 20 minutes to bring out their flavor. Check and stir once or twice during this time so that they do not burn.

4. Remove the seeds from the cardamom pods and discard the pods. You will have 2 tablespoons of seeds.

5. Grind the spices together. We find the Varco Spice and Coffee Grinder made by Moulinex (check the mail-order listings) best for this, but you may use a blender or a mortar with pestle.

Grind the cinnamon sticks first (you will have about 1 tablespoon), then combine the remaining spices as you grind them. The grinding should be done in small batches.

Do not grind the spices to a powder, but leave them with a bit of texture.

6. When all of the spices have been ground, mix them thoroughly together and store the garam masala in an airtight spice jar.

Important Note: All of the spices may be obtained by mail order which we recommend for optimum freshness, unless, of course, you have a spice shop nearby.

SALADS FOR ANY SEASON

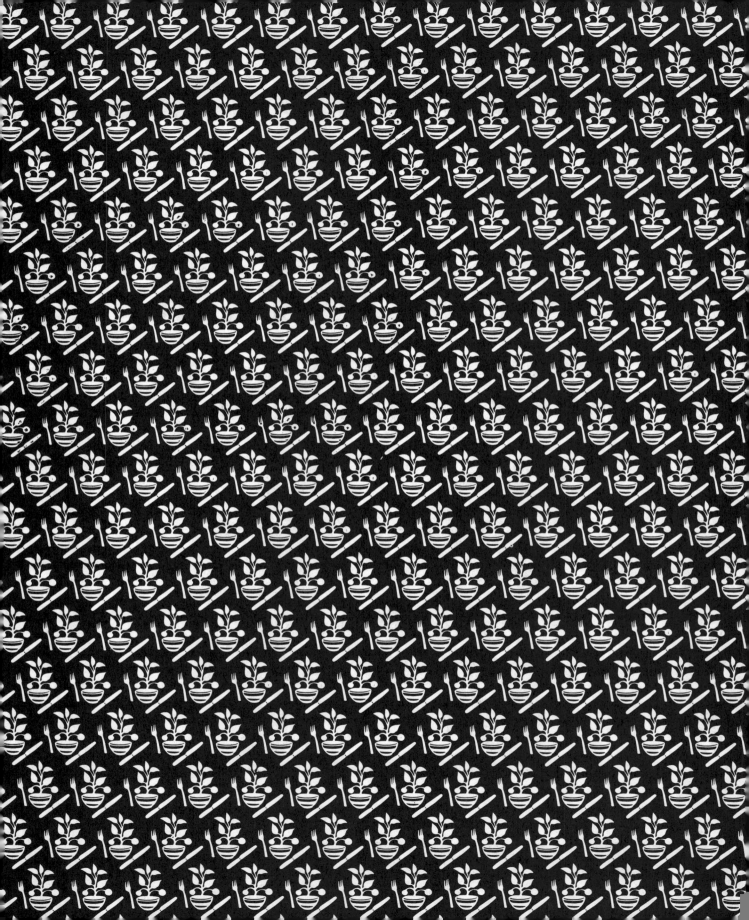

SALADS FOR ANY SEASON

Too often, people serve salads indifferently, if at all, and this is an unfortunate mistake. One can almost forgive a poorly prepared meal if it is saved at the end with a crisp and imaginative salad. So, give your salads the same thought that you give to any other course of a meal and present them accordingly. Clear the table, bring in fresh bread, cheese (if it is appropriate), and serve your salads on *large* plates.

We prepare salads twice a day. Lunch will generally consist of just a composed salad, cheese, and bread. In the evenings, our salad is usually tossed and served at the end of the meal. We like the practice of serving the salad after the main course as it means the host or hostess can then relax with the guests with no thoughts of oven temperatures or last-minute disasters.

Most of our salads are quite simple to prepare and have interchangeable ingredients. If a salad calls for Boston lettuce, try it next time with Bibb lettuce. You will also find that cutting or chopping your ingredients using different techniques will alter the flavors slightly.

Vary your choice of fresh herbs. On some mornings our garden is fragrant with the smell of tarragon and we feel we must have it in one of our salads. Other days, perhaps basil will captivate us. Whatever our ingredients, we are sure to use the best ones that are in season.

As each of our salads has its own individual dressing, we include only the recipes for the two separate dressings that remain constant—Mayonnaise and Mother's Salad Dressing. Even the proportions for a vinaigrette dressing will vary, depending upon the ingredients in a salad.

PURCHASED SALAD GREENS AND VEGETABLES

Caring for and storing purchased salad ingredients differs from the storing of vegetables brought in fresh from the garden. If the items are perishable, logically, you should buy only amounts that you can use within one week. Where we live, we must drive quite a way to find good produce, so it is better to buy in large quantities. Often supermarkets, like ours, will get shipments only once or twice a week, so find out what those days are. If you have to drive there, plan the trip on the days the produce is the freshest. If the displayed vegetables look worn-out, ask what's in the back. Don't buy tired vegetables.

Washing and storing greens

Salad greens are the most perishable produce items and as soon as we return from the store, we carefully wash them. Stored, unwashed, in their original wrappings, they rapidly lose their freshness. For greens that come in "heads," try to leave the larger ones intact as you wash them. Open up the leaves and run cold water between them. For smaller heads, such as Boston, that can be dried in a salad spinner, separate the leaves as you wash without bruising them. Allow the greens to drain either in the dish rack in the sink or spread out on towels for a few minutes before drying.

To store the greens, shake as much water as possible from the large heads and place them in airtight plastic bags to which you have added several paper towels. The paper towels will continue to absorb excess moisture. Close tightly and store in the refrigerator. If the greens were very fresh when purchased, they will stay so for about a week.

For the smaller heads which have been pulled apart, dry first in the salad spinner, then store as for the large heads. Do not attempt to dry greens such as romaine, escarole, or endive in a spin drier. It only damages them. Also, the leaves should never be cut until it is time to prepare your salad.

Storing other salad vegetables

Most other salad vegetables will benefit by being washed before storing. We like to have our salad ingredients ready to use so that making our salads is a pleasure, not a chore, with washing and attempts at freshening them done at the last minute. Obviously, we do not wash some things, and carrots, radishes, and celery can be stored, unwashed, in their original wrappings.

We feel mushrooms should never be washed, but only wiped with damp paper towels. We store them in their boxes with a few holes punched in the wrapping, as they prefer a bit of air, but we use them very quickly. If there are no wrappings on your vegetables, place them in plastic bags. Cucumbers should be washed and stored in airtight plastic bags. Peppers should be washed, but do not require wrapping. (Recently, we read to store bell peppers at room temperature—don't do it. We did and they were soft within 2 days.)

We have found it helpful to line our refrigerator drawers with paper towels which we change weekly. This helps to control moisture and keeps the drawers clean.

We do store lemons at room temperature if they are very hard and if they will be used within a few days. Otherwise, we wash and refrigerate them. If they are selling for a good price, we buy several dozen at a time. They keep for a couple of weeks in the refrigerator. We keep onions, garlic, and potatoes at room temperature, either in hanging baskets or in bowls on the floor. Potatoes should be used within 1 week.

VEGETABLES FROM THE GARDEN

With the exception of corn, we pick all of our fruits, vegetables, and herbs early in the morning as soon as the dew has dried. Herbs hold their oils (flavors) in their leaves at this time of the day. As the temperature rises, the oils will go back into their root systems. We have noticed this in particular with tarragon. In the morning, the garden is heavily scented with tarragon, but by late in the day, the aroma is gone.

Picking order

If there is a lot to be picked, we pick the most fragile items such as the herbs and salad greens first and bring them back into the house, rinse, and put them away. It is very important to clean and refrigerate them promptly, for if they are kept out even for an hour, they will never recover their original crispness.

Then it's back into the garden for the bulkier vegetables. As beans and tomatoes are susceptible to disease, we pick them last when we are certain the dew has completely dried. If the leaves are wet, it is easy to spread diseases with your hands or clothing. Also, never smoke in your garden and, if you do smoke, it is advisable to wash your hands before handling your plants as you can infect some plants with tobacco mosaic disease.

Storing garden produce

For the vegetables that need to be bagged before refrigeration, such as salad greens, herbs, and cucumbers, we use Ziploc or Bes-pak plastic bags. Ziploc bags are completely airtight, but unfortunately, they do not make a size larger than 1 gallon. Bespak makes bags which they label Turkey Freezer Bags that have a 2-gallon capacity. These are perfect for large amounts of salad greens. We line all of our plastic bags with a white paper towel before placing the vegetables inside. The towel will absorb any excess moisture. Also, we do not force the air from the bags containing salad greens, as they seem to stay crisper with it. With a little care, we are able to rinse and re-use the bags over and over again. We save the paper towels for little cleaning jobs. We prefer the white Viva paper towels, as they have no odor. Some paper towels have a strong odor that can be transmitted to your vegetables. Do not use colored towels as the colors may bleed onto your vegetables and some dyes are potentially dangerous.

And finally, corn! We have been told so often to pick our corn when the pot of water is boiling, that if we are found picking corn in the early morning, it is because we are having it for breakfast.

HOMEMADE MAYONNAISE BY HAND

With all due respect for our regional commercial brand of mayonnaise, a very popular favorite in North Carolina, we still like to make our own, and by hand. Some of it has to do with the challenge of not curdling the egg yolks, but more important, we feel our balance of ingredients (slightly more dry mustard and wine vinegar) cuts the heaviness of the oils better than most recipes for homemade mayonnaise. We find wine vinegar preferable to lemon juice for, in order to give the mayonnaise some "bite," too much lemon juice must be added, resulting in a bitter taste.

If you are making mayonnaise for the first time and are fearful that it might curdle, have an extra egg or two ready at room temperature. However, if you are extremely careful in adding the initial oil, this is unlikely to happen. It is more likely your arm will tire from the whisking since it could take up to ½ hour to add all the oil. Keep in mind that the resulting mayonnaise, in both texture and taste, is worth every minute and sore muscle.

To rectify a curdled mayonnaise, beat another egg yolk in a clean bowl until it is thick. Gradually beat in the curdled mayonnaise and finally the remaining oil.

Makes about 1 ¾ cups mayonnaise

2 egg yolks, at room temperature
1 teaspoon dry mustard
½ teaspoon salt
¼ teaspoon freshly ground white pepper
2 tablespoons white wine vinegar
½ cup olive oil
¾ cup corn oil

1. In a small, deep bowl, beat the egg yolks with a wire whisk. Add the dry mustard, salt, white pepper, and wine vinegar. Whisk again until the dry ingredients have dissolved. The yolks should be thick.

2. Gradually begin adding the combined oils, drop by drop. Whisk constantly, keeping your eyes on the drops of oil, not on the contents of the bowl. The mayonnaise will start to thicken after you have added about ¼ cup of the oil.

At this point, you may begin to add the oil by teaspoons, then by tablespoons, and finally in a steady stream.

3. When all of the oil has been added and the mayonnaise is thick and smooth, using a rubber spatula, scrape the contents of the bowl into a glass container. Cover and refrigerate the mayonnaise if it is not to be used right away. The mayonnaise will be at its best if used within 1 week.

MAYONNAISE MADE IN A BLENDER OR FOOD PROCESSOR

Only on rare occasions do we make our mayonnaise in a blender or processor. Even though it is extraordinarily easy to make, the texture is not the same and this seems to affect the taste. Made by hand, mayonnaise is solidly thick, but with a machine it is somewhat fluffy because of the whole egg being used rather than just the yolk.

Makes about 2 cups

2 whole eggs, at room temperature
1 teaspoon dry mustard

½ teaspoon salt
¼ teaspoon freshly ground white pepper
2 tablespoons white wine vinegar
½ cup olive oil
1 cup corn oil

1. Break the eggs into the bowl of your blender or processor (use the steel blade). Add the dry mustard, salt, white pepper, and wine vinegar. Cover and blend for 3 to 5 seconds.

2. With the motor still running, remove the plastic or rubber stopper from the cover of the blender or the pusher from the processor and begin adding the combined oils in a slow, steady stream until all the oil is used. Blend only until the mayonnaise is thick.

3. Scrape the mayonnaise into a glass container, cover, and refrigerate if the mayonnaise is not to be used right away. The mayonnaise will keep for 1 week.

MOTHER'S SALAD DRESSING

In general, we feel our salad dressings should be made fresh for each salad, but this one is the exception. It makes a very pleasant change from regular olive-oil dressings. Try it on any salad, particularly on avocados and tomatoes, or on fruit salads. Prepare the dressing one day before you plan to use it so that the flavors can meld.

Makes about 1½ cups

2 teaspoons dry mustard
2 teaspoons salt
2 teaspoons sweet paprika
¼ cup sugar
1 large clove garlic
1 small onion
½ cup white wine vinegar
1 cup corn oil

1. Into a glass jar with a tight-fitting cover (we use a pint or quart canning jar), measure the dry mustard, salt, sweet paprika, and sugar. Break up any lumps in the dry ingredients.

2. Peel the garlic and onion, but leave them whole. Stick a toothpick in each and add them to the jar. This prevents them from getting into salads by mistake.

3. Add the wine vinegar and corn oil to the jar. Close tightly and shake the jar until the dry ingredients have dissolved and the liquids are combined. Refrigerate until ready to use.

WINTER SALADS

A HEARTY WINTER COLESLAW

We use a food processor to accomplish the tasks of shredding and chopping vegetables for this delicious wintertime coleslaw. It does the job swiftly and effectively. The slaw goes particularly well with the Fried Chicken recipes on page 106. Also, we often use it in halves of a Pita Bread (see pages 172 and 174) combined with sliced avocados for a sandwich at lunch.

If you wish to serve the slaw as a salad course, surround it with Boston lettuce, either on one large serving platter or on individual salad plates. Sliced avocados, sprinkled with lemon juice and additional sprouts, make an inviting presentation.

As winter cabbages do not have the tender flavor of spring or early summer cabbages, make the coleslaw on the day you plan to serve it. It will keep for several days, but the cabbage will pass its peak for freshness if held longer.

Serves 4 to 6

¾ cup homemade Mayonnaise (see pages 195 and 196)

½ cup Yogurt (see page 67)

½ teaspoon salt

¼ teaspoon freshly ground black pepper

½ cup coarsely chopped dill pickles

½ cup coarsely chopped canned Colorado peppers or mildly hot peppers, packed in brine

4 tablespoons juice from the pickles and/or peppers

2-pound winter cabbage

2 large carrots

1 medium onion, chopped fine

2 cups finely chopped parsley, loosely packed

2 cups mung-bean sprouts (for growing instructions, see page 39)

1. Prepare the dressing for the coleslaw. In a small mixing bowl, whisk the mayonnaise and yogurt together. Add the salt, black pepper, chopped pickles, and peppers (do not seed the peppers), along with 4 tablespoons of their juice. Whisk to blend. Set aside.

2. Discard the outer leaves from the cabbage. Quarter and core the cabbage. If you are using a food processor, cut the quarters to fit the feed tube. Fit the processor with the medium shredding disk and shred the cabbage fine.

   Or, you may shred the cabbage by hand using the medium side of a hand grater or a cabbage cutter, if you have one. Place the shredded cabbage in a large mixing bowl.

3. Scrape the carrots with a vegetable peeler and shred them in the processor fitted with the medium shredding disk or by hand on the medium side of the hand grater. Add to the cabbage.

4. Add the onion, parsley, and mung-bean sprouts to the other ingredients. Toss to mix. Add the reserved salad dressing and toss again. Cover and refrigerate the coleslaw if it is not to be served immediately.

A WARM WINTER POTATO SALAD

We like to serve this salad warm with small, individual pots of Pesto (see page 309) and thick slices of crusty bread. Pickled Eggs (see page 152) are also a tasty accompaniment.

Serves 4 to 6

2½ pounds medium-size boiling potatoes
½ pound Hot Sausage (see page 45)
1 tablespoon olive oil
½ cup homemade Mayonnaise (see pages 195 and 196)
½ teaspoon salt
¼ teaspoon freshly ground black pepper
2 tablespoons wine vinegar
1 medium onion, cut into thin, lengthwise slivers
2 cups coarsely chopped celery
1 cup finely chopped parsley, tightly packed
1 teaspoon crumbled dried oregano or winter savory

1. Scrub the potatoes. Steam them for 20 to 30 minutes, just until they are tender.

2. Prick the sausages with the point of a knife in 5 or 6 places. Place the olive oil in a skillet over medium-low heat and add the sausages. Sauté the sausages for about 20 minutes, turning them frequently, until they are nicely browned. Remove them from the heat and cover to keep warm.

3. While the potatoes are steaming and the sausages are sautéing, prepare the remaining ingredients for the salad. Place the mayonnaise in a small bowl and whisk in the salt, black pepper, and wine vinegar. Whisk until the mixture is smooth. Set aside.

4. In another bowl, toss together the onion, celery, parsley, and oregano or winter savory. Set aside.

5. When the potatoes are tender, remove them from the heat. Peel them as soon as they are cool enough to handle. Place the uncut potatoes in your salad bowl.

6. When all of the potatoes have been peeled, cut them into 1- to 1½-inch chunks. Add the mayonnaise dressing to the potatoes and toss until they are lightly coated.

Add the tossed vegetables from the other bowl and toss again.

Quickly cut the sausages into ¼-inch slices. Toss them into the salad and serve immediately.

Note: For all of our potato salads, we have specified amounts for the dressings. However, you may find that sometimes you will need more than we have listed. Some potatoes (generally mealy ones) will absorb an enormous amount of liquid; at other times, a moderate amount of dressing will be sufficient. Always sample your salad before serving and add more dressing as the potatoes require. A dry potato salad is definitely undesirable.

CELERY CABBAGE SALAD WITH YOGURT VINAIGRETTE DRESSING

With all the variations of salads we make using fresh celery cabbage, this very simple one is our favorite. The texture and delicate flavor of the cabbage have center stage.

Serves 4 to 6

2-pound celery cabbage
1 medium onion
1 teaspoon dry mustard
½ teaspoon salt
⅛ teaspoon freshly ground white pepper
1 small clove garlic, minced fine
2 tablespoons mild wine vinegar
⅓ cup olive oil
3 heaping tablespoons Yogurt (see page 67)

1. Discard any outer leaves of the cabbage that are blemished or tough. Wash the cabbage and cut it lengthwise into quarters. Remove the core. Shred the cabbage fine and place it in a large bowl.

Peel and slice the onion thin, breaking the slices into ringlets. Add to the cabbage and toss thoroughly. If you do not plan to serve the salad right away, cover the bowl with plastic wrap and refrigerate.

2. In a small bowl, combine the dry mustard, salt, white pepper, minced garlic, and wine vinegar. Whisk just to mix and dissolve the dry ingredients.

Add the olive oil in a steady stream, whisking constantly. Continue whisking after all the oil is added until you have a thick emulsion. Set aside until you are ready to dress the salad.

3. Just before you are ready to serve the salad, add the yogurt to the dressing and whisk again. Pour the dressing over the salad and toss lightly until all the cabbage is coated with the dressing.

WINTER CORN SALAD

In this recipe we use corn and bell peppers, frozen from the summer, and our canned Colorado peppers. You may use a good quality of commercially frozen corn kernels, fresh bell peppers, and substitute mildly hot peppers packed in brine for the Colorados. Serve this salad at lunch on salad greens or at dinner as a vegetable accompaniment to fish or chicken. Crusty chunks of bread will be welcome at either time.

Serves 4 to 6

4 cups frozen corn kernels, partially defrosted (see Note)
2 large bell peppers, preferably red, fresh or frozen, cut into ⅓-inch dice (see Note)
1 tablespoon corn oil
¼ teaspoon salt
¼ teaspoon freshly ground black pepper
1 medium onion, preferably red, cut into thin slivers
1½ cups celery, chopped into ¼-inch dice
⅓ cup unseeded, coarsely chopped canned Colorado peppers or mildly hot peppers, packed in brine
¼ cup finely chopped parsley or celery leaves
½ cup mung-bean sprouts (for growing instructions, see page 39)
⅓ cup Mother's Salad Dressing (see page 197)

1. Let the corn and bell peppers, if frozen, partially defrost for about an hour before you begin the salad.

2. Place the oil in a skillet over medium heat. Add the diced peppers, sprinkle them with salt, and sauté until they are just tender but

still crisp. The moisture should evaporate from the skillet.

Add the corn and black pepper, toss, and cook the mixture until the corn is hot. Remove the skillet from the heat.

3. Put the onion, celery, Colorado peppers, and parsley into a salad bowl and add the mung-bean sprouts and the reserved corn and bell peppers. Toss to mix and add the salad dress-

ing. Toss again until the ingredients are thoroughly combined. This salad is best served at room temperature.

Note: To absorb any excess water, allow the corn to partially defrost in a bowl lined with paper towels. If you are using frozen peppers, spread them on a paper towel to defrost before dicing.

CAULIFLOWER AND RED PEPPER SALAD

Serve this multicolored salad as part of a buffet or as a first course during the holiday season. If possible, use red and yellow bell peppers.

Serves 6 to 8

1½-pound head cauliflower
Small piece of lemon
3 large red bell peppers (or a combination of red and yellow), fresh
     or frozen (see Note)
2 tablespoons olive oil
2 large cloves garlic, minced
¼ teaspoon salt
¼ teaspoon freshly ground black pepper
1 tablespoon wine vinegar
2 cups coarsely chopped celery
1½ cups finely chopped parsley
1 cup alfalfa sprouts (for growing instructions, see page 39)

Dressing:
1 teaspoon dry mustard
½ teaspoon salt
¼ teaspoon freshly ground white pepper
½ teaspoon freshly ground dried hot red pepper
1 clove garlic, minced

3 tablespoons lemon juice
⅓ cup olive oil

1. Remove any outer leaves from the cauliflower. Rinse and core the cauliflower and break it into flowerets no larger than 2 inches in diameter.

In a 1½-quart saucepan, arrange the cauliflower stem side down. Add the small piece of lemon to prevent discoloration while cooking. Pour in water to a depth of 1 inch, cover, and bring to a boil over medium heat. Parboil for only 10 minutes, then drain and run cold water over the cauliflower. Set aside.

2. Core and seed the peppers. Cut them lengthwise into julienne strips, ¼ inch thick.

3. Heat the olive oil in a skillet and add the peppers and garlic. Sprinkle with salt and black pepper and toss just to mix.

Cover and cook over medium heat for 15 minutes, tossing occasionally. After 15 minutes, remove the peppers from the heat and toss with the vinegar. Set aside, uncovered.

4. While the peppers are cooking, prepare the salad dressing. In a bowl, combine the dry mustard, salt, white pepper, hot red pepper, garlic, and lemon juice. In a thin, steady stream add the olive oil, whisking constantly, until the dressing is thick and smooth.

5. Add the cauliflower, celery, and parsley to the dressing and toss thoroughly. Arrange the vegetables in the center of a serving platter, re-forming the cauliflower to resemble the original head. Surround the platter with the julienne strips of pepper. They require no further dressing.

Sprinkle the alfalfa sprouts over the entire salad, fluffing them as you do so to create a confetti appearance.

6. Serve the salad at room temperature or chilled, as you prefer.

Note: We freeze our peppers, cored, seeded, and quartered so a minimum amount of work is necessary when we are ready to use them. For ease in handling, we let them defrost for about an hour on paper towels before cooking. Slightly defrosted, the cooking time will be the same as if we used fresh.

JERUSALEM ARTICHOKE AND MUNG-BEAN SPROUT SALAD

When the winter is really bleak and the garden looks as if nothing is growing, we bundle up and go digging for Jerusalem artichokes. And with some searching, we often find enough parsley to accompany them. However, this salad is so good it is worthy of a trip to the supermarket to buy the ingredients, if need be.

Serves 4 to 6

1 pound Jerusalem artichokes
1 cup mung-bean sprouts (for growing instructions, see page 39)
1½ cups chopped parsley, tightly packed
1 teaspoon dry mustard
¼ teaspoon freshly ground white pepper
1 small clove garlic, minced
1 tablespoon lemon juice
1 tablespoon soy sauce
¼ cup olive oil

1. Scrub the artichokes. With a small knife, peel and slice them into ¼-inch pieces. The peeling can be rather tedious depending upon the shape of the artichokes. Try to find ones that are uniform and not too gnarled.

Place the slices in a salad bowl. Add the sprouts and the parsley. Toss to mix.

2. Prepare the dressing. In a small bowl, combine the mustard, pepper, garlic, lemon juice, and soy sauce. In a steady stream, begin adding the olive oil, whisking constantly until all the oil is used. The dressing should be smooth. Do not add salt as the soy sauce replaces it.

3. Pour the dressing over the salad and toss.

RADISH AND TWO-SPROUTS SALAD

If you still have radishes in your garden as late as December, use them in this unusual salad. Even though they may be large with a rather sharp flavor, they work very nicely with the other ingredients. Of course, store-bought radishes work equally well. This particular salad is ideal for stuffing into a Pita (see pages 172 and 174).

Serves 4 to 6

¾ pound radishes
1 cup mung-bean sprouts (for growing instructions, see page 39)
1 cup alfalfa sprouts (see page 39)
1 medium red onion, sliced thin
1 cup coarsely chopped parsley
12 ripe olives, pitted and cut into slivers
½ teaspoon salt
¼ teaspoon freshly ground black pepper
2 tablespoons olive oil
2 tablespoons lemon juice

1. Wash and trim the radishes. Shred them, using either the coarse side of a grater or a food processor. Place the shreds in a salad bowl and add the two kinds of sprouts.

Break the onion slices into rings and add them along with the parsley and slivered olives to the salad bowl.

2. Sprinkle the salad with the salt and pepper. Pour on the oil and then the lemon juice. Toss and serve.

BEET, AVOCADO, AND SAUERKRAUT SALAD

We can make this salad when almost nothing is left in the garden and we are relying on what we have frozen, stored, and canned. We do have to buy avocados and if bad weather has killed the last of the celery cabbage, we purchase a Boston lettuce. Serve this salad either as a first course or to follow the main course or even as a light lunch.

Serves 4 to 6

1 pound beets (with their tops)
1 pint Sauerkraut (see page 137)
2 teaspoons dry mustard
½ teaspoon freshly ground black pepper
1 teaspoon minced garlic
3 tablespoons lemon juice
2 tablespoons soy sauce
½ cup olive oil
½ pound celery cabbage or Boston lettuce
2 large, ripe avocados
2 medium red onions, peeled and sliced thin
1 cup mung-bean sprouts (for growing instructions see page 39)
Dill Pickle slices (see page 135), Pickled Eggs (see page 153), and ripe olives for garnishing

1. Prepare the beets. Place them in a saucepan with water to cover and boil until tender. Drain the beets, peel, and cut them lengthwise into ¼-inch julienne strips. Chill the julienne strips before composing the salad.

2. Drain the sauerkraut in a colander and run cold water over it to remove excess salt. Squeeze the water from the kraut and refrigerate the kraut until you are ready to prepare the salad.

3. In a small mixing bowl, prepare the salad dressing. Blend together the dry mustard, black pepper, and garlic. Whisk in the lemon juice and soy sauce.

In a slow, steady stream, pour in the olive oil, whisking constantly until the dressing is smooth and thick. Set aside.

4. Select a large serving platter and arrange the celery cabbage or Boston lettuce on it. Break the leaves into pieces and place the most attractive ones around the rim of the platter.

5. Arrange the sauerkraut on top of the leaves, leaving a 2-inch margin of leaves showing. Fluff the kraut to create volume.

6. Halve the avocados. Remove the pits and peel, and cut each half into 6 lenghwise slices. Divide the slices and the beets into individual portions, depending upon whether you will be serving 4 or 6. Arrange the portions alternately around the platter on top of the sauerkraut.

7. Break the slices of onion into rings and scatter them over the other ingredients. Top the onion rings with the mung-bean sprouts.

8. Pour the salad dressing over the salad, lightly coating all of the ingredients. Garnish the platter with the ripe olives and pickles and, if you are serving the salad as a lunch, add the Pickled Eggs.

AVOCADO AND GRAPEFRUIT SALAD WITH A CORIANDER SEED DRESSING

That old standby, Avocado and Grapefruit Salad, seemed ready for a refurbishing and this recipe does just that. The salad should be served as a luncheon course, as a first course at dinner, or as part of a buffet. It may be arranged on individual plates or on a large platter. Double or triple the recipe according to the number of guests. The dressing may be placed on the salad before serving, or for a buffet the dressing may be served from a bowl with the guests helping themselves.
Serves 4

1 cup Yogurt (see page 67)
2 teaspoons coriander seeds
¼ teaspoon salt
¼ teaspoon freshly ground white pepper
2 tablespoons lemon juice
⅓ cup olive oil

1 small head Boston lettuce
2 cups alfalfa sprouts (for growing instructions, see page 39)
2 medium, white grapefruits
2 large, ripe avocados

1. About 3 hours before you plan to make the salad, place the yogurt in a small sieve, lined with cheesecloth. Place the sieve over a bowl and refrigerate it. Let the whey drain from the yogurt. You should have approximately ½ cup of thickened yogurt and ⅓ cup of whey after draining.

2. When you are ready to make the salad, prepare the dressing first. (The avocados should be prepared last so that they will not darken.) Toast the coriander seeds in a small skillet over low heat for about 5 minutes to bring out their flavor. Grind the toasted seeds.

3. With a rubber spatula, scrape the thickened yogurt into a small bowl. Whisk in the coriander seed, salt, white pepper, and lemon juice. In a slow, steady stream, add the olive oil, whisking constantly, until the dressing is smooth and thick.

4. Rinse the leaves of Boston lettuce and dry them either by patting them with paper towels or in a salad spinner. Tear the leaves into pieces small enough so that a knife will not be necessary at the table. Rearrange the leaves in an attractive manner circling the outsides of the individual plates or platter.

5. In the centers of the plates or platter, make a thin layer using 1 cup of the alfalfa sprouts, fluffing them apart as you do so.

6. Peel the grapefruits and carefully cut out the individual segments, making sure that they are free of any white pith or membrane. Place the segments in a sieve, placed over a bowl, to drain them of excess juice. Save the juice for another use.

Cut the avocados in half lengthwise. Remove the pits and peel the halves. Cut each half into 4 lengthwise slices.

7. Arrange the slices of grapefruit and avocado in an alternating pattern on top of the alfalfa sprouts on the plates or platter. Sprinkle the slices with the remaining 1 cup of sprouts, fluffing them out as before. Divide the dressing among the individual servings, spreading about 3 tablespoons of the dressing across the midsection of the sliced fruits.

If you are serving the salad on a platter, either spread all of the dressing on the sliced fruits, as suggested above, or serve it separately in a small bowl.

Note: For additional recipes using coriander seeds and yogurt, see the recipe index for Spring Endive Salad, Coriander Sauce, An Autumn Coleslaw, and Fresh Fruit with a Yogurt and Coriander Sauce.

SPAGHETTI SQUASH SALAD

Noting the crunchiness of leftover cooked spaghetti squash, we felt it would make an unusual salad and it does. Not only is it an unexpected ingredient for a salad, it is very festive looking, fit for a holiday occasion as part of a party buffet.

Make the salad one day ahead so that the spaghetti squash will be very crisp and will have absorbed the flavor of the vinaigrette dressing. Double the recipe if there is a larger crowd.

Serves 8 to 10

2½-pound spaghetti squash
½ cup roasted red peppers, cut into thin, 1-inch-long julienne strips
1 small onion, coarsely chopped
2 medium stalks celery, coarsely chopped
½ cup finely chopped parsley
1 teaspoon dry mustard
½ teaspoon salt
¼ teaspoon freshly ground white pepper
2 tablespoons white wine vinegar
1 large clove garlic, minced
⅓ cup olive oil

1. To cook the squash, preheat the oven to 350°F. Line a heavy baking sheet that has sides with aluminum foil. Place the squash on the baking sheet and pierce it with a fork in 8 or 9 places. Bake the squash, whole, for 1 to 1½ hours. The time will depend upon the age of the squash. When it is done, the fork will easily pierce the outer shell.

2. Remove the baking sheet from the oven and when the squash is cool enough to handle, cut it in half lengthwise. Remove the seeds and fiber.

With a tablespoon, scrape out the flesh, which is the "spaghetti," in a bowl. If the stem is still attached, use it as a "handle" to hold the squash. Fluff the spaghetti as you remove it. There should be 6 or more cups.

Add the red pepper, onion, celery, and parsley. Toss just enough to mix the vegetables.

3. Prepare the vinaigrette dressing. In a small bowl, mix the dry mustard, salt, and white pepper. Add the vinegar and garlic. Whisk until the dry ingredients have dissolved.

In a thin, steady stream, begin adding the olive oil, whisking constantly, until all the oil has been added and the dressing is thick and smooth.

4. Pour the sauce over the vegetables and toss again, using two forks to fluff up the spaghetti. Cover with plastic wrap and refrigerate overnight. Toss once again before the salad is served. The salad will remain crisp for 3 or 4 days.

SPAGHETTI SQUASH SALAD WITH ORANGES AND ALMONDS

This second recipe for a spaghetti squash salad is as convivial as our first. It, too, goes well with traditional holiday fare such as turkey and ham.

We use only half a baked squash in this dish, but if you wish to serve a larger gathering, double the recipe. The salad must be made at least one day ahead, and it can be made 2 or 3 days ahead if kept covered and refrigerated. Refrigerate or freeze any remaining squash to use for a Spaghetti Squash and Sprout Frittata (see page 295).

Serves 4 to 6

2½- to 3-pound spaghetti squash
1 medium red onion, sliced thin
1 cup coarsely chopped celery
3 medium oranges, peeled, cut into ¼-inch crosswise slices, and
    seeded
½ cup Mother's Salad Dressing (see page 197)
1 cup slivered almonds

1. Preheat the oven to 350°F.

2. Line a heavy baking sheet that has sides with aluminum foil. Place the spaghetti squash on the baking sheet and pierce it with a fork in 8 or 9 places. Bake the squash for 1 to 1½ hours. The fork should easily pierce the outer shell when it is done.

3. When it is tender, remove the baking sheet from the oven and let the squash cool until it can be handled. Cut the squash in half lengthwise and remove the seeds and fiber around the seeds.

With a tablespoon, scrape the "spaghetti" from the shell in a bowl, fluffing the threads as you go.

4. Place the onion, celery, and orange slices in another bowl. Measure 3 cups of the spaghetti and add it to the bowl. Pour on the salad dressing and toss.

Cover with plastic wrap and refrigerate for at least 12 hours so that the squash will be very crisp. Reserve the remaining squash for another recipe (see above).

5. On the day that you serve the salad, toast the slivered almonds. You may do this on a baking sheet in a preheated 225° F oven for about 15 minutes or in a skillet over low heat on top of the stove. Stir the almonds as they toast so that they do not burn. They should be golden brown in color.

6. Arrange the salad on a serving platter and sprinkle the almonds on top. If you wish to garnish the salad with lettuce, use Boston or another pale variety to pick up the color of the celery.

WINTER ENDIVE SALAD

Along about the middle of January there isn't much left in our garden, and what there is, we are tired of. Our hunger for fresh greens and even a store-bought waxed cucumber drives us to the supermarket. There, to our delight, is an abundance of vegetables from warmer climates — green curled endive, firm red onions, and perfect avocados. We go overboard and buy everything in sight. Six avocados at a time! These salads bring a little spring to our winter meals. Of course, in May we will feel nothing equals those first spring greens we pick.

Serves 4 to 6

¾ pound curly leaf endive
1 large red onion
½ pound cucumbers
1 large, ripe avocado
1½ cups mung-bean sprouts (for growing instructions, see page 39)
2 tablespoons lemon juice
½ teaspoon salt
2 tablespoons olive oil

1. Rinse the endive and dry it with paper towels. Remove any blemished areas and cut the endive leaves into 1½-inch lengths. Place the endive in a large salad bowl.

2. Peel the red onion and cut it in half lengthwise and then crosswise, into ⅛-inch-thick slices. Add the onion to the salad bowl and toss to mix.

3. If the cucumbers are waxed, peel them. Cut the cucumbers into ¼-inch-thick rounds, and add them to the salad bowl, and toss again. (Tossing the bulkier ingredients as you add them makes for better distribution and a crisper salad. Too much tossing after the dressing is added often wilts the ingredients and makes them seem soggy.)

4. Cut the avocado in half lengthwise. Remove the pit and peel the halves. Cut each half into 4 to 6 long slices. Add them to the salad bowl, but do *not* toss.

Add the mung-bean sprouts to the salad and sprinkle the salad with the lemon juice.

5. If you plan to serve the salad right away, sprinkle with the salt and add the olive oil. Toss very gently and serve.

If you are not serving the salad immediately, cover the bowl tightly with plastic wrap and place it in the refrigerator. The lemon juice will prevent the avocado from darkening. Just before serving, add the salt and olive oil and toss gently.

SPRING SALADS

SALAD OF LEAF LETTUCE

In May, when the leaf lettuces have been thinned, the heads become luxurious. The most beautiful is the Ruby, which we plant as we would a bed of flowers. It is too early for much else in the garden, so we make a salad of leaf lettuce and spring onions along with a little celery and sprouts for texture.

The salads can include only one variety of lettuce or a combination of several. With the Ruby lettuce, we use immature Red Hamburger onions for a salad ablaze with color. The dressing should be light, as the flavors of leaf lettuces are subtle.

Serves 4 to 6

1 pound leaf lettuce (Ruby, Royal Oak Leaf, Black Seeded Simpson)
3 or 4 very small spring onions
1 cup coarsely chopped celery
1 cup alfalfa sprouts (for growing instructions, see page 39)
½ teaspoon dry mustard
½ teaspoon salt
¼ teaspoon freshly ground white pepper
2 tablespoons lemon juice
4 tablespoons olive oil
3 tablespoons Yogurt (see page 67)

1. Wash the leaf lettuce carefully, as it is fragile. Pull the leaves from the base and lay them on paper towels to drain. Pat dry.

Tear the leaves into 3- to 4-inch pieces and place them in a salad bowl.

2. Chop the spring onions, including some of the green tops, into small pieces after first removing the root ends. Add the onions, celery, and alfalfa sprouts to the lettuce and toss to mix.

3. Prepare the dressing by dissolving the dry mustard, salt, and white pepper in the lemon juice. Whisk in the olive oil and, when it is thoroughly combined, whisk in the yogurt.

4. The moment you are ready to serve the salad, pour the dressing over it and toss gently until the leaf lettuce is thinly and evenly coated. Once the dressing is added, the salad must be served immediately, as the lettuce can quickly wilt under the weight of even a light dressing.

A Salad of Thinnings from the Garden

This salad is perhaps enjoyed more than any other during the year, if only because it announces the arrival of spring. The young leaves from our lettuces with the first radishes and spring onions seem unrivaled.

Since it is almost impossible to space lettuce seeds so they require no thinning, we allow the plants to grow thickly until they are about 4 or more inches tall. Then we thin them by pulling the extra plants and using them for salads. The combinations are almost endless since we grow so many varieties. One day it might be a salad of Ruby, a few beet top greens, and Roquette (Arugula), and another day, Boston, Bibb, and Royal Oak Leaf. Other days, we might combine them all.

The important thing to remember is to treat the thinnings as the tender plants they are and not to overpower them with a heavy dressing.

Serves 4 to 6

1 pound young salad thinnings of any combination
3 or 4 small spring onions
1 dozen small radishes
½ teaspoon salt
¼ cup olive oil
2 tablespoons lemon juice

1. Wash the greens and remove the root ends if you have pulled whole plants. Dry the leaves. If they are very tender, this might best be done by gently patting them with paper towels. Cut or tear the leaves into 2½-inch pieces and place them in a large salad bowl.

2. Cut the root ends from the spring onions. Slice the onions, including the green tops, into ¼-inch pieces. Trim the ends from the radishes and slice them as thin as possible. Add the onions and radishes to the salad bowl. Toss just to mix.

3. Sprinkle the salad with salt. Pour on the olive oil, distributing it evenly. Then add the lemon juice. Toss gently and serve.

A SIMPLE SPRING SPINACH SALAD

Except for the avocado, this salad is composed of the first spring crops from our garden. Our fall sowing of Melody and/or Bloomsdale spinach is making a healthy showing along with the first spring onions and radishes. We plant Red Hamburger onions to grow to a medium size, but we always pull a dozen or so early to use as spring onions.

Our radishes are Crimson Giant. They are so tasty and so perfect in shape that usually we serve them unadorned except for a tiny dish of coarse salt to dip them into. Serve this simple spinach salad with crusty bread and bowls of ripe and green olives alongside.

Serves 4 to 6

1 pound fresh spinach (leaves only)
1 dozen large radishes
3 or 4 small spring onions or 1 small onion
1 large, ripe avocado
3 tablespoons lemon juice
½ teaspoon salt
¼ teaspoon freshly ground white pepper
⅓ cup olive oil

1. Wash the spinach and remove the stems. Dry the leaves, either by patting them with paper towels or in a salad spinner. If the leaves are very large, tear them in half. Place the leaves in a large salad bowl.

2. Remove the ends from the radishes. Cut into thin slices and add them to the salad bowl. Trim the ends from the spring onions and cut them crosswise into ¼-inch slices, using some of the green tops. (If you are using a small onion, peel and slice it thin.) Add the onions to the salad bowl and toss the ingredients.

3. Cut the avocado in half lengthwise and remove the peel. Discard the pit and cut each half into 6 lengthwise slices. Add to the salad bowl.

Immediately sprinkle the slices with the lemon juice, followed by the salt and white pepper. Pour the olive oil over the surface and toss gently. Serve as soon as possible so that the spinach will not have time to wilt or the avocado to darken.

SPINACH SALAD WITH SPROUTS AND CHEESE

We sow spinach seeds late every summer, hoping for a fall crop. Although our harvest is never abundant, the plants winter over and we are rewarded with spinach as the first green ready for spring picking.

A more classic spinach and cheese salad would use feta cheese, but we have found our Pressed Cottage Cheese works admirably. If we wish to make this salad in the winter, we buy fresh spinach packaged by Too Goo Doo Farms, Yonges Island, S. C. Who can resist such a fetching name?

Serves 4 to 6

1 pound fresh spinach
4 or 5 small spring onions, or 1 medium white or red onion
1 cup mung-bean sprouts (for growing instructions, see page 39)
6 ounces Pressed Cottage Cheese (see page 95) or feta cheese
1 teaspoon dry mustard
¼ teaspoon freshly ground black pepper
1 small clove garlic, minced
2 tablespoons red wine vinegar
1 tablespoon soy sauce
⅓ cup olive oil

1. Wash the spinach and remove the stems. Dry the leaves either by patting them with paper towels or in a salad spinner. Tear the leaves into 2½-inch pieces and place them in a large salad bowl.

2. If you are using spring onions, remove the root ends and chop the onions coarsely, including most of the green tops. If you are using a regular onion, slice it ⅛ inch thick and separate the slices into rings.

3. Add the onions and the mung-bean sprouts to the spinach and toss just to mix. Cut the cheese into cubes about ½ inch square and add to the salad, but do not toss.

4. Prepare the dressing. In a small bowl, whisk together the dry mustard, black pepper, garlic, red wine vinegar, and soy sauce.

When the mustard has dissolved, add the olive oil in a steady stream, whisking constantly, until the dressing is smooth. Do not add salt, as the soy sauce replaces it.

5. Pour the dressing over the salad and toss gently but thoroughly. The cheese may break up a bit, but it should not become softened by too heavy a tossing.

A SEASONAL TOSSED SALAD

Although the ingredients for this salad vary from season to season they are always of top quality and, if not, they are eliminated. In winter, tomatoes are out, so we increase the amounts of the other ingredients slightly. But in the very late spring, we are able to savor that most luscious of fruits in our tossed salads.

We do not specify the variety of salad green, as it should be whatever is freshest and in season. Use a combination of greens for a contrast in taste and texture. We like to combine curly leaf endive (chicory) with a milder-flavored green. Although we enjoy carrots in other salads, they are not appropriate here. Nor do we feel wine vinegar should be used in place of the lemon juice in the dressing.

Do not cut your ingredients into tiny pieces, as is too often done in tossed salads. A simple tossed salad should have substance.

Serves 4 to 6

1 large bell pepper
2 medium stalks celery
1 small onion, sliced thin
2 medium unwaxed pickling cucumbers, sliced thin
½ pound fresh salad greens (see above)
2 ripe tomatoes
1 large avocado
1 cup alfalfa or mung-bean sprouts (optional; for growing
    instructions, see page 39)
1 tablespoon finely chopped fresh basil or snipped dill (if available)
½ teaspoon salt, or to taste
¼ cup olive oil
2 tablespoons lemon juice

1. Core and seed the bell pepper. Cut it into chunks just a little over 1 inch in diameter. Trim the ends of the celery stalks and cut the stalks into ½-inch crosswise slices. Use the green leaves of the celery stalks, if they are still very fresh. Place the pepper and celery in a large salad bowl along with the onion and cucumbers. Toss to mix the ingredients. (We use our hands.)

2. Tear the salad greens into chunks no smaller than 2 inches in diameter. Add to the salad bowl and toss the ingredients again.

3. Core the tomatoes and cut each tomato into 8 wedges. Halve the avocado and discard the pit. Peel and cut each half into 4 lengthwise slices. Add the tomatoes and avocado to the bowl along with the sprouts and fresh herb.

4. Sprinkle the salad ingredients with the salt. Pour the olive oil over the surface and then the lemon juice. Toss the salad, using a wooden salad spoon and fork, just to coat the ingredients with the dressing. Serve immediately.

Note: The salad may be prepared ahead up to Step 3 and refrigerated for a few hours, if it is tightly covered with plastic wrap. Do not add the tomatoes or avocado until serving time.

SPRING COLESLAW

The ingredients in this coleslaw are delicately balanced so that the incomparable freshness of each can be savored. The cabbage (Early Jersey Wakefield for us), onions, and peas are still young and at their peak for flavor. The parsley and tarragon plants are sporting their youngest, most fragrant leaves.

Serves 4 to 6

1 teaspoon dry mustard
½ teaspoon salt
¼ teaspoon freshly ground white pepper
2 tablespoons white wine vinegar
⅓ cup olive oil
½ cup Yogurt (see page 67)
2 cups fresh garden peas (2 pounds before shelling) or ½ pound sugar snap peas
2-pound head young cabbage
3 or 4 spring onions or 1 small onion, chopped fine
1 cup finely chopped parsley, tightly packed
1 tablespoon finely snipped fresh tarragon leaves

1. In a small bowl, prepare the dressing for the coleslaw. Mix together the dry mustard, salt, and white pepper. Whisk in the wine vinegar. In a slow, steady stream, add the olive oil, whisking constantly, until the mixture is smooth and thick. Whisk in the yogurt. The dressing will thin when the yogurt is added. Set aside.

2. Prepare the peas. If you are using fresh garden peas, cook them for only 1 minute in lightly salted, boiling water. Drain immedi-

ately and run cold water over the peas to stop the cooking process and to preserve the color.

If you are using sugar snap peas, string them and cut them into 1-inch pieces. They will be used raw. Set the peas aside.

3. Discard any tough or blemished outer leaves from the cabbage. Quarter the cabbage and remove the core. Shred each quarter fine by hand, using a chef's knife. (Do not use a food processor for this particular coleslaw.

The chef's knife will give the desired crisply cut edge.)

4. Place the shredded cabbage in a large salad bowl. Add the onions, parsley, tarragon, and sugar snap peas, if you are using them. Toss the ingredients, using your hands. Add the dressing and toss again, this time with wooden spoons. If you are using garden peas, add them after tossing in the onions, parsley, and tarragon. At the same time, add the dressing and toss. The coleslaw may be served either right away or several hours later after it has been slightly chilled. The salad will be at its prime for only 1 day. After that, the vegetables will begin to lose their sweetness.

SPRING ENDIVE SALAD

Curly leaf endive (sometimes called chicory lettuce) and alfalfa sprouts tossed with a coriander seed dressing form an ingenious alliance for a spring salad. We like the addition of the sliced avocado, but only if the avocado is still of a superior quality. Do not use one if it has become "bready" in texture as sometimes happens as the weather warms.

Serves 4 to 6

3 teaspoons coriander seeds
½ cup Yogurt (see page 67)
½ cup homemade Mayonnaise (see pages 195 and 196)
2 tablespoons lemon juice
¼ teaspoon salt
¼ teaspoon freshly ground white pepper
¾ pound curly leaf endive
3 cups alfalfa sprouts (for growing instructions, see page 39)
6 small spring onions or 1 medium onion
1 large avocado

1. In a small skillet over low heat, toast the coriander seeds for about 5 minutes to bring out their flavor. Stir so that they do not burn. Grind the seeds.

2. In a small bowl, prepare the salad dressing. Whisk together the yogurt and mayonnaise until the mixture is smooth. Add the ground coriander seed, lemon juice, salt, and white pepper. Whisk again and set the dressing aside.

3. Cut the leaves of the endive into 1½-inch pieces and place them in a large salad bowl. Add the alfalfa sprouts, pulling the threads apart to fluff them. Remove the root ends and any core from the spring onions. Slice them thin, using most of the green tops. If you are using a regular onion, peel and slice it thin. Add the onions to the salad bowl. Toss the ingredients with your hands.

4. Cut the avocado in half lengthwise. Peel the

halves and remove the pit. Cut each half into 6 long slices. Add the slices to the salad and toss once more with your hands.

5. Pour the dressing over the salad and toss, this time with your salad fork and spoon. Serve immediately.

Note: The salad and the dressing can be made ahead, covered and refrigerated, but do not cut or add the avocado until just before you plan to serve.

SPRING POTATO SALAD

Fresh tarragon or fresh basil used in a salad of "new" potatoes show off their special affinity for the vegetable. Use either herb but not a combination of the two. In fact, the flavor each imparts to the salad is so different, this recipe could be considered as two.

Serves 4 to 6

3 pounds medium-size "new" or boiling potatoes
5 tablespoons dill pickle juice
1 cup coarsely chopped celery
1 cup coarsely chopped onions
2 tablespoons finely chopped fresh tarragon or 3 tablespoons finely chopped fresh basil
½ cup coarsely chopped dill pickles
1 tablespoon capers
¼ teaspoon freshly ground black pepper
½ cup homemade Mayonnaise (see page 195 and 196)
Additional pickles for garnish (optional)

1. Wash but do not peel the potatoes. Steam them for about ½ hour until they are just tender. The time will depend upon the size and freshness of the potatoes. "New" potatoes will cook very quickly.

2. Cover the bottom of a shallow dish with 3 tablespoons of the dill pickle juice.

3. When the potatoes are tender, immediately remove them from the heat. When they have cooled slightly, make a small slit with a knife around the middle of each potato. Peel back the skin from the slit.

As the potatoes are peeled, place them, uncut, in the shallow dish. Gently move them about in the pickle juice to absorb the liquid.

4. When the potatoes have cooled to room temperature, cut them into smaller pieces. We find this cooling period before cutting helps to keep the potatoes from breaking apart as the salad is mixed. If you are lucky enough to have

very small potatoes, there is no need to cut them. In any case, do not cut them into pieces smaller than 1½ inches in diameter.

5. Add the chopped celery, onions, and the herb to the potatoes and toss to mix.

6. In a small bowl, prepare the dressing by combining the chopped pickles, capers, black pepper, and the remaining 2 tablespoons of pickle juice with the mayonnaise. Pour the dressing over the salad and gently toss until the vegetables are evenly coated. Since the pickles and capers are salty, we do not add any salt.

7. The salad may be kept under refrigeration until you are ready to serve, but bring it back to room temperature before serving.

To serve, transfer the salad to a serving dish and garnish it with additional slices of pickles or more chopped basil, if you are using basil as your herb. Do not use additional tarragon, as the flavor is too powerful.

HERBED POTATO SALAD

For this spring potato salad, the freshness and flavor of the potatoes must be the best. If you are a grower or can buy Red Pontiac or Lady Finger potatoes (available from Gurney Seed; see the mail-order listings) they are recommended. The dressing for the salad is light and the herbs are at their tenderest and sweetest in the spring so that the potatoes are in no way camouflaged. Even parsley is dispensed with!

Serves 4 to 6

3 pounds potatoes (see above)
1 teaspoon salt
1 teaspoon freshly ground white pepper
1 teaspoon dry mustard
1 teaspoon finely minced garlic
¼ cup white wine vinegar
½ cup olive oil
½ cup Yogurt (see page 67)
¼ pound small, sweet onions, sliced thin
4 tablespoons finely chopped fresh basil
3 tablespoons finely snipped fresh chives
2 tablespoons finely snipped fresh dill leaves
2 tablespoons finely snipped fresh tarragon leaves

1. Wash the potatoes. Steam them until they are just tender, but not soft. The time will depend upon the size and freshness of the potatoes.

2. While the potatoes are steaming, prepare the salad dressing. In a small bowl, combine the salt, pepper, dry mustard, and garlic. Whisk in the vinegar.

In a slow, steady stream, whisk in the olive oil until the mixture is smooth and thick. Whisk in the yogurt. The dressing will thin when the yogurt is added.

Pour approximately one third of the dressing into a large, shallow dish and set aside the rest.

3. As soon as the potatoes are tender, remove them from the heat and drain them to prevent further cooking. Peeling the potatoes is optional. If the skins are very thin and in good condition, we do not peel them. Place the whole potatoes, peeled or unpeeled, into the dish with the dressing. Let them cool briefly—about 5 minutes—before cutting them.

If you have firm, waxy potatoes, cut them into ¼-inch slices. If they do not slice well, cut them into chunks about 1½ inches in diameter. As you cut the potatoes, gently move them about so that they will absorb the dressing.

4. Add the sliced onions and the remainder of the dressing to the dish. Toss the ingredients thoroughly. Add the herbs and toss once again, this time more gently.

5. Transfer the salad to a salad bowl or platter. Serve at room temperature.

STRING BEAN AND MUSHROOM SALAD

Use only the freshest string beans for this salad and cook them for such a short amount of time that none of the crunchiness is lost. The mushrooms must be pure white and very firm. The dressing is light so that the flavors of both vegetables can be appreciated.

For individual portions, serve the salad on lettuce leaves that have been sprinkled with a little salt, black pepper, and lemon juice. Boston lettuce would be our first choice.

Serves 4 to 6

1 pound fresh string beans
1 teaspoon salt
¼ teaspoon freshly ground black pepper
1 teaspoon dry mustard
3 tablespoons lemon juice
1 small clove garlic, minced
⅓ cup olive oil
1 medium onion, sliced thin

1 dozen radishes, sliced thin
1 cup chopped parsley, loosely packed
½ cup mung-bean sprouts (for growing instructions, see page 39)
½ pound fresh, medium-size mushrooms
¼ cup snipped fresh dill leaves (if available)

1. Bring a large pot of water to a boil. String the beans, if necessary, and snip off the ends. Rinse.

When the water comes to a rapid boil, add ½ teaspoon of the salt. When the water returns to a boil, add the string beans. Cook for only 3 minutes.

Drain promptly and run cold water over the beans to stop the cooking process and to preserve the color. Drain the beans on a towel.

2. Prepare the salad dressing in your salad bowl. Dissolve the remaining ½ teaspoon of salt, black pepper, and dry mustard in the lemon juice.

Add the minced garlic and whisk in the olive oil in a steady stream until the dressing is smooth.

3. Cut the string beans into 2-inch lengths and add them to the salad bowl. Separate the

onion slices into rings as you add them to the bowl. Add the radishes, parsley, and mung-bean sprouts.

Remove the stem ends from the mushrooms, then wipe them with damp paper towels. Slice them thin and add to the salad, along with the snipped dill, if it is available. Toss the salad so that it is coated with the dressing.

FAVA BEAN SALAD

Although you might not think of flat beans as typical in a spring salad, fava beans are the exception. They must be planted early as they do not fare well in summer heat. We plant ours the last week of February and they are ready to harvest by the first week of June.

Fava beans, sometimes known as English broadbeans, are not very popular as a market vegetable, although they can often be found in Italian specialty markets. For the home gardener, they are easy to grow and have a flavor that is sweeter than a lima bean.

Serve this salad as part of a cold supper, on a buffet table, or carry it on a picnic. Arrange the salad either in a bowl or on a platter and surround it with leaves of spring lettuce.

Serves 4 to 6

3 ounces pancetta (Italian bacon, see page 54)
1 tablespoon olive oil plus ⅓ cup
2 large green bell peppers
1 teaspoon dry mustard
¼ teaspoon salt
¼ teaspoon freshly ground black pepper
4 tablespoons lemon juice (about 1 lemon)
1 teaspoon minced garlic
4 cups fava beans (about 4 pounds before shelling)
2 cups coarsely chopped celery
3 or 4 spring onions, including most of the green tops, sliced thin, or
    1 medium onion, chopped coarse
3 jalapeño peppers, fresh or canned, minced fine but not seeded
3 tablespoons minced fresh basil, if available (Do not use dried.)
¼ cup finely chopped fresh parsley
¼ cup finely chopped celery leaves

1. Cut the pancetta into ¼-inch dice. Place 1 tablespoon of the olive oil in a 10-inch skillet over low heat. Add the pancetta and sauté the dice until they are rendered of their fat and have lightly browned.

2. Core and seed the bell peppers and cut them into 1-inch julienne strips, ¼ inch in diameter. (If you are using frozen peppers, let them defrost a little on paper towels before cutting.)

When the pancetta has lightly browned, add the bell peppers to the skillet. Toss and increase the heat to medium low. Sauté the peppers for 15 minutes, tossing frequently so that they do not brown. Remove the skillet from the heat to cool briefly.

3. While the pancetta and peppers are sautéing, prepare the salad dressing in your salad bowl. Dissolve the dry mustard, salt, and black pepper in the lemon juice. Add the minced garlic.

In a slow, steady stream, whisk in the remaining ⅓ cup of olive oil. Whisk until the dressing is smooth and thick.

4. In a 2-quart saucepan, bring 1 quart of lightly salted water to a boil. Add the fava beans, cover and simmer over medium-high heat until they are barely tender. They should not become soft.

If the beans are very young and under 1 inch in length, this will take from 5 to 7 minutes. (If you are using frozen beans, let them defrost before cooking; again, the cooking time will be only about 5 minutes.) Drain the beans in a sieve and run cold water over them to stop the cooking process.

5. Add the drained fava beans to the salad dressing. Toss just to coat the beans with the dressing. Add the celery, onions, jalapeño peppers, basil, parsley, and celery leaves. Toss again.

Remove the pancetta and bell peppers from the skillet with a slotted spoon, leaving behind any fat or oil, and add them to the salad. Toss again, this time more thoroughly. Serve the salad at room temperature.

COTTAGE CHEESE WITH VEGETABLES AND HERBS

This versatile salad is welcome during the spring months as the garden begins to bear its first vegetables. It keeps very well, so we try to have a pot on hand in the refrigerator for easy lunches, arranging the salad on a platter and garnishing it with olives and dill pickles. Often we spread the cheese on slices of freshly made bread for open-faced sandwiches.

Serves 4 to 6

1 recipe homemade Cottage Cheese (see page 88)
12 radishes, chopped fine
5 tablespoons finely chopped celery
3 tablespoons finely chopped red onion
1 tablespoon finely chopped jalapeño pepper, fresh or canned
2 tablespoons minced fresh parsley
2 tablespoons minced fresh dill
2 tablespoons minced fresh chives
¾ cup alfalfa or mung-bean sprouts (for growing instructions, see page 39)
½ teaspoon salt
½ teaspoon freshly ground white pepper

1. Crumble the Cottage Cheese into a mixing bowl. Add all the ingredients to the cottage cheese, reserving ¼ cup of the sprouts and 1 tablespoon of one of the minced herbs for garnish. Thoroughly but gently mix the ingredients with a fork, being careful not to cream the cottage cheese.

2. Arrange the salad on a platter, individual plates, or in a pot as suggested above. Sprinkle with the remaining ¼ cup of sprouts and the reserved tablespoon of minced herb.

A LUNCHEON PRESENTATION

Later in the season, add finely chopped cucumbers to this salad. Drain the chopped cucumbers in a sieve for ½ hour before adding to the salad to rid them of excess liquid. Add finely chopped bell peppers (any color), a bit of chopped tomato, and use fresh basil as one of your herbs. Use your own judgment as to the amount of each addition.

For a more elegant presentation of this salad, prepare individual plates, surrounding the cheese with leaves of spring lettuce. Ruby lettuce is our first choice as it picks up the red of the radishes and onion. Garnish the salads with ripe olives and slices of pickle and top them with more sprouts, a dollop of homemade Mayonnaise, and a sprinkling of a fresh, minced herb.

Summer Salads

Ripe Tomato Salads

All of the hard work in the garden is forgotten once we begin to harvest our first ripe tomatoes. For the first few days, we cut them into thick slices or wedges and eat them just as they are. Perhaps after three or four days we will lightly salt them with coarse salt, and only after a week will we think of adding other ingredients to make a full-fledged salad.

Rather than giving individual recipes for tomato salads, we are offering suggestions for serving. If you have wonderful, ripe tomatoes, feature them, making the other ingredients secondary. There will be too many months when the taste of summer tomatoes will be only memory. Allow 1 large tomato (6 to 8 ounces) per person.

1. Tomatoes are perhaps most attractive when arranged on a platter. Core and peel the tomatoes (if you must) and cut them into ½-inch slices. Arrange the slices in an overlapping fashion around the platter. Garnish the slices with a chopped fresh herb (basil is our choice). The dressing can be as simple as just salt, olive oil, and lemon juice, or prepare a light vinaigrette dressing. Mother's Salad Dressing (see page 197) would be an affinitive choice.

Additional garnishes could be a handful or so of fluffed alfalfa sprouts or mung-bean sprouts. Ripe and green olives are especially good with tomatoes.

2. For a more elaborate arrangement, alternate the tomato slices with thin slices of Pressed Cottage Cheese (see page 95), thin sliced rings of red onion, and thin rings of bell peppers (any color).

3. For a more assertive dressing serve Pesto (see page 309) thinned with additional olive oil so that it can be spooned over the tomato slices.

4. The thicker pesto can be used as a stuffing for hollowed-out and drained cherry tomatoes. They make very tasty hors d'oeuvres. For larger tomatoes, core and cut them in half crosswise. Drain the halves, cut side down, on paper towels for ½ hour to remove excess liquid. Spread the halves with a thin layer of the pesto.

Both the cherry tomatoes and tomato halves can be placed under a broiler and then served as a vegetable course. Preheat the broiler. Arrange the stuffed tomatoes or tomato halves spread with pesto in a lightly oiled gratin dish. Place the gratin dish about 6 inches under the broiler and broil the tomatoes for 5 to 10 minutes, depending upon their size. The tomatoes should be heated through and the tops bubbling. Do not let the pesto burn.

5. Tomatoes, cut into thick wedges, are best in a tossed salad. The salad can be entirely of tomatoes with any of the simple dressings already suggested, or add thinly sliced onions, bell peppers, and cucumbers.

Marinated Cucumbers with Dill

Almost to the day, we seem to pick our first crop of cucumbers on the first day of summer. Salting and allowing the cucumbers to drain for ½ hour before making the salad not only crisps them, but removes bitterness. Keep in mind that the bitterness in cucumbers is concentrated near the stem end, so always slice your cucumbers from the blossom end and discard the last ½ inch near the stem if it seems bitter. Toss the marinated cucumbers with salad greens, add radishes and sprouts, or serve it in Pita (see pages 172 and 174).

Serves 4 to 6

1¼ pounds unwaxed cucumbers
1 teaspoon salt
1 medium onion
3 tablespoons snipped fresh dill
½ teaspoon sugar
¼ teaspoon freshly ground white pepper
2 tablespoons white wine vinegar
¼ cup olive oil

1. Wash and scrub the cucumbers. Do not peel, but cut them into ⅛-inch slices. Place the slices in a colander or sieve.

Sprinkle them with the salt and let stand for ½ hour. Toss occasionally during this time.

2. In the meantime, peel the onion and cut it in half lengthwise and then crosswise into ⅛-inch slices.

With a pair of kitchen shears, snip the dill fine.

3. Prepare the salad dressing by whisking together the sugar, white pepper, and vinegar. Whisk in the olive oil slowly so that the dressing is smooth.

4. After ½ hour, pat the cucumber slices with paper towels to dry them. There is no need to rinse the slices as no further salt is added to the salad.

Place the slices in a medium-size salad bowl. Add the onion and dill. Pour on the dressing and toss the ingredients well.

5. Cover the salad bowl with plastic wrap and chill for several hours before serving. Because of the preliminary salting, the salad will actually stay crisp for several days.

The salad may be served as a salad course on a bed of lettuce or it makes an excellent dish as part of a cold buffet. An even nicer idea is to serve it as part of a summer picnic.

EARLY SUMMER COLESLAW

This coleslaw is especially good in the early summer. We grow Early Jersey Wakefield cabbage, as the flavor is finer and the leaves more tender than most cabbages. It is easy to distinguish at the market with its pointed head.

At the same time that the cabbage is at its prime, we have our first carrots, cucumbers, and fresh dill, but it is still too early for bell peppers or tomatoes.

Serves 6 to 8

1 tablespoon dry mustard
1 teaspoon salt
¼ teaspoon freshly ground white pepper
½ teaspoon freshly ground dried hot red pepper
3 tablespoons lemon juice
1 small clove garlic, minced
½ cup olive oil
2-pound cabbage
2 cups carrots
3 medium-size unwaxed cucumbers
1 small onion
2 cups alfalfa sprouts (for growing instructions, see page 39)
1 tablespoon snipped fresh dill leaves

1. Prepare the dressing by placing the dry mustard, salt, white pepper, and red pepper in a small bowl. Add the lemon juice and garlic and whisk until the dry ingredients dissolve.

Add the olive oil in a slow, steady stream, whisking constantly. The dressing should be smooth and thick. Set aside.

2. Remove the tough outer leaves from the cabbage. Cut the cabbage into quarters lengthwise, and remove the core. Shred the cabbage fine, either with a chef's knife, a cabbage cutter, or a food processor.

If using a food processor, cut the cabbage into pieces to fit the feed tube and fit the machine with the medium shredder. Place the shredded cabbage in a large salad bowl.

3. Peel and shred the carrots, using the coarse side of a grater or, again, the medium shredder of the processor.

Wash, but do not peel the cucumbers. Slice them into ¼-inch rounds. Peel and slice the onion thin.

Add the carrots, cucumbers, and onion to the cabbage along with the alfalfa sprouts and dill leaves.

4. Toss the salad lightly, making sure that the alfalfa sprouts are separated from each other. Add the dressing and toss again.

The salad may be served at this time or covered with plastic wrap and refrigerated overnight.

A MIDSUMMER COLESLAW

Prepare this coleslaw the day before you plan to serve it so that the flavors have time to mingle, but add the tomatoes just before serving. With tomatoes, cucumbers, and peppers at their best and a few heads of cabbage still in the garden, this makes a perfect coleslaw for a late July or August picnic. The fresh dill leaves can be tricky to grow in the summer heat, so if the plants have gone to seed, we substitute fresh basil.

Serves 6 to 8

¾ pound small unwaxed pickling cucumbers
1 teaspoon salt
1 teaspoon sugar
½ teaspoon freshly ground white pepper
1 small clove garlic, minced
2 tablespoons white wine vinegar
⅓ cup olive oil
½ cup Yogurt (see page 67)
2-pound cabbage
1 large bell pepper
¼ pound small, sweet onions, preferably from the garden
5 tablespoons snipped fresh dill leaves or 3 tablespoons finely
    chopped fresh basil
1 pound ripe tomatoes or ½ pound cherry tomatoes

1. Trim and discard the ends of the cucumbers. Slice the cucumbers into ⅛-inch-thick rounds and place them in a colander or sieve. Sprinkle with ½ teaspoon of the salt. Toss just to mix and let the cucumbers drain for ½ hour to draw out excess moisture.

2. Prepare the dressing for the coleslaw. In a small mixing bowl, combine the remaining ½ teaspoon of salt, sugar, white pepper, and garlic. Add the wine vinegar and whisk to mix. In a slow, steady stream, pour in the olive oil, whisking constantly, until the mixture is smooth and thick. Whisk in the yogurt. The dressing will thin when the yogurt is added. Set aside.

3. Discard any tough outer leaves from the cabbage, cut it into quarters lengthwise, and remove the core. Shred the cabbage fine, either with a chef's knife or a cabbage cutter. (A food processor shreds the cabbage too fine for this coleslaw.) Place the shredded cabbage in a large mixing bowl.

4. Core, seed, and halve the bell pepper. Cut each half into ¼-inch lengthwise strips. Cut the strips into 1½-inch lengths. Add to the cabbage in the mixing bowl. Pat the cucumber rounds dry with paper towels and toss them with the cabbage and bell pepper.

5. Peel and slice the onions thin. Add them to the mixing bowl along with the dill or basil. Toss again and pour on the dressing. Toss once more. Tightly cover the bowl and refrigerate the coleslaw for at least 12 hours before serving.

6. About 45 minutes before you are ready to serve the salad, core and seed the tomatoes. Chop them coarsely and let them drain in a colander or sieve for ½ hour to rid them of excess liquid. Just before serving, toss them with the coleslaw. (If you are using cherry tomatoes, they do not require draining. They may be added whole to the coleslaw if they are very small, or cut in half, if they are large.)

RED CABBAGE SALAD

Red cabbage, as spectacular as it is to look at, can be so assertive in a salad that it overwhelms any other ingredients. In experimenting, we have found that an anchovy dressing adds the needed tangy note. Also, red cabbage with its hard crispness can be difficult to munch if it is not very finely shredded. We find the medium shredding disk of a food processor perfect for shredding red cabbage.

   The variety of red cabbage that we grow in our garden is Ruby Ball Hybrid, which matures early, has a very small core, and seems impervious to cabbage worms. The salad will serve 4 to 6 as a salad course, or 6 to 8, if the salad is served as an accompaniment to a meat or fish course.

   Serves 4 to 6, or 6 to 8 (see above)

2-ounce tin flat filets of anchovies
1 teaspoon dry mustard
½ teaspoon freshly ground black pepper

½ teaspoon freshly ground dried hot red pepper
1 small clove garlic, minced
¼ cup red wine vinegar
¼ cup olive oil
½ cup Yogurt (see page 67)
2-pound head red cabbage
½ pound small, sweet onions, preferably red
2 tablespoons capers or 1 tablespoon Fresh Green Coriander Seeds
   (see page 57)
2 tablespoons finely snipped fresh tarragon leaves or 5 tablespoons
   finely chopped fresh basil

1. Prepare the salad dressing. Empty the tin of anchovies with its oil into a small mixing bowl. With the back of a fork, mash the filets into a pulp. Add the dry mustard, black and red peppers, and garlic to the bowl. Whisk in the vinegar.

    In a slow, steady stream, whisk in the olive oil until the dressing is smooth. Whisk in the yogurt. Set the dressing aside.

2. Discard any tough or damaged outer leaves from the cabbage, quarter it, and remove the core. Shred the cabbage fine in a food processor fitted with the medium shredding disk. If you do not have a food processor, shred the cabbage as fine as possible by hand. Place it in a large salad bowl.

3. Peel and slice the onions thin. If the onions are more than an inch in diameter, break the slices into rings. Add the onions to the salad bowl along with the capers or coriander seeds, and the tarragon or basil. (If the capers have been preserved in salt, you may wish to rinse away the salt, as the dressing is already salty from the anchovies.)

4. Toss the ingredients to mix and add the salad dressing. Toss once more to incorporate the dressing. The salad may be served right away or, tightly covered, it will keep for 24 hours under refrigeration. Serve the salad from the salad bowl or arrange it on a platter lined with lettuce leaves. Ruby lettuce will carry out the color scheme.

Note: When purchasing anchovies, read the label, as some brands require refrigeration. Having neglected to do this once and having lost several tins, we find it easier just to refrigerate all brands if they will not be used in a few days.

SUMMER HERBED POTATO SALAD

Some of the ingredients for this salad are the same as for the Spring Potato Salad, but with the addition of the season's fresh peas and a lighter dressing, it is an altogether different salad. The dressing is purposely more delicate so as not to conceal the sweet flavor of the fresh peas.

We have listed alternatives, but try to use the ingredients listed first. The alternatives may be used in another season when the fresh are not available. If you are substituting a dried herb for the fresh, use only 1 teaspoonful.

Serves 4 to 6

2½ pounds medium-size "new" or boiling potatoes
1 teaspoon dry mustard
1 teaspoon salt
½ teaspoon freshly ground black pepper
4 tablespoons lemon juice
1 small clove garlic, minced
½ cup olive oil
2 cups fresh peas (2 pounds before shelling) or one 10-ounce package
    of frozen, defrosted
½ cup thinly sliced spring onions or 2 small onions sliced thin
1 cup coarsely chopped celery
4 tablespoons fresh basil or dill, or 2 tablespoons fresh tarragon,
    chopped fine

1. Scrub the potatoes. If they are very new, they may peel themselves, which is so much the better.

Steam the potatoes until they are tender. This will depend upon the size and newness of the potatoes. The time could be from 15 minutes to ½ hour. Pierce with a fork to test.

2. While the potatoes are steaming, prepare the salad dressing and the other ingredients. In a small bowl, dissolve the dry mustard, salt, and black pepper in the lemon juice. Add the minced garlic.

Whisk and begin adding the olive oil in a steady stream, continuing to whisk until all of the oil is added. Add the oil slowly so that the dressing does not separate, but becomes very smooth and thick.

3. If you are using fresh peas, cook them in boiling water in a 2-quart saucepan for no more than 2 minutes. Drain immediately and run cold water over them to stop the cooking process.

If you are using defrosted frozen peas, place them in a small saucepan. Cover and cook over medium heat for about 3 minutes, just until they are heated through. There will be enough moisture in the peas so that no water need be added to the saucepan and no draining will be necessary afterward. Set aside.

4. When the potatoes are tender, remove them from the heat and drain.

As soon as you are able to handle them, make a small slit with a knife around their midsections. Peel back the skin from the slit. As the potatoes are peeled, place them, uncut, in a shallow dish. (A shallow dish will make the mixing easier and will not break up the potatoes.)

Pour the salad dressing over the potatoes and move them about to absorb some of the dressing before you add the other ingredients.

5. When the potatoes have cooled, cut them

into pieces no smaller than 1½ inches in diameter. Allowing the potatoes to cool first keeps them from falling apart when they are cut.

6. Add the peas, onions, celery, and herb to the potatoes and toss gently to mix thoroughly. Transfer the salad to your serving dish and serve at room temperature.

As fresh peas lose their special sweetness very quickly, do not make the salad more than a few hours before you will be serving it.

A SUMMER SALAD, RADIANT WITH MARIGOLD PETALS

Until recently, the only thing in our garden that we did not eat were our marigolds. However, once we found out that they were not poisonous, we had a field day preparing salads, as the color is magnificent when marigold petals are added to a salad. And they are quite tasty, too! This particular salad is actually two recipes, as the onions can be tossed with the dressing, basil, and marigold petals and served as a salad on its own. It is excellent with an Indian dinner.

We use our Red Hamburger onions when they are no larger than 1½ inches in diameter. They are very sweet when they are this small. Serve this luminescent salad as part of a buffet or as a first course at dinner.

Serves 4 to 6

½ teaspoon freshly ground white pepper
½ teaspoon freshly ground dried hot red pepper
1 teaspoon finely minced garlic
1 tablespoon finely chopped fresh ginger root
4 tablespoons lemon juice
1 tablespoon soy sauce
½ cup olive oil
1 pound small, sweet red onions
½ pound red leaf lettuce
3 unwaxed pickling cucumbers, approximately 3½ inches long
1 large, ripe mango (about 12 ounces)
1 large, ripe avocado (about 12 ounces)
1 cup orange marigold petals, loosely packed (about 1 large blossom)
½ cup finely chopped fresh basil, loosely packed
Additional marigold blossoms for garnish (optional)

1. Prepare the salad dressing. In a small mixing bowl, combine the white and red peppers, garlic, and ginger root. Whisk in the lemon juice and soy sauce. In a slow, steady stream, whisk in the olive oil until the dressing is smooth. Set aside.

2. Peel the onions and, with a small knife, remove the core so there will be no hint of bitterness. Cut the onions into slices no thicker than ⅛ inch. Break the slices into rings and place them in a small bowl. Toss the rings with approximately half of the dressing.

Cover the bowl with plastic wrap and refrigerate the onions as you complete the salad.

3. On a large serving platter, arrange the leaves of lettuce, using the prettiest leaves around the rim.

4. Trim the ends of the cucumbers, but do not peel them. Cut each cucumber into 4 lengthwise strips. Peel the mango and cut it into 12 lengthwise slices, resembling the wedged shapes of the cucumbers as closely as possible. Peel the avocado. Cut it in half lengthwise, and remove the pit. Cut each half into 6 lengthwise slices.

5. Divide the cucumber, mango, and avocado slices into 4 or 6 individual groups, depending upon how many you will be serving. Arrange the individual groups in an alternating pattern on the platter, leaving a 1½-inch margin of lettuce showing on the outside. Distribute the remaining dressing evenly over the platter.

6. Gently pull the petals from the marigold blossom and discard the white, threadlike tips. Toss the petals and basil with the onions and arrange them in the center of your platter. Garnish the platter with additional marigold blossoms, if you wish. Serve the salad immediately.

BEET AND CUCUMBER SALAD

This is a vivid salad to serve in the early summer while one waits for those first tomatoes and peppers to mature on the plants.

Serves 4 to 6

1½ pounds fresh beets (tops removed)
1 pound unwaxed pickling cucumbers (about 12 cucumbers, 3 to 4 inches long)
½ teaspoon salt
¼ pound small red onions
½ cup homemade Mayonnaise (see pages 195 and 196)
½ cup Yogurt (see page 67)
½ teaspoon freshly ground white pepper
3 tablespoons finely snipped fresh dill leaves

½ pound red leaf lettuce
4 to 6 small flower heads of dill for garnish (if available)

1. Cook the beets in boiling water until they are tender. The time will be from 15 minutes to ½ hour, depending upon their size. Do not over-cook.

Drain and peel them while they are still hot. Refrigerate the beets, whole, until you are ready to arrange the salad.

2. Cut the cucumbers crosswise into slices just under ¼ inch in thickness. Place them in a sieve and sprinkle with the salt.

Toss to mix in the salt and let the cucumbers drain for ½ hour to draw out excess moisture. This will also help them to retain their crispness.

3. Peel the onions and cut them crosswise into ¼-inch slices. Break the slices into rings if the onions are larger than 1 inch in diameter.

4. When the cucumbers have drained for ½ hour, pat them dry with paper towels. Combine them with the onions in a small bowl.

Cover and chill the mixture in the refrigerator for ½ hour.

5. Prepare the salad dressing. In a small mixing bowl, whisk together the mayonnaise, yogurt, and white pepper. When the mixture is smooth, fold in the snipped dill leaves.

Cover and refrigerate until you are ready to serve the salad.

6. On a large serving platter, arrange the leaves of red leaf lettuce. Rim the outside of the platter with the prettiest leaves.

7. Cut the beets from top to bottom into ¼-inch slices. Cut the slices, again lengthwise, into ¼-inch julienne strips.

Arrange the strips in a circular pattern on the red leaf lettuce, leaving a 2-inch margin of lettuce on the outside of the platter and an area in the middle of the platter for the cucumber and onion mixture.

8. Place the cucumber and onion mixture in the center of the platter and arrange the flower heads of dill in an appealing fashion.

9. Present the platter at the table or on the buffet with the salad dressing in a bowl next to it. The dressing should be spooned on top just as the salad is served.

KOHLRABI AND RED ONION SALAD

Serve this sprightly salad as a salad course on a bed of curly greens or just as it is, as an accompaniment to a cold fish or chicken dish. It will stay crisp, even at room temperature, so that it is transportable for an outdoor summer gathering. When selecting your kohlrabi and onions, try to find ones that are uniform in size and no larger than 2 inches in diameter. Both vegetables must be young and the onions very sweet.

Serves 4 to 6

1 teaspoon salt
1 teaspoon freshly ground white pepper
4 tablespoons lemon juice
½ cup olive oil
2 pounds young kohlrabi, without their tops (see above)
1 pound sweet red onions (see above)
6 tablespoons snipped fresh dill leaves

1. Prepare the salad dressing in a small mixing bowl. Combine the salt, white pepper, and lemon juice. Whisk until the salt dissolves. In a slow, steady stream, whisk in the olive oil until the dressing is smooth. Set aside.

2. Peel the kohlrabi bulbs and slice them crosswise into rounds no thicker than ⅛ inch. If they are sliced thicker, their flavor will overpower that of the sweet onions. Place the rounds in a large salad bowl.

3. Peel the onions and cut them crosswise into ⅛-inch slices. Break the slices into rings and place them in the salad bowl. Add the snipped dill and toss the ingredients to mix.

4. Pour the dressing over the salad and toss again. The salad may be served right away or it will keep, tightly covered, in the refrigerator for several days.

LIMA BEAN AND YELLOW TOMATO SALAD

The ingredients in this salad make an unexpectedly lovely color scheme. The dressing is purposely unassertive so that the sweetness of the lima beans can be discerned. For individual servings, line the salad plates with a pale salad green, such as Boston lettuce. For a buffet, the recipe should be doubled or tripled and can be served from a salad bowl.

Serves 4

2 cups fresh lima beans (about 2½ pounds before shelling)
2 large yellow tomatoes, such as Sunray
½ teaspoon salt
2 large green bell peppers, 1 green and 1 yellow if available
1 medium onion
¼ teaspoon freshly ground black pepper
¼ cup olive oil
2 tablespoons lemon juice
4 tablespoons finely chopped parsley

1. Shell the lima beans and rinse them in a colander.

2. Core and seed the yellow tomatoes, but do not peel them.

Chop the tomatoes into cubes about ½ inch in diameter. Place them in a sieve and sprinkle with the salt. Toss to mix and let the tomatoes drain for ½ hour to rid them of excess liquid.

3. In a large pot, bring 2 quarts of water to a boil. Add the lima beans and cook at a boil, partially covered, for 4 to 5 minutes, depending upon the size of the beans. Watch them, as limas froth as they cook and may boil over.

Drain immediately in the colander and run cold water over the beans to stop the cooking process.

4. Core and seed the bell peppers. Chop them coarsely into ½-inch pieces. Peel the onion and chop it fine.

Place the bell peppers and onion in a mixing bowl and add the lima beans and drained tomatoes. Season with the black pepper.

Pour the olive oil over the surface and then the lemon juice. Toss lightly and thoroughly. Taste for salt. We feel the salt that was mixed with the chopped tomatoes is sufficient, but you may wish to add more.

5. Just before serving, sprinkle each individual salad with a tablespoon of the chopped parsley.

SUMMER CORN SALAD

Serve this multicolored salad as part of a summer supper. It also travels well for a picnic.
Serves 4 to 6

2 pounds ripe tomatoes
2 medium unwaxed cucumbers
1¼ teaspoons salt
6 ears fresh corn (about 5 cups)
1 fresh green bell pepper
2 mildly hot fresh peppers, such as Colorado or Yellow Banana,
    or ½ teaspoon freshly ground dried hot red pepper
1 medium onion
¼ cup finely chopped fresh basil
¼ cup finely chopped parsley
2 teaspoons dry mustard
½ teaspoon freshly ground black pepper
3 cloves garlic, minced
2 tablespoons red wine vinegar
⅓ cup corn oil

1. Core and seed the tomatoes, but do not peel them. Chop them coarse and place them in a sieve placed over a bowl. Do not peel the cucumbers, but chop them coarsely and add them to the sieve.

Sprinkle the tomatoes and cucumbers with ¼ teaspoon of the salt. Toss to distribute the salt. Drain for about ½ hour to draw out excess moisture; otherwise, the salad will contain too much liquid. (The liquid can be saved for another use, as it is quite tasty.)

2. Shuck the ears of corn and remove the silk. Drop the corn into a large pot of boiling water, salted with ½ teaspoon of the salt.

Cover the pot and when the water returns to a boil, remove the pot from the heat and let the corn sit, covered, for 10 minutes. Drain the corn and run cold water over the ears to cool them.

Cut the kernels from the cobs and place the kernels in a large salad bowl.

3. Core and seed the green bell pepper and the mildly hot peppers if you are using them. Chop the peppers coarsely and add them to the corn.

Peel and chop the onion fine, adding it to the salad bowl.

Add the chopped basil and parsley along with the drained tomatoes and cucumbers. Toss, just to mix.

SUMMER CORN AND LIMA BEAN SALAD

Vary the Summer Corn Salad by omitting the cucumbers and adding 2 cups of fresh lima beans (about 2½ pounds before shelling). The amount of corn should be only 2½ cups instead of 5 (you will need about 3 ears).

Follow each step as in the corn salad recipe, disregarding the instructions for the cucumbers. After shelling the lima beans, cook them for 5 minutes in the boiling, salted water *before* you cook the corn. Use a steam basket for this or the Everything Pot for easy removal.

Run cold water over the cooked beans to stop the cooking process. They may be added to the salad at any point.

Continue with the recipe for the corn salad. For added color, use a combination of red and yellow tomatoes.

4. Prepare the salad dressing. In a small bowl, combine the dry mustard, the remaining ½ teaspoon of salt, black pepper, garlic, and dried hot red pepper if you are using it. Add the wine vinegar and whisk until the dry ingredients dissolve.

In a steady stream, whisk in the corn oil until the dressing is thick and smooth. Pour the dressing onto the salad and toss thoroughly.

ROMANO BEAN SALAD

We grow Romano Italian Pole beans not only for their unique flavor, but because the vines are pretty all summer long, creating a fence of privacy in the garden. And as long as we keep picking, these broad-podded, stringless beans keep producing.

Serves 4 to 6

1 teaspoon dry mustard
1 teaspoon freshly ground black pepper
2 teaspoons minced garlic
¼ cup red wine vinegar
½ cup plus 1 tablespoon olive oil
3 ounces pancetta (Italian bacon, see page 54)
1½ pounds Romano beans
¼ cup water
1½ cups coarsely chopped celery
¾ pound sweet onions, preferably red, peeled and sliced thin
¼ cup finely chopped fresh basil

1. Prepare the dressing in your salad bowl. Place the dry mustard, black pepper, garlic, and wine vinegar in the bowl and whisk, just to blend.

In a slow, steady stream, whisk in the ½ cup of olive oil until the dressing is smooth and thick. (Because of the saltiness of the pancetta, no salt is used in the dressing.) Set aside.

2. Cut the pancetta into ¼-inch dice. Heat the remaining 1 tablespoon of olive oil in a 10-inch skillet over low heat. Add the pancetta dice and sauté until they have given up their fat and have lightly browned and crisped. Do not drain. This will take about 15 minutes.

3. Meanwhile, prepare the remaining ingredients for the salad. Break off and discard the tip ends of the Romano beans. It is not neces-sary to string them. Break each bean into 3 pieces. If the beans are very fresh, you will hear a distinct snap.

4. When the pancetta has browned, add the ¼ cup of water to the skillet. Increase the heat to medium-high and add the Romano beans.

Cook the beans with the pancetta, toss-ing almost constantly, for 6 to 8 minutes. The beans should cook only long enough to re-move the rawness of flavor. Do not let them become soft.

5. Toss the Romano beans and pancetta with the dressing in the bowl. Add the celery, on-ions, and basil and toss again. The salad may be served while it is still warm or a short time later at room temperature. It is at its best if served soon after completion.

OCTOBER BEAN SALAD

We delight in this salad all year long, but especially in the summer when we pick those speckled October bean pods from the vines. (Why they are called October beans is unclear, as our crop matures in August, and in New York we found them in the markets in September.) What we do not eat during the summer months, we freeze for winter.

Instead of October beans (Dwarf French Horticultural), you may use beans such as cranberry, Great Northern, and flageolet. If the beans are dried, use 2 cups and follow the instructions on the package for the cooking time.

The ingredients are very flexible—eliminate or add as you please. What else we will be serving decides whether or not we will use the tuna fish. The salad can be made a day ahead and will keep for several days under refrigeration. We often serve the salad with Pickled Eggs, any of the Roasted or Sautéed Peppers (check the index), and wedges of ripe tomatoes.

If fresh herbs are not available, use a teaspoon of dried oregano or wild thyme, not basil.

Serves 4 to 6

4 cups shelled October beans (2 pounds before shelling)
1 medium onion
2 cups celery
½ cup coarsely chopped canned Colorado Peppers, or mildly hot
      peppers, packed in brine
1 cup finely chopped parsley
3 tablespoons finely chopped fresh basil
3 tablespoons snipped fresh chives
7-ounce can tuna, packed in olive oil (optional)

Dressing:
2 teaspoons dry mustard
½ teaspoon salt
½ teaspoon freshly ground black pepper
3 tablespoons red wine vinegar
2 large cloves garlic, minced
⅓ cup olive oil

1. Bring a large pot of water to a boil. Add the October beans and cook just until they are barely tender. Begin testing them after 8 minutes. They must remain firm, but not taste raw. The cooking time can vary from less than 10 minutes to 15 minutes. (If using frozen beans, let them defrost slightly before cooking. The cooking time will approximate that of fresh beans.)

When the beans have cooked to your taste, drain them immediately in a colander and run cold water over them to stop the cooking process.

2. While the beans are cooking, prepare the dressing in your salad bowl. Dissolve the dry mustard, salt, and black pepper in the vinegar.

Add the minced garlic and whisk in the olive oil in a thin stream until the dressing is smooth and thick.

3. Toss the beans with the salad dressing before they have completely cooled so that they will remain plump.

4. Peel the onion and cut it in half lengthwise. Cut each half into ⅛-inch slices and break the slices apart. Add to the salad bowl.

Cut the stalks of celery crosswise into ⅓-inch slices. Add to the salad bowl along with the Colorado peppers, which have been coarsely chopped, but not seeded. Add the herbs to the salad.

5. If you are using the tuna, add it along with its oil to the other ingredients. Break the tuna into chunks about ½ inch in diameter. Toss the salad so that all of the ingredients are mixed with the dressing.

A GOLDEN SUMMER SALAD

The number of new varieties of vegetables that have been developed in recent years is extraordinary. Some we are vehemently opposed to, like the square tomato, but others are quite exciting, either in their flavors, sizes, disease resistance, or brilliant colors. Color is something we are particularly interested in and today it is possible to grow a full garden with one range of color. This salad features the yellow and golden vegetables, but if it is impossible to find all of the ingredients with the proper colors, the salad is still lovely with red and green substitutions.

When selecting your vegetables, try to find ones of a uniform size. The beets, tomatoes, and bell peppers should be approximately the same size so that they will look more attractive when the salad is composed. The varieties of golden salad vegetables we grow are Gold Rush Hybrid zucchini, Burpee's Golden beets, Sunray tomatoes, and Golden Bell peppers.

Serve the salad as part of a buffet, following the main course at dinner, or as the main course itself at a luncheon. A selection of cheeses and freshly made bread should accompany the salad. If the salad is served as the main course, it will serve 4. If it is part of a buffet, 6 to 8 can be served.

Serves 4 to 8 (see above)

½ pound small yellow zucchini (5 × 1½ inches)
1¼ teaspoons salt
1½ pounds medium yellow beets (without their tops)
1 teaspoon dry mustard
½ teaspoon freshly ground black pepper
1 teaspoon minced garlic
3 tablespoons white wine vinegar
½ cup olive oil
4 small yellow onions, peeled and sliced thin
4 large yellow tomatoes
4 large yellow bell peppers
4 tablespoons finely chopped fresh basil

1. Trim and discard the ends of the zucchini. Do not peel, but slice the zucchini into ¼-inch rounds. Place them in a colander or sieve and sprinkle with ¼ teaspoon of the salt. Toss to

mix and let the zucchini drain for ½ hour to draw out excess liquid.

2. Cook the unpeeled beets in boiling water until they are just tender. Do not overcook.

3. Meanwhile, prepare the salad dressing. In a small bowl, combine the remaining 1 teaspoon of salt, dry mustard, black pepper, and garlic. Add the wine vinegar and whisk to mix the ingredients.

In a slow, steady stream, pour in the olive oil, whisking constantly, until the dressing is smooth and thick.

4. When the beets are just tender, drain them and, as soon as you are able to handle them, peel and cut them into crosswise slices, ⅓ inch thick. Place the slices in a small bowl and toss them with ¼ cup of the salad dressing. Cover and refrigerate them until you are ready to arrange the salad platter.

5. After the zucchini rounds have drained for ½ hour, pat them dry with paper towels. Place them in another bowl and toss them with the sliced onions. Cover and refrigerate. The salad may be prepared several hours ahead of time to this point.

6. Core the tomatoes and cut them into ⅓-inch-thick crosswise slices (peeling is optional). Carefully core the bell peppers and cut them into ⅓-inch-thick crosswise rings. Discard the seeds and, with a small knife, remove any white membrane.

7. Select a large salad platter and arrange the sliced tomatoes, sliced beets, and bell pepper rings in an alternating pattern on the platter, leaving a small amount of space in the center of the platter. Place the tossed zucchini and onions in the center with a little of the mixture extending onto the other vegetables.

8. Whisk the remaining salad dressing if it has begun to separate and pour it over the salad, coating all of the vegetables lightly. Sprinkle the surface of the salad with the chopped basil just before serving.

FALL SALADS

AN AUTUMN COLESLAW

The blending of yogurt with freshly ground coriander seed creates a new sensation for satiated taste buds. Before blending, the yogurt must be "hung" for several hours to extract the whey, thereby ensuring a thicker dressing. It is also very important that the cabbage be finely shredded. Our fall variety in the garden is Surehead, which is recognizable by its flat head.

Serves 6 to 8

1 cup Yogurt (see page 67)
2 teaspoons coriander seeds
½ teaspoon salt
½ teaspoon freshly ground white pepper
3 tablespoons lemon juice
⅓ cup olive oil
2-pound fall cabbage
1 cup coarsely chopped parsley (see Step 5)
2 cups coarsely chopped celery (see Step 5)

1. About 3 hours before you plan to make the coleslaw, place the yogurt in a small sieve lined with cheesecloth. Place the sieve over a bowl and refrigerate it.

When the whey has drained from the yogurt, you will have about ½ cup of thickened yogurt in the cheesecloth and ⅓ cup of whey in the bowl. (The whey will continue to drain from the yogurt the longer it is "hung," so if you plan to hang it longer than 3 hours, use more yogurt in order to have ½ cup.)

2. Toast the coriander seeds in a small skillet over low heat for about 5 minutes to bring out their flavor. Grind the seeds.

3. When the yogurt has thickened, scrape it into a small bowl with a rubber spatula and prepare the salad dressing. Whisk in the coriander seed, salt, pepper, and lemon juice.

Add the olive oil in a slow, steady stream, whisking constantly, until the dressing is smooth. Set aside.

4. Discard the outer leaves of the cabbage and quarter and core it. Shred the cabbage fine, either by hand on the medium side of a grater or with a cabbage cutter, or in a food processor fitted with the medium shredding disk.

Place the shredded cabbage in a large salad bowl.

5. Chop the parsley and celery coarsely. If you are using a food processor, remove the shredding disk and fit the processor with the metal blade for chopping. Add the parsley and celery to the salad bowl. Toss just to mix.

6. Pour the dressing over the salad ingredients and toss again.

If the coleslaw is not to be served right away, cover it with plastic wrap and refrigerate it. This coleslaw will be good for several days, so it can be made in advance.

AN AUTUMN POTATO SALAD

In late fall, as the weather begins to cool, we like to add pancetta to potato salads. If there has not yet been a killing frost, we use a bell pepper from the garden. Otherwise, we use our frozen, quartered peppers that have been slightly defrosted before cutting. For ½ cup, you will need one 6-ounce fresh bell pepper or 4 large, frozen quarters. You may also use purchased roasted peppers. In that case, they need only be drained and cut into julienne strips.

Serves 4 to 6

2½ pounds medium-size boiling potatoes
3 ounces pancetta (Italian bacon, see page 54)
1 tablespoon plus ⅓ cup olive oil
½ cup julienne strips of bell or roasted peppers (see above)
1 teaspoon crumbled dried or fresh rosemary
1 teaspoon dry mustard
½ teaspoon freshly ground black pepper
1 teaspoon minced garlic
4 tablespoons wine vinegar
1½ cups coarsely chopped celery (about 3 medium stalks)
⅓ cup coarsely chopped canned Colorado Peppers
    or mildly hot peppers packed in brine
3 tablespoons liquid from the Colorado peppers
½ cup finely chopped parsley

1. Scrub the potatoes. Steam them for 20 to 30 minutes just until they are tender.

2. Cut the pancetta into ¼-inch dice. Heat the tablespoon of olive oil in a 10-inch skillet over

low heat. Add the pancetta and sauté until it is rendered of its fat and the dice have browned. This will take about 15 minutes. Stir several times so that the dice brown evenly. Do not drain.

3. Cut the bell or roasted peppers into 1½ x ¼ inch julienne strips. When the pancetta has browned, add the peppers to the skillet. Sprinkle with the rosemary. Toss and increase the heat to medium.

Sauté, uncovered, for 10 minutes, tossing several times with wooden spoons. The peppers should absorb most of the liquid in the skillet. Set aside.

4. While the potatoes are steaming and the pancetta and peppers are sautéing, prepare the salad dressing. In a small bowl, combine the dry mustard, black pepper, and garlic. Whisk in the wine vinegar.

In a slow, steady stream, whisk in the remaining ⅓ cup of olive oil. Whisk until the dressing is smooth and thick. Set aside.

5. When the potatoes are tender, remove them from the heat and drain. As soon as you are able to handle them, remove the skins. Place the peeled potatoes in a shallow dish. Let them cool slightly before cutting them into 1½-inch chunks.

6. Add the pancetta, sautéed peppers, and any liquid remaining in the skillet to the potatoes. Toss to mix and pour on the dressing. Toss again. Add the celery, Colorado peppers (seeding is optional), pepper liquid, and parsley. Toss, and serve at room temperature.

CABBAGE AND FINOCCHIO SALAD

Some years our fall garden provides us with a crop of finocchio (Florence fennel) that will be fully developed, but often frost kills it before the bulbs are much larger than 1½ inches in diameter. Despite these small crops, we can still enjoy the aniselike flavor by using large amounts of the leaves if the bulbs are tiny. Combined with celery cabbage and tossed with a soy sauce dressing, this is a simple but unusual salad.

Serves 4 to 6

1-pound Chinese celery cabbage (or part of a larger head)
1 bulb finocchio about 2 inches in diameter, or part of a larger bulb
1 cup snipped finocchio leaves, loosely packed
1 small onion, sliced thin
1 teaspoon dry mustard
¼ teaspoon freshly ground white pepper
1 small clove garlic, minced
1 tablespoon lemon juice
1 tablespoon soy sauce
¼ cup olive oil

1. If you are using an elongated celery cabbage, cut the leaves into pieces about 2 inches in diameter.

If you are using a squat celery cabbage, cut it into chunks as you would a head of lettuce. Place the cut cabbage into a large salad bowl.

2. Remove the core end and coarsely chop the finocchio bulb. Add it to the salad bowl along with the snipped finocchio leaves and the sliced onion, breaking the slices into rings.

Toss the salad just to mix.

3. Prepare the salad dressing. In a small bowl, combine the dry mustard, white pepper, minced garlic, lemon juice, and soy sauce. Whisk to dissolve the dry mustard.

Add the olive oil in a steady stream, whisking constantly, until all the ingredients are mixed and the dressing is smooth. Pour over the salad, and this time toss thoroughly so that the salad is evenly coated with the dressing.

SALAD WITH TWO CABBAGES

This salad is deceptive in its simplicity, but it is quite capable of holding its own as a course at any fine dinner.
Serves 4 to 6

1 pound celery cabbage
3 kohlrabi, about 1½ inches in diameter
1 medium onion
½ cup chopped parsley
½ teaspoon salt
¼ teaspoon freshly ground black pepper
2 tablespoons olive oil
2 tablespoons lemon juice

1. Wash and drain the celery cabbage. Cut it in half lengthwise and remove the core. If your celery cabbage is larger than 1 pound, cut it into pieces and refrigerate the unused portions. It keeps very well under refrigeration.

For the salad, cut the cabbage into pieces as you would a head of lettuce, with no piece larger than 1½ inches square. Place the cabbage pieces into a salad bowl.

2. Cut the leafy greens with their stems from the kohlrabi, reserving them for another use (boiled or for soups). Rinse the bulbs and peel them.

With a sharp knife, cut the bulbs into matchstick pieces, no longer than 1¼ inches. Do not use a food processor for this. Add the strips to the cabbage.

3. Peel and slice the onion thin. Break the slices into rings and add them to the salad bowl along with the chopped parsley. Toss just to mix.

4. Sprinkle the salad with the salt and pepper and pour on the olive oil, followed by the lemon juice. Toss until the ingredients are lightly coated with the oil and lemon juice.

If the salad is not to be served right away, it will hold for several hours in the refrigerator, covered with plastic wrap.

CARROT, PARSLEY, AND SPROUT SALAD

Serve this as a salad course or as a light lunch with a pot of Yogurt (see page 67) and Round Loaves with Cracked Wheat and Whole-Wheat flour Bread (page 24). The salad also keeps very well, so that it can be made a day ahead.

Serves 4 to 6

1 pound carrots
1 small onion, minced
3 cups chopped curly parsley, tightly packed
2 cups alfalfa sprouts (for growing instructions, see page 39)
½ teaspoon salt
¼ teaspoon freshly ground black pepper
3 tablespoons olive oil
⅓ cup freshly squeezed lemon juice

1. Cut off and discard both ends of the carrots. Peel the carrots, using a vegetable peeler. Then shred them, using the vegetable peeler or a food processor, fitted with the medium shredding disc. This should yield 5 cups of shredded carrots with pieces no longer than 2 inches (see Note).

2. Place the shredded carrots in a large salad bowl and add the onion, parsley, and the alfalfa sprouts. Toss thoroughly, fluffing the vegeta-bles so that the salad is light and airy.

3. Add the salt, black pepper, and olive oil. Sprinkle the lemon juice over the salad and toss once again before serving.

Note: Do not mistake "shredded" for the "finely grated" consistency we call for in our Carrot Cake. One pound of carrots, finely grated, will yield only 2 cups and the texture will be incorrect for this recipe.

PARSLEY SALAD

All through the fall our parsley bed is still lush, so we try to use as much as we can before a few severe frosts kill it. This salad improves when aged a bit, so make it one day ahead. Do not add the radishes until just before serving as they will eventually "bleed" after being sliced. Serve this either as a salad course or stuffed into Pita Bread (see pages 172 and 174).

Serves 4 to 6

2 cups finely shredded carrots (see Step 1)
2 cups coarsely chopped celery
1 medium onion, chopped coarsely
4 cups coarsely chopped curly parsley leaves, tightly packed
½ cup Mother's Salad Dressing (see page 197)
1 dozen radishes

1. Peel the carrots and shred them using a hand grater or food processor. Place them in a large salad bowl along with the celery and onion.

2. Add the chopped parsley to the other ingredients tossing the salad just to mix. Add the salad dressing and toss thoroughly.

Cover the salad bowl with plastic wrap and refrigerate overnight.

3. Just before serving, slice the radishes and add them to the salad. Toss again.

ROMAINE LETTUCE SALAD WITH BLUE CHEESE AND SPROUTS

Romaine lettuce is available most of the year so this salad can be prepared during any season. We feel it is best served when little else is fresh at the market or in the garden. Combined with freshly grown sprouts and a mild, creamy blue cheese such as Maytag, the sweetness of the lettuce will not be masked.

Serves 4 to 6

1 pound Romaine lettuce
1 small onion, sliced thin
10 radishes, sliced thin

1 cup chopped fresh parsley
1 cup alfalfa sprouts (for growing instructions, see page 39)
3 ounces blue cheese
3 tablespoons olive oil
¼ teaspoon salt
¼ teaspoon freshly ground black pepper
2 tablespoons lemon juice

1. Wash the Romaine lettuce, carefully removing each leaf as you do so. Drain and pat dry. Break the leaves into pieces 2 to 3 inches in diameter (see Note). As you break the leaves, place them into a large salad bowl.

2. Add the slices of onion, broken into rings, along with the radishes and parsley. Add the alfalfa sprouts, pulling them into fluffy threads as you do so. Toss the salad just to mix.

3. Crumble the blue cheese onto the salad, with the pieces no larger than ⅓ inch. Pour the olive oil over the salad. Sprinkle with the salt, black pepper, and lemon juice. Toss again to mix thoroughly. Serve as soon as possible.

Note: Romaine lettuce bruises more than most lettuces, so tearing it is better than cutting with a knife. For this same reason, it is best not to make the salad too far in advance, for even when the leaves are broken, the breaks will begin to darken within a few hours.

TUNA AND PASTA SALAD

The ingredients in this salad are similar to those used in the October Bean Salad (see Page 237). In fact, quite often we make this salad and add 2 cups of cooked October beans when we want a robust main-course salad for a cold supper. Depending upon what is available, serve the salad on a platter and surround it with Dill Pickles, Pickled Eggs, Virginia's Green Tomato Pickles (see the recipe index), olives, and cucumbers. It may just be a quirk with us, but we feel the flavor of fresh tomatoes is altered when combined with tuna, so we do not suggest that you use them on your platter. But we do encourage you to have lots of crusty bread on the table.

For your dried pasta, use any of the small tubular pastas, such as penne or macaroni, or the spiral pastas, or even the small "seashells" and "little wheels." Several of our mail-order sources carry numerous varieties.

Serves 4 to 6

3 large bell peppers, preferably red
2 tablespoons plus ¼ cup olive oil
½ teaspoon freshly ground dried hot red pepper
2 teaspoons dry mustard
¼ teaspoon freshly ground black pepper
1 tablespoon minced garlic
3 tablespoons wine vinegar
1 tablespoon salt (for cooking the pasta)
½ pound dried pasta (see above)
1 cup coarsely chopped celery
1 medium onion, chopped coarsely
2 cans tuna, 7 ounces each, packed in olive oil
½ cup finely chopped parsley
4 tablespoons finely chopped fresh basil (if available)

1. Core and seed the bell peppers. Cut the peppers into julienne strips 2 inches long by ¼ inch wide.

2. Place 2 tablespoons of the olive oil in a 10-inch skillet over medium-low heat. Add the bell peppers, and sprinkle them with the hot red pepper and toss.

   Sauté the peppers, covered, for about 8 minutes. Remove the cover and sauté for another 2 to 3 minutes, so that most of the moisture will evaporate. Set aside.

3. In a large pot, bring 4 quarts of water to a boil.

4. While the peppers are sautéing and the water is coming to a boil, prepare the salad dressing. Place the dry mustard, black pepper, and garlic in your salad bowl. Whisk in the wine vinegar.

   In a slow, steady stream, pour in the remaining ¼ cup of olive oil, whisking constantly, until the dressing is smooth and thick.

5. Add the salt to the boiling water and when the water returns to a boil, add the pasta. Cook until *al dente* (cooked but firm to the bite).

6. Drain the pasta and toss it with the salad dressing while it is still hot.

   Add the celery, onion, and sautéed peppers to the salad bowl and toss again. Add the tuna with its oil, flaking the tuna into ¾-inch chunks as you add it. Sprinkle with the parsley and basil and toss again. Do not break up the tuna. Serve the salad at room temperature.

CHICKPEA SALAD

We eat this salad with gusto at any time of the year, but perhaps appreciate it most in the fall when the garden is dwindling and the evenings are often still too warm for more substantial fare.
Serves 4 to 6

1½ cups dried chickpeas (½ pound)
1½ teaspoons salt
1 teaspoon coriander seeds
1 teaspoon cumin seeds
1 teaspoon dry mustard
½ teaspoon freshly ground black pepper
1 teaspoon minced garlic
2 tablespoons lemon juice
⅓ cup olive oil
½ cup Yogurt (see page 67)
1 medium onion, chopped coarsely
2 cups coarsely chopped celery
2 cups finely chopped parsley
2 two-inch jalapeño peppers, fresh or canned, chopped fine
1 teaspoon Fresh Green Coriander Seeds (see page 57)
or 1 tablespoon finely chopped coriander leaves

1. Begin the preparation of the chickpeas several hours before you are ready to make the salad. Rinse and pick over the dried chickpeas, discarding any that are blemished or broken.

Place the chickpeas in a heavy 2½-quart saucepan. Add water to cover them by 1 inch. Cover the saucepan and bring the chickpeas to a boil over medium heat.

Remove the saucepan from the heat and let it sit, still covered, for 1 hour. This step eliminates an overnight soaking.

2. After 1 hour, return the saucepan to the stove and add ½ teaspoon of the salt. Simmer the chickpeas, partially covered, over medium-low heat for about 45 minutes. They should not lose their crunchiness.

Drain the chickpeas in a colander and set aside. You should have about 4 cups of cooked chickpeas.

3. Toast the coriander and cumin seeds in a small skillet over low heat for about 5 minutes to bring out their flavors. Grind the seeds.

4. Prepare the salad dressing. Place the coriander and cumin seeds, dry mustard, the remaining 1 teaspoon of salt, black pepper, and garlic in your salad bowl. Whisk in the lemon juice. Continue whisking until the ingredients are combined.

In a slow, steady stream, pour in the olive oil, whisking constantly until the dressing is smooth and thick. Whisk in the yogurt. At this point the dressing may no longer look smooth, but once the salad ingredients are added, this will not be noticeable.

5. Add the chickpeas to the salad bowl and mix with a wooden spoon until the chickpeas are well coated with the dressing. Add the onion and celery and, this time, toss with two wooden spoons.

Add the parsley and jalapeño peppers and lightly toss again.

6. If you are using Fresh Green Coriander Seeds, toss them into the salad when you add the parsley and jalapeño peppers. If you are using fresh coriander leaves, sprinkle them on top of the salad just before serving.

The salad should be served at room temperature.

BROWN RICE SALAD

The corn and peppers we freeze make up into a delicious salad that is harmonious with an autumn menu. Of course, the salad can also be prepared during the summer months when the produce is fresh.

Serves 4 to 6

2 cups raw brown rice
2 large bell peppers, fresh or frozen
2 cups corn kernels, fresh (3 medium ears) or frozen
2 tablespoons plus ½ cup olive oil
2 teaspoons dry mustard
1 teaspoon salt
½ teaspoon freshly ground black pepper
½ teaspoon freshly ground dried hot red pepper
1½ tablespoons minced garlic
4 tablespoons lemon juice
1 medium onion, chopped fine
2 cups mung-bean sprouts (for growing instructions, see page 39)
2 tablespoons finely chopped fresh basil or parsley

1. Cook the brown rice, following the instructions for Basic Brown Rice (see page 74). You will have about 5 cups of cooked rice.

Let the rice remain in the saucepan, covered, until you are ready to add it to the salad bowl.

2. If you are using fresh bell peppers, core, seed, and cut them into julienne strips 1-inch long by ¼-inch thick.

If you are using frozen bell peppers, let them defrost on paper towels just enough so that you can cut them into the julienne strips.

3. Prepare the corn. If you are using fresh corn, shuck it, remove the silk, and cut the kernels from the cobs.

If you are using frozen cut corn, let it defrost on paper towels until the kernels can be separated from each other.

4. Place 2 tablespoons of the olive oil in a 10-inch skillet over medium-low heat. Add the bell peppers and sauté, covered, for about 10 minutes. Toss several times. The strips should remain crisp.

5. While the bell peppers are sautéing, prepare the salad dressing. Place the dry mustard, salt, black and red peppers, and minced garlic in your salad bowl. Add the lemon juice and whisk to blend.

In a slow, steady stream, pour in the remaining ½ cup of olive oil, whisking constantly, until the mixture is smooth and thick.

6. When the bell peppers have sautéed for 10 minutes, add the corn. Toss the ingredients to mix them.

Cover the skillet and sauté for another 5 minutes or until the corn is barely tender. Do not overcook the vegetables as they must retain their textures.

Remove the skillet from the heat and let the mixture cool briefly.

7. Add the brown rice and chopped onion to the salad bowl and toss them thoroughly with the dressing.

Add the peppers and corn with any liquid that might remain in the skillet. Toss again.

Add the mung-bean sprouts and toss once more, but more gently. Sprinkle with the chopped basil or parsley. Serve the salad at room temperature.

WILD RICE SALAD

Wild rice is an expensive treat that we cannot resist indulging in several times a year. We feel it is at its best in a simple salad. Served at room temperature, the flavor of the rice is predominant over everything else.

Serves 4 to 6

1½ cups raw wild rice
3 cups water
1 teaspoon salt
1 teaspoon dry mustard
¼ teaspoon freshly ground black pepper
2 tablespoons mild white wine vinegar
⅓ cup olive oil
2 medium stalks celery, chopped coarse
1 medium onion, minced
1 red bell pepper, chopped coarse
1 teaspoon crushed dried rosemary
1 cup chopped parsley
1 dozen ripe olives

1. Wash the wild rice by placing it in a 1½-quart saucepan filled with water. Swish it around in the water and drain it in a sieve.

2. Rinse the saucepan and add the 3 cups of water and ½ teaspoon of the salt. Bring to a boil and add the wild rice. Cover and simmer over low heat for 45 minutes.

Several times while the rice is cooking,

stir and fluff it with a fork. Do not overcook.

3. For the vinaigrette dressing, dissolve the dry mustard, the other ½ teaspoon of salt, and the black pepper in the wine vinegar. Add the olive oil in a steady steam, whisking constantly until the sauce is thick and smooth.

4. In 45 minutes, the rice should have absorbed

all the liquid from the saucepan. Place the cooked rice in a large bowl and toss it with the celery, onion, bell pepper, and rosemary.

Add the vinaigrette dressing and toss.

5. To serve, arrange the salad on a platter and surround it with the chopped parsley and ripe olives.

A LATE FALL SALAD WITH JERUSALEM ARTICHOKES

Jerusalem artichokes, sometimes called sunchokes, are becoming increasingly popular and can be found in most supermarkets. They are an extremely easy vegetable to grow, but do not plant them unless you have plenty of space and want to keep them in the garden "forever."

Serves 4 to 6

½ teaspoon salt
¼ teaspoon freshly ground white pepper
2 tablespoons lemon juice
¼ cup olive oil
1 cup thinly sliced Jerusalem artichokes (about ½ pound)
2 cups coarsely chopped celery stalks with their leaves
2 cups finely shredded carrots
2 canned Colorado peppers or mildly hot peppers, packed in brine
2 tablespoons liquid from the peppers
1 ripe avocado
1 cup coarsely chopped parsley
2 cups alfalfa sprouts, loosely packed (for growing instructions, see page 39)

1. Prepare the salad dressing. In your salad bowl, blend together the salt, white pepper, and lemon juice. In a slow, steady stream, whisk in the olive oil until the dressing is smooth.

2. Scrub and peel the artichokes. Cut the tubers into ⅛-inch slices. The diameter of the slices will be irregular in size as are the tubers, but this is not important as long as they are thinly sliced. Place the slices in the salad bowl and toss with the dressing. The lemon juice will prevent the slices from discoloring as you prepare the remaining ingredients.

3. Add the celery, carrots, peppers, and 2 tablespoons of the pepper liquid to the salad bowl. Toss the ingredients thoroughly.

4. Just before you are ready to serve the salad, peel the avocado and cut it into 1-inch cubes. Add the cubes along with the parsley and alfalfa sprouts to the salad bowl. Toss once more, but more gently this time.

JULY

A MONTH OF SUMMER VEGETABLES

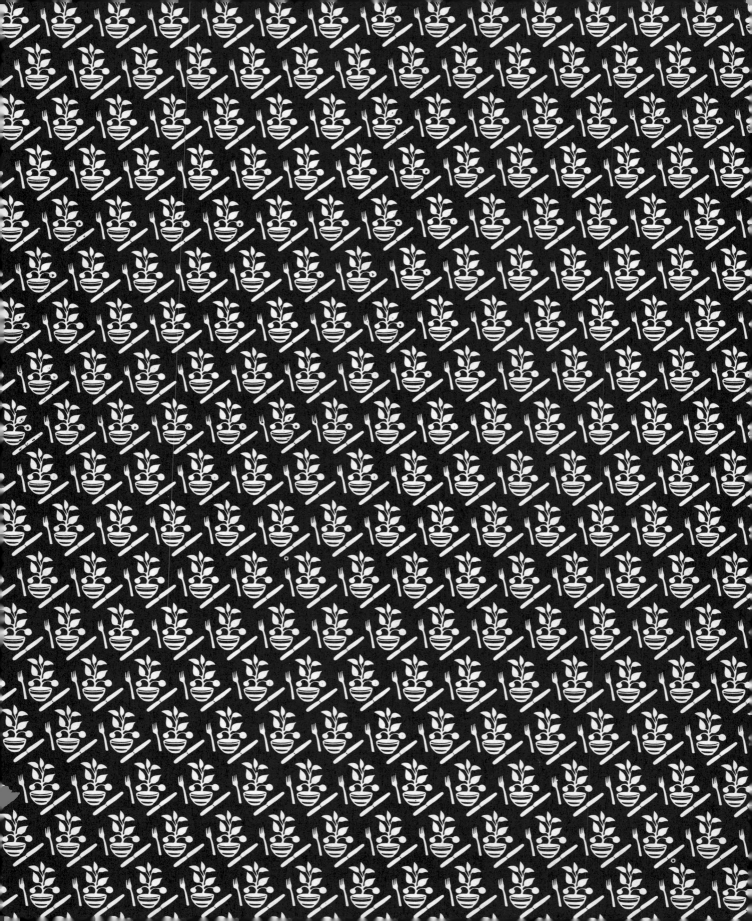

A Month Of Summer Vegetables

With a surfeit of spring and summer vegetables in the garden, it is often difficult to choose what we should eat next and how we should prepare these marvels we have grown. Fortunately, whether sautéed, baked, braised, fried or even scorched, fresh vegetables taste best when they are simply and quickly prepared. This is a bonus when most of the day has been spend picking, shelling, freezing, and beginning the first canning.

The July chapter seems an appropriate time to personally acknowledge Doctors Calvin Lamborn and M.C. Parker of the Gallatin Valley Seed Co. in Idaho for their development of the edible-podded sugar snap pea. We have grown these sweet peas for several years and they are so good that each year we anxiously await our first crop. Unfortunately, the birds find them just as sweet as we do so we must net the vines. However, since the birds spend all their time trying to get at the sugar snaps, they leave our other varieties of peas alone.

Sautéed Sugar Snap Peas

It is interesting to note that sugar snap peas are sweeter cooked than they are raw. Our recipe for sugar snaps differs from the usual in that we feel olive oil is much better for sautéing the peas than is butter. Butter gives the peas too much of a cloying flavor. Often we counter the sweetness by adding a little lemon juice and/or hot red pepper.

Serves 4

1 pound sugar snap peas
2 tablespoons olive oil
1 teaspoon minced garlic
½ teaspoon salt
¼ teaspoon freshly ground white pepper
1 teaspoon lemon juice (optional)
½ teaspoon freshly ground dried hot red pepper (optional)
2 tablespoons minced, fresh basil leaves, if available

1. String the sugar snap peas using your fingers or a small knife. Begin at the very tip of each pea and pinch or cut it in order to grasp the string. Pull the string to the opposite end of the pea.

Pinch off or cut away the stem end and continue pulling the string down the other side of the pea until it is removed. This will take only a few minutes. Leave the sugar snap peas whole.

Begin warming your serving bowl.

2. Place the olive oil in a 10-inch skillet over medium heat. Add the garlic and sauté for only 1 minute. Do not let it burn.

3. Add the sugar snap peas. Sprinkle them with the salt and white pepper.

Increase the heat to medium-high and sauté the peas for 2 to 3 minutes depending upon their size. They must not be overcooked or they will lose their crispness. Toss the peas with two wooden spoons as they sauté.

4. Just before serving, sprinkle with the lemon juice and/or hot red pepper, if you are using them. Toss, and add the minced basil. Serve immediately from a heated serving bowl.

SAUTÉED SUGAR SNAP PEAS WITH MUSHROOMS

As mushrooms are readily available in most markets, they make a perfect companion to sugar snap peas. The mushrooms sautéed with fresh ginger root and garlic bring out, rather than diminish, the sweetness of the peas.

Serves 4

½ pound sugar snap peas
1 pound fresh firm mushrooms
2 tablespoons olive oil, plus 1 teaspoon
1 teaspoon finely minced garlic
1 tablespoon finely chopped fresh ginger root
½ teaspoon salt
¼ teaspoon freshly ground black pepper
¼ teaspoon freshly ground dried hot red pepper

1. String the sugar snap peas using your fingers or a small knife. Begin at the very tip of each pea and pinch or cut it in order to grasp the string. Pull the string to the opposite end of the pea. Pinch off or cut away the stem end and continue pulling the string down the other side of the pea until it is removed. This goes quickly. Leave the sugar snap peas whole.

2. Trim and discard the ends from the mushrooms. Wipe the mushrooms with damp paper towels to clean them. Slice the mushrooms thin.

3. Begin warming your serving bowl. Heat 2 tablespoons of the olive oil in a 10-inch skillet. Add the garlic and ginger root and sauté over medium heat for 1 minute. Add the mushrooms and sprinkle them with the salt and black pepper.

Sauté the ingredients until the mushrooms have given up their liquid and it has completely evaporated. Toss frequently. The skillet may be set aside at this point if you are not ready to serve.

4. Add the sugar snap peas to the skillet only minutes before you are ready to serve as they must not be overcooked. Increase the heat to medium high and add the sugar snap peas. Sprinkle them with the red pepper and dribble on the remaining 1 teaspoon of olive oil.

Toss the ingredients with two wooden spoons for no more than 2 to 3 minutes. The peas should become hot, but should lose none of their crispness. Serve immediately from a heated serving bowl.

SAUTÉED SUGAR SNAP PEAS AND BELL PEPPERS

Serve this recipe as a vegetable course or toss it with fettuccine for a sumptuous pasta dish. For dazzling color, use red bell peppers.

Serves 4

3 large bell peppers
2 tablespoons olive oil
1 teaspoon minced garlic
½ teaspoon salt
¼ teaspoon freshly ground black pepper
½ pound sugar snap peas
½ teaspoon freshly ground dried hot red pepper

1. Core, halve, and seed the bell peppers. Cut each half into 4 lengthwise strips, removing any white pith along the ribs of the peppers.

2. Heat the olive oil in a 10-inch skillet over medium-low heat. Add the bell peppers and garlic. Sprinkle with the salt and black pepper. Toss the ingredients with two wooden spoons.

Cover the skillet and sauté the peppers for about 15 minutes, until they are just tender. Toss several times as the peppers are sautéing. Begin warming your serving bowl.

3. String the sugar snap peas, using your finger or a small knife. Begin at the very tip of each pea and pinch or cut it in order to grasp the string. Pull the string to the opposite end of the pea. Pinch off or cut away the stem end and continue pulling the string down the other side of the pea until it is removed. This operation goes very quickly. Leave the sugar snap peas whole.

4. Just minutes before you are ready to serve, increase the heat to medium high and add the sugar snap peas. Sprinkle them with the hot red pepper.

Tossing the ingredients constantly, sauté for only 2 to 3 minutes, depending upon the maturity of the peas. They must not be overcooked or they will lose their crispness. Serve immediately from a heated serving bowl.

SAUTÉED CARROTS

Cooked carrots were never very appealing to us until we started growing our own tiny carrots, Baby Nantes. It is almost as if we had discovered a new vegetable. We tried them sautéed and found, if they are left whole and barely cooked, they are delicious.

Fortunately, commercial growers must have decided this too, as we are able to find baby or finger carrots in the supermarkets when ours are out of season in the garden. The carrots should be no longer than 3½ inches in length and less than 1 inch in girth.

Serves 4

1 pound baby or finger carrots (see above)
½ cup water (approximately)
2 tablespoons unsalted butter
½ teaspoon salt
¼ teaspoon freshly ground white pepper
1 teaspoon lemon juice (optional)
2 tablespoons of a minced, fresh spring herb, such as basil, mint,
    or dill; or 1 tablespoon of fresh tarragon

1. Remove the ends from the carrots. Scrape them only if necessary. Very small carrots will not need to be scraped. Leave the carrots whole.

2. Pour water into a heavy, 10-inch skillet to a depth of about ¼ inch, just to film it. Add the carrots, cover, and bring to a simmer over medium-low heat. Cook for 4 minutes, shaking the skillet across the burner several times so that the carrots move about.

Uncover and test the carrots by piercing several with the point of a knife. You should be able to pierce them just to the core with the carrots still remaining very crisp. Very small carrots will be done in this amount of time.

If they are not and the water has evaporated from the skillet, add a little more water and continue to cook the carrots, testing them every few minutes.

3. When the carrots are just barely tender and the water has evaporated, remove the cover and add the butter, salt, and white pepper. Toss the ingredients and increase the heat to medium high.

Sauté for about 2 minutes, until the carrots have absorbed the butter. Toss the carrots as they sauté.

Just before serving, sprinkle the carrots with the lemon juice, if you are using it, and the minced herb of your choice.

SAUTÉED SUMMER CROOKNECK SQUASH

To us, this is the most delicious way to prepare these prolific summer squash. We like to serve them surrounding a platter of freshly made and lightly dressed fettuccine for our main course at dinner. The cooking time for the squash will be less than 5 minutes, so cook your pasta as the squash sauté. The squash should be served immediately so that they will still retain their crispness.

Serves 4

1½ pounds baby Summer Crookneck squash (3½ inches long)
2 tablespoons corn oil
½ teaspoon salt
¼ teaspoon freshly ground black pepper

1. Trim the stems of the squash to ⅓ inch. If there are blossoms at the opposite ends, remove them. Leave the squash whole and pierce each one with the point of a knife in 3 or 4 places. This will keep them from splitting as they sauté.

2. Heat the corn oil in a heavy, 10-inch skillet over medium-high heat. Add the squash and sprinkle with the salt and pepper. Toss with two wooden spoons to coat the squash evenly with the oil and seasonings.

3. Cover the skillet and sauté the squash just until they are barely tender. Shake the skillet back and forth so that the squash will sauté evenly. The skins may brown lightly in spots, which will only add flavor; however, it is essential not to overcook the squash. If they are very small, the total cooking time will be 3 to 5 minutes. Watch them carefully and serve as soon as they are ready, as they will soften and possibly collapse upon standing.

SAUTÉED STRING BEANS

We are able to prepare this recipe summer or winter, as we freeze 1-pound packages of our beans whole after first scalding them for 3 minutes in boiling water. The Blue Lake Stringless variety, which is a perfect, tender bean, does not require stringing even when it has grown to 6 inches in length, and it retains its texture even after having been frozen for many months.

Sautéed String Beans is equally good hot or cold. Served hot, it goes well with almost any meat course. Serve it cold on any salad platter or as part of a cold buffet.

Serves 4 to 6

1 pound string beans, fresh or frozen
3 tablespoons olive oil
4 large cloves garlic, minced
½ teaspoon salt
¼ teaspoon freshly ground black pepper
Herb of your choice (see Step 3)
1 tablespoon red wine vinegar

1. Prepare the string beans. If you are using fresh beans, cut off the ends, string them if necessary, and wash under cold water. Do not cut them, but leave them whole. Drain and wipe dry.

If you are using frozen beans, remove them from the freezer about an hour or so before you are ready to cook them, and spread them on paper towels to absorb moisture as they defrost. Otherwise, if you sauté them while they are still frozen, they will lose their crisp texture.

2. Heat the olive oil in a skillet and add the beans, the minced garlic, salt, and black pepper. Toss with wooden spoons to mix.

If your beans are fresh, cover the skillet and cook for about 5 minutes over medium heat. Uncover and sauté for a few more minutes until the beans are cooked, but still very

crisp. The cooking time will depend upon the variety of string bean.

If your beans have been frozen and are defrosted, sauté them, uncovered, over medium heat just until the beans are very hot.

3. When the beans are cooked, add the herb of your choice. In the summer, we would use 2 tablespoons of a fresh herb, such as chopped basil, French tarragon, or dill.

In the winter months with frozen beans, our choice would be 1 teaspoon of dried oregano, wild thyme, or winter savory.

4. At the same time that you add the herb of your choice, add the vinegar. Toss the ingredients and sauté for only a moment.

Serve immediately or chill in the refrigerator, covered, for several hours if you wish to serve the beans cold.

SAUTÉED NEW POTATOES

At our farmers' market, the new potatoes are sorted by size with some no larger than 1 to 1½ inches in diameter. For some reason, they are the least popular and therefore very inexpensive. To us, *they* are choice. This recipe will work just as well with larger new potatoes, but they will take longer to cook. Potatoes other than new will not taste as good.

Serves 4 to 6

2 pounds new potatoes, none larger than 2½ inches in diameter
3 tablespoons olive oil
¼ cup water
1 teaspoon salt
½ cup finely chopped parsley

1. Scrub the potatoes. Sometimes the skins of new potatoes will be so thin that they will scrub away. You may scrub them off, but we prefer to leave them on.

2. Pour the olive oil into a heavy, 10-inch skillet with a cover. Add the potatoes and toss them about to coat them with the olive oil. Add the water, cover, and steam the potatoes over medium heat until they are tender and the water evaporates.

Give the skillet a few good shakes to move the potatoes about. With very tiny potatoes, the cooking time could be no more than 10 minutes or up to 20 for larger potatoes. Pierce them with a fork to test. Do not let them overcook.

3. When the potatoes are tender, sprinkle them with the salt and chopped parsley. Turn the heat to medium-high and sauté, shaking the pan and tossing them for about 5 minutes until the skins brown. Use a spatula to loosen them if they begin to stick to the pan.

The parsley will become crusty, giving it added flavor. Serve immediately as an accompaniment to almost anything including egg, chicken, or fish dishes.

SAUTÉED NEW POTATOES WITH A GREMOLADA GARNISH

For an enticingly pretty dish, use new potatoes whose skins are so thin that they scrub away as you wash them. The yellow and green of the gremolada garnish will make a striking contrast with the whiteness of the potatoes. As the new potatoes coincide with our first fresh dill, we include dill in the gremolada although it normally is just a mixture of garlic, lemon peel, and parsley.

You may also use other small potatoes, if they are very fresh. In that case, whether you peel them or leave the skins on, as we sometimes prefer to do, is up to you.

Serves 4 to 6

2 pounds new potatoes, none larger than 2½ inches in diameter
1½ tablespoons finely chopped garlic (about 4 large cloves; see Step 3)
1½ tablespoons finely chopped lemon peel (about 1 lemon; see Step 3)
½ cup finely chopped parsley, tightly packed (see Step 3)
2 tablespoons finely snipped dill (see Step 3)
2 tablespoons olive oil
½ teaspoon salt
¼ teaspoon freshly ground white pepper

1. Scrub the potatoes with a stiff vegetable brush, scrubbing away the skins if they are very thin (see above).

2. Steam the potatoes until they are tender, but not mushy. The time will depend upon the size and newness of the potatoes. Very small, fresh potatoes may take no longer than 10 minutes. Larger potatoes may take 20 minutes.

3. While the potatoes are steaming, prepare the gremolada. This must be done by hand with a chef's knife as the ingredients must have cleanly chopped edges. Peel and chop the garlic fine. Cut the peel from the lemon, making lengthwise julienne strips. Chop the strips fine. Chop the parsley fine. Using kitchen shears, snip the dill leaves fine.

Chop all the ingredients together just enough to combine them. Do not overchop, as each ingredient must retain its own identity.

Begin warming your serving dish.

4. Place the olive oil in a 10-inch skillet over medium-high heat. Add the steamed potatoes and sprinkle them with the salt and pepper.

Toss with wooden spoons until the potatoes are evenly coated with the oil, salt, and pepper. Do not let the potatoes stick to the skillet.

5. Remove the skillet from the heat and toss the potatoes with the gremolada. Serve immediately in a heated serving dish.

A GRATIN OF NEW POTATOES WITH ONIONS

Potatoes and onions baked in a rich, reduced stock will appear to be copiously caloric, but in fact the opposite is true. This dish is most enjoyed made in the spring and early summer, when new potatoes and fresh herbs are available. However, it is still excellent at other times using boiling potatoes and dried herbs. If the skins appear tough, it may be necessary to peel the potatoes.

In the cooler months, use dried herbs, such as tarragon, wild thyme, rosemary, winter savory, or bay leaves. Use only 2 teaspoons of a dried herb and if you are using bay leaves, insert 2 or 3 imported leaves into the potato mixture, removing them before serving.

Turkey stock is preferred in this dish, but you may use Chicken Stock. If you are using stock left from the Mock Vitello Tonnato on page 107, it need not be reduced.

Serves 4 to 6

4 cups turkey or Chicken Stock (see page 109)
1 pound onions
2 pounds new potatoes, of a uniform size
4 tablespoons fresh tarragon or 5 tablespoons fresh basil, chopped
fine or 2 teaspoons of a dried herb (see above)
1 teaspoon salt
½ teaspoon freshly ground black pepper
2 tablespoons olive oil

1. Preheat the oven to 425° F.

2. In a 1½-quart saucepan, bring the stock to a full simmer over high heat. Continue to briskly simmer (not a full boil) until the stock is reduced to 2 cups.

3. Peel the onions and cut them in half lengthwise. Slice the halves thin, breaking the slices apart.

Scrub the potatoes, but do not peel them. Cut away any blemishes or eyes. Cut the potatoes into thin, ⅛-inch slices.

4. Place the onions and potatoes into a 14-inch oval gratin dish. Toss them with the tarragon or basil, reserving 1 tablespoon of the herb for garnish.

Pack the vegetables down slightly in the dish to make a tidy layer.

5. Pour 1½ cups of the reduced, simmering stock over the vegetables. Sprinkle with the salt and black pepper and dribble the olive oil over the surface. (Depending upon the amount in your stock, you may use less salt. The stock becomes saltier as it is reduced.)

6. Bake the gratin for about 1 hour on the middle level of your oven. The time can vary, depending upon the potatoes. If your potatoes are very new, they may be tender within 45 minutes.

Check the gratin after 45 minutes and add the remaining ½ cup of stock if the mixture seems dry. The onions will be giving off their liquid as they bake, so more stock will probably be unnecessary.

At serving time, the vegetables should be tender, having absorbed all of the stock, and the gratin should be a golden brown on top. Sprinkle with the remaining tablespoon of tarragon or basil just before serving.

Note: This gratin may also be made using whey instead of stock. In this case, do not reduce the whey. Use 1½ cups of whey when you begin the baking, adding more if needed.

FARMERS' MARKET POTATOES

One of our favorite friends at the farmers' market gave us this recipe for roasted potatoes. It is deceptive that anything so simple should taste so good, particularly when prepared with potatoes from the first spring crop.

In winter, we find that, if they are very fresh, potatoes from the store work just as well. However, there will be a difference in cooking time; the spring potatoes will roast faster. We like to serve the potatoes with the Fried Fish on page 115.

Serves 4 to 6

1½ pounds medium potatoes
2 tablespoons olive oil
Salt and freshly ground black pepper, to taste

1. Select potatoes that are uniform in size and very firm. The lengthwise measurement should be from 2 to 2½ inches. Depending upon size, you will have 6 to 8 potatoes. Wash and dry the potatoes, but do not peel them.

2. Preheat the oven to 425° F.

3. Cut the potatoes in half lengthwise and place them, cut side up, in a single layer in an ungreased baking pan or Pyrex pie plate. Brush the cut surfaces with the olive oil and sprinkle each potato half with salt and pepper.

If the potatoes should overlap slightly, it does not matter, but at some point during the cooking time, turn them around so that the entire surface can brown.

4. Roast the potatoes on the middle rack of the oven for 45 minutes to 1 hour. The fresher your potatoes, the faster they will cook.

Test after 45 minutes to see if they are tender. The potatoes should be crisp and golden brown. They may even puff a bit. Serve immediately. We find them best picked up and eaten like chips or fries.

SAUTÉED PEPPERS

The advantage that the Sautéed Peppers have over the Roasted Peppers on page 265 is that they can be prepared at any time of the year from peppers that have been quartered and frozen.

The red bell peppers are the most desirable for sautéing, as the olive oil makes them glisten with color. Serve them hot or cooled to room temperature as part of an antipasto platter or as a vegetable accompaniment. Needless to say, they are perfect partners for the Hot Sausage on page 45 or with many pasta dishes.

Serves 4 to 6

6 large fresh red or green bell peppers (about 6 ounces each) or the equivalent amount of frozen, quartered peppers
2 tablespoons olive oil
1½ tablespoons minced garlic
½ teaspoon salt
¼ teaspoon freshly ground black pepper
½ teaspoon freshly ground dried hot red pepper
1 tablespoon red wine vinegar

1. If you are using fresh bell peppers, core, seed, and quarter them.

If you are using frozen bell peppers, let the quarters defrost slightly on paper towels before sautéing them.

2. Place the olive oil in a heavy, 10-inch skillet over medium-low heat. Arrange the peppers skin side up in the skillet. Sprinkle the peppers with the garlic, salt, and black pepper. Do *not* mix.

Cover the skillet and sauté the peppers for 15 minutes.

3. Uncover the skillet and increase the heat to medium. Sprinkle the peppers with the hot red pepper and vinegar.

Lightly toss with two wooden spoons for 2 to 3 minutes to take the edge off the vinegar and to reduce the liquid in the pan.

Serve right away or at room temperature. The peppers will keep, covered, in the refrigerator for 3 or 4 days.

A FEW NOTES ABOUT PEPPERS

Whether they be sweet, mildly hot, hot or even freshly ground peppercorns, our recipes use peppers abundantly.

Remember, when handling fresh hot peppers, wear rubber gloves, if possible, and never touch your eyes, mouth, nose, and ears. The tissue in these areas is extremely sensitive to pepper oils. After working with the hot peppers, wash your hands and rubber gloves thoroughly.

ROASTED PEPPERS WITH A CHOICE OF TWO DRESSINGS

We have included two methods of roasting peppers, one for a gas stove, the other for an electric. Either way roasted peppers are delicious served with one of the two suggested dressings.

Serve the roasted peppers as part of an antipasto, as a vegetable side dish, as a relish (if they are cut into julienne strips), and especially with the Hot Sausage on page 45. Select only bell peppers with thick walls, otherwise they will roast away.

Makes about 5 cups

10 large, firm bell peppers (about 6 ounces each; red and green combined, if available)
1 recipe dressing (see below)

Method for a gas stove

Place each pepper directly on a medium flame on top of the stove. As each side of the pepper chars, turn it with two forks until it is totally blackened. (The aroma will be irresistible.)

Method for an electric oven

1. Place your rack in the upper third of the oven about 6 inches under the broiler. Preheat the broiler.

2. Line a large, heavy baking sheet with aluminum foil. Fold the sides of the foil to form an edge all around, as the peppers will release some liquid as they broil.

3. Trim the pepper stems so that they are flat against the peppers. Arrange the peppers, stem ends down, on the foil.

Place the baking sheet in the oven and roast the peppers until they are charred on the exposed surface. This will take about 5 minutes. Turn the peppers to char on another side.

Continue to do this until the peppers are completely blackened. The peppers may not remain exactly as you place them and the baking sheet will probably buckle, but this is no cause for concern. The total cooking time will be about 20 minutes.

4. Remove the baking sheet from the oven and as soon as you are able to handle the peppers, peel off the charred skins.

As each pepper is peeled, core, halve, and seed it. Depending upon the dressing you will be using and the size you wish the peppers to be, you may either quarter them or cut them into julienne strips, 2 inches long by ¼-inch wide. Do not be too particular about removing all of the charred skin or, if the flesh itself has charred, do not worry as this is what gives the peppers their unique flavor.

AN OIL AND GARLIC DRESSING FOR ROASTED PEPPERS

6 large cloves garlic, peeled and halved
1 teaspoon coarse salt (kosher or freshly ground sea salt)
3 tablespoons olive oil

1. Prepare the roasted peppers. After peeling, coring, and seeding them, cut the peppers into 1½-inch-wide lengthwise strips.

Place the strips in a medium-size bowl. Add the garlic, salt, and olive oil. Toss until the peppers are well coated with the dressing.

Cover the bowl tightly with plastic wrap and let the peppers marinate in the dressing for 2 hours at room temperature.

2. After 2 hours remove the pieces of garlic, as they will overpower the peppers if left in. The peppers may be served right away or refrigerated and served at a later time. They will keep for about 5 days in the refrigerator.

A VINAIGRETTE DRESSING FOR ROASTED PEPPERS

The roasted peppers are deliciously but decidedly hot with this dressing, and it is possible that the first time you prepare them you may want to use only half the amounts of dry mustard, garlic, and hot pepper.

> **2 teaspoons dry mustard**
> **1 teaspoon salt**
> **½ teaspoon freshly ground black pepper**
> **2 tablespoons minced garlic**
> **2 jalapeño peppers, fresh or canned, or 1 teaspoon freshly ground dried hot red pepper**
> **3 tablespoons wine vinegar**
> **½ cup olive oil**

1. In a medium-size mixing bowl, place the dry mustard, salt, black pepper, and garlic. If you are using jalapeño peppers, core and chop them fine. Removing the seeds is optional. Left in, the dressing will be *much* hotter.

Add the jalapeño peppers or the hot red pepper to the mixing bowl along with the wine vinegar. Whisk just to mix the ingredients.

In a slow, steady stream, pour in the olive oil, whisking constantly, until the dressing is smooth and thick.

2. Peel and cut the roasted peppers, mixing them into the dressing as you do. The peppers may be cut to any size you wish, from quarters to 2- × ¼-inch julienne strips.

Toss the peppers thoroughly in the dress-ing. They may be served as soon as you have completed the recipe or refrigerated for up to a week.

Note: The peppers prepared with this dressing freeze very well, which is a bonus when peppers are very expensive in the winter months. We freeze as many pints as we have time and peppers. They need only to be defrosted to be enjoyed.

BRAISED BEET TOPS

When our beets are ready for picking we feel the tops are as tasty as the roots and have devised this dish to do them justice.
Serves 4

2 pounds beet tops
2 tablespoons olive oil
1 medium onion, chopped fine
1 teaspoon minced garlic
½ cup water (approximately)
¼ teaspoon salt
¼ teaspoon freshly ground black pepper
¼ teaspoon freshly ground dried hot red pepper
1 tablespoon red wine vinegar

1. Carefully wash the beet tops. Do not dry them. Trim the ends of the stems if they are tough and cut them into 1-inch pieces.

Chop the leaves coarsely into 2½- to 3-inch pieces.

2. Heat the olive oil in a 3-quart saucepan. Add the onion and garlic. Sauté them over medium-low heat until they have wilted.

3. Add the beet stems and toss them with the onions and garlic. Add water to the saucepan to a depth of ¼ inch.

Cover the saucepan and braise the beet stems for 5 minutes.

4. Add the beet leaves, salt, and two peppers. You may have to add the leaves gradually as they wilt down. There should be sufficient water clinging to the leaves so that no more will need to be added. Toss to mix.

Partially cover the saucepan and braise the beet tops for 20 to 25 minutes over low heat. Stir occasionally.

Begin warming your serving bowl.

5. Just before serving, add the wine vinegar and toss the ingredients. Increase the heat to medium and cook the beet tops for another 2 minutes, just to take the "edge" off the vinegar. Serve immediately in a heated serving bowl.

PEAS AND BEANS FRESH FROM THE GARDEN

The simplest preparation is the best for these vegetables when picked from the garden or purchased unshelled. We begin to pick our peas and fava beans the end of May and the limas in early summer, but our basic recipe is the same for all three.

Our portions are generous, as we cannot resist the vegetables at their peak of freshness and crispness. You will need 5 pounds of unshelled peas, fava beans, or lima beans for 4 cups, shelled.

Serves 4

4 cups shelled green garden peas, fava beans, or lima beans (see above)

1 teaspoon salt
1 tablespoon unsalted butter
¼ teaspoon freshly ground white pepper
2 tablespoons of a minced, fresh herb, such as basil, dill, tarragon, or parsley

1. Bring 1 quart of water to a boil in a 2½-quart saucepan. When the water comes to a boil, add ½ teaspoon of the salt and the shelled vegetable of your choice.

Cover and bring the water back to a boil over medium-high heat and carefully time the cooking of the peas or beans. Garden peas will be done in 2 minutes (less, if they are very tiny) and fava or lima beans in just 4 minutes.

Begin warming your serving bowl.

2. Drain the vegetable in a sieve and return it to the warm saucepan, placed off the heat. Add the butter, the remaining ½ teaspoon of salt, and the white pepper. Toss, so that the peas or beans are lightly coated with the butter. Transfer to a heated serving bowl. Sprinkle with the fresh herb you have chosen.

SCORCHED TOMATOES

These tomatoes may be served as a vegetable course with any meal. They are delicious hot or cold.

Use only tomatoes that weigh about ½ pound apiece and that preferably have not been waxed. If they have been waxed, wash them thoroughly. The yogurt is optional. Add it if you want to tame the spices or if you want a creamier consistency.

Serves 4 to 6

3 pounds firm ripe tomatoes
3 tablespoons unsalted butter
2 medium onions, chopped fine
1 tablespoon minced garlic
½ teaspoon salt
½ teaspoon freshly ground black pepper
2 tablespoons peeled and finely chopped fresh ginger root
1 teaspoon Garam Masala (see page 190)
½ cup Yogurt (see page 67), at room temperature

1. Preheat the broiler, placing the rack about 6 inches under the heat.

2. Line a baking sheet that has sides with aluminum foil. Place the whole tomatoes core

side down on the foil. Broil the tomatoes for 10 minutes, until the skins blister and split.

Lift the tomatoes with two wooden spoons and turn them core side up. Broil for another 10 minutes. The skins may begin to char, which is desirable.

3. While the tomatoes are charring, melt the butter over medium-low heat in a heavy, 2½-quart saucepan.

Add the onions, garlic, salt, and black pepper. Sauté, stirring occasionally, until the onions wilt and begin to color.

4. When the skins of the tomatoes are nicely blistered and a bit charred, remove the baking sheet from the oven.

As soon as you are able to handle the tomatoes, pull away and discard the skins.

Core the tomatoes and if there are many obvious seeds, remove them. A few will not matter. Chop the tomatoes coarsely, reserving the liquid. The chopped pieces should be no smaller than ½ inch in diameter.

5. Add the ginger root and Garam Masala to the saucepan. Stir and sauté for 1 minute and add the chopped tomatoes with their liquid. Turn the heat to high and bring the ingredients to a full simmer.

Continue to cook over high heat, stirring the ingredients frequently with a wooden spoon until almost all of the liquid from the tomatoes evaporates. As the mixture thickens, push the tomatoes across the saucepan with the back of the spoon. The saucepan should "clean" where you have pushed and you will hear a sound, almost like scorching. Do this frequently and do not let the tomatoes burn. It may take up to ½ hour for the mixture to thicken.

6. When the ingredients have become quite thick, remove the saucepan from the heat. You may serve the tomatoes at this point, but if you wish to add the yogurt, let the mixture cool for about 5 minutes. Then stir in the yogurt.

Serve the tomatoes hot or cold.

FRIED MUSHROOMS

Fried mushrooms served with Coriander Sauce (see below) go very well with the Fried Fish on page 115. Fry the mushrooms first and keep them hot in a serving dish lined with paper towels in a warm oven while you fry the fish using the same oil. (Remove the paper towels before serving.)

Serves 4

1 pound firm, medium-size fresh mushrooms
1 egg
1 teaspoon of water
½ cup all-purpose, unbleached flour
½ teaspoon salt
¼ teaspoon freshly ground black pepper
1 teaspoon freshly ground coriander seed

½ teaspoon freshly ground dried hot red pepper
Corn oil for frying

1. Remove the ends from the mushroom stems. Wipe the mushrooms with damp paper towels to clean them.

2. In a small bowl, beat the egg with the teaspoon of water.

3. In another bowl, mix together the flour, salt, black pepper, coriander seed, and hot red pepper.

4. In a heavy skillet, heat the corn oil to 375°F or until a cube of bread browns instantly. The oil should be to a depth of 1 inch, but the skillet should not be more than half full. We use our 10½-inch cast-iron skillet.

5. When the corn oil is hot, dip the mushrooms one at a time into the egg mixture and then into the seasoned flour, coating them evenly.

Lower each mushroom as it is coated into the hot oil and fry for about 2 minutes, turning once with a spatula. Do not crowd the skillet.

The dipping and coating is best done using your hands, rather than trying to work with utensils.

6. When the mushrooms are golden brown on both sides, remove them with a slotted spatula from the oil to a dish lined with paper towels to drain.

Serve the mushrooms immediately, if possible, or keep them hot in a warm oven.

CORIANDER SAUCE

This recipe is actually two entirely different recipes, depending upon the fresh herb you use. With fresh parsley, the sauce is mild, but with fresh coriander leaves, it is agreeably pungent.

Makes about 1½ cups

1 cup homemade Mayonnaise (see pages 195 and 196)
½ cup Yogurt (see page 67)
2 tablespoons lemon juice
¼ teaspoon salt
¼ teaspoon freshly ground black pepper
1 teaspoon freshly ground coriander seed
4 tablespoons finely minced onion
1 cup finely chopped parsley, loosely packed
    or ¼ cup finely chopped fresh coriander

1. In a small bowl, whisk together the mayonnaise, yogurt, lemon juice, salt, black pepper, and coriander seed.

Blend in the onion and parsley or coriander leaves, reserving a small amount of the chopped herb for garnish.

2. Serve the sauce at room temperature in a serving bowl or in individual pots for each guest, sprinkled with the reserved herb.

FRIED GREEN TOMATOES

We are very fond of Fried Green Tomatoes, particularly at the end of the gardening season when there are no ripe tomatoes left on the vines.

Often, they are served for breakfast, using leftover bacon fat for the frying, or with a fried-fish dinner, frying the tomatoes first in the hot corn oil and then the fish.

Use only very hard green tomatoes which show no signs of ripening, so that they will remain firm and tart after frying.

Serves 4 to 6

1¼ to 1½ pounds very hard green tomatoes
Corn oil for deep frying
1 whole egg
1 cup yellow cornmeal
Salt and freshly ground black pepper, to taste

1. Wash and core the tomatoes, but do not peel or seed them. Cut them horizontally into slices about ½-inch thick. Place them in a single layer on paper towels until ready to fry.

2. Heat the corn oil in a heavy skillet to about 375° F or until a cube of bread browns instantly.

The depth of the oil should be ½ inch if you are only frying the tomatoes and 1 inch if you will be frying fish afterward. When deep frying, it is dangerous to add additional cold oil to hot oil already in the skillet.

3. In a small bowl, beat the egg well. Measure the cornmeal into a separate bowl. When the oil is hot, moisten a slice of tomato in the beaten egg and dip it into the cornmeal, coating it evenly.

With a slotted spatula or tongs, lower the tomato into the hot oil and continue with the next slice until all have been fried. The slices of tomato will sink to the bottom of the skillet, but should return to the surface almost instantly. If they do not, the oil is not hot enough.

After they have fried for about a minute or so and the edges begin to brown, turn and fry for another minute. Do not crowd the pan.

4. When the slices are lightly browned on both sides, remove them with a slotted spatula or tongs to a warm, ovenproof platter lined with paper towels. Salt and pepper to taste. Do not cover them, but keep warm in a low oven until ready to serve.

SOUTHERN FRIES

We are not sure that these fried potatoes are strictly Southern, but we have not encountered them outside the South. Whatever their origin, cut by hand into thick wedges they have a homey quality, very unlike the fast-food variety with its impersonal perfection.

You must use a deep-fryer with a basket. Our deep-fryer is nonelectric, aluminum, 9½ inches in diameter by 4 inches deep, and with a cover. For frying the potatoes, we pour in corn oil to a depth of 2 inches, which is 4 cups of oil in our fryer. After frying potatoes, we save the oil, storing it in the refrigerator, as it can be used again.

Allow at least 1 large Idaho potato per person and possibly more, as these are often eaten intemperately.

Serves 4

4 large Idaho potatoes
4 cups corn oil
1 teaspoon coarse salt (kosher or sea salt, freshly ground)

1. Peel the potatoes and cut them in half lengthwise. Cut each half into 4 lengthwise wedges.

Place the wedges in a bowl of cold water for ½ hour to draw out the starch and to prevent discoloration.

2. Heat the corn oil, covered, in a deep fryer with the basket removed, to 375° F or until a bread cube browns instantly.

3. Drain the potatoes on paper towels, drying them thoroughly before frying. If they are not properly dried, the oil will foam up when the potatoes are lowered into the basket.

4. Place one third of the dried potatoes in the fryer basket and lower them slowly into the heated oil. Fry the potatoes for 10 minutes. They will be lightly browned.

If they are browning too quickly, adjust the heat. Move the potatoes about with a wooden spoon to brown them evenly.

Drain the potatoes on a double layer of paper towels and continue with a second and third batch until all of the potatoes are fried.

At this point, the potatoes may remain on the paper towels for up to an hour or until you are ready for the second frying, which must be done just before serving.

5. When you are about ready to serve, if the oil has cooled, reheat it to 375° F. Again lower the potatoes, placed in the basket, into the heated oil. Fry them in three batches, this time for only 2 minutes.

This second frying insures a very crispy and golden-brown potato, whereas the first frying was for cooking purposes only.

6. Drain the potatoes on paper towels and sprinkle them with the salt. Toss them about to distribute the salt. Serve immediately. (If they must be held, place them in a dish lined with paper towels, in a warm oven.)

FRIED OKRA

Fried Okra, with its hot, spicy flavor, served with Fried Fish, Mother's Grits, and Country Cornbread (see recipe index), is country living at its best.

Serves 4

1 pound fresh okra pods, no longer than 2½ inches
1 teaspoon coriander seeds
3 tablespoons corn oil
½ teaspoon salt
½ teaspoon freshly ground dried hot red pepper
1½ tablespoons coarsely chopped garlic

1. Wipe the okra pods with damp paper towels to clean them. Trim the stems to within ⅛ inch of the pods, being careful not to cut into them.

2. Toast the coriander seeds in a small skillet over low heat for about 5 minutes to bring out their flavor. Grind the seeds.

3. Place the corn oil in a heavy, 10-inch skillet over medium-high heat. When the oil is hot, add the okra. Sprinkle it with the salt, coriander seed, hot red pepper, and garlic.

Begin tossing immediately, using a spatula in one hand and a wooden spoon in the other. Continue to toss the ingredients for 4 to 6 minutes, depending upon the size of the okra.

The okra should remain very crisp. Do not let it overcook. The pods should show no signs of softening. The garlic may brown and crisp, but that, too, gives added flavor. Do not discard it.

Serve the okra immediately for optimum crispness.

ZUCCHINI FRITTERS

We like to prepare these fritters on "Fish Night," frying them just before we fry our fish. Not only do we get double usage from the oil, but the house is filled with the aroma of the Garam Masala, rather than the fish.

We grow two varieties of zucchini. Our staple variety is Burpee Hybrid zucchini, which consistently performs well, and the other, which we are using for the first time, is Black Magic zucchini, a new variety. The plants are compact and the zucchini are a very dark green with an extremely firm texture so that they are good keepers.

Makes about 30 fritters; serves 4 to 6

1 pound zucchini
½ teaspoon salt
2 tablespoons unsalted butter
1 medium onion, chopped fine
½ teaspoon freshly ground black pepper
1 teaspoon Garam Masala (see page 190)
Corn oil for frying
1 cup all-purpose, unbleached flour
1 teaspoon baking powder
2 eggs, slightly beaten

1. Trim and discard the ends of the zucchini. Cut the zucchini into thin, julienne strips, no more than 1½ inches long. A food processor or Mouli-Julienne fitted with the medium shredding disk works perfectly for this step. If you have no equipment that will julienne the zucchini, it can be done by hand or even shredded on the medium side of a hand grater.

Place the zucchini in a colander or sieve and toss the strips with the salt. Let the zucchini drain for ½ hour to draw out excess moisture.

2. In a 10-inch skillet over medium-low heat, melt the butter. Add the onion and sauté it until it wilts, but does not brown. Remove from the heat, if you are not ready to add the zucchini.

3. When the zucchini has drained for ½ hour, take up small handfuls and squeeze it to rid it of as much liquid as possible. Add the zucchini to the skillet with the onion. Sprinkle with the pepper and garam masala. Toss and sauté the mixture over medium heat until all of the moisture evaporates from the skillet. Be careful that the vegetables do not burn.

Remove the skillet from the heat and let the ingredients cool for about 10 minutes. (At this point, you could serve the zucchini as an excellent vegetable dish.)

WHAT TO BUY OR ORDER NOW

July is probably the only month in the year when we may not be visited by the United Parcel Service delivering something we've ordered. But, it is time to take stock of canning ingredients and jars. Some supermarkets will be running low or preparing to put canning items away for the season. We try to have several dozen more jars, lids, and bands on hand than we think we will need. Even if they are not used this season, they will be the next and if the price goes up over the year, we will have made a little savings.

This also holds true for vinegar as we make second plantings of cucumbers and beets and, depending upon the yields, we may do second cannings.

Lastly, a close watch is kept for specials on lemons and onions which we use in either our frozen Pesto or Canned Tomato Sauce.

4. In a heavy, 10-inch skillet (preferably cast iron) or a wok, pour in corn oil to a depth of 1 inch, but no more than half full. Heat the oil to about 360°F. The fritters fry very quickly so the oil must not be as hot as for most frying, otherwise they will burn on the outside and the inside will not be done. If you do not have a deep-frying thermometer, use a little guesswork by dropping tiny bits of the fritter batter into the oil to gauge the heat.

5. While the oil is heating, begin warming your serving bowl. Sift the flour and baking powder together into a medium-sized mixing bowl. Add the eggs and blend them in thoroughly. Add the zucchini mixture and blend it in.

6. When the oil is hot, scoop up a roughly rounded teaspoon of the batter and, with the back of another spoon, slide the batter into the hot oil. The fritter will expand as it fries.

Turn the fritter with a slotted spatula as soon as the edges begin to brown. This will be less than 30 seconds. Brown on the other side for another 30 seconds or until the fritter is golden brown all over.

Remove the fritter with the spatula and place it in a heated serving bowl, lined with several paper towels, to drain. Continue in this manner until all of the batter has been used, being careful not to crowd the skillet or wok as you fry the fritters. Adjust the temperature of the cooking oil when necessary.

7. Serve the fritters as soon as possible, removing the paper towels before bringing the serving bowl to the table.

AND IN OUR GARDEN

Very little is planted in the garden in July unless there is space and then we plant more beans. Most of our time is spent weeding, watering and picking. Working in the intense heat, the wounds of summer begin to appear. Sunburn is not a problem as our skins have been gradually exposed as the weather warmed. Unusual fatigue was a problem until we increased our intake of bananas to replace potassium loss. Combined with yogurt, bananas keep our energies at their highest levels.

We do develop something we call "Pesto Thumb" which comes from picking so much basil that the leaves dye the nail indelibly green. And, on the other hand, we also burn from "Garlic Fingers" caused by peeling so many cloves for our pickles, pesto and tomato sauce. To top it off, our systems are a bit acidic from the gluttonous eating of tomatoes. For these ailments, the arrival of winter is the cure.

Note: If you are serving Fried Fish with the fritters, Coriander Sauce (see page 271) makes a good accompaniment for both dishes.

AUGUST

APPETIZING
ONE-DISH MEALS

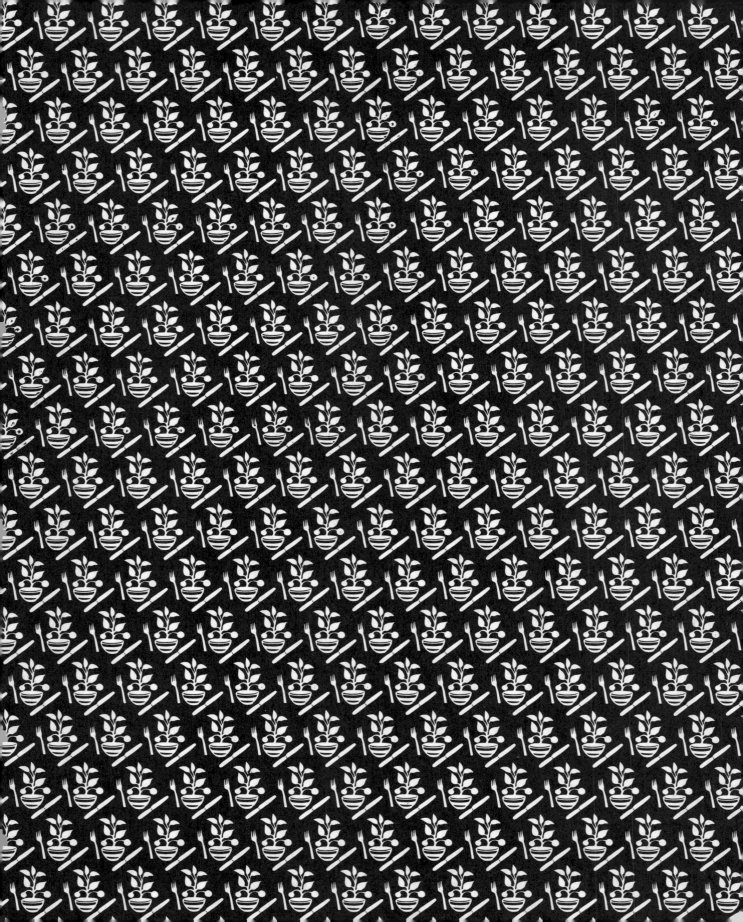

APPETIZING ONE-DISH MEALS

After so many months of looking somewhat sad in the garden, in August the eggplants become beautiful with their purple flowers. Quickly they begin to bear glossy, dark fruits which we prepare for immediate consumption. Those we can't eat, and there are many, we prepare as Eggplant Sauté and freeze for winter use.

Beside eggplants, bushels of tomatoes and peppers are gathered daily along with Swiss chard and our first spaghetti squash. In one or more combinations, these vegetables produce appetizing and easily prepared one-dish summer suppers that are particularly welcome on days when kitchen space is at a premium due to canning and freezing. We think of tians (closely related to gratins), frittatas (generous Italian omeletlike creations), and pizzas as perfect dishes to prepare in our busy kitchen. Once the basic techniques are learned, little thought is required—just imagination for varying your ingredients. In other seasons, other ingredients will proffer themselves. With or without a garden, these recipes can be enjoyed all year long.

EGGPLANT SAUTÉ

Use this recipe for preparing Caponata (see page 281) or as part of the filling for the pizza on page 288. Both recipes follow the basic sauté.

The sauté is excellent on pasta just as it is. For 4 servings, toss 2 cups of the Eggplant Sauté with one recipe of freshly made spaghetti or fettuccine. Have plenty of Parmesan or Romano cheese for sprinkling on top of each serving.

Makes 4 pints (8 cups)

2 pounds firm eggplant
1 teaspoon salt
1 pound mushrooms
3 medium onions
4 large cloves garlic
⅓ cup olive oil
3 large red bell peppers
1 large green bell pepper
2 pounds ripe tomatoes
2 fresh cayenne peppers, each 4 inches, or 1 teaspoon
    freshly and coarsely ground dried hot red pepper
½ teaspoon freshly ground black pepper
3 tablespoons of a finely chopped fresh herb, such as basil, thyme,
    oregano; or 1 tablespoon of fresh rosemary; or 1 teaspoon of a
    dried herb

1. Cut the eggplant(s), unpeeled, into lengthwise slices ⅜-inch thick. Cut the slices into ⅜-inch strips. Cut the strips into ⅜-inch dice.

Spread the dice on paper towels and sprinkle them with the salt. Let them drain for 30 minutes to remove excess moisture and bitterness.

2. Trim and discard the ends from the mushroom stems, then wipe the mushrooms with damp paper towels. Chop them coarsely and set aside.

3. Peel and chop the onions coarsely. Peel and mince the garlic. Heat the olive oil in a 12-inch skillet. Add the onion and garlic and sauté over medium heat until they wilt and begin to color.

Add the mushrooms and sauté them until they have given up their moisture and it has evaporated.

4. Meanwhile, core and seed the bell peppers and chop them coarsely. Set aside.

5. Peel the tomatoes by first immersing them in boiling water for 30 seconds to loosen their skin. Core, seed and chop the tomatoes coarse, and set them aside.

6. If you are using fresh cayenne peppers, mince but do not seed them. Set aside.

7. When the mushrooms have given up their liquid and it has evaporated, squeeze the eggplant dice between fresh paper towels to dry them. Add them to the skillet with the chopped bell peppers. Sprinkle the ingredients with either the cayenne peppers or dried hot red pepper and black pepper.

Continue to cook over medium heat for 15 minutes, tossing frequently with wooden spoons.

8. Add the chopped tomatoes and the herb of your choice to the skillet and cook for another 15 minutes, still tossing with the wooden spoons, until the tomatoes have given up their liquid and it has evaporated.

9. The sauté is now ready to be used for pizza or pasta. Additional seasoning and a chilling period in the refrigerator are necessary if you wish to serve caponata.

Note: To freeze the eggplant sauté, let it cool to room temperature. Place the mixture in freezer containers, leaving a 1-inch headspace. Label the containers and freeze them.

CAPONATA

Serve Caponata as an appetizer, as part of an antipasto, or as a vegetable side dish with meats, chicken, or fish. You may vary the ingredients according to your taste, adding more vinegar if you wish. We do not recommend making caponata for freezing. Make the Basic Eggplant Sauté and freeze it, but add the caponata ingredients later for a fresher-tasting cold dish.

Makes about 5 cups

3 ounces pancetta (Italian bacon, see page 54), diced and sautéed, or thinly sliced salami, cut into julienne strips (both are optional)
1 tablespoon olive oil, if you are using pancetta
¼ cup pignolia (pine) nuts
6 ripe olives
2 tablespoons red wine vinegar
½ recipe Eggplant Sauté (see page 279)

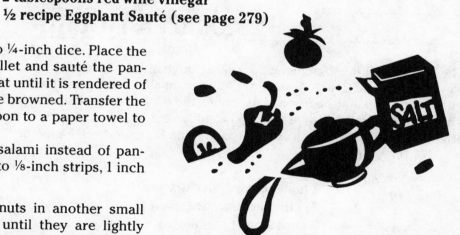

1. Cut the pancetta into ¼-inch dice. Place the olive oil in a small skillet and sauté the pancetta over very low heat until it is rendered of its fat and the dice have browned. Transfer the dice with a slotted spoon to a paper towel to drain.

If you are using salami instead of pancetta, cut the slices into ⅛-inch strips, 1 inch long.

2. Toast the pignolia nuts in another small skillet over low heat until they are lightly browned. Stir often so that they do not burn.

3. Pit the olives and cut them into thin, lengthwise slivers.

4. *If you are preparing the caponata at the same time that you are making the eggplant sauté*, add the pancetta (or salami), olives, and vinegar to the eggplant mixture during the last 5 minutes of cooking. The vinegar must have a little cooking time to remove its "edge." After the caponata has cooled, add the pignolia nuts.

Refrigerate the mixture, covered, for several hours or overnight before serving. The flavor will be at its best several days later and the caponata will keep for a week in the refrigerator. When serving, let the caponata come to room temperature.

If your eggplant sauté is cold or frozen, reheat it in a saucepan just until it is hot. Proceed with the directions in Step 4, giving the mixture, with the added ingredients, 5 minutes of cooking time.

PIZZA

More and more, pizza is being made at home, where it is receiving its deserved place as a truly delectable one-dish meal. Pizzas are perfect for showing off your creativity and once you have made our versions, we encourage you to experiment with your own.

A baking stone will produce a pizza far superior to one baked in a pan. The crust will cook uniformly throughout and the possibilities of burned or soggy crusts will be eliminated. However, if you are timid about beginning your first pizzas by sliding them from your peel (paddle) to the hot stone, buy a pizza pan (they are inexpensive) and use it until you are an "expert." The 14-inch black-steel, deep-dish pizza pan from Brookstone (see the mail order listing) will give you a far better crust than the aluminum pans. Whether baked on a stone or in a pan, always cut your pizza slices with kitchen sheers. It is the easiest way and the pans are easily damaged if you use a knife or pizza cutter.

BASIC PIZZA DOUGH

The amounts of the ingredients for pizza dough always remain the same, but as with our breads, you may vary the flours. Always use 1 cup of an all-purpose, unbleached flour for 1 of the 2 cups. The second cup may be more of the unbleached, or a whole-wheat or semolina flour, as we prefer. The semolina flour will give the crust a golden color and more texture than ordinary flour. Do not attempt to make the dough with only semolina flour, as it will be too dry and crumbly to knead.

For one 14-inch pizza

> **1 tablespoon active dry yeast**
> **¾ cup warm water (105° F)**
> **2 cups flour (see above)**
> **½ teaspoon salt**
> **1 tablespoon olive oil**

1. Using a 1-cup measuring cup, dissolve the yeast in the warm water.

2. *If you are making the pizza dough in a food processor*, fit it with the metal blade and add the flour and salt. With a few On/Off motions, mix them.

When the yeast has dissolved, add the olive oil to it. Do not stir. With the motor on, pour the yeast mixture through the feed tube. Within 30 seconds, the dough will form a moist ball. Remove it from the bowl and knead again on your floured work surface, just to further shape the ball of dough.

Place the dough in a mixing bowl with a 1½-quart capacity. Cover with a towel and let the dough rise in a warm spot (80°F) until it has doubled in bulk. This will take 1 hour.

If you are making the pizza dough by hand, measure the flour onto your work surface and sprinkle the flour with the salt. Make a well in the center of the flour.

When the yeast has dissolved, add the olive oil to it. Do not stir. Pour the yeast mixture into the well.

Working with the fingers of one hand, begin mixing the flour into the liquids. Work from the inside, bringing small amounts of the flour into the liquids until a soft dough is formed. Keep a scraper in the other hand to avoid an overflow.

When the flour has been incorporated into the liquids and you have a soft dough, begin to knead the dough until it is smooth. This will take about 5 minutes. Flour your work surface if the dough is sticking to it.

Cover with a towel and let the dough rise in a warm spot (80°F) until it has doubled in bulk. This will take about 1 hour.

BAKING STONES FOR PIZZA

Buy the best quality of baking stone available. We recommend a round stone as thick as you can possibly get. This thickness is a definite plus, as thinner models are more likely to crack in the oven. The thinner stones are all right for breads, but for obvious reasons, not very good for pizzas with their fillings.

Respect your stone and handle it with care. Never touch it when it is hot. Let the stone cool before removing it. If your pizza is ready to be removed from the stone and you need the oven for another use, just leave the stone inside and proceed with your other baking.

Never clean the stone with any kind of detergent. It will absorb the detergent and the flavor of your pizzas will be affected. If it becomes soiled, use a metal scraper or scouring pad (without soap) with hot water to clean it.

PREPARING AND BAKING YOUR PIZZA

Whether you are baking your pizza on a baking stone or in a pizza pan, the oven rack should be in the lower third of the oven. The filled pizza will be heavy, so prior to preheating the oven, you might want to practice sliding some similar object from the peel onto the baking stone. The peel must be given a strong forward thrust for the pizza to leave the peel. (The first few times we used the baking stone, we had visions of the pizza landing on the floor of the oven, but so far it has not happened.)

Instructions for a baking stone

1. About half an hour before you plan to bake your pizza, place your baking stone in the lower third of your oven. Preheat the oven to 450°F.

2. When your pizza dough has doubled in volume, scrape it from the bowl onto your floured work surface. Do not knead, but punch the dough down and press it into a circle.

Work the dough as little as possible; if it is overworked, it will become brittle as it bakes. Press the dough into a circle 16 inches in diameter. Try to do this with your hands positioned flat on the dough. If the dough is too resistant, roll it with a rolling pin.

3. Fold the circle of dough in half and unfold it onto your wooden peel, which has been generously sprinkled with cornmeal. Fold 1 inch of the outside edge of dough in to form a

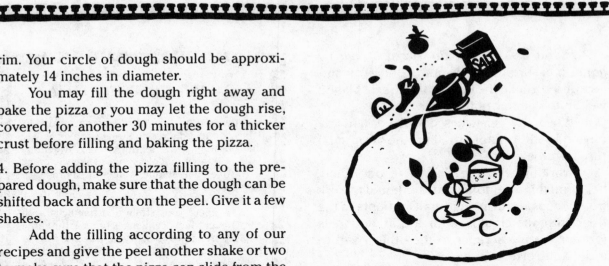

rim. Your circle of dough should be approximately 14 inches in diameter.

You may fill the dough right away and bake the pizza or you may let the dough rise, covered, for another 30 minutes for a thicker crust before filling and baking the pizza.

4. Before adding the pizza filling to the prepared dough, make sure that the dough can be shifted back and forth on the peel. Give it a few shakes.

Add the filling according to any of our recipes and give the peel another shake or two to make sure that the pizza can slide from the peel without sticking. Only then open the oven door.

If the pizza should refuse to leave the peel, prod it off with a wide spatula. (Clean your peel by rubbing the excess cornmeal into the surface to absorb any overflow of filling. Do not use water, as the peel will warp. Brush off the cornmeal.)

5. Bake the pizza for 25 to 30 minutes until it is bubbling and the top is lightly colored.

6. To remove the pizza from the baking stone, pull the oven rack halfway out from the oven. Hold a round serving platter or an aluminum pizza pan just under the rack and, with the aid of a spatula, slide the pizza from the baking stone onto your platter or pan.

7. Place your serving platter or pizza pan on a large, thick mat as it will be very hot and could remove the finish from your table.

8. Let the pizza cool for about 5 minutes or so, then cut it first in half with kitchen shears, and then cut each half into 4 serving pieces.

Instructions for a pizza pan

1. Oil the bottom and sides of your pizza pan with 1 tablespoon of olive oil.

2. When your pizza dough has doubled in volume, follow Step 2 above, except press or roll the circle of dough to the 14-inch diameter of your pizza pan.

3. Fold the circle of dough in half and unfold it into your pizza pan. With your fingers held together and straight out, press the dough from the center to the sides until a rim is formed on the outside of the pan.

Again, you may fill the dough and bake the pizza right away, or you may let it rise, covered, for another 30 minutes for a thicker crust.

4. Fill the prepared pizza dough with your filling and bake it for 25 to 30 minutes in your oven until it is bubbling and the top is lightly colored.

5. Bring the pizza, still in the pan, to the table. Place it on a large, thick mat, as the extreme heat can ruin your table.

6. Let the pizza cool for 5 minutes or so, then cut it in half with kitchen shears and then cut each half into 4 serving pieces.

Note: When using metal pans, be careful not to cut into the pan with the shears. If you are using the black steel pan, be extra careful. When washing it, use only a brush, not a scouring pad to clean it. Dry the pan immediately and thoroughly in a warm oven.

SAUSAGE PIZZA

This pizza has all the familiar ingredients. It calls for adding the onions and peppers to the filling raw, rather than sautéed. Each method has its own merits and if you prefer, you may lightly sauté the vegetables in a little olive oil first.

Serves 4

1 recipe Basic Pizza Dough, using half semolina flour (see page 282)
½ pound Hot Sausage (see page 45)
1 pound fresh mushrooms
3 tablespoons olive oil
½ teaspoon freshly ground dried hot red pepper, plus additional (see Step 11)
1 teaspoon dried oregano
2 large bell peppers
2 medium onions
2 cups coarsely grated Swiss Gruyère cheese (6 ounces)
2 cups well-drained and coarsely chopped canned tomatoes

1. Prepare your pizza dough, using 1 cup all-purpose, unbleached flour and 1 cup semolina flour.

2. While the dough is rising, begin the preparation of the filling. Prick the sausages with the point of a knife in 5 or 6 places.

Place the sausages in a saucepan and cover them with water. Simmer, partially covered and over medium-low heat, for 10 minutes. Drain the sausages and set them aside.

3. Trim and discard the ends from the mushroom stems. Wipe the mushrooms with damp paper towels, and slice them thin.

Place 2 tablespoons of the olive oil in a 10-inch skillet over medium-low heat. Add the mushrooms and sprinkle them with the red pepper and oregano. Toss and sauté the mushrooms until they give up their liquid and it evaporates. This will take about 15 minutes.

4. Place your oven rack in the lower third of the oven and preheat the oven to 450°F. If you are using a baking stone, place it in the oven at this time.

5. Core, halve, and seed the bell peppers. Cut the halves into ¼-inch lengthwise strips. Cut each strip in half. Set aside.

6. Peel the onions and cut them in half lengthwise. Cut the halves into lengthwise slivers. Set aside.

7. When the pizza dough has doubled in volume, follow the instructions for preparing your pizza dough on page 283, for either a baking stone or pizza pan.

8. Sprinkle the prepared pizza dough with 1 cup of the grated cheese. In evenly distributed layers, add half the onions, bell peppers, mushrooms, and tomatoes.

9. Make a second layer the same as the first. Cut the sausages into ¼-inch crosswise slices and arrange them evenly on the filling. Press them lightly into the top layer of tomatoes.

Dribble the remaining 1 tablespoon of olive oil over the surface of the pizza.

10. Place the pizza in the oven and bake it, following the instructions on page 283, for either a baking stone or pizza pan.

Bake the pizza for 25 to 30 minutes until it is bubbling hot and the crust is golden brown.

11. When serving, place a small bowl filled with freshly and coarsely ground dried hot red pepper on the table so that additional pepper may be sprinkled on the slices for those who wish it.

Note: You can use fresh, ripe tomatoes for the pizza. It is difficult to estimate the amount that will be needed, as that is determined by the amount of water in the tomatoes. You will need at least 2½ pounds.

Peel, core, seed, and chop the tomatoes coarse. Place them in a sieve and sprinkle them with ½ teaspoon of salt. Toss to mix in the salt and let the tomatoes drain for ½ hour, pressing down on them occasionally to exude the water.

In Step 3, after the mushrooms have given up their liquid and it has evaporated, add the drained tomatoes. Increase the heat to medium and sauté the vegetables, stirring, until the excess liquid evaporates from the tomatoes. Proceed with the recipe as given.

A RED OR YELLOW SUMMER PIZZA

With the wide choice of color in summer vegetables, it is fun to make this pizza either with all red vegetables or all yellow vegetables. In our garden, we purposely grow a selection of yellow vegetables. The yellow Sunray tomatoes have a special flavor of their own and, when cooked, their color becomes a vivid orange. Choose your onions, bell peppers, and tomatoes to fit your color scheme.

We specify using Italian Fontina as one of the cheeses as its lightness goes well with the fresh vegetables. You may substitute mozzarella cheese, but be careful of the brand you use. We find most mozzarella to be much too salty and therefore do not use it.

Serves 4

1 recipe Basic Pizza Dough (see page 282)
3 pounds fresh, ripe tomatoes
½ teaspoon salt
¾ pound onions
3 tablespoons olive oil
1½ tablespoons minced garlic

3 large bell peppers
1 pound fresh mushrooms
¼ teaspoon freshly ground black pepper
¼ cup finely chopped fresh basil
3 cups coarsely grated Italian Fontina cheese (9 ounces)
½ cup freshly grated Parmesan or Romano cheese

1. Prepare your pizza dough, using the flours of your choice.

2. While the pizza dough is rising, prepare the filling. Peel the tomatoes by first immersing them in boiling water for 30 seconds to loosen the skins. Core, seed, and chop the tomatoes coarsely and place them in a sieve. Sprinkle them with the salt and toss.

Let the tomatoes drain for ½ hour to draw out excess liquid. Press down upon them occasionally to exude more liquid. (Save this liquid to use later as part of a soup stock.)

3. Peel the onions and cut them in half lengthwise. Cut each half into thin lengthwise slivers.

4. Place 2 tablespoons of the olive oil in a 10-inch skillet over medium-low heat. Add the onions and garlic. Sauté until the onions wilt.

5. Core, halve, and seed the bell peppers. Cut them into lengthwise julienne strips, ¼-inch thick. Add the strips to the skillet when the onions have wilted. Toss to mix.

Cover the skillet and sauté the vegetables, still over medium-low heat, for 10 minutes.

6. Trim and discard the ends from the mushroom stems, then wipe them with damp paper towels. Slice the mushrooms thin and add to the skillet after the bell peppers have sautéed for 10 minutes. Sprinkle the vegetables with the black pepper. Toss and increase the heat to medium high.

Sauté the vegetables, tossing often, until the mushrooms have given up their liquid and it evaporates.

7. When the liquid has evaporated from the mushrooms, add the drained tomatoes to the skillet. Tossing constantly, sauté the vegetables until any additional liquid from the tomatoes evaporates.

Remove the skillet from the heat and add the fresh basil.

8. Place your oven rack in the lower third of the oven and preheat the oven to 450°F. If you are using a baking stone, place it in the oven at this time.

9. When the pizza dough has doubled in volume, follow the instructions for preparing your pizza dough on page 283, for either a baking stone or pizza pan.

10. Sprinkle the prepared pizza dough with 1 cup of the Fontina cheese. Making an even layer, spread half of the sautéed vegetables over the cheese. Cover the vegetables with another cup of the cheese. Add the remaining vegetables, making another even layer. Cover with the remaining cup of the Fontina cheese.

Sprinkle the filling with the Parmesan or Romano cheese and dribble the remaining 1 tablespoon of olive oil evenly over the surface.

11. Place the pizza in the oven and bake it, following the instructions on page 283, for either a baking stone or pizza pan.

Bake the pizza for 25 to 30 minutes until it is bubbling hot and the crust and filling are a light golden brown.

EGGPLANT PIZZA

If you use frozen Eggplant Sauté for this pizza, remove it from the freezer several hours ahead and let it defrost and come to room temperature before combining it with the tomatoes or tomato sauce.

Serves 4

1 recipe Basic Pizza Dough, using half semolina flour (see page 282)
2 cups Eggplant Sauté (see page 279)
1 cup well-drained canned tomatoes or 1 cup Tomato Sauce
   (see pages 310 and 311)
3 tablespoons Pesto (optional; see page 309)
2 cups coarsely grated Swiss Gruyère cheese (6 ounces)
2 teaspoons olive oil

1. Make your pizza dough, using 1 cup all-purpose, unbleached flour and 1 cup semolina flour.

2. When the dough has doubled in volume, follow the instructions for preparing your pizza dough on page 283, for either the baking stone or pizza pan.

3. Place your oven rack in the lower third of the oven and preheat the oven to 450°F. If you are using a baking stone, place it in the oven at this time.

4. In a mixing bowl, combine the eggplant sauté with the tomatoes or tomato sauce.

5. If you are using the pesto, spread the 3 tablespoons evenly over the surface of the prepared pizza dough.

6. Sprinkle the dough with 1 cup of the grated cheese. Cover the cheese with half the eggplant and tomato mixture.

   Make another layer with the remaining cheese and cover it with the remaining eggplant and tomato mixture.

7. Dribble the olive oil over the surface of the pizza and place the pizza in the preheated oven, following the instructions on page 283, for either a baking stone or pizza pan.

SWISS CHARD PIZZA

The filling for this pizza is basically a tian mixture (a tian is another form of gratin) and is quite different from the fillings one usually encounters.

Serves 4

1 recipe Basic Pizza Dough, using half whole-wheat flour
(see page 282)
2 pounds Swiss chard (leaves and ribs)
3 ounces pancetta (Italian bacon, see page 54)
2 tablespoons olive oil
2 medium onions
4 large cloves garlic
1 pound fresh mushrooms
½ teaspoon freshly ground black pepper
2 cups coarsely grated Swiss Gruyère cheese (6 ounces)
2 eggs, slightly beaten
¼ cup freshly grated Parmesan cheese

1. Prepare your pizza dough, using 1 cup all-purpose, unbleached flour and 1 cup whole-wheat flour.

2. While the dough is rising, begin the preparation of the filling.

Wash and drain the Swiss chard. Trim and discard the ends of the ribs. Place each leaf face down on your work surface and cut out the rib.

Coarsely chop the leaves and ribs separately. The leaves should be chopped into 1-inch pieces and the ribs into pieces no larger than ¼ inch. Set aside.

3. Cut the pancetta into ¼-inch dice. Place 1 tablespoon of the olive oil in a large skillet and sauté the pancetta over low heat until it is rendered of its fat and has lightly browned. Do not drain.

4. Peel and chop the onions coarsely. Peel and mince the garlic. Trim and discard the ends from the mushroom stems, then wipe the mushrooms with damp paper towels. Slice the mushrooms thin.

5. When the pancetta has browned, add the onions and garlic to the skillet. Sauté over medium heat until they have wilted.

Add the mushrooms and black pepper. Sauté the mushrooms until they have given up their moisture and it has evaporated.

6. Add the chopped Swiss chard to the skillet and sauté just until it has wilted. Remove the skillet from the heat and let it cool briefly.

7. Place your oven rack in the lower third of the oven and preheat the oven to 450°F. If you are using a baking stone, place it in the oven at this time.

8. When the pizza dough has doubled in volume, follow the instructions for preparing your pizza dough on page 283, for either a baking stone or pizza pan.

9. When the mixture in the skillet has cooled for a brief time, add the grated Swiss Gruyère cheese and mix the ingredients with a wooden spoon. Add the eggs and mix again.

10. Spoon the filling into your prepared pizza dough, spreading it evenly across the surface and to the outside rim.

Sprinkle the pizza with the grated Parmesan cheese and dribble the remaining 1 tablespoon of olive oil over the surface.

11. Place the pizza in the oven and bake it, following the instructions on page 283, for either a baking stone or pizza pan.

Bake for 25 to 30 minutes until the surface is slightly gratinéed.

BASIC TIAN

A Tian is closely related to a gratin. Generally, it contains Swiss chard, spinach, or zucchini or a combination of these vegetables. Rice and eggs are used as binders for the mixture and the baking is like that of a gratin. Our basic recipe uses only Swiss chard, but you may add spinach, zucchini, or even string beans for variations. If you should wish to add spinach, use 1 pound of fresh spinach leaves that have been coarsely chopped, adding them to the mixing bowl with the 3 pounds of chopped Swiss chard.

For zucchini, add 1 pound, unpeeled and coarsely shredded. Lightly salt the zucchini and let it drain in a colander for ½ hour to remove excess liquid. Squeeze it dry before adding to the tian mixture.

Only if you combine all three vegetables should you reduce the Swiss chard to 2 pounds and increase the eggs to 3 rather than 2.

Use string beans (½ pound) only with the Swiss chard. The string beans should be given a 3-minute blanching in boiling, salted water, drained and rinsed with cold water and then cut into 1-inch pieces.

We prefer the flavor of brown rice cooked in whey in our tians, but you may use white rice. Often, we will add ½ pound of sautéed mushrooms to the mixture for variety. Serve the tian as you would any vegetable gratin. We are satisfied to have the tian as our main course, followed with a salad and crusty bread, but it may be served as a first course or as an accompaniment to meats.

Serves 4 to 6

½ cup raw brown rice
2 tablespoons olive oil, plus ¼ cup
3 ounces pancetta (Italian bacon, see page 54), cut into ¼-inch dice
3 pounds Swiss chard (leaves and ribs)
1 cup finely chopped parsley
2 medium onions, chopped fine
1½ tablespoons finely chopped garlic
1 fresh cayenne pepper, 4-inches long, unseeded and minced,
    or ½ teaspoon freshly ground dried hot red pepper
½ teaspoon freshly ground black pepper
2 cups coarsely grated Swiss Gruyère cheese (6 ounces)
2 eggs, lightly beaten
¼ cup freshly grated Parmesan or Romano cheese

1. Prepare the brown rice, following the instructions given on page 74. Set aside.

2. Heat 1 tablespoon of the olive oil in a small skillet. Add the diced pancetta and sauté over very low heat until the dice have been rendered of their fat and have lightly browned. Do not drain.

3. Rinse and pat the Swiss chard dry. Place the leaves face down on your work surface and cut out the ribs. Coarsely shred the leaves and chop the ribs fine. Place the chard in a large mixing bowl.

4. Preheat the oven to 375° F.

5. Add the parsley, onions, garlic, fresh cayenne (or dried hot red pepper), and black pepper to the Swiss chard. Toss the mixture with large wooden spoons or your hands.

6. Add the brown rice, rendered pancetta with the fat, Gruyère cheese, and eggs to the mixing bowl. Toss again, this time very thoroughly, so that the mixture is dense.

7. Oil a 17-inch oval gratin dish with 1 tablespoon of the olive oil. Add the chard mixture and pack it firmly into the gratin dish. Smooth the surface.

Sprinkle with the Parmesan or Romano cheese and dribble the remaining ¼ cup of olive oil evenly over the surface.

8. Bake the tian on the middle rack of the oven for about 1 hour, until the liquids have been absorbed and the surface has gratinéed.

EGGPLANT GRATIN

This is our version of Eggplant Parmigiana. Finding almost all mozzarella cheese unpalatable due to its extreme saltiness, we use our homemade Cottage Cheese, creamed with a little heavy cream. This makes for a lighter dish. Brushing the fried eggplant slices with Pesto also adds an unusual touch.

The most difficult part of this recipe is selecting your eggplant. We specify 2 pounds, which may be either 2 medium eggplant or 3 smaller ones. They *must* be very firm or the slices will not fry properly. Soft eggplant slices will soak up the oil like sponges. Crisp slices, quickly fried, are delicious just as they are.

Serves 4 to 6

2 pounds eggplant (see above)
½ teaspoon salt
6 ounces homemade Cottage Cheese (see page 88), at room
    temperature
½ cup heavy cream
2 cups corn oil for frying
2 cups Tomato Sauce (see pages 310 and 311)
½ cup Pesto (see page 309)
⅓ cup freshly grated Parmesan cheese
1 tablespoon olive oil

1. Remove the stem section from the eggplants. Do not peel, but cut the eggplants into lengthwise slices, ⅓ inch thick. By cutting them lengthwise, the slices will not curl when they are fried.

Spread the slices on paper towels and sprinkle them with the salt. Let the slices drain for ½ hour. This will draw out excess moisture and rid the eggplant of any bitterness.

2. Meanwhile, cream the cottage cheese with the heavy cream and prepare the other ingredients so they will be ready to use. (This is assuming that the tomato sauce and pesto were made in advance.)

3. Preheat the oven to 400°F.

4. Heat the corn oil in a heavy, 10-inch skillet to 375° F or until a bread cube fries instantly.

Dry each slice of eggplant by pressing it between paper towels. Lower the slices into the hot oil. Turn the slices once. This goes very quickly if the oil is at the proper temperature. It should take no longer than 1 minute on each side for the eggplant slices to become a rich golden brown.

Remove at once with a slotted spatula to a platter lined with paper towels to drain. Place more paper towels between the layers as the slices are fried.

5. Spread ½ cup of the tomato sauce over the bottom of a 14-inch oval gratin dish. Arrange one-third of the eggplant slices over the sauce. Brush the slices with one-third of the pesto, covering the pesto with one-third of the creamed cottage cheese.

Make a second and third layer the same as the first, beginning with ½ cup of the tomato sauce, and one-third of the eggplant, pesto, and cottage cheese.

Spread the remaining ½ cup of tomato sauce on top. Sprinkle the gratin with the Parmesan cheese and dribble the olive oil over the surface.

6. Bake on the middle level of the oven for 30 minutes. The gratin will be bubbling and the top lightly browned. It will be very hot, so a short rest before serving is advised.

Serve with freshly made fettuccine, tossed only with butter and a little salt. The pasta can be cooked and tossed while the gratin rests for 5 to 10 minutes.

MUSHROOM AND SPINACH FRITTATA

Italian Frittatas are incomparable for spring and summer menus. They might best be described as very substantial omelets that instead of being folded are served open faced and cut into wedges. Ours are ample enough to be served as the main course for a summer meal, followed with a salad that does not include any of the vegetables that are in the frittata.

For this variation use *only* fresh spinach. A half pound is needed for the recipe, but if the spinach has long stems attached to the leaves, purchase 10 ounces or so. The mushrooms must be very firm and white so that the texture and whiteness will not be destroyed when they are sautéed.

Serves 4

½ pound fresh spinach
1 pound fresh, firm mushrooms
6 tablespoons unsalted butter
3 tablespoons minced shallots
2 large cloves garlic, minced
½ teaspoon salt
½ teaspoon freshly ground black pepper
8 eggs, at room temperature
1 cup homemade Cottage Cheese (see page 88), at room temperature
¼ cup freshly grated Parmesan cheese
1 tablespoon olive oil

1. Carefully wash the spinach and remove the stems. Place in a colander to drain. Remove the ends from the mushroom stems. Slice the mushrooms thin.

2. In a 12-inch omelet pan or a large skillet with sloping sides, heat 2 tablespoons of the butter. Add the shallots and garlic. Sauté over medium-low heat until they have softened. Use only a wooden spoon to stir, so as not to damage your pan.

Add the sliced mushrooms, salt, and black pepper. Turn the heat to medium and sauté until the mushrooms give up their liquid and it evaporates. Remove the pan from the heat to cool.

3. In a large mixing bowl, beat the eggs until they are light. Chop the drained spinach fine (do not turn it into a purée) and add it to the eggs along with the cottage cheese. Stir to blend and then add the mushroom mixture from the omelet pan. Stir again.

4. Preheat the broiler.

5. Wipe the omelet pan clean with a paper towel and place it back on the stove over medium-high heat. Add the remaining 4 table-spoons of butter. When the butter is hot and bubbling, pour in the egg mixture. Quickly give the pan a few vigorous shakes back and forth across the burner surface to make sure that the frittata does not stick. Immediately turn the heat to medium low.

Continue to cook the frittata, without stirring, for about 10 minutes. Lift the edges with a fork to check that it is not sticking. If it is sticking, carefully lift it with a spatula and give the pan another shake or two.

6. When the egg mixture has set but the top is still a little runny, sprinkle the frittata with the Parmesan cheese and dribble the olive oil over the surface.

Place the pan 6 inches under the broiler, for 1 or 2 minutes until the cheese has melted and colored ever so slightly. The eggs should no longer be runny, but the frittata should not be dry.

7. With the aid of a spatula, slide the frittata onto a serving platter. You may serve the frittata immediately, cutting it into wedges, or it may cool to room temperature. The fresh flavor of the vegetables will be more pronounced at room temperature.

CABBAGE AND TOMATO FRITTATA

Use an early variety of summer cabbage, such as Early Jersey Wakefield, for the frittata, as the cabbage must be tender in texture and more delicate in flavor than winter varieties. For the cheese, you may use any of the Cheddars, Italian Fontina, or a Gruyère.

Serves 4

1 medium onion
1 pound cabbage
1 pound ripe tomatoes
2 tablespoons olive oil
½ teaspoon salt
¼ teaspoon freshly ground black pepper
8 eggs, at room temperature
1 cup coarsely grated cheese
4 tablespoons finely chopped fresh basil
1 jalapeño pepper, fresh or canned, chopped fine
4 tablespoons unsalted butter

1. Peel and chop the onion coarsely. Remove the outer leaves and quarter and core the cabbage. Shred the quarters fine either on the medium side of a hand grater or in a food processor fitted with the medium shredding disk. Peel, core, and seed the tomatoes. Chop the tomatoes coarse and place them in a sieve over a bowl for about 20 minutes to drain them of excess liquid. Toss and gently press down on the tomatoes to rid them of most of their liquid. After draining, you will have about 1 cup of tomatoes. Save the liquid for another use.

2. Heat the olive oil in a 12-inch omelet pan or large skillet with sloping sides. Add the chopped onion and shredded cabbage. Sprinkle with the salt and black pepper. Sauté over medium heat, tossing occasionally with a wooden spoon, until the vegetables are wilted and most of the moisture has evaporated from the pan.

Try to keep the cooking time to a minimum to preserve the color and texture of the cabbage. Add the chopped tomatoes and cook just until their moisture has evaporated. Remove the pan from the heat to cool.

3. In a large mixing bowl, beat the eggs until they are light. Add the grated cheese, 3 tablespoons of the fresh basil, and the jalapeño pepper. Stir in the vegetable mixture from the omelet pan.

4. Preheat the broiler. Also, begin warming your serving platter.

5. Wipe the omelet pan clean with a paper towel and place it back on the stove over medium-high heat. Add the butter.

When the butter is hot and bubbling, pour in the egg mixture. Quickly give the pan a few vigorous shakes back and forth across the burner surface to make sure that the frittata does not stick. Immediately turn the heat to medium low.

Continue to cook the frittata, without stirring, for about 10 minutes. Carefully lift the edges with a spatula and give the pan another shake to prevent the frittata from sticking.

6. When the eggs are set, but still a little runny on the surface, and the cheese has melted, place the frittata 6 inches under the broiler. Broil for 1 or 2 minutes, just until the surface lightly browns and the eggs are no longer runny.

7. Using a spatula, slide the frittata onto a heated serving platter. Sprinkle with the remaining 1 tablespoon of chopped basil. This frittata is best eaten while it is still hot.

SPAGHETTI SQUASH AND SPROUT FRITTATA

Spaghetti squash with its crisp texture and golden yellow color pairs admirably with eggs for an unusual frittata. Serve the frittata with Tomato Sauce (see pages 310 and 311), Hot Tomato Sauce (see page 352), or Tomato and Yogurt Sauce (see below).

If the frittata is to be served hot, the sauce should be hot. If the frittata is to be served at room temperature, the sauce, likewise, should be at room temperature. Allow ½ cup for each guest.

The spaghetti squash may be baked several days ahead or you may use frozen, if it is on hand. Let it defrost in a sieve to drain it of its liquid before preparing the frittata.

Serves 4

3 cups of the "spaghetti" from a 2½- to 3-pound baked spaghetti squash
3 medium onions
4 large cloves garlic
4 tablespoons olive oil
½ teaspoon salt
½ teaspoon freshly ground black pepper
8 eggs, at room temperature
1½ cups alfalfa sprouts (for growing instructions, see page 39)
½ cup freshly grated Parmesan or Romano cheese
4 tablespoons unsalted butter
2 tablespoons minced fresh basil or parsley for garnish

1. Preheat the oven to 350°F.

2. Line a heavy baking sheet that has sides with aluminum foil. Place the spaghetti squash on the baking sheet and pierce it with a fork in 8 or 9 places. Bake the squash until tender, 1 to 1½ hours. A fork should easily pierce the shell.

When the squash is tender, remove the baking sheet from the oven and let the squash cool until it can be handled. Cut the squash in half lengthwise and remove the seeds and fiber surrounding the seeds.

With a tablespoon, scrape the "spaghetti" from the shell. Measure the 3 cups needed for the frittata and reserve the remaining spaghetti (about 3 cups) for another use.

3. Peel the onions and cut them in half lengthwise. Cut each half into thin slices. Peel and mince the garlic.

4. In a 12-inch omelet pan or large skillet with sloping sides, heat 3 tablespoons of the olive oil. Add the onions and garlic. Sprinkle with the salt and black pepper. Sauté over medium heat until the vegetables have wilted.

Add the spaghetti squash and stir with a wooden spoon, just to mix. Remove the pan from the heat and set aside to cool slightly.

5. In a large mixing bowl, beat the eggs until they are light. Add 1 cup of the alfalfa sprouts and ¼ cup of the cheese to the eggs. Stir to mix and blend in the cooled vegetables from the omelet pan.

6. Preheat the broiler.

7. Wipe the omelet pan clean with a paper towel. Place the pan over medium-high heat and add the butter. When the butter is hot and bubbling, add the egg mixture. Quickly give the pan a few vigorous shakes back and forth across the burner to make sure that the frittata is not sticking. Immediately turn the heat to medium low.

Cook the frittata for about 10 minutes until the eggs are set, but still runny on the surface. Carefully lift it with a spatula and give the pan a few more shakes to prevent the frittata from sticking.

8. Sprinkle the frittata with the remaining ½ cup of alfalfa sprouts and ¼ cup of cheese. Dribble the remaining 1 tablespoon of olive oil over the surface. Place the omelet pan 6 inches under the broiler for 1 to 2 minutes until the frittata is lightly colored.

9. Using a spatula, slide the frittata onto a serving platter. Sprinkle with the minced fresh herb. Serve while the frittata is hot or later when it is at room temperature.

Note: You may vary this frittata by adding Pesto (see page 309). In Step 8, just before you sprinkle the frittata with the sprouts and cheese, spread 3 tablespoons of pesto on the surface. Continue with Steps 8 and 9. Serve this frittata with Pesto and Cream Sauce (see page 351).

TOMATO AND YOGURT SAUCE

If you have freshly made or home-canned Tomato Sauce on hand, this delectable sauce can be made in a matter of minutes. It also stretches out that precious tomato sauce if you are running low. Besides frittatas, we enjoy the sauce, hot or cold, with eggs or simply prepared fish dishes.

Purchased plain yogurt is acceptable, but do not use a commercially prepared tomato sauce or a recipe other than ours. Remember, too, that the tomato sauce can be made with yellow tomatoes for unexpected color.

Makes 1½ cups

1 cup Tomato Sauce (see pages 310 and 311)
½ cup Yogurt (see page 67), at room temperature
1 tablespoon any minced fresh herb (optional)

1. If you wish to serve the sauce cold, whisk the yogurt into the tomato sauce. Cover and refrigerate until you are ready to serve.

2. If you wish to serve the sauce hot, bring the tomato sauce, placed in a small saucepan, to a simmer over medium heat. Add the yogurt (see page 68), whisking it in, until the sauce is creamy and smooth. Bring back to a simmer and serve immediately. Garnish with a tablespoon of a fresh, minced herb if you wish.

SPAGHETTI SQUASH AND YELLOW ZUCCHINI FRITTATA

If you do not have a garden, you may have difficulty finding the squash blossoms called for in this recipe. They are optional and, although tasty, are added more for color than for flavor.

Pick only the male flowers, as obviously the female will be bearing the squash later. It is easy to distinguish between the two. The female flower will show a tiny bulbous growth where the blossom connects with the stem. This is the squash forming. Pick the flowers early in the morning as soon as the dew has fallen from the petals.

Carefully wash the flowers with a fine spray of water to remove any insects. Trim the stems to ¼ inch and refrigerate the flowers in a tightly-closed plastic bag, lined with a paper towel, until you are ready to prepare the frittata.

Serve this frittata with ½ cup of Tomato Sauce (see pages 310 and 311) for each guest. If you are fortunate enough to also have yellow tomatoes, make the sauce with them.

Serves 4

3 cups of the "spaghetti" from a 2½- to 3-pound baked spaghetti
  squash
3 medium onions
¾ pound small yellow zucchini (green may be used, if the yellow are
  not available)
4 large cloves garlic
4 tablespoons olive oil
½ teaspoon salt
½ teaspoon freshly ground black pepper
6 to 8 squash blossoms, optional (see above)
5 tablespoons unsalted butter
8 eggs, at room temperature
½ cup freshly grated Parmesan or Romano cheese
2 tablespoons minced fresh basil or parsley for garnish

1. Prepare the spaghetti squash as in Steps 1 and 2 for Spaghetti Squash and Sprout Frittata (page 295). This may be done ahead.

2. Peel the onions and cut them in half lengthwise. Cut each half into thin slices. Trim the ends from the zucchini and slice the zucchini into ⅛-inch rounds. Peel and mince the garlic.

3. In a 12-inch omelet pan or a large skillet with sloping sides, heat 3 tablespoons of the olive oil. Add the onions, zucchini, and garlic. Sprinkle with the salt and pepper.

   Sauté over medium heat until the vegetables have wilted and the moisture has evaporated from the pan.

   Add the spaghetti squash and stir with a wooden spoon, just to mix. Set the pan aside, off the heat, to cool slightly.

4. While the vegetables are sautéing, in another small skillet quickly sauté the squash blossoms (if you are using them) in 1 tablespoon of the butter. Toss them about until they have absorbed the butter and wilted. This will take only a minute. Set aside.

5. In a large mixing bowl, beat the eggs until

WHAT TO BUY OR ORDER NOW

Although the weather is much too hot to order any perishables, August is a good time to order flower bulbs and possibly some garden equipment for the following year, from the fall garden catalogs. Many also offer the straightforward bushel and half-bushel harvest baskets. Thinking ahead, we order these now and later fill them with our breads, which we will give as holiday gifts come December.

Fall catalogs from our other mail-order sources will be arriving soon, and again we will look for baskets, tins or other interesting containers to hold our canned goods when we give them as presents.

they are light. Add ¼ cup of the cheese and the cooled vegetables from the omelet pan. Stir to blend.

6. Preheat the broiler.

7. Wipe the omelet pan clean with a paper towel. Place the pan over medium-high heat and add the remaining 4 tablespoons of butter. When the butter is hot and bubbling, add the egg mixture. Give the pan a few vigorous

shakes back and forth across the burner surface to make sure that the frittata is not sticking. Immediately turn the heat to medium-low.

Cook the frittata for about 10 minutes until the eggs are set, but still a little runny on the surface. Do not stir. Carefully loosen the frittata with a spatula and give the pan a few more shakes to prevent the frittata from sticking.

8. Arrange the sautéed squash blossoms over the top of the frittata and sprinkle them with the remaining ¼ cup of cheese. Dribble the remaining 1 tablespoon of olive oil over the surface.

9. Place the omelet pan 6 inches under the broiler for 1 to 2 minutes or just until the eggs are no longer runny and the surface has lightly colored.

10. With the aid of a spatula, slide the frittata onto a serving platter. Sprinkle with the minced basil or parsley. Serve while the frittata is hot, or later, at room temperature, cutting it into wedges.

AND IN OUR GARDEN

In the midst of gathering our heaviest yields of summer garden produce, it is time to plant our fall garden. Where there is space, we plant snow peas, sugar snap peas, kale, cabbages, finocchio (fennel), radishes, beets and lettuces. In the summer heat, they will sprout within days. With some of the vegetables, we are taking the chance that they will reach maturity before a killing frost. Others will appreciate the nip of cold weather in late fall. It is worth the effort though, if we succeed and have more red leaf lettuce and a few peas before winter.

Throughout August and September, we freeze and dry our cayenne peppers as soon as they turn red on the plants. If you have cayenne peppers you'd like to freeze cut them so that about ¾ inch of the stem is left on the pepper. Then they need only be placed in an airtight, plastic bag and frozen. They will retain their color and may be used just as you would use fresh, hot peppers.

To dry the peppers, string them through the short stems on heavy thread (linen or silk twist) and hang them until they are thoroughly dried. They may be left hanging indefinitely or unstrung and stored in a container, open or closed. The hotness will remain however they are kept. If you are stringing the peppers, do it the same day that they are picked as the stems will dry, making it difficult to push a needle through. By late September, we will have several dozen strings hanging from the kitchen ceiling. They make cheerful gifts during the holiday season.

Toward the end of the month, we also pick the last of our perennial herbs for freezing and drying. To pick them later, as cold weather approaches, stimulates the plants to put on new growth at a time when the strength of perennial herbs should be going to their root systems. When there is frost forecasted never run and cut all the herbs in sight — it will probably be the last time you will see them.

SEPTEMBER

PASTA

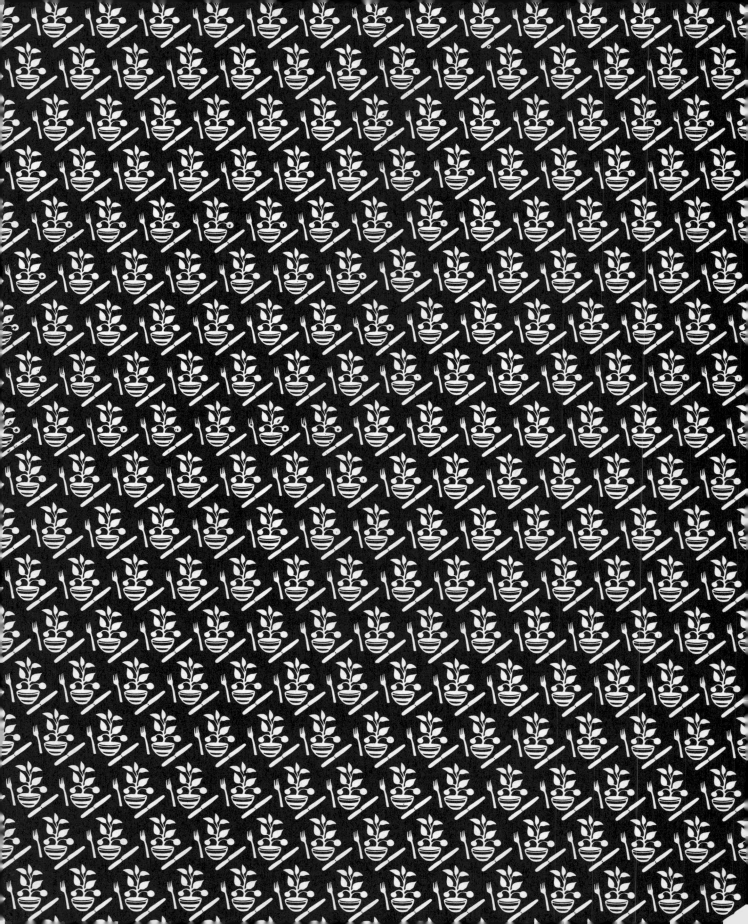

PASTA

Homemade pasta is so rewarding that we think there is no substitute. We prepare and serve it three times a week, and have worked out an easy basic recipe that can be used with all of our various flours.

If you are making pasta for the first time, we suggest that you prepare the Basic Egg Dough for Fettuccine before proceeding to the slightly more difficult flour combinations, and, finally, to the Spinach Fettucine.

Our instructions include the methods for making the pasta entirely by hand, or by using a food processor and rolling machine. Since we consume so much, we use a food processor and a rolling machine, but occasionally we will still make the pasta by hand, so as not to lose our "touch." Even by hand, it is possible, after some practice, to complete your pasta in less than a half hour.

The nonelectric pasta rolling machines are very reasonable in price and make it possible to make what we refer to as "spaghetti" in our recipes. The shape is actually square rather than round, but this does not diminish the quality of the pasta in any way.

Almost all of our recipes call for either spaghetti or fettuccine, for which you will need no special equipment. We have purchased the electric Simac "Pastamatic" and the Spaghetti/Noodle Maker attachment kit for our Kitchen Aid food preparer, primarily to make tubular pasta. Both work very well and are recommended for those who would like to make all the pasta shapes. We have not had the occasion to use other electric machines, but we have read good reports on most of them. (The electric machines come with their own specific instructions that should be followed.)

HOW TO USE OUR PASTA RECIPES

Most of our pasta recipes claim to serve four. These are average-size portions, so if you are serving a recipe as the main course to hearty pasta eaters, you may wish to increase the amount of pasta and the sauce. This is easily done by keeping in mind that you must use 1 egg for every 1 cup of flour and increase the amount of water accordingly.

If we are serving two guests plus ourselves, we generally make our pasta dough using 3 cups of flour and 3 eggs—our pasta appetites are *very* hearty. Our freshly made pasta, using 2 cups of flour, is the equivalent of ¾ pound of a commercial, dried pasta.

Some of our recipes suggest making the pasta before the sauce and letting it hang to dry. Others will designate a point during the preparation of the sauce when there will be time to prepare the pasta.

If you are a beginner at pasta making, we suggest that you make the pasta first to give yourself ample time. As you become faster, you will be able to make the pasta as the sauce is cooking.

The pasta pot

We strongly suggest that you purchase a pasta pot that has a perforated basket for draining. This eliminates draining the pasta in a colander in the sink. There are many on the market today. Ours is made of graniteware and is called "The Everything Pot," and we use it literally for everything: pasta, steaming potatoes, blanching vegetables for freezing, and as our stock pot. There are models in aluminum as well and many come with additional insert baskets for other purposes.

We cook our pasta in 4 quarts of liquid, which is sufficient. Sometimes, depending upon the recipe, we use half water and half whey. The whey will foam up as it boils, so it must be closely watched. Always use 1 tablespoon of salt in the boiling water (or water and whey), but do not add it until just before you are going to add the pasta. If added ahead, the salt will give an unpleasant taste to the water and affect the pasta itself.

Although salt is always used in the pasta's cooking water, it is often eliminated from the sauces. This is because many of the recipes contain pancetta or a cheese which is salty in itself. Do not add more salt.

When is it done?

The cooking time for the pasta is approximate. If the cut pasta has hung to dry for only a few minutes, the cooking time could be as little as 30 seconds. If the weather is dry and the pasta has been hanging for an hour or so, the cooking time may be 2 minutes or longer. You will have to judge, but do not overcook the pasta. It must be *al dente*. That is, it should be a little firm "to the teeth." We begin to test as soon as the water returns to a boil.

Serving pasta

In our instructions, we call for pasta to be cut to approximately a 10-inch length. We find this a proper length for serving. When we first began making pasta, we rolled it out as long as we could. It is fun, but there is a point where your arms cannot reach to toss it. Also, your guests should be taken into consideration and not confronted with yard-long strands of pasta on their plates.

Pasta dishes cool quickly, so always toss your pasta with the other ingredients on a heated serving platter or in a bowl, and serve it on heated plates.

We find the heating pad made especially for plates to be very efficient. To heat our serving platter, we place it on a crumpled pad of aluminum foil over the back burner of the stove (the burner should be *off*) where the oven exhausts its heat. The oven should be turned on to somewhere between 300° − 400°F. Do *not* warm your platter or plates directly in the oven unless they are metal. Even oven-proof dishes can crack if they are empty.

The point of making pasta fresh is to consume it right away. Therefore, we do not recommend drying or freezing it. If you must do so, it will keep its freshness better if it is frozen. To freeze, let the strands of pasta dry for about 10 minutes after cutting. They should not stick together, but should be pliable. Drop the strands into a plastic bag. Tightly close the bag and freeze the pasta. Do *not* defrost before cooking. Drop the frozen pasta into boiling, salted water and watch the cooking time closely, adding an additional 2 or 3 minutes.

Basic Egg Dough for Spaghetti and Fettuccine

Makes approximately ¾ pound pasta

> **2 cups all-purpose, unbleached flour**
> **¼ teaspoon salt**
> **2 eggs, at room temperature**
> **2 tablespoons water (approximately)**

Preparing the dough by hand

1. Measure the flour onto your work surface and sprinkle it with the salt.

2. Lightly beat the eggs with the water, make a well in the center of the flour, and pour in the egg mixture.

3. Using a fork or the fingers on one hand, begin mixing the flour into the egg mixture, working from the inside to the outside of the well. Hold a metal scraper in your other hand, in case of spillovers.

Work rapidly and, as soon as you can gather up the dough, begin kneading. Add more water, 1 tablespoon at a time, if the dough is very dry.

4. Knead vigorously for about 5 minutes, until the dough is very smooth.

With a metal scraper or knife, cut the dough into 4 equal pieces. Knead each piece briefly to form a flattened ball. Wrap the pieces of dough in plastic wrap and let them rest for about 15 minutes before rolling. This will allow the gluten in the flour to relax. (Refrigerate the dough if you do not plan to roll it out within that time.)

Rolling and cutting the dough by hand

If you will be rolling and cutting the dough by hand, plan on preparing fettuccine since spaghetti must be cut too thin to be a practical job by hand.

1. When the pieces of dough have rested for 15 minutes, roll them out. Begin by lightly flouring your work surface. Slightly flatten one piece of the dough with a heavy rolling pin and then starting from the center, roll the dough into a long rectangle, approximately 20 inches long by 5 inches wide.

Continue to flour your work surface when necessary and turn the dough over several times as you roll. As the dough begins to thin out, you will be able to roll it with a strong, forward thrust (never back and forth). This thrust makes it easier to roll the dough to the desired thinness.

Roll the dough uniformly so that the outside edges are not thinner than the body of the dough.

2. When the dough has been rolled to the desired thinness (approximately 1/16 inch), lay it flat on a cloth towel, or over the back of a

chair, coat hanger, or whatever you may improvise. (The wooden pasta dryers are very handy, but not essential.)

Continue with the remaining pieces of dough until all have been rolled out.

3. Let the strips of pasta dough dry for about 15 minutes before cutting them. The drying time will depend somewhat upon the weather. The dough should still be damp to the touch, but not sticky. If, when you begin to fold over the dough, it appears to be sticking together, just unroll it and let the dough hang a little longer.

Fifteen minutes is generally the amount of time needed for the pasta to be ready for cutting, but if the weather is very dry, the time will be shorter. On the other hand, if it is *very* humid (which sometimes is the case for us), the pasta will seem to be getting wetter rather than drying. If that should happen, just dust the strips of dough liberally with flour before folding and cutting.

4. When the dough is ready for cutting, working from a narrow end, fold 3 inches of the dough over and onto itself until you have a flat, rectangular roll about 3 × 5 inches (the original width of the strip). Do not press down upon the dough as you fold or the dough may stick to itself.

5. Cut each strip as soon as it is folded. Use a chef's or other large knife for cutting. With firm and even pressure on the knife, cut across the folded edges of the rolled dough at ¼-inch intervals. Be careful to cut the dough evenly. Each strip can be cut entirely before unfolding the strands, but if the dough looks as though it might be sticking, cut only a few strands at a time and unfold them before cutting more.

6. As the strands are cut and unfolded, again allow them to dry as described in Step 2. They need only about 5 minutes of drying time, just to be certain that they will not stick together.

You may wish to cut the pasta to a shorter length (10 inches) before cooking.

Preparing the dough in a food processor

1. Place the flour and salt in the bowl of a food processor, fitted with the metal blade. Blend the flour and salt with several On/Off motions.

2. In a cup, lightly beat the eggs. With the processor on, pour the eggs through the feed tube. Immediately add the water and process until the dough leaves the sides of the bowl and forms a ball.

Add more water, 1 tablespoon at a time, if the dough does not form a ball within 30 seconds.

3. Remove the dough from the processor and cut it into 4 equal pieces. Knead the pieces briefly and form flattened balls.

Wrap the pieces of dough in plastic wrap and let them rest for about 15 minutes before rolling. This rest allows the gluten in the flour to relax. (Refrigerate the dough if you do not plan to roll it out within that time.)

Rolling and cutting the dough with a nonelectric pasta machine

A nonelectric pasta machine will allow you to roll out and cut either spaghetti or fettuccine. Most models also have extra attachments that will cut the dough to other widths. However, we have found the two built-in widths sufficient: the narrow head (⅛-inch) for spaghetti and the wider head (¼-inch) for fettuccine. With the machine you should be able to roll and cut your dough in less than 15 minutes.

1. When the pieces of dough have rested for 15 minutes, proceed to roll them out. Slightly flatten one end of the dough between your fingers or with a rolling pin. Dust the dough with flour and run it through the widest roller setting on your machine (usually #8).

Fold the dough into thirds and run it through the widest setting again. Always send folded dough through the rollers with the folded sides running parallel to the sides of the machine. Otherwise, you may create air bubbles. For a second time, fold the dough into thirds and send it through the widest setting. By this time you should have a smooth dough.

If, by chance, your dough should break or tear, just continue to fold and roll on the widest setting until the dough is smooth. Dust the pieces of dough with flour as necessary.

2. When your dough is smooth, turn your machine to a narrower setting. You may run the dough through each of the width settings, but for speed, we skip from #8 to #6 to #4, and so forth, running the dough twice through each setting. Roll the dough to the thinness you prefer. We roll our fettuccine to the next to the last setting (#2) and our spaghetti, a little thicker (#3).

For spaghetti and fettuccine, it will be easier if the dough is not rolled to the full width of the rollers. The strips of dough should measure approximately 20 inches long by 5 inches wide when you have completed the rolling process.

3. As each strip of dough is rolled out, place it flat on a cloth towel or over the back of a chair, on coat hangers, or preferably, on a wooden pasta dryer. Allow the strips of dough to dry for about 10 minutes before cutting them. The drying time will depend upon the weather, and you should watch them closely. If the air is very dry, you may be able to cut the pasta almost as soon as it is rolled out, or if the weather is humid, 15 minutes of drying time will be required. If the weather is extremely humid, it may be necessary to dust the strips of dough in order to send them through the cutting gears.

4. When the dough is ready for cutting, insert the handle from your machine into one of the cutting gears, depending upon whether you are making spaghetti or fettuccine. With kitchen shears, cut each strip of dough into two 10-inch halves just before inserting it into the gears. Insert the cut end into the gears. The gears will more readily accept a cut edge than one that has slightly dried. Repeat until all of the pasta has been cut.

If you wish to cook the pasta right away, it will need to hang only long enough to be sure that the strands will not stick together, about 5 minutes.

BASIC EGG DOUGH VARIATIONS

As with our breads, in our pastas we also like to experiment with different flours. (See page 14 for a more detailed description of flours.) And although in our recipes we specify the type of pasta to use with a particular sauce, this should not restrict you from varying them according to your preferences. In almost every type of pasta we make, the recipe is identical to the Basic Egg Dough except for the combinations of flours. The two exceptions are the use of semolina flour and the addition of spinach.

SPINACH FETTUCCINE

Use only fresh spinach for the fettuccine, as frozen spinach compromises the flavor. Do not attempt to make spinach spaghetti from this pasta. It is too difficult to cut to such a narrow width.

> ¾ **pound fresh spinach**
> 2 **eggs, at room temperature**
> 2 **cups all-purpose, unbleached flour**
> ¼ **teaspoon salt**
> **Water (only if needed)**

1. Wash the spinach well and discard the stems. Cook the spinach in the water clinging to the leaves just until they have wilted. Drain and run cold water over the spinach to cool it and to help it retain its bright-green color. In small handfuls, squeeze the spinach to remove any liquid. Chop the spinach fine, either with a chef's knife or in a food processor.

2. Beat the eggs lightly and add the spinach. Mix thoroughly.

Proceed with the instructions for preparing the pasta dough either by hand or in a food processor, treating the spinach and egg mixture as you did the egg mixture in the basic recipe. Add water, a tablespoon at a time, if the pasta dough seems too dry. Most likely, none will be necessary.

3. Roll and cut the dough for fettuccine following the instructions for the Basic Egg Dough.

WHOLE-WHEAT AND BUCKWHEAT SPAGHETTI OR FETTUCCINE

For 1 of the 2 cups of flour, substitute either whole-wheat or buckwheat flour. Before adding the eggs and water to the flours and salt, make sure that the two flours are well mixed. Otherwise, follow the instructions for the Basic Egg Dough.

If you use the unbleached flour from Walnut Acres, which gives the pasta exceptional flavor, use 1 cup of their flour to 1 cup of an all-purpose, unbleached flour from the store. Using any of these flours alone makes for difficult kneading and rolling, but by combining them with a store-bought flour, the flavor is maintained without laborious work.

SEMOLINA SPAGHETTI

Semolina flour is next to impossible to knead and roll if it is not used in combination with a commercial, all-purpose, unbleached flour. Use 1 cup of semolina flour to 1 cup of the unbleached flour, mixing them thoroughly along with the salt before adding the eggs and water. The semolina flour will give you a superior and truly *al dente* spaghetti. Do not use the semolina flour for fettuccine as these noodles should be tender.

PARMESAN AND ROMANO CHEESES

The quality and authenticity of these cheeses is vital to the success of your pasta dishes. Rather than using a substitute, your recipe will be better with the cheese eliminated. Two of our mail-order sources supply fine quality Parmesan and Romano.

Parmesan cheese is made from cow's milk and Romano from sheep's milk. Your true Parmesan cheese will have little dots all over the surface of the yellowish (never black) crust, stamping out the words parmigiano-reggiano. If it does not, the cheese is not Parmesan. There are many Romano cheeses, so you must rely on the honesty of your source. Sometimes there are variations in the Romano cheeses we order, but our sources always supply an excellent quality.

Both cheeses keep very well under refrigeration, so we order large amounts at one time—up to 10 pounds. When storing the cheeses, do *not* wrap them in aluminum foil; the salt in the cheese will eat into the foil. We wrap our cheeses in plastic wrap and then place the chunks in plastic bags. Every week or so we take them from the refrigerator to check them. If any mold is developing, we cut it away and wipe the surfaces of the cheeses with a cloth that has been dipped in vinegar. By doing this, we can successfully keep both cheeses for up to six months. We do not recommend freezing any cheese.

Several of our recipes will say to use either Parmesan or Romano and others will specify one or the other. When only Parmesan is listed, it should be used, as Romano will be too sharp. It is good to have a choice between the two, since Parmesan is close to double in price, but sometimes this is not possible.

Since Parmesan is so expensive, we always grate it by hand; a food processor does not do an adequate job. Romano, on the other hand, can be grated in a food processor with success. Most important, though, always grate your cheeses just when you will be using them.

PESTO

The proportions given here are plenty for several pasta with pesto dinners. (If you wish to make Pesto in quantity for freezing, see page 155.)

Our pesto is thicker than most, so when you use it on freshly made pasta, you may wish to toss the pasta with a little extra olive oil before adding the pesto. The amount of pesto to use depends on your taste. For any of our pasta recipes use from ¼- to ½-cup of pesto. Toss the pasta and pesto together on a heated serving platter so that the pesto is warmed when tossed.

Makes about 2 cups

4 cups fresh, young basil (¼-pound), leaves *only*, tightly packed
¾ cup pignolia (pine) nuts, pecans, or walnuts
1 cup freshly grated Parmesan or Romano cheese
4 large cloves garlic
2 tablespoons lemon juice
1 cup olive oil
½ teaspoon salt
¼ teaspoon freshly ground black pepper

Method for a food processor

1. Preheat the oven to 225°F.

2. Rinse the basil then dry it with paper towels or in a salad spinner.

3. Toast the nuts on a baking sheet in the oven for about 15 minutes to bring out their flavor. Stir occasionally to make sure they don't burn. Allow the nuts to cool, then chop them fine in the food processor fitted with the metal blade.

4. Place the chopped nuts in a small mixing bowl and combine them with the grated cheese.

5. Peel the garlic and add it to the work bowl of the processor; chop it fine. With the garlic still in the bowl, pack in the basil. Sprinkle the leaves with the lemon juice. The lemon juice not only adds zest, but it keeps the basil leaves from darkening.

6. With the motor on, add the olive oil in a thin stream through the feed tube. Process until the mixture is a smooth purée. Add the puréed mixture to the cheese and nuts. Add the salt and pepper and mix with a wooden spoon.

Method for a blender

1. Follow Steps 1 through 4 in the instructions for the food processor method, using the blender to chop the nuts.

2. Place half of the garlic, peeled, in the blender and chop fine. With the garlic still in the blender, add half the basil and 1 tablespoon of the lemon juice. Pour ½ cup of the olive oil over the ingredients and purée. Add the puréed mixture to the cheese and nuts.

3. Repeat Step 2 with the remaining garlic, basil, lemon juice, and olive oil. Add this to the mixing bowl. Add the salt and pepper. Mix thoroughly with a wooden spoon.

TOMATO SAUCE FROM FRESH TOMATOES

This recipe is a smaller version of the Tomato Sauce discussed in the canning chapter on page 140. Use it tossed with one of the freshly made pastas.

Makes 1 quart

6 pounds ripe tomatoes
¼ cup olive oil
1 medium onion, coarsely chopped
1½ tablespoons minced garlic
1 teaspoon salt
¼ teaspoon freshly ground black pepper
2 tablespoons minced, fresh basil leaves, or 1 teaspoon dried
oregano or dried wild thyme

1. Wash, core, and seed the tomatoes, but do not peel them. When puréed, the peel will add thickness and flavor to the sauce. Cut the tomatoes into chunks about 1½ inches in diameter.

If you are using plum tomatoes, cut each one in half lengthwise and remove the seeds. Set aside in a mixing bowl.

2. Heat the olive oil in a heavy, 3-quart saucepan. Add the onion and garlic. Sauté over medium-low heat until the onion has wilted and is just beginning to color.

3. While the onion and garlic are sautéing, purée the tomatoes in a food processor, blender, or in a food mill fitted with the medium blade. Return the puréed tomatoes to the mixing bowl.

4. Purée the onions and garlic and return them to the saucepan. Add the puréed tomatoes along with the salt, black pepper, and herb of your choice. Stir and bring the ingredients to a simmer over medium heat.

5. Continue to simmer, uncovered, until the tomato sauce is quite thick. This may take 1½ hours, depending upon the type of tomato you are using. Reduce the heat if the sauce begins to splatter. Stir often with a wooden spoon to prevent the sauce from sticking or burning.

TOMATO SAUCE FROM CANNED TOMATOES

This recipe is excellent whether you use purchased or home-canned tomatoes. In testing various purchased brands we found a great discrepancy in the amount of tomatoes the cans yielded. One pound, twelve-ounce cans varied from 1⅓ cups to just under 2 cups of tomatoes. On the other hand, one quart of our drained tomatoes consistently yielded 2 cups of tomatoes. Because of these variations, we can only approximate the amount of sauce the tomatoes will yield.

Makes 1 quart (approximately)

¼ cup olive oil

1 medium onion, chopped coarse

1½ tablespoons minced garlic

2 cans tomatoes, each 1 pound 12 ounces, or 1½ quarts home-canned tomatoes (see page 138), with liquid

Salt to taste

¼ teaspoon freshly ground black pepper

2 tablespoons minced fresh basil, or 1 teaspoon dried oregano or dried wild thyme

1. Heat the olive oil in a heavy, 3-quart saucepan. Add the onion and garlic. Sauté over medium-low heat until the onion has wilted and is just beginning to color.

2. When the onion has wilted, purée the onion and garlic in batches along with the tomatoes and the tomato liquid. This may be done in a food processor, blender, or the ingredients may be passed through a food mill fitted with the medium blade.

3. Place the puréed ingredients into the saucepan. Add salt to taste (keep in mind that the tomatoes may have been salted), the pepper, and the herb of your choice. Stir, cover, and bring the ingredients to a simmer over medium heat.

4. Continue to simmer the sauce, uncovered, until it is quite thick. The time will depend upon the amount of liquid that is in the tomatoes. It could take as little time as 45 minutes or, more likely, a little over an hour. Reduce the heat if the sauce begins to splatter. Stir often with a wooden spoon.

SPAGHETTI WITH A SAUCE OF FRESH TOMATOES

For this pasta recipe, we have combined uncooked, ripe tomatoes with that much neglected garnish called gremolada. Gremolada is a lovely combination of chopped parsley, garlic, and lemon peel and is rarely encountered except with osso buco. However, we feel it enhances a variety of foods such as potatoes, soups, and particularly tomatoes.

In summer months when fresh basil is available, we substitute it for the parsley. The amount of raw garlic is not overwhelming, but it must be very fresh with no signs of aging.

Serves 4

1 recipe freshly made Spaghetti (¾ pound; see page 305)

3½ pounds ripe tomatoes

1 teaspoon salt, plus 1 tablespoon (for cooking the pasta)
4 large cloves garlic
1 lemon, for the peel (about 1½ tablespoons)
½ cup finely chopped fresh parsley or basil, tightly packed
2 eggs, at room temperature
¾ cup freshly grated Parmesan or Romano cheese
1 teaspoon freshly ground dried hot red pepper
3 tablespoons unsalted butter

1. Prepare the spaghetti and let it hang to dry as you make the sauce.

2. Core and seed the tomatoes, but do not peel them. Coarsely chop the tomatoes so that the pieces are between ½-inch and ¾-inch in diameter.

Place the tomatoes in a large sieve placed over a bowl. Toss the tomatoes with 1 teaspoon salt and let them drain for ½ hour to rid them of excess liquid. The draining is essential and prevents a watery sauce. (The liquid may be saved for another use.)

3. Prepare the garlic and lemon peel for the gremolada by hand, using a chef's knife. Peel and chop the garlic fine. Cut the peel from the lemon, making lengthwise julienne strips. Be sure none of the white membrane is attached. Chop the strips fine.

Chop the garlic, lemon peel, and basil together just to combine the ingredients. The gremolada should be chopped fine, but the ingredients must remain crisp and not lose their individual identities. Set aside in a small bowl.

4. In a large pot, bring 4 quarts of water to a boil. Also begin warming your serving platter and plates.

5. While waiting for the water to boil, prepare the remaining ingredients. In a small bowl, beat the eggs and add the Parmesan or Romano cheese and the hot red pepper. Stir with a fork to combine.

Arrange all of the ingredients (the butter, the egg and cheese mixture, the tomatoes, and the gremolada) by your heated serving platter so that they will be ready to toss with the pasta as soon as it is drained.

6. Add 1 tablespoon of salt to the boiling water. When the water returns to a boil, add the spaghetti. Cook until *al dente*, which could take less than 2 minutes if the pasta has not dried too long.

7. Drain the pasta and toss it with the butter on a heated serving platter. Immediately add the egg and cheese mixture and toss again. Add the tomatoes and toss once more to distribute them throughout the spaghetti. Sprinkle with the gremolada and give one final, light tossing before serving.

A WINTER VERSION OF
SPAGHETTI WITH A SAUCE OF FRESH TOMATOES

Not content to be deprived of the preceding recipe for half the year, we worked out a winter solution using our canned tomatoes.

 If you do not have your own home-canned tomatoes, use the best purchased brand you can find because the tomatoes are not cooked. Essentially, the recipe remains the same except that salt is eliminated and fresh parsley is substituted for the basil.

Serves 4

1 recipe freshly made Spaghetti (¾ pound; see page 305)
2 cups well-drained, canned tomatoes
1 tablespoon salt (for cooking the pasta)
4 large cloves garlic
1 lemon, for the peel
½ cup finely chopped fresh parsley, tightly packed
2 eggs, at room temperature
¾ cup freshly grated Parmesan or Romano cheese
1 teaspoon freshly ground dried hot red pepper
3 tablespoons unsalted butter

1. Prepare the spaghetti and let it hang to dry as you make the sauce.

2. Drain the tomatoes in a sieve placed over a bowl for about 15 minutes to remove excess liquid. (If you are using purchased tomatoes, you will need a 1-pound, 12-ounce can for the 2 cups.) Coarsely chop the drained tomatoes.

3. Continue with Steps 3 through 7 in the preceding recipe, substituting parsley for the basil.

SEMOLINA SPAGHETTI
WITH
MUSHROOMS AND TOMATOES

Wanting an alternative to the usual combination of mushrooms and cream, we concocted this simple, appetizing sauce. We feel canned tomatoes are best for this sauce, as the flavor is more concentrated than with fresh tomatoes.

If you prefer fresh, use two cups of peeled, cored, seeded, and coarsely chopped tomatoes. Drain them in a sieve, placed over a bowl, for ½ hour or so, pressing on the pulp to remove excess liquid. Reserve the liquid.

Serves 4

1 recipe freshly made Semolina Spaghetti (¾ pound; see page 308)
1 pound fresh mushrooms
5 tablespoons unsalted butter
1 tablespoon olive oil
1 tablespoon minced garlic
½ teaspoon salt, plus 1 tablespoon (for cooking the pasta)
½ teaspoon freshly ground dried hot red pepper
1 cup well-drained, coarsely chopped canned tomatoes
3 tablespoons liquid from the drained tomatoes
½ cup chopped parsley

1. Prepare the semolina spaghetti and let it hang to dry as you make the sauce.

2. Trim off the ends from the mushroom stems. Wipe the mushrooms with damp paper towels, then slice them thin. We prefer to slice them by hand, as the mushrooms seem to retain their shape and texture better than if done in a food processor.

3. Melt 3 tablespoons of the butter with the olive oil in a skillet over medium heat. Add the mushrooms and the garlic. Sprinkle with ½ teaspoon salt and the red pepper. Mix with a wooden spoon and sauté the mixture until the mushrooms give up their liquid and begin to brown slightly.

4. Meanwhile, in a large pot, bring 4 quarts of water to a boil. Also begin warming your serving platter and dishes.

5. When the mushrooms begin to brown, add the well-drained tomatoes to the skillet. Make sure that your drained measure is 1 good cup.

Increase the heat slightly and sauté the mixture just until the tomatoes are hot. Stir just to blend the ingredients.

6. When the sauce is almost ready, add 1 tablespoon of salt to the boiling water. When the water returns to a boil, add the semolina spaghetti. Cook until *al dente*, which could take less than 2 minutes if the pasta has not dried too long.

7. Drain and toss the spaghetti in a heated serving platter with the remaining butter, 3 tablespoons of reserved liquid from the drained tomatoes, and the parsley.

8. If you are using a round serving platter, arrange the sauce in the center of the spaghetti. If you are using an oval platter, arrange the sauce lengthwise down the middle.

Serve immediately on heated plates, giving each guest a portion of the spaghetti and topping it with a serving of sauce. Because the sauce is so pure and pretty as is, do not serve cheese.

SEMOLINA SPAGHETTI WITH MUSHROOMS AND PEPPERS

Try preparing this dish with red or yellow bell peppers, or even better, a combination of the two. If only green are available, the pasta will still be delicious, but not as colorful. In the winter months, we use our bell peppers frozen from the summer crop. When using frozen peppers, let them defrost on paper towels to absorb the excess moisture before cutting and adding them to the skillet. No cheese is needed, but you may serve it, if you wish.

Serves 4

> 1 recipe freshly made Semolina Spaghetti (¾ pound; see page 308)
> 1 tablespoon olive oil
> 2 ounces pancetta (Italian bacon, see page 54), cut into ¼-inch dice
> 4 large bell peppers, fresh or frozen
> 1 pound fresh mushrooms, thinly sliced
> 1½ tablespoons minced garlic
> ¼ teaspoon freshly ground black pepper
> 1 teaspoon freshly ground dried hot red pepper
> 1 tablespoon salt (for cooking the pasta)
> 3 tablespoons unsalted butter
> 1 cup freshly grated Parmesan cheese (optional)

1. Prepare the semolina spaghetti and let it hang to dry as you make the sauce.

2. Place the olive oil in a 10-inch skillet over very low heat and add the diced pancetta. Sauté until the pancetta is rendered of its fat and the dice have lightly browned. Do not drain.

3. While the pancetta is sautéing, core and seed the bell peppers, if you are using fresh. Cut the peppers, both fresh or frozen, into lengthwise julienne strips, ¼ inch in diameter.
   Trim off the ends from the mushroom stems. Wipe the mushrooms with damp paper towels, and slice them thin.

4. When the pancetta dice have lightly browned, add the bell peppers, garlic, and black pepper to the skillet. Raise the heat to medium low and sauté the ingredients, uncovered, for 10 minutes. Toss occasionally with wooden spoons.

5. Meanwhile, in a large pot, bring 4 quarts of water to a boil. Also begin warming your serving platter and plates.

6. After the bell peppers have sautéed for 10 minutes, add the sliced mushrooms and hot red pepper to the skillet. Toss and increase the heat to medium. Sauté until the mushrooms give up their liquid.

The liquid should not completely evaporate before the sauce is tossed with the pasta. If the pasta is not ready, lower the heat under the skillet, just to keep the sauce hot.

7. When the sauce is almost ready, add 1 tablespoon of salt to the boiling water. When the water returns to a boil, add the semolina spaghetti. Cook until *al dente*, which could be less than 2 minutes if the pasta has not dried too long.

8. Drain the spaghetti and toss it on a heated serving platter with the butter.

Arrange the sauce over the spaghetti and present the platter at the table before tossing the ingredients. Toss as you are serving. Pass the cheese, if desired.

WHOLE-WHEAT SPAGHETTI WITH A MUSHROOM SAUCE

To offset what would be a rather mild sauce, we have added freshly ground hot red pepper. If you prefer the sauce less lively, cut down on the amount, but do not eliminate the pepper entirely.
Serves 4

1 recipe freshly made Whole-Wheat Spaghetti (¾ pound; see page 308)
1 pound fresh mushrooms
5 tablespoons unsalted butter
1 tablespoon olive oil
½ teaspoon salt, plus 1 tablespoon (for cooking the pasta)
1 tablespoon freshly ground dried hot red pepper
1 cup heavy cream, at room temperature
¼ cup minced parsley

1. Prepare the whole-wheat spaghetti and let it hang to dry as you make the sauce.

2. Trim off the ends from the mushroom stems. Wipe the mushrooms with damp paper towels and slice them thin. (We prefer to slice them by hand, as the mushrooms seem to retain their shape and texture better than if done in a food processor.)

3. In a skillet, melt 3 tablespoons of the butter with the olive oil over medium heat. Add the sliced mushrooms and sprinkle with the ½ teaspoon salt. Sauté until the mushrooms give

up their liquid and begin to brown slightly.

4. Meanwhile, in a large pot, bring 4 quarts of water to a boil. Also begin warming your serving platter and plates.

5. Add the pepper to the mushrooms. Stir, just to mix, with a wooden spoon. Add the heavy cream and stir again.

Bring to a simmer and cook until the cream has been reduced by one-fourth.

6. When the sauce is ready, add the tablespoon of salt to the boiling water. Return the water to a boil and add the spaghetti. Cook until *al dente*, which should take 2 to 3 minutes if the pasta has not dried too long.

Drain, then toss the spaghetti in a heated serving dish with the remaining butter. Add the mushroom sauce and toss briefly. Sprinkle with the minced parsley and serve immediately on heated plates.

MOIRA'S SPAGHETTI WITH ANCHOVY SAUCE

This recipe was given to us by our friend, Moira Henry, over ten years ago and it continues to be as exciting for us now as the first time we prepared it. Originally it was given to Moira by a Spanish friend, and although the origin is uncertain, the reception it receives from anchovy lovers is positively impassioned.

Don't be intimidated by the large amounts of anchovies or the way the sauce looks as it cooks—just wait and indulge!

Serves 4

> 9 cloves garlic, peeled but left whole
> 3 tablespoons olive oil
> 2 cans flat filets of anchovies, each 2 ounces
> 1 recipe freshly made Whole-Wheat Spaghetti (¾ pound; see page 308)
> 1½ cups of water
> 1 tablespoon wild thyme
> ½ teaspoon freshly ground black pepper
> 1 teaspoon freshly ground dried hot red pepper
> 1½ cups chopped parsley
> 1 tablespoon salt (for cooking the pasta)

1. Using the saucepan in which you will serve the pasta, sauté the garlic in the olive oil over low heat. When the garic has browned slightly add the anchovies with their oil. Turn off the

heat and cover the pan. Let rest for 20 minutes.

2. During this time, begin preparing the whole-wheat spaghetti dough.

3. After 20 minutes, turn the heat to medium low and add the water, thyme, black pepper, red pepper, and parsley. Do not add salt. Simmer uncovered for 45 minutes, stirring occasionally.

   The garlic will become very soft and, if you wish, you may mash it with a fork and blend it into the sauce. The anchovies will have disintegrated on their own.

4. While the sauce is simmering, roll out and cut the pasta. Bring 4 quarts of water to a boil in a large pot. Also begin warming your dinner plates.

5. When the sauce is ready, add the salt to the boiling water, and when it returns to a boil, add the whole-wheat spaghetti. Cook until *al dente* which should take 2 to 3 minutes if the pasta has not dried too long. Drain the pasta and add it to the anchovy sauce. Toss and serve immediately on hot plates.

MOIRA'S ORIGINAL RECIPE

Fry 6 to 9 garlic cloves in enough olive oil to cover the bottom of a frying pan. As soon as the garlic begins to brown (be careful not to burn), empty two 2-ounce cans of anchovies into the frying pan (oil and all), turn off the heat, and cover the pan. Keep the flame off for 15 to 20 minutes, then turn the flame onto a low simmer, add 1½ cups of water, and season heavily with thyme, black pepper, hot red pepper, and a whole bunch of chopped parsley. Simmer for approximately 45 minutes. Add the spaghetti (cooked *al dente*) to pan and toss. Serve immediately.

FETTUCCINE ALL'ALFREDO

This simply prepared sauce allows the taste of freshly made fettuccine to be fully appreciated. Basically, our recipe differs very little from the classic Fettuccine all'Alfredo except that we simmer and reduce the heavy cream to remove some of that "ultra-pasteurized" flavor. If you are able to buy "real" cream, this step is not necessary.

A pinch of nutmeg is usually tossed with the fettuccine, but often we eliminate it and instead add finely chopped parsley for color and flavor. We list ¼ cup of the finely chopped herb, but as we are very fond of it, on occasion we add as much as a full cup. In season, we use fresh basil instead.

Serves 4

▼▼

1 recipe freshly made Fettuccine (¾ pound; see page 305)
1 cup heavy cream, at room temperature
2 eggs, at room temperature
1 cup freshly grated Parmesan cheese
1 tablespoon salt (for cooking the pasta), plus ½ teaspoon
¼ teaspoon freshly ground white pepper
Pinch of freshly grated nutmeg, optional
4 tablespoons unsalted butter, cut into small pieces
¼ cup finely chopped parsley or basil (optional)

1. Prepare the fettuccine and let it hang to dry as you prepare the sauce.

2. In a small saucepan, bring the heavy cream to a slow simmer over medium-low heat. When the cream comes to a simmer, turn the heat to low. Whisk the cream every few minutes and continue to let it simmer until it has been reduced to approximately ⅔ cup.

3. In a small bowl, lightly beat the eggs and stir in ¾ cup of the grated cheese.

4. In a large pot, bring 4 quarts of water to a boil. Also begin warming your serving platter and dinner plates. Add 1 tablespoon of salt to the boiling water and when it returns to a boil, add the fettuccine. Cook just until *al dente*,

which should take 2 to 3 minutes if the pasta has not dried too long.

5. Drain the fettuccine and place it on the heated serving platter. Sprinkle with the ½ teaspoon salt, white pepper, and nutmeg, if you are using it. Add the butter and quickly toss the pasta. Add the reduced heavy cream and toss again. Add the egg and cheese mixture and toss once more. Sprinkle with the remaining ¼ cup of cheese and the parsley, if you are using it.

If you should be using a full cup of chopped parsley, toss ¾ of it with the pasta at the same time that you add the butter, reserving the remaining ¼ cup for garnish.

Serve the fettuccine immediately on heated plates.

FETTUCCINE ALLA CARBONARA

Although it is traditional to serve this sauce with spaghetti, we prefer it with fettuccine. Also, we like it a bit hot so you may wish to add less red pepper.

Slab or sliced bacon can be substituted for the pancetta (Italian bacon, see page 54). Blanch the bacon for 2 minutes and drain before sautéing it. You may also substitute Romano cheese for the Parmesan.

Serves 4

1 recipe freshly made Fettuccine (¾ pound; see page 305)
¼ pound pancetta, cut into ¼-inch dice
1 tablespoon olive oil
5 cloves garlic, minced
¼ cup dry white wine or vermouth
2 eggs, at room temperature
½ cup heavy cream, at room temperature
½ cup freshly grated Parmesan cheese
1 tablespoon salt (for cooking the pasta)
½ teaspoon freshly ground black pepper
1 teaspoon freshly ground dried hot red pepper
¼ cup chopped parsley

1. Prepare the fettuccine. Let it hang to dry as you prepare the sauce.

2. In a large pot, bring 4 quarts of water to a boil. Also begin warming your dinner plates.

3. While the water is coming to a boil, sauté the pancetta in the olive oil over very low heat. If possible, use a saucepan in which you can serve the completed dish.

Sauté the pancetta until it has given up its fat and begun to brown. Add the minced garlic. Sauté for only a moment or two then add the wine.

Turn the heat to medium, let the wine evaporate entirely; then return the heat to low.

4. In a small bowl, mix the eggs, the heavy cream, and the cheese.

5. When the water is boiling rapidly, add the salt to the pot. When the water returns to a boil, add the fresh pasta. Cook until *al dente*, which should take 2 to 3 minutes if the pasta has not dried too long.

Drain and add the pasta to the saucepan containing the pancetta, garlic, and wine mixture. Toss briefly and add the egg mixture. Toss again, adding the black pepper, the red pepper, and the parsley. Serve immediately on heated plates.

FETTUCCINE WITH AVOCADOS AND CREAM

Inspired by the combination of fresh tomatoes, gremolada, and spaghetti (see Spaghetti with a Sauce of Fresh Tomatoes, page 312), we wanted to experiment with other fresh fruits that would work well with gremolada (a garlic, lemon peel, and herb garnish) and pasta. Selecting avocados resulted in a pasta dish that is incomparable. Again, there is little actual cooking involved and all ingredients should be ready to toss with the fettuccine before it has been placed in the pot to cook.

It goes without saying that the avocados must be in perfect condition, as their fresh, green color is one of the distinctive features of this unusual recipe.

Serves 4

> 1 recipe freshly made Fettuccine (¾ pound; see page 305)
> ¼ cup pecans
> 2 teaspoons finely chopped garlic (see Step 3)
> 1½ tablespoons finely chopped lemon peel (about 1 lemon; see Step 3)
> 3 tablespoons finely chopped fresh basil or ¼ cup finely chopped
>   parsley (see Step 3)
> 1 cup heavy cream, at room temperature
> 2 large ripe avocados
> 2 tablespoons lemon juice
> 2 tablespoons unsalted butter
> 1 tablespoon salt (for cooking the pasta), plus ½ teaspoon
> ¼ teaspoon freshly ground white pepper
> ¾ cup freshly grated Parmesan cheese
> 1 cup alfalfa sprouts (for growing instructions, see page 39)

1. Prepare the fettuccine and let it hang to dry as you prepare the other ingredients.

2. Toast the pecans in a small skillet over low heat for about 5 minutes to bring out their flavor and crisp them slightly. Chop them fine and set them aside.

3. Prepare the gremolada by hand, using a chef's knife. Peel and chop the garlic fine. Cut the peel from the lemon into lengthwise julienne strips. Clean away any attached white membrane. Chop the strips fine. Chop the basil leaves fine.

Chop the three ingredients together just enough to mix them, but make sure that they are neither overchopped nor become soft.

4. In a small saucepan, bring the cream to a simmer over medium-low heat. Let the cream

simmer, stirring it occasionally, until it has been reduced to ⅔ cup.

5. In a large pot, bring 4 quarts of water to a boil. Also begin warming your serving dish and plates.

6. While the water is coming to a boil, cut the avocados in half lengthwise. Remove the pit and peel the halves. Cut each half into 8 lengthwise slices and then cut each slice in half.

Place the avocados in a small bowl and immediately sprinkle them with the lemon juice so that they will not discolor. Add the gremolada and toss lightly, just to mix.

7. Place all of your prepared ingredients for the pasta close to your heated serving dish, so that the fettuccine can be tossed immediately after being cooked and drained.

8. Add 1 tablespoon of salt to the boiling water. When the water returns to a boil, add the
fettuccine. Cook just until *al dente*, which
should be no more than 2 to 3 minutes if the
pasta has not dried too long.

9. Drain the fettuccine and place it in your
heated serving dish. As quickly as you can,
toss the fettuccine with the butter, ½ teaspoon
salt, and white pepper.

Add the simmering cream and ½ cup of
the Parmesan cheese. Toss again, so that the

fettuccine is nicely coated with the cream and
cheese.

Add the avocado mixture and gently mix
it into the pasta.

10. Sprinkle the remaining ¼ cup of cheese
over the surface. Then top with the alfalfa
sprouts, pulling them apart into threads as
you do so and, finally, scatter on the pecans.

11. Serve immediately with a gentle touch so
as not to damage the avocado slices.

FETTUCCINE WITH CABBAGE AND ONIONS

With an abundance of home-grown cabbage throughout most of the year, we are constantly experimenting with new recipe ideas. This one is for quite a hearty winter dish which might best be served as the main course, followed by a salad and bread, and a light dessert of fruit and cheese. The slow braising of the vegetables brings out a sweetness that combines nicely with the sharpness of the Romano cheese. The hot red pepper adds an agreeably piquant flavor to complete the dish. For a truly robust meal, serve the Hot Sausages on page 45.

Serves 4

1 pound yellow onions
½ cup olive oil
4 cloves garlic, minced
1 pound cabbage
1 tablespoon salt (for cooking the pasta), plus extra
1 recipe freshly made Fettuccine (¾ pound; see page 305)
¾ cup freshly grated Romano cheese
¾ cup chopped parsley
1 teaspoon freshly ground dried hot red pepper

1. Slice the onions thin. You may do this in a food processor or, if doing them by hand, first

cut the onions in half, top to bottom, then slice each half crosswise into pieces ⅛-inch thick.

2. In a heavy casserole, heat the olive oil. Add the onions and toss over medium heat until they are thoroughly coated with the oil.

Continue tossing occasionally until the onions begin to take on some color. This will take about 10 minutes. Do not let them burn. Add the minced garlic. Toss again, cover, and turn the heat to low.

Braise for ½ hour, tossing every 10 minutes or so to make sure the onions do not burn.

3. Meanwhile, core and shred the cabbage. When the onions have braised for ½ hour, add the cabbage to the pot and stir together thoroughly. Salt to taste, keeping in mind that the cheese will be salty. Cover and continue braising over low heat for another 20 minutes tossing occasionally.

4. While the onions, garlic, and cabbage are braising, prepare the fettuccine. Let the pasta hang to dry until you are ready to cook it.

5. Begin warming your serving platter and dinner plates.

Bring to a boil 4 quarts of water. When it is boiling, add 1 tablespoon of salt. When the water returns to a boil, add the pasta. Cook until *al dente*, which should take 2 to 3 minutes if the pasta has not dried too long, then drain.

6. Spoon 1 cup or more of the braised vegetables into your heated serving dish. Add the drained pasta and toss with the vegetables. Add the rest of the vegetables with their liquid, ½ cup of the cheese, ½ cup of the parsley, and the teaspoon of red pepper. Toss thoroughly. Sprinkle with the remaining cheese and parsley. Serve immediately on heated plates.

FETTUCCINE WITH SAUTÉED CARROTS AND CHEESE

When we first started making our own pasta, we were intrigued by the idea of using vegetables for coloring and flavor in the pasta dough itself. After trying beets, carrots, and spinach, we found spinach to be the only vegetable worth the trouble involved. Neither beets nor carrots imparted any perceptible flavor and both lost most of their color when cooked. (The beet fettuccine was amazing to look at before cooking, but not particularly appetizing—unless one is fond of cotton candy!)

Therefore we originated this recipe so we could enjoy carrots with pasta. Sautéed and seasoned before being added to pasta, they glisten with their orange color. Try to use very small carrots so that they may be left whole. We grow a variety, Baby Nantes, which do not even need scraping. For the herb, we use basil or mint when they are in season, and parsley at other times.

Serves 4

1 recipe freshly made Fettuccine (¾ pound; see page 305)
¾ pound baby or finger carrots
4 tablespoons unsalted butter
4 tablespoons minced shallots or 1 medium onion, chopped fine
1½ tablespoons minced garlic
¼ cup dry, white wine or vermouth
¼ cup water
½ teaspoon salt, plus 1 tablespoon (for cooking the pasta)
¼ teaspoon freshly ground white pepper
½ teaspoon freshly ground dried hot red pepper (optional)
½ cup chopped parsley or 4 tablespoons chopped fresh basil or mint
2 cups coarsely grated Italian Fontina cheese (6 ounces)

1. Prepare the fettucine and let it hang to dry as you prepare the other ingredients.

2. Trim the ends from the carrots and scrape them, if necessary. If the carrots are longer than 2½ inches, cut them crosswise into pieces about 2 inches long. Set aside.

3. In a 10-inch skillet, melt 3 tablespoons of the butter over medium-low heat. Add the shallots and garlic and sauté them just until they wilt.

Add the carrots and toss briefly so that the ingredients are well mixed. Add the wine or vermouth and the water to the skillet. Sprinkle the carrots with the ½ teaspoon salt, white pepper, and red pepper, if you are using it. (We like the addition of red pepper as it counters the sweetness of the carrots in a very pleasant way.) Cover the skillet and turn the heat to medium high.

Cook the carrots only long enough so that they can be pierced with the point of a knife. They must not overcook. The very small carrots will cook in about 4 minutes. Toss several times as they are cooking. Remove the cover and continue to toss so that most of the moisture evaporates from the pan.

4. While the carrots are cooking, bring 4 quarts of water to a boil in a large pot. Also begin warming your serving dish and dinner plates.

5. When the carrots are almost cooked, add 1 tablespoon of salt to the boiling water. When the water returns to a boil, add the fettuccine. Cook only until *al dente*, which should take only 2 to 3 minutes if the pasta has not dried too long.

6. Drain the fettuccine and place it in your heated serving dish. Toss the pasta quickly with the remaining 1 tablespoon of butter and the herb of your choice.

Immediately add the Fontina cheese. Toss again until the cheese is distributed throughout the pasta. It will melt as you toss. Add the ingredients from the skillet. Toss once more and serve on heated plates.

FETTUCCINE WITH CAULIFLOWER, MUSHROOMS, AND FONTINA

The addition of hot red pepper perks up the cauliflower in this lavish pasta dish. Follow it with a large, simply dressed salad filled with greens.

Serves 4

1 recipe freshly made Fettuccine (¾ pound; see page 305)
1½-pound cauliflower
1 teaspoon salt, plus 1 tablespoon (for cooking the pasta)
1 pound small, perfect, fresh mushrooms
3 tablespoons olive oil
1½ tablespoons minced garlic
1 cup heavy cream, at room temperature
1 teaspoon freshly ground dried hot red pepper
2 tablespoons unsalted butter
2 cups coarsely grated Italian Fontina cheese (6 ounces)
1 cup finely chopped parsley

1. Prepare the fettuccine and let it hang to dry as you cook and assemble the other ingredients.

2. Break the cauliflower into flowerets. Trim and discard any tough areas on the stem ends. Place the flowerets, stems down, in a 2-quart saucepan. Sprinkle them with ½ teaspoon of the salt. Add water to a depth of 1 inch, cover the saucepan and simmer the cauliflower over medium heat for 10 minutes.

   Drain the cauliflower in a colander and run cold water over the flowerets to stop the cooking process. The cauliflower must remain crisp. Set aside.

3. Trim off the ends from the mushroom stems and wipe the mushrooms with damp paper towels.

4. Place the olive oil in a 10-inch skillet over medium-low heat. Add the mushrooms and garlic. Sprinkle them with the remaining ½ teaspoon of salt. Sauté the mushrooms until they give up their moisture and it evaporates.

   Stir or shake the ingredients several times so that the garlic does not burn and the mushrooms lightly brown on all sides. This will take about 15 minutes.

5. Meanwhile, bring 4 quarts of water to a boil in a large pot. Begin warming your platter and plates.

6. In a small saucepan, bring the heavy cream to a simmer over medium-low heat. Let it simmer, whisking occasionally, until it is reduced to approximately ½ cup. This will take 10 minutes or so.

7. When the mushrooms have lightly browned, add the cauliflower to the skillet. Sprinkle the vegetables with the red pepper. Toss, and cover the skillet. Turn the heat to very low as you cook the pasta.

8. Add 1 tablespoon of salt to the boiling water and when it returns to a boil, add the fettuccine. Cook until *al dente*, which will be about 2 minutes, if the pasta has not dried too long.

9. Drain the fettuccine and place it on a large, heated serving platter. Quickly toss the pasta with the butter, simmering cream, Fontina cheese, and ¾ cup of the parsley. The Fontina cheese will melt as it is tossed.

Add the vegetables from the skillet and toss once more. Sprinkle the pasta with the remaining ¼ cup of parsley. Serve immediately on heated plates.

FETTUCCINE WITH SNOW PEAS

Snow peas add a refreshing crispness to this velvety spin-off from Fettuccine all'Alfredo. We grow our own (Drawf Gray Sugar is the variety we prefer), but store-bought fresh or frozen snow peas are surprisingly good. Allow the frozen variety to defrost some before cooking. Then the cooking time can be very brief. Either way, be careful not to overcook them.

Serves 4

1 recipe freshly made Fettuccine (¾ pound; see page 305)
½ pound fresh snow peas or one 10-ounce package, frozen
1 egg, at room temperature
½ cup heavy cream, at room temperature
1 cup freshly grated Parmesan cheese
¼ teaspoon freshly ground white pepper
4 tablespoons unsalted butter
3 large cloves garlic, minced fine
1 tablespoon salt (for cooking the pasta)
3 tablespoons finely chopped fresh basil, if available,
    or fresh parsley

1. Prepare the fettuccine and let it hang to dry as you prepare the sauce.

If you are using frozen snow peas, spread them on a paper towel to defrost slightly.

2. In a small bowl, beat the egg and combine with the heavy cream, ¾ cup of the Parmesan cheese, and the white pepper. Set aside.

3. In a large pot, bring 4 quarts of water to a boil. Also begin warming your serving platter and dinner plates.

4. In a skillet, melt 2 tablespoons of the butter over medium heat. Add the garlic and sau-

té it for a minute or so (do not let it brown). Add the snow peas and sauté them, tossed with the garlic, for an additional 2 minutes.

Turn the heat to very low while you cook the pasta.

5. Add the salt to the boiling water and when it returns to a boil, add the fettuccine. Cook until *al dente*, which should take only 2 to 3 minutes if the pasta has not dried too long.

6. Place the remaining 2 tablespoons of butter on the heated serving platter. Drain the fettuccine and place it on the platter.

7. Add the egg, heavy cream, and cheese mixture and toss to mix. Add the snow peas and garlic and toss again. Sprinkle with the remaining ¼ cup of cheese and the minced basil or parsley. Serve immediately on heated plates.

FETTUCCINE WITH CHINESE CELERY CABBAGE, SNOW PEAS, AND MUNG-BEAN SPROUTS

Combining Chinese celery cabbage, snow peas, and mung-bean sprouts with their familiar accompaniments—fresh ginger and soy sauce—makes for an out-of-the-ordinary dish when tossed with fettuccine. Do not overcook the cabbage or it will lose its texture and color.
Serves 4

1 recipe freshly made Fettuccine (¾ pound; see page 305)
¼ pound fresh snow peas or ½ package frozen
2-pound Chinese celery cabbage
4 tablespoons olive oil
1 medium onion, chopped coarsely
1 tablespoon minced garlic
½ teaspoon salt, plus 1 tablespoon (for cooking the pasta)
¼ teaspoon freshly ground black pepper
2 tablespoons finely chopped fresh ginger root
3 tablespoons soy sauce
½ teaspoon freshly ground dried hot red pepper
1 cup mung-bean sprouts (for growing instructions see page 39)

PASTA

¼ cup finely chopped spring onions
2 tablespoons finely chopped fresh coriander, if available,
or ¼ cup finely chopped fresh parsley

1. Prepare the fettuccine and let it hang to dry as you prepare the other ingredients.

2. If you are using frozen snow peas, let them defrost slightly on paper towels.

3. Discard the outer leaves from the cabbage. Quarter, core, and shred the cabbage fine by hand, using a chef's knife.

4. In a 3-quart saucepan, heat 2 tablespoons of the olive oil over medium-low heat. Add the onion and garlic and sauté until they have wilted slightly.

5. Add the shredded cabbage to the saucepan, tossing it with the onions and garlic. Sprinkle with ½ teaspoon salt and the black pepper. Cover the saucepan and braise over medium heat for 10 minutes, tossing several times.

6. In a large pot, bring 4 quarts of water to a boil. Also begin to warm your plates. Add the tablespoon of salt to the boiling water and when it returns to a boil, add the fettuccine. Cook just until *al dente*, which will take only 2 to 3 minutes if the pasta has not dried too long.

7. While the pasta is cooking, add the ginger, 2 tablespoons soy sauce, the hot red pepper, and snow peas to the cabbage mixture. Toss thoroughly and cook, uncovered, for 2 to 3 minutes over medium heat.

8. Drain the fettuccine and place it on a heated serving platter. Toss the pasta with the remaining olive oil and soy sauce, and the mung-bean sprouts.
    Immediately add the ingredients from the saucepan and toss again. Garnish the pasta with the spring onions and coriander or parsley. Serve on heated plates.

Spinach Fettuccine
with
Sugar Snap Peas

All of the ingredients must be ready to use when preparing this recipe. The sugar snap peas should be sautéed at the same time that the fettuccine is being cooked and neither should take more than 2 minutes to cook. We prefer olive oil for sautéing the sugar snaps as we feel butter combined with the very sweet peas is cloying.

Serves 4

1 recipe freshly made Spinach Fettuccine (¾ pound; see page 308)
½ pound sugar snap peas
1 egg, at room temperature
½ cup Yogurt (see page 67), at room temperature
1 cup freshly grated Parmesan cheese
3 tablespoons olive oil
1 teaspoon minced garlic
1 tablespoon salt (for cooking the pasta)
2 tablespoons unsalted butter, cut into pieces
½ teaspoon freshly ground white pepper
1 cup finely chopped parsley

1. Prepare the spinach fettuccine and let it hang to dry as you prepare the other ingredients.

2. String the sugar snap peas using your fingers or with a small knife. Begin at the very tip of each pea and pinch or cut it in order to grasp the string; pull the string to the opposite end of the pea.

Pinch off or cut the stem away and continue pulling the string down the other side of the pea until the string is completely removed. (This goes very quickly.)

3. In a large pot, bring 4 quarts of water to a boil. Also begin warming your serving platter and dinner plates.

4. In a small bowl, lightly beat the egg. Whisk in the yogurt. When the mixture is smooth, whisk in ¾ cup of the Parmesan cheese.

5. In a 10-inch skillet, heat 2 tablespoons of the olive oil over medium-low heat. Add the minced garlic and sauté just until wilted, but not browned. Turn the heat down to very low.

6. Arrange the remaining ingredients (the remaining tablespoon of olive oil, the butter, white pepper, the egg and cheese mixture, parsley, and the remaining ¼ cup of Parmesan cheese) on your work area so that they can be speedily tossed with the fettuccine.

7. Add 1 tablespoon of salt to the boiling water and when the water returns to a boil, add the fettuccine. Cook just until *al dente*, which will be only 2 to 3 minutes if the pasta has not dried too long.

8. Simultaneously, add the sugar snap peas to the skillet containing the garlic. Increase the heat to medium and sauté the peas for *only 2 minutes*, tossing frequently.

9. Drain the fettuccine and place it on a heated serving platter. Toss the pasta with the olive oil, butter, and white pepper.

Add the egg and cheese mixture and ¾ cup of the parsley. Toss again and add the sugar snap peas. Toss once more and sprinkle the pasta with the remaining ¼ cup of Parmesan cheese and the ¼ cup of parsley.

Serve immediately on heated plates.

FETTUCCINE WITH TOMATO AND YOGURT SAUCE

Heavy cream is used so often in pasta dishes that include tomatoes, we felt that substituting yogurt could add a new, special quality. Even though tomatoes and yogurt are acidic, combining them results in a silken blending that counterbalances the spicy pancetta (Italian bacon, see page 54) and hot red pepper.

Pesto is optional, but we like the contribution it makes in flavor as well as in color. Since the fettuccine is not tossed with the sauce, make the spinach variety to complete a color scheme of red and green. Use only our recipes for Tomato Sauce.

Serves 4

1 recipe freshly made Fettuccine (¾ pound; see page 305)
1 tablespoon olive oil
2 ounces pancetta, cut into ¼-inch dice
2 cups Tomato Sauce (see pages 310 and 311)
1 cup Yogurt (see page 67), at room temperature
1 tablespoon salt (for cooking the pasta)
1 teaspoon freshly ground dried hot red pepper
1 cup freshly grated Parmesan or Romano cheese
½ cup Pesto (see page 309), optional
½ cup minced fresh basil or parsley for garnish if you are not using pesto

1. Prepare the fettuccine and let it hang to dry as you prepare the other ingredients.

2. Heat the olive oil in a small skillet and add the pancetta. Sauté over very low heat until the dice have lightly browned and given up their fat.

3. In a large pot, bring 4 quarts of water to a boil. Also begin warming your serving platter and dinner plates.

4. In a 1½-quart saucepan, bring the tomato sauce to a simmer over medium heat. Slowly whisk in the yogurt (see page 68) and reduce the heat to low. Continue to whisk occasionally as the pasta is cooked.

5. Add the salt to the boiling water, and when it returns to a boil, add the fettuccine. Cook just until *al dente*, which should take 2 or 3 minutes if the pasta has not dried too long.

6. Drain the fettuccine and place it on the heated serving platter. Toss the pasta with the sautéed pancetta, undrained, and the hot red pepper. Pour the tomato and yogurt sauce over the center of the pasta, but do not toss.

Give each guest a serving of the pasta and some of the sauce on the heated plates. Sprinkle each serving with ¼ cup of the grated cheese and top with a tablespoon or so of pesto. If you are not using pesto, sprinkle the top with the minced herb.

FETTUCCINE WITH SHRIMP

One recipe suggests another. We developed this one after finding that tomato sauce blended so well with yogurt for Fettuccine with Tomato and Yogurt Sauce (see page 331). In this recipe the fettuccine is liberally sauced, but the sauce has so many nuances of flavor that the extra amount is relished.

Serves 4

1 recipe freshly made Fettuccine (¾ pound; see page 305)
1½ pounds fresh, unshelled shrimp
1 tablespoon olive oil
4 tablespoons unsalted butter
1 medium onion, chopped fine
1½ tablespoons finely chopped garlic
½ teaspoon salt, plus 1 tablespoon (for cooking the pasta)
¼ teaspoon freshly ground black pepper
¼ cup dry, white wine or vermouth
1 tablespoon flour
1 cup liquid from the drained tomatoes
2 cups well-drained and coarsely chopped canned tomatoes
2 tablespoons lemon juice
1 teaspoon freshly ground dried hot red pepper
2 cups Yogurt (see page 67), at room temperature
4 tablespoons finely minced fresh dill

1. Prepare the fettuccine and let it hang to dry as you make the sauce.

2. Peel and clean the shrimp. (See How to Shell and Clean Shrimp, page 120.) Set aside.

3. In a 2½-quart saucepan, heat the olive oil and 2 tablespoons of the butter. Add the onion and garlic. Sprinkle with the ½ teaspoon salt and black pepper and sauté over medium heat until the onions have wilted.

Add the white wine or vermouth and simmer over medium-high heat until the wine has almost evaporated.

4. Turn the heat down to medium and whisk in the flour. When the sauce begins to bubble, add the cup of liquid from the drained tomatoes. Continue whisking until the mixture thickens.

Add the drained tomatoes and turn the heat low. Let the mixture simmer, uncovered, while you cook the pasta and shrimp. Whisk occasionally.

5. In a large pot, bring 4 quarts of water to a boil. Also begin warming your serving bowl and plates.

6. In a 10-inch skillet, melt the remaining 2 tablespoons of butter over medium high heat. Add the shrimp and sprinkle them with the lemon juice and red pepper. Toss with two wooden spoons and sauté just until the shrimp are pink.

7. While the shrimp are sautéing, gradually whisk the yogurt into the saucepan (see page 68) with the tomatoes. Add the dill. Increase the heat to medium low and bring the ingredients to a simmer.

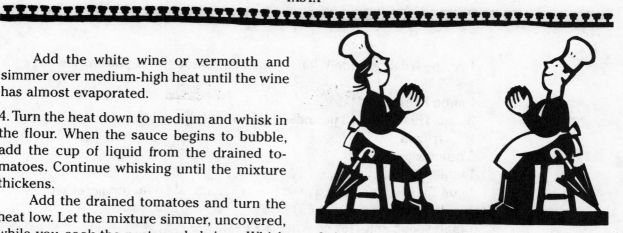

8. As soon as the shrimp have turned pink, add them to the saucepan. They must not overcook or they will become tough.

9. Quickly cook the pasta. Add 1 tablespoon of salt to the boiling water and when it returns to a boil, add the fettuccine. Cook until *al dente*, which should be about 2 to 3 minutes if the pasta has not dried too long.

10. Drain the fettuccine and place it in a heated serving bowl. Add the sauce and toss. Serve immediately on heated plates.

Note: For a variation, use 2 tablespoons of minced, fresh tarragon leaves instead of the dill and 1 cup of heavy cream, at room temperature, instead of the yogurt. Add them as you would the dill and yogurt.

PASTA WITH SIX P'S

This is our traditional pre-Marathon dinner. Although only one of us is a runner, we originated this recipe to satisfy the need for those extra carbohydrates the evening before a race. Only then did we realize the preponderance of P's.

If you are preparing the pasta for marathoners, this recipe will serve only 2. At other times, it should serve 4. Use salt only for cooking the pasta; the salt contained in the pancetta (Italian bacon, see page 54) and cheese will take care of the rest. On nonmarathon occasions, heavy cream may be used in place of the yogurt.

Serves 2 to 4

1 recipe freshly made Whole-Wheat Pasta dough (¾ pound; see page 308)
1 pound boiling potatoes
2 cups fresh peas (2 pounds before shelling) or 1 ten-ounce package frozen
2 ounces pancetta
1 tablespoon olive oil
1 cup Yogurt (see page 67) or heavy cream, at room temperature
½ cup Pesto (see page 309)
1 tablespoon salt (for cooking the pasta)
½ teaspoon freshly ground black pepper
1 cup finely chopped fresh parsley
1 cup freshly grated Parmesan cheese

1. Prepare the pasta dough and roll it out. Using kitchen shears, cut the rolled dough into strips 4 inches long by ½-inch wide.

Spread the strips on a cloth towel until you are ready to cook them.

2. Scrub the potatoes and steam them whole over low heat until they are just tender. Drain and allow to cool. When they are cool enough to handle, peel and cut them into 1-inch cubes. Cover the cubes to keep them warm.

3. Shell the peas or, if you are using frozen, let them defrost slightly.

4. Cut the pancetta into ¼-inch dice. In a 10-inch skillet, place the olive oil over very low heat and add the pancetta. Sauté until the dice have been rendered of their fat and have browned. Do not drain.

5. In a large pot, bring 4 quarts of water to a boil. Also begin warming your plates.

6. In a small saucepan over low heat, bring the yogurt (see page 68) or cream to just under a simmer. Whisk in the pesto. Keep the ingredients warm over very low heat, whisking occasionally.

7. Add the salt to the boiling water and when it returns to a boil, add the pasta. Cook until *al dente*, which could take 2 to 3 minutes if the pasta has not dried too long.

8. While the pasta is cooking, add the peas to the skillet with the pancetta. Cook the peas, tossing occasionally, just to heat them.

9. Drain the pasta and place it on a heated serving platter. Toss the pasta with the pancetta and peas. Add the black pepper, chopped parsley, and ¾ cup Parmesan cheese and toss again.

Add the warm potato cubes and yogurt (or cream) and pesto mixture. Toss a third time and sprinkle the remaining ¼ cup of Parmesan cheese on the surface. Serve immediately on heated plates.

WHOLE-WHEAT FETTUCCINE WITH A GARLIC SAUCE

This combination occurred to us one evening when we were enjoying Baked Whole Heads of Garlic. We thought *they* are such a luscious favorite that combined with fettuccine, they must be ambrosial. As with the whole heads, there is no hint of harshness in the garlic sauce, only a sublime tastiness.

Serves 4

1 recipe Baked Whole Heads of Garlic (see page 161),
    using ½-pound garlic
1 recipe freshly made Whole-Wheat Fettuccine (¾ pound;
    see page 308)
½ cup heavy cream, at room temperature
1 tablespoon salt (for cooking the pasta), plus ¼ teaspoon
2 tablespoons unsalted butter
¼ teaspoon freshly ground black pepper
1 cup chopped parsley

1. Prepare the baked garlic. The garlic cloves will be slipped from their skins before adding them to the pasta so it is not necessary to have perfect heads for baking, but do make sure to use a full ½ pound.

2. While the heads of garlic are baking, prepare the whole-wheat fettuccine. Let it hang to dry while you complete the sauce.

3. Have the remaining ingredients ready to use. About 10 minutes before the garlic is ready, bring 4 quarts of water to a boil in a large pot. Also begin warming your serving platter and dinner plates.

4. Place the baked heads of garlic in a sieve over a small saucepan. Quickly slip the cloves from their skins, discarding the skins and stems. This is done over a saucepan to catch any precious liquid the garlic may express.

5. Add the garlic cloves and the heavy cream to the liquid in the saucepan. (There will probably be very little liquid.) Let the mixture simmer over low heat.

6. Add the tablespoon of salt to the boiling water. When the water returns to a boil, add the fettuccine. Cook just until *al dente*, which will take 2 or 3 minutes, if the pasta has not dried too long.

7. Drain the fettuccine and place it on a heated serving dish. Toss with the butter, ¼ teaspoon of salt, pepper, and ¾ cup of the parsley.
Add the garlic and cream mixture and toss again. By this time, the cloves of garlic will have melted into the cream and will not be evident in the sauce. Sprinkle the pasta with the remaining ¼ cup of chopped parsley and serve immediately on heated plates.

BUCKWHEAT FETTUCCINE WITH THREE CHEESES

The cheese sauce for the fettuccine can be prepared within minutes, so have all of the ingredients lined up, ready to use.

The cottage and Parmesan cheeses are basic to the sauce but the third cheese can vary slightly. Try it with an Italian gorgonzola, which we sometimes use, or a Maytag Blue, which is milder. Both are delicious and both are available by mail order. The buckwheat flavor pairs perfectly with the creamy sauce and the sprouts add a likewise agreeable touch.

Serves 4

1 recipe freshly made Buckwheat Fettuccine (¾ pound;
    see page 308)
4 ounces blue cheese
1 cup homemade Cottage Cheese (see page 88)
1 cup Yogurt (see page 67)
1 egg
¾ cup freshly grated Parmesan cheese
½ teaspoon freshly ground white pepper
3 tablespoons unsalted butter
1 tablespoon salt (for cooking the pasta)
1 cup alfalfa sprouts, loosely packed (for growing instructions,
    see page 39)

1. Prepare the buckwheat fettuccine and let it hang to dry as you begin the sauce.

2. In a small bowl, cream together the blue cheese, cottage cheese, and ½ cup of the yogurt.

In another small bowl, beat the egg with the remaining yogurt, ½ cup of the Parmesan cheese, and the pepper.

3. In a large pot, bring 4 quarts of water to a boil (see Note). Also begin warming your dinner plates.

4. In a shallow saucepan, large enough to hold the pasta, melt the butter over medium-low heat. (By using a large saucepan, the pasta can be mixed directly into the sauce, so that none will be lost.)

When the butter has melted, add the blue cheese mixture. Stir until the cheeses melt into a creamy consistency. Reduce the heat to low while you cook the pasta.

5. Immediately add the salt to the boiling water and as soon as the water returns to a boil, add the pasta. Buckwheat fettuccine cooks very quickly and will be ready in less than 1 minute, if you like it *al dente* and it has not dried too long.

6. Drain the pasta and quickly toss it with the sauce in the pan. Add the egg mixture and toss again.

Sprinkle the remaining Parmesan cheese over the pasta, topping it with the alfalfa sprouts. Separate the sprouts into threads as you add them. Serve from the saucepan onto heated plates.

Note: If you have whey on hand, use it for half of your liquid for cooking the pasta. Whey adds a very special taste to buckwheat pasta.

A GRATIN OF CAULIFLOWER AND RED PEPPERS WITH FETTUCCINE

This colorful gratin, with its generous amount of dried hot red pepper (use less if a teaspoon seems too much), makes for delicious eating on a cold evening. Use salt only in the boiling water in which the pasta is cooked; the cheeses supply enough in the finished dish.

Serves 4

1 recipe freshly made Fettuccine (¾ pound; see page 305)
2-pound head cauliflower
1 small slice of lemon
3 large red bell peppers (¾ pound), fresh or frozen,
    or 1 cup good quality canned pimientos
2 tablespoons unsalted butter, plus 1 teaspoon
2 large cloves garlic, minced
1 teaspoon finely chopped fresh or dried rosemary
1 teaspoon freshly ground dried hot red pepper
2 cups Yogurt (see page 67), at room temperature
2 cups coarsely grated Italian Fontina cheese (6 ounces)
1 tablespoon salt (for cooking the pasta)
¼ cup freshly grated Parmesan cheese

1. Prepare the fettuccine and let it hang to dry as you prepare the cauliflower, bell peppers, and sauce.

2. Remove the outer leaves and trim any blemishes from the head of cauliflower. Cut out the thick core.

Rinse the head and cut or break it into 1½- to 2-inch flowerets. Place the flowerets in a 2-quart saucepan, stems down. Add the slice of lemon (this will help prevent discoloration) and pour in water to a depth of 1 inch.

Cover the saucepan and bring water to a simmer over medium heat. Cook for 10 minutes. Immediately remove the saucepan from the heat and drain the cauliflower in a sieve. Run cold water over the flowerets to stop the cooking process. Let them remain in the sieve while you prepare the bell peppers and sauce.

3. If you are using fresh or defrosted red bell peppers, core and seed them. If you are using frozen, let them defrost on paper towels. Drain canned pimientos in a sieve. Cut whichever peppers you are using into ¼-inch-wide julienne strips, 1½-to 2-inches long.

4. Using the same saucepan, melt 2 tablespoons of the butter. Add the strips of pepper, the garlic, rosemary, and hot red pepper. Sauté, covered, over medium-low heat until the bell peppers are tender. This will take about 10 minutes if the peppers are fresh or frozen, and 5 minutes if canned pimientos.

5. Meanwhile, bring 4 quarts of water to a boil in a large pot. Also begin warming your dinner plates.

Preheat the oven to 400° F.

6. When the bell peppers are tender, stir in the yogurt with a wooden spoon (see page 68). Bring to a full simmer over medium heat and stir in the Fontina cheese. Stir until the cheese has melted and turn the heat to low as you cook the pasta.

7. Just before you are ready to cook the pasta, add the salt to the boiling water. When the water returns to a boil, add the pasta. Cook just until *al dente*, which should take 2 or 3 minutes if the pasta has not dried too long.

Butter a 14-inch oval gratin dish with the remaining teaspoon of butter. Drain the pasta and place it in the gratin dish.

8. Add half of the simmering sauce to the pasta and toss thoroughly. Arrange the reserved cauliflower over the top and cover with the remaining sauce.

Sprinkle the Parmesan cheese over the top and place the gratin dish on the middle rack of the oven for about 20 minutes until the sauce is bubbling and the top is lightly browned. Serve immediately.

WHAT TO BUY OR ORDER NOW

In September, 90-degree days are not unusual where we live so, fearing spoilage, we mail-order very little. Instead we begin to make lists of what we will need and if the weather does cool by the last week of the month, we will be ready to call in or mail out our orders.

AND IN OUR GARDEN

During early September, work continues in the garden just as in August with large hauls of tomatoes, peppers and beans, all of which must be canned or frozen. As the plants or vines finish their production for the season, we cut them to the ground in foot-long pieces. Some plants, such as tomatoes and peppers, we pull up by the roots so that no diseases can harbor in the soil. All of this, we let dry out and then decompose slightly on top of the soil. A week or so later, we till it back into the soil. This saves the work of keeping a compost bin.

In late September, it is time to pick our winter squash. The stems will have dried and turned brown. We cut the squash, leaving 1½ inches of the stem attached and use our "wire plant cages" (page 64) to let them cure in the sun for a few days before storing them in a cool place for the winter. As the crops dwindle and our harvest baskets are no longer needed, we scrub them and let them dry in the sun before putting them away. This is not done without a certain amount of sadness for a season that is ending. In preparation for the coming year, we plant a bed of spinach seeds, knowing that the small plants will winter over and greet us early in the spring.

OCTOBER

GOOD OLD COUNTRY CORN

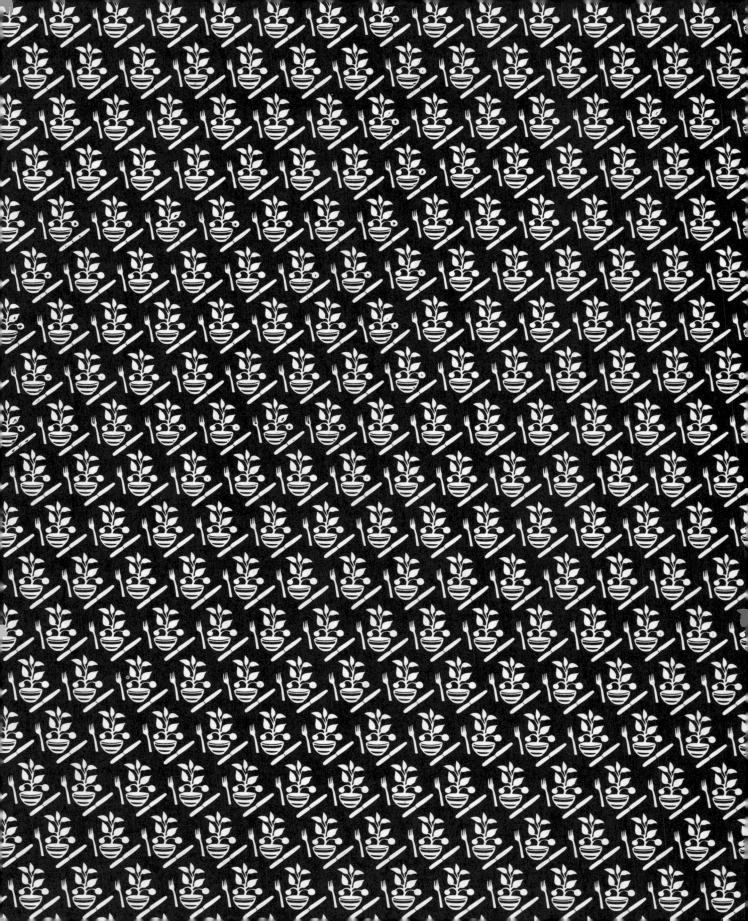

Good Old Country Corn

In our admiration for this phenomenal grain, we have given corn a chapter all its own. As perhaps with no other crop, one could almost exist on corn and its by-products: corn syrup, cornstarch, cornmeal, grits, animal feed, fuel and whiskey. In several Central American countries, even corn smut is considered a delicacy. Corn smut, by the way, is a disease caused by a fungus which attacks the ears of corn. The smut grows rapidly, forming a huge black mass of spores. To see smut for the first time is an unnerving experience. To present it on the table to the uninitiated would be paralyzing. On a happier note, a strain of perennial corn has been found in Mexico and developers are hopeful that they can cross it with a sweet corn, thereby breeding an edible corn that is perennial.

In our area, corn is the main farm crop and a favorite in the home garden. Silver Queen ranks well above the rest as the preferred variety. We seem to be in a minority growing only the yellow varieties.

Although there is none in our garden in October, we associate the month with corn, anyway. Perhaps it is because of the dried ears on display all over or because we choose this month to visit Linney's Mill, when the farmers bring their trucks filled with dried ears to be ground into feed. Today, instead of burlap sacks, old colorfully printed sheets are sewn into sacks. The loaded trucks form a patchwork of dazzling color.

It should be noted that not all of our corn recipes appear in this chapter. Corn Soup fit in nicely with the other yogurt-base soups in March, and three of our salads using corn naturally seemed to go with the other salad recipes.

Country Cornbread

This bread can be prepared with ease at the end of a long day when there is not time for concentrated baking.

Serves 4 to 6

1 egg
1 cup Buttermilk (see page 96)
3 tablespoons corn oil, plus a small amount for oiling the baking pan
2 tablespoons natural honey
⅔ cup all-purpose, unbleached white flour
1 tablespoon baking powder
½ teaspoon baking soda
½ teaspoon salt
¾ cup yellow cornmeal

1. Preheat the oven to 425° F.

2. Rub an 8½-inch round cake pan with a little of the corn oil.

In a mixing bowl, beat the egg with the buttermilk, corn oil, and honey. In another bowl, sift together the unbleached white flour, baking powder, baking soda, and salt. Add the cornmeal and mix.

Add the dry ingredients to the liquids and stir just enough to blend.

3. Pour the mixture into the cake pan. Smooth the surface and bake for 20 minutes. Serve immediately, cutting the bread into wedges.

CORNMEAL MUFFINS

Muffins taste best when baked in tins which are *not* the nonstick kind. We tested this by baking half the batter in just an ordinary aluminum tin and the other half in a tin with a nonstick surface. It was as if we had used two different batters. Cast iron is even better.

For this recipe, as in any using baking soda and baking powder, it is extremely important to sift the two with the flour. Once, being in a great hurry, we eliminated this step and one muffin had a clump of soda in it. The taste was indescribably foul.

Makes 12 muffins

1 cup yellow cornmeal
¾ cup all-purpose, unbleached white flour
½ teaspoon baking soda
1 teaspoon baking powder
½ teaspoon salt
2 eggs
1 cup Buttermilk (see page 96)
3 tablespoons corn oil plus an additional tablespoon for oiling the muffin tin

1. Preheat the oven to 425° F Lightly oil the muffin tin.

2. Place the cornmeal in a mixing bowl. In another, smaller bowl, combine the flour, baking soda, baking powder, and salt. Sift these ingredients into the cornmeal, and mix.

3. Lightly beat the eggs with the buttermilk and the 3 tablespoons of corn oil, then add them to the dry ingredients. Mix just enough to moisten. Spoon the batter into the tin.

4. Bake for 25 minutes until golden brown. Remove the muffins from the oven and if they are not to be served immediately, lift each from its cup and turn it on its side; this prevents the muffins from "sweating." Reheat briefly when you are ready to serve them.

Variations: For larger, richer muffins, this recipe can be varied in several ways. Add any of the following ingredients to the liquid mixture before mixing with the dry ingredients. Otherwise, the recipe remains the same: 2 cups fresh or frozen corn kernels; or 1 cup coarsely grated Cheddar cheese; or ½ teaspoon dried hot red pepper (or all three).

HUSH PUPPIES

In the South, Hush Puppies are often considered a must with fried fish. Some recipes say to fry the hush puppies in the oil after frying the fish, but we prefer to fry them first, while the oil is clean, then keep them warm in the oven, lightly covered with foil. No harm is done if you prefer to do them last. Of all fried breads, hush puppies are the easiest to make.

Makes 2 dozen or so

> **2 cups yellow cornmeal**
> **1 teaspoon baking powder**
> **½ teaspoon baking soda**
> **½ teaspoon salt**
> **¼ teaspoon freshly ground black pepper**
> **2 eggs**
> **1 cup Buttermilk (see page 96)**
> **Corn oil for deep frying**

1. Sift the cornmeal with the baking powder, baking soda, salt, and black pepper into a bowl.

Beat the eggs with the buttermilk, then add them to the dry ingredients. Using a wooden spoon, blend together until the batter is thick and smooth.

2. Pour corn oil into a heavy skillet to a depth of at least 1 inch. Heat the oil to 375° F or until ½ teaspoon of the batter dropped into the oil browns instantly.

3. Drop the batter by tablespoonfuls into the hot oil.

Do not crowd the pan, frying only 6 to 8 hush puppies at a time. They fry very quickly and should be turned only once. The frying time for each will be less than 2 minutes. Do not worry if the shapes are irregular or have "puppy tails."

4. When golden brown on all sides, remove each hush puppy with a slotted spoon to a heated dish, lined with paper towels, to drain.

Serve hot with unsalted butter or, as we prefer, with Pesto (see page 309).

Variations: This recipe is basic, but you may add 1 small, finely minced onion and/or 1 teaspoon fresh ground dried hot red pepper to the batter. To serve the hush puppies as an hors d'oeuvre, add to the batter the minced onion and 3 tablespoons of finely minced pancetta (Italian bacon, see page 54) that has been sautéed until crisp and brown.

CORN DROP BISCUITS

These effortless biscuits go well with salads or with soups, particularly tomato soups. The red pepper is optional or you may use a smaller amount if a full tablespoon seems too hot for you.

Makes about 3 dozen biscuits

> 2½ cups corn kernels, fresh (3 large ears) or frozen
> 2 eggs
> ½ cup Buttermilk (see page 96)
> ¼ cup corn oil
> 1 tablespoon natural honey
> 1 tablespoon freshly ground dried hot red peppers (optional)
> 1 cup yellow cornmeal
> 1 cup all-purpose, unbleached flour
> 1 teaspoon baking powder
> ½ teaspoon baking soda
> 1 teaspoon salt

1. If you are using fresh corn, shuck the ears, remove the silk, wash and cut the kernels from the cob. If you are using frozen corn, place the kernel in a sieve to defrost and drain. No preliminary cooking is necessary for either.

2. Preheat the oven to 425° F.

3. In a large mixing bowl, beat the eggs. Add the buttermilk, corn oil, honey, hot red pepper,

and corn. Stir with a wooden spoon, just enough to blend the ingredients.

4. In a smaller bowl, sift together the cornmeal, flour, baking powder, baking soda, and salt. Add the dry ingredients to the liquid ingredients and stir again until well blended.

5. Drop little mounds of batter by the heaping spoonful (actual measure should be about 2

tablespoons) onto a large, ungreased, aluminum baking sheet. Leave ¾ inch of space between each biscuit.

6. Bake the biscuits on the middle rack of the oven for 20 minutes. They should be golden brown. Remove the baking sheet from the oven and let the biscuits rest for a minute or two. After this short rest, they can easily be removed from the baking sheet with a metal spatula.

7. Serve very hot in a basket lined with a cloth.

SPOON BREAD WITH CHEESE

For the cheese in our spoon bread, we usually combine leftover bits and pieces—aged Colby, Cheddar, Italian Fontina, even Romano. If using Romano, use only ¼ cup and make up the rest of the cup with a milder cheese such as Fontina.

Serves 4 to 6

3 tablespoons unsalted butter
3 cups milk, at room temperature
½ cup water or whey
½ teaspoon salt
1½ cups yellow cornmeal
3 eggs, well beaten
1 cup coarsely grated cheese (see above)
1 teaspoon freshly ground dried hot red pepper

1. Preheat the oven to 350°F.

2. Rub the inside of a 1½-quart casserole with 1 tablespoon of the butter and set aside.

   Rinse a 1½-quart saucepan with cold water. Do not dry, but add the milk, water or whey, and salt. The cold water will help to prevent the milk from burning in the bottom of the saucepan.

   Cover the saucepan and bring the liquid to just under a boil over medium heat.

3. When the liquid is almost boiling, add the cornmeal in a slow, steady stream, whisking constantly so that it does not lump. Cook the cornmeal while continuing to whisk until it is thick and bubbling. This will take 5 minutes.

4. Remove the saucepan from the heat and, using a wooden spoon, beat the remaining 2 tablespoons of butter into the cornmeal. Add the eggs and beat vigorously until blended. Fold in the cheese and red pepper.

5. Pour the cornmeal mixture into the greased casserole. Smooth the surface and bake on the middle rack of the oven for 45 minutes. Spoon out immediately to serve.

   This bread goes well with Hot Sausage or Fried Fish, along with A Mess of Greens (see the recipe index).

CORNMEAL CRACKERS

Our cornmeal crackers, contrary to the usual, rather bland versions, are not only colorful, but assuredly zesty.

Makes 26 crackers

1 cup yellow cornmeal
½ cup all-purpose, unbleached white flour
1 teaspoon salt
1 tablespoon sweet paprika
1 teaspoon freshly ground dried hot red pepper
⅓ cup milk
3 tablespoons corn oil

1. In a bowl, combine the cornmeal, flour, salt, paprika, and red pepper. In a separate cup mix the milk and corn oil and add them to the dry ingredients. Blend together with a fork.

2. Place the dough on a work surface and knead for about 3 minutes until it forms a cohesive mass. If it seems too dry, dribble additional milk onto the dough and knead again. Cut it into 4 pieces and knead each piece briefly. Let the dough rest for 5 minutes.

3. Preheat the oven to 350°F. After the dough has rested, roll out each piece ⅛-inch thick. If the dough is crumbly and falls apart, gather it up and roll out again.

Cut the crackers with a 3-inch biscuit cutter. As you cut the crackers, place them on an ungreased baking sheet. (Do not use a heavy iron baking sheet, as the crackers will burn on the bottoms.) Gather up all scraps of dough, knead briefly, and roll out again until all the dough is used.

4. Prick the crackers all over with the tines of a fork. Bake for 15 minutes. Do not remove the crackers from the baking sheet until they have cooled. Store in an airtight container.

CORN PUDDING

Since this is a dish we are more likely to prepare in cooler weather, we use corn frozen from our summer crop. Serve the pudding with ham, poultry, or fish, preferably fried.

Serves 4 to 6

3 cups corn kernels, fresh (4 to 5 medium ears) or frozen
1 tablespoon unsalted butter

4 eggs, at room temperature
1 cup heavy cream, at room temperature
1 cup Yogurt (see page 67), at room temperature
2 tablespoons corn oil
½ teaspoon salt
1 teaspoon freshly ground dried hot red pepper
1 medium onion, chopped fine

1. Prepare the corn. If you are using fresh corn, shuck the ears, remove the silk, wash, and cut the kernels from the cob.

For frozen corn, place the kernels in a sieve to defrost and drain.

2. Preheat the oven to 325° F

3. Rub the inside of a 1½-quart casserole with the butter.

In a mixing bowl, beat the eggs with the heavy cream, yogurt, corn oil, salt, and red pepper until smooth. Add the chopped onion and the corn. Blend thoroughly.

4. Pour the mixture into the casserole. Place the casserole in a shallow pan, then half fill the pan with hot water.

Bake the pudding in the oven for about 1¼ hours. The top should be nicely browned and a knife inserted into the center of the pudding should come out clean. Serve at once.

CORN PANCAKES

We prepare our pancakes in an iron skillet, but they can be made on a griddle or nonstick frying pan if you wish. The pancakes have their place at breakfast or brunch (try them with dollops of yogurt and preserves), but we enjoy them unadorned, served with fish or chicken at dinner.

Makes about 24 pancakes, each 3 inches

1½ cups corn kernels, fresh (about 2 ears) or frozen
½ cup yellow cornmeal
½ cup all-purpose, unbleached flour
1 teaspoon baking powder
½ teaspoon baking soda
¼ teaspoon salt
¼ teaspoon freshly ground black pepper
2 eggs
1 cup Yogurt (see page 67)
2 tablespoons unsalted butter
2 to 4 tablespoons corn oil

1. Prepare the corn. If you are using fresh corn, shuck the ears, remove the silk, wash, and cut the kernels from the cobs. If you are using frozen corn, place the kernels in a sieve to defrost and drain.

2. Into a medium-size bowl sift together the cornmeal, flour, baking powder, baking soda, salt, and black pepper.

    In a smaller bowl, beat the eggs. Add the yogurt and corn. Stir to mix. Blend the liquid ingredients into the dry ingredients. Let the batter rest for ½ hour before making the pancakes.

3. Preheat the oven to 200°F.

4. When you are ready to cook the pancakes, melt the butter with 2 tablespoons of the corn oil over medium heat in your skillet. Ladle the batter onto the skillet, allowing approximately 3 tablespoons of batter for each pancake.

    Cook the pancakes for about 2 minutes on one side or until the edges begin to brown and the surface starts to bubble. Using a spatula, turn the pancakes over and cook for another 2 minutes. They should be golden brown.

5. Continue in this manner until all of the batter has been used, keeping the completed pancakes hot in the warm oven as you cook the rest. Add more corn oil if necessary and adjust the heat if the skillet becomes too hot.

GINGERED CORN

Use a very sweet variety of corn for this lively vegetable course. We grow two varieties, Sugar Sweet and Kandy Korn E. H., that are well described by their names. As with most corn-base dishes, this one goes excellently with fish or chicken.

Serves 4 to 6

4 cups corn kernels, fresh (5 or 6 medium ears) or frozen
2 tablespoons unsalted butter
1 teaspoon olive oil
1 medium onion, chopped fine
2 tablespoons peeled and finely chopped fresh ginger root
1 teaspoon finely chopped garlic
½ teaspoon salt
½ teaspoon freshly ground dried hot red pepper
¼ teaspoon freshly ground black pepper
½ cup water, if needed

1. If you are using fresh corn, shuck, silk, and cut the kernels from the cobs.

    If you are using frozen cut corn, let it drain on paper towels for about ½ hour to defrost slightly.

2. Combine the butter and olive oil in a 10-inch skillet over medium-low heat. Add the onion and sauté it, stirring occasionally, until it wilts and begins to color.

3. Add the ginger root and garlic to the skillet and sauté for 1 minute. Add the corn and sprinkle it with the salt and red and black peppers. Stir the ingredients to mix. Increase the heat to medium.

If you are using fresh corn, add the ½ cup of water to the skillet. Cover the skillet and cook just until the corn is tender.

If you are using frozen corn, the water will probably not be necessary—in fact, there may be excess moisture. In that case, cook the corn uncovered until it is tender so that the moisture will evaporate. The cooking time for either corn will be only 5 to 8 minutes, depending upon the size of the kernels and the variety.

BASIC POLENTA

Although polenta from Italy and grits from the South are similar they certainly are not the same, and it is gratifying to have a choice between the two when we want a warming and wholesome "meal." We enjoy polenta in its simplest form, served directly from the pot onto serving plates and topped with a bit of butter, or we utilize the basic polenta recipe to create others. Often, we will use whey instead of water for an exceedingly nourishing and tasty variation.

Serves 4 to 6

2 quarts water or whey
1 teaspoon salt
2 cups yellow cornmeal

1. In a heavy 3-quart pot or casserole, bring the water or whey to a boil.

If you are using whey, remember that it froths as it boils and care must be taken that it does not boil over the sides of the pot. When the liquid comes to a boil, add the salt.

2. Place the cornmeal in a bowl from which you can easily grab up small handfuls. Holding a small amount of cornmeal in one hand, steadily let it fall into the boiling liquid, sifting it through your fingers as you do so.

Whisk continually, so that the polenta does not lump, until all of the cornmeal is added.

3. Reduce the heat to medium low and continue to whisk until the polenta is too thick for the whisk to be effective. At this point, switch to a wooden spoon. Stir until the polenta is very thick. This will take from 30 to 45 minutes.

4. Serve the polenta from the pot or transfer it to a serving platter. The presentation will depend upon what you are serving with the polenta. It may be that you would wish to add only butter or freshly grated cheese and a sprinkling of parsley. Or you may surround the polenta with Tomato Sauce or Pesto and Cream Sauce (see the recipe index).

BAKED POLENTA

There are two very easy methods for baking polenta, and the accompaniments can vary according to what else is being served. Try the dish with any of the sauces that follow — Pesto and Cream, Blue Cheese or Hot Tomato — or other sauces containing tomatoes and/or mushrooms. If you wish, add finely diced and sautéed pancetta (Italian bacon, see page 54) to the polenta itself before baking.

The baking time is quite flexible. We have served the baked polenta after only ½ hour in the oven, and, at times, after an hour's baking. With longer baking, the polenta will develop a browner crust, both top and bottom. Baked polenta is exceedingly hot inside, so it is best to let it rest briefly before serving.

Serves from 4 to 6

1 recipe freshly prepared Polenta (see page 349)
1 tablespoon unsalted butter, plus an additional tablespoon (optional)
¼ cup freshly grated Parmesan or Romano cheese (optional)
Freshly chopped basil or parsley as garnish

In addition, for Method 2, one *of the following:*
2 ounces blue cheese, crumbled
½ pound Italian Fontina cheese, coarsely shredded
½ pound dry homemade Cottage Cheese (see page 88)

Method 1

1. Preheat the oven to 400°F while you prepare the polenta.

2. Rub a gratin dish (a 14-inch oval, if possible) with the unsalted butter. While the polenta is still very hot, spoon it into the gratin dish, smoothing the surface flat.

Bake the polenta on the middle rack of the oven for 30 minutes or until browned to your liking. During the last 10 minutes of baking you may spread more butter on the surface and sprinkle it with ¼ cup freshly grated Parmesan or Romano cheese. This, again, is optional.

3. Just before serving, surround the polenta with the accompaniment of your choice. If you are using the Pesto and Cream Sauce, a sprinkling of freshly chopped basil will add color. Parsley could be used with the other choices.

Method 2

1. While the polenta is still very hot, spoon it out onto a wooden board, a marble surface, or a large platter. Spread it with the back of your wooden spoon so that it is no more than ½ inch thick. Let the polenta cool briefly.

2. Preheat the oven to 400°F.

3. Rub a gratin dish (a 14-inch oval, if possible) with the unsalted butter. Cut the polenta into pieces to fit the gratin dish so that there

will be enough for two layers. (Tradition holds that polenta, like dumplings, should be cut with a string as metal supposedly ruins the taste. However, a stainless knife is quite satisfactory.)

Make one layer of polenta in the gratin dish, fitting the cut edges together.

4. Cover the layer with cheese and, again, the choice is yours. If you will be serving the polenta with the Blue Cheese Sauce, sprinkle the layer with 2 ounces of crumbled blue cheese.

If you will be serving a tomato-base sauce, sprinkle the layer with ½ pound coarsely shredded Italian Fontina cheese.

For the Pesto and Cream Sauce, spread the layer with ½ pound of dry, homemade Cottage Cheese.

5. Make your second layer of polenta as you did the first, covering all of the cheese. Bake the polenta on the middle rack of the oven for about 30 minutes, again brushing the surface with butter and sprinkling it, depending upon your sauce, with ¼ cup of grated Parmesan or Romano cheese for the final 10 minutes of baking. Serve the sauce of your choice from a separate bowl, spooning a little sauce over or alongside each serving of polenta. Sprinkle with the basil or parsley.

PESTO AND CREAM SAUCE

In this sauce, the piquancy of the pesto is tamed by the heavy cream. It is unusually good with polenta, pasta, and even fish.
Makes about 1¼ cups

> **2 cups heavy cream, at room temperature**
> **½ cup Pesto (see page 309)**
> **¼ teaspoon freshly ground black pepper**

1. In a small saucepan, bring the heavy cream to a boil over medium heat. Continue to boil, whisking occasionally until the cream is reduced to 1 cup.

2. Whisk in the pesto and the black pepper. Bring to just a simmer and serve immediately.

BLUE CHEESE SAUCE

When serving this sauce with Baked Polenta, try to use Gorgonzola cheese, as it is a more authentic accompaniment, or you may use a mild blue cheese such as Maytag Blue. With either cheese, this is a pleasing and complementary sauce for the polenta.
Makes about 1½ cups

½ cup heavy cream, at room temperature
4 ounces Gorgonzola or blue cheese, crumbled
½ to 1 cup Yogurt (see page 67), at room temperature
¼ teaspoon freshly ground white pepper

1. In a small saucepan bring the heavy cream to a boil over medium heat. Whisk in the crumbled cheese and yogurt (see page 68). The amount of yogurt will depend upon how thick or thin you prefer the sauce. Keep in mind that as soon as the sauce cools even slightly, it will begin to thicken because of the cheese. Add the pepper.

2. Continue to whisk until the sauce is smooth and bubbly. If the sauce is not to be served immediately, keep it over low heat at a slow simmer. Whisk occasionally and add more yogurt if it becomes reduced.

Note: When made with Gorgonzola cheese, this sauce is also wonderful on pasta.

HOT TOMATO SAUCE

Makes 1½ cups

1 medium onion
4 large cloves garlic
2 tablespoons olive oil
2 cups canned tomatoes
½ teaspoon of a dried herb such as oregano, wild thyme, or basil
1 teaspoon freshly ground dried hot red pepper
½ teaspoon salt, if the canned tomatoes are unsalted

1. Peel and chop the onion fine. Peel and mince the garlic. Heat the olive oil in a 1½-quart saucepan. Add the onion and garlic and sauté over medium heat until wilted.

Add the tomatoes with their liquid, the dried herb, the hot red pepper, and salt if you are using it.

2. Bring the ingredients to a simmer and cook, uncovered, until the sauce has thickened. This will take about 20 minutes. Stir occasionally, breaking up the tomatoes if they do not do so on their own, but leave them in small chunks.

A GRATIN WITH INDIVIDUAL MOLDS OF POLENTA

This is captivating, and a different treatment from the usual recipes for polenta. For the individual molds, use any small containers that have a ½- to ⅔-cup capacity. We use porcelain ramekins, but 6- or 7-ounce tins from canned goods will work just as well.

You may substitute Romano cheese for the Parmesan, but the cottage cheese must be homemade and no other cheese will work as well as the Italian Fontina. We often prepare this gratin when we have just a small amount of leftover canned tomatoes that contain too much liquid for most recipes, but are too precious to discard.

Serves 4

> 1 recipe Polenta (see page 349)
> 1½ cups canned tomatoes, with their liquid
> ¾ pound homemade Cottage Cheese (see page 88)
> 4 tablespoons unsalted butter
> 1 heaping tablespoon flour
> 1 teaspoon freshly ground black pepper
> 1 tablespoon finely chopped fresh basil or 1 teaspoon dried basil
> 2 cups coarsely grated Italian Fontina cheese (6 ounces)
> ½ cup finely grated Parmesan cheese
> Additional ¼ cup finely chopped fresh basil or fresh parsley, for
>   garnish

1. Prepare the polenta. Have ready 8 individual molds and when the polenta is very thick, immediately fill each mold. Press down upon the polenta to make sure the mold is completely filled. Smooth the surface.

It is not necessary to butter the molds, but it is necessary to fill them while the polenta is hot because as it cools, it becomes a very solid mass and is difficult to spoon into the molds.

Set the filled molds aside to cool while you prepare the sauce.

2. Purée the tomatoes with their liquid. It is easy with such a small amount to press them through a sieve into a bowl.

In another bowl, cream the cottage cheese by mashing the curds with the back of a spoon.

3. Preheat the oven to 400°F.

4. In a 2-quart saucepan, melt 3 tablespoons of the butter over medium-low heat. Add the flour, whisking constantly, and when it begins to bubble, whisk in the puréed tomatoes. Add the black pepper and the fresh or dried basil.

Simmer, continuing to whisk, until the mixture thickens slightly.

Add the cottage cheese, ½ cup at a time. The cottage cheese may have a curdled appearance, but do not worry about it. When the cottage cheese has been incorporated, use a wooden spoon to stir in the Fontina cheese, ½ cup at a time.

Turn the heat to low while you prepare the gratin dish. Stir occasionally, making sure that the sauce does not burn on the bottom.

5. Rub a 16-inch oval gratin dish with the remaining tablespoon of butter. On your work surface, unmold the polenta. Run a small knife around the edge of each mold, turn it upside down and give it a tap. The molded polenta will come out easily. Arrange the molded polenta in the gratin dish, spacing them evenly apart.

6. Spoon the sauce over the polenta and around it into the gratin dish. Sprinkle the Parmesan cheese over the top and bake on the middle rack of the oven for 30 minutes. The polenta should be a golden brown (it will be very hot inside) and the sauce bubbling. Sprinkle the gratin with the ¼ cup of chopped basil or parsley and serve immediately, giving each guest 2 molds of polenta and the sauce.

MOTHER'S GRITS

We can understand when someone from outside the South expresses a disdain for grits (possibly because they have never tasted them), but for Southerners to feel the same is shocking! Obviously, they were not raised on a recipe as delicious as this one.

If you are a hearty breakfast type, serve the grits at that time of the day. We have them for supper with Hot Sausages (see page 45). If you prefer, use white grits instead of the yellow variety we suggest.

Serves 4 to 6

> 3 cups water
> 1 teaspoon salt
> 1 cup yellow grits
> 2½ cups milk, at room temperature
> 4 tablespoons unsalted butter
> 2 eggs, well beaten
> ½ teaspoon freshly ground black pepper
> 1 teaspoon minced hot red pepper, fresh or dried (optional)

1. In a 1½-quart saucepan, bring the water and salt to a boil over medium heat. Very slowly pour in the grits, whisking constantly to prevent lumps. Continue whisking until the mixture begins to bubble.

Add the milk, ½ cup or so at a time,

whisking to incorporate. When the mixture becomes too thick to continue whisking, switch to a wooden spoon and stir vigorously.

2. Lower the heat and continue cooking, stirring often, for 30 minutes. The grits should cook at a "slow bubble." Do not cover.

3. The grits will be cooked within the 30 minutes and could be served as is with dabs of butter. However, to have Mother's, remove the saucepan from the heat and beat in the butter, followed by the beaten eggs and black pepper. Add the hot red pepper, if you wish, and serve immediately, piping hot.

FRYING GRITS AND POLENTA

The method for frying grits and polenta is the same. They can be enjoyed at any meal during the day, served with jams and preserves at breakfast and with any of the suggested sauces for Basic Polenta (see page 349) when served at other times. Our instructions will generously serve 8 or more. We do this as the cooked grits and polenta will keep in the refrigerator for a week and the slices can be cut as needed. However, you may halve the recipes, if you wish.

Serves 8 or more (see above)

1 recipe Mother's Grits or Basic Polenta (see page 349)
Unsalted butter, as needed, for the bread-loaf pans and frying

1. Prepare the recipe for grits or polenta. While the mixture is still very hot, spoon it into two lightly buttered bread-loaf pans, approximately 8½ × 4½ × 2⅝ inches. Pack the mixture in firmly and smooth the surface. Cool at room temperature for ½ hour. Then cover the loaf pans with plastic wrap and refrigerate them for 2 hours or until needed.

2. When you are ready to fry the grits or polenta, unmold them onto a platter. Cut the loaves crosswise into slices ½-inch thick.
Begin warming your serving platter.

3. In a heavy, 10-inch skillet, heat 3 tablespoons of butter over medium heat. When the butter is hot (do not let it burn), add as many of the slices as will fit comfortably in the skillet. Fry the slices on one side for about 3 minutes or until they are crusty and a golden brown. Turn

them with a spatula and fry on the other side for another 3 minutes. As the slices are fried, remove them to the heated platter, arranging them in an overlapping fashion.

Add more butter to the skillet as it is needed and continue to fry until all of the slices are used. Serve immediately, giving each guest 2 or 3 slices.

Nannie Fraley's Livermush

Like grits, livermush is not properly appreciated. Just the name seems to upset some people. Originally, livermush was made so that every part of the hog at hog-killing time in late autumn could be used. When we were children, many families made enough to last through the winter. Today, it is rare to find anyone who is still making true livermush, and when such a person is found, the recipe is usually a well-kept secret. A good livermush can be prized as much as a good country ham. Our recipe makes a modest amount, manageable for those timid of the hog's head.

Makes about 3¾ pounds, either as 2 loaves or 4 pints

1 pound pork liver
1 pound fresh, boneless, lean pork (such as from the shoulder)
2 quarts water
1 tablespoon salt
1 teaspoon freshly ground black pepper
1 teaspoon freshly ground dried hot red pepper
1 teaspoon finely crumbled dried sage leaves
2 cups yellow cornmeal

1. Cut the liver and pork meat into 2-inch cubes. Do not remove the fat from the meat. Place the cubes in a large, heavy pot or casserole with a 4- to 5-quart capacity. Cover the meat with the water and add the salt. Bring to a simmer.

   Cook, covered, over low heat for about 3 hours or until the meat is so tender that it breaks apart when pierced with a fork. Do not skim the liquid during this time.

2. Drain the liver, meat, and liquid through a colander lined with cheesecloth and placed over a bowl. Reserve the liquid.

   Grind the liver and the meat together either in a food processor or in a food grinder fitted with the fine plate.

3. Wipe your pot with a damp paper towel to remove any sediment. Return the ground liver and meat to the pot along with the reserved

AND IN OUR GARDEN

Up until the middle of October, we still have a few vegetables from our summer garden. The tomatoes are small and mostly green, but the pepper plants flourish until the first frost. This is a good opportunity to can recipes using green tomatoes, such as Green Tomato and Apple Chutney and Virginia's Green Tomato Pickles. We also prepare Billie's Jalapeño Pepper Relish, using both the peppers and green tomatoes. (All three recipes appear in the May chapter.) With luck, our first frost might be late, but when it occurs, the hot pepper plants blacken and die. This also means the end of our okra, cucumbers and basil, so we harvest daily no matter how small the yields.

Even a fall garden can be beautiful and since ours is much smaller than the summer garden, there is time to clean the vacant areas. If there is nothing else in the garden, the Chinese cabbages and fennel are spectacular sights.

liquid. You should have about 4½ to 5 cups of meat and about 6 cups of liquid. Add the black pepper, hot red pepper, and sage. Bring to a full simmer over medium heat.

4. Have the cornmeal placed in a bowl close to your pot. When the liquid is simmering, begin adding the cornmeal. Grab a small handful and let it pass through your fingers into the liquid. At the same time, whisk constantly, to prevent lumps. Switch to a wooden spoon when the mixture becomes too thick for a whisk. There should be no lumps.

5. When all of the cornmeal has been added, turn the heat to *very* low and continue to cook the livermush, uncovered, for another 45 minutes. Stir constantly or the livermush will burn easily on the bottom of the pot. The mixture should be very thick and your spoon will stand unaided.

6. While the livermush is still hot, put it in ungreased containers for cooling and shaping. Generally, livermush is placed in loaf pans. In this case, you will need two loaf pans, 8½ × 4½ × 2⅝ inches. Pack the livermush down as densely as possible so that it will be smooth for slicing.

If we are planning to freeze the livermush, we put it in four 1-pint plastic containers with lids, leaving ½-inch headspace.

7. Let the livermush stand, uncovered, at room temperature for 1 hour to cool. If you plan to use the livermush within 1 week, cover it with plastic wrap and refrigerate overnight before using. If it is not to be used within the week, freeze it.

8. When the livermush has chilled overnight, unmold it. Run a knife around the edges and invert the container onto a plate. The livermush will fall onto the plate for slicing.

9. When you are ready to serve the livermush,

WHAT TO BUY OR ORDER NOW

By now the weather has cooled, so throughout the month of October we buy and mail order in bulk. It's best to plan ahead so as not to order any staple or perishable items after the middle of November when they are likely to be caught up with, and delayed by, holiday parcels. In addition to the perishable foods, this is the best time to order nuts, dried fruits, and dried beans. Ordered now, they will come from this year's harvest and therefore be at their freshest. We order all of the pecans we will need for the year and freeze them. This is a considerable amount as we will use them in our Pesto next summer.

At the farmers' market, we stock up on the various honeys that are sold. They are bottled in quart canning jars and we prefer to buy the ones that contain the honeycomb. Our friend and expert beekeeper, Elgy Henderson, sells both a light and dark variety. The spring honey is called Poplar and the later honey, Bright Bay. Another local beekeeper has a very dark honey as his bees feast on the flowers of wild blackberries.

In October many of the farmers sell our favorite apple, the Stayman Winesap with its crisp, tart and spicy flavor. We buy them, along with a huge pumpkin for Halloween.

---

cut it into slices ½-inch thick. Fry the slices in a skillet with a small amount of butter, oil, or bacon fat over medium heat. This will take about 3 minutes for each side. The outsides should be a crusty brown and the insides still soft. Allow 2 slices per serving.

10. Serve the fried livermush for breakfast or supper. Eggs, grits, and thick biscuits are traditional accompaniments. Have plenty of butter and jam to be passed around the table. At supper, serve with Fried Okra (see page 274) or "A Mess of Greens" (see page 365).

NOVEMBER

REAPING THE REWARDS

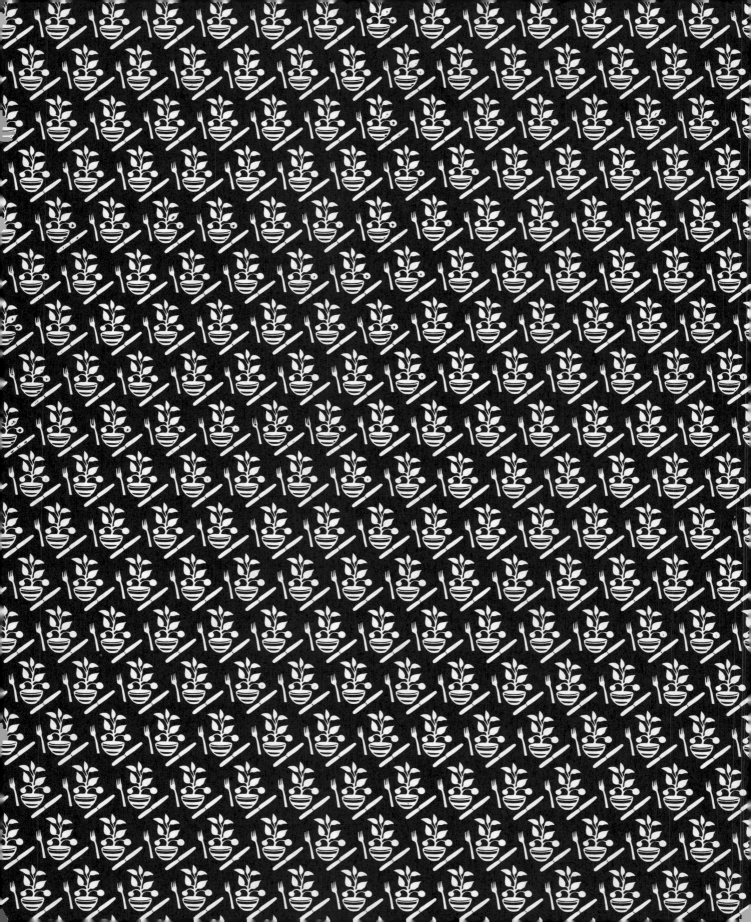

Reaping the Rewards

November is a month to relax and to begin to enjoy the rewards from our summer work. We make it a point to never open our home-canned goods until now. Enough time has passed so that we are hungry for all that we've frozen or canned.

Dinner can be prepared almost instantly. Warming recipes come to mind in the chilly November air — hearty soups, a rich fondue, stick-to-the-ribs dishes with greens and cabbages from the garden, and a bracing casserole of October beans. Fortified, we can tackle the 12-pound pumpkin left from Halloween.

Wild Rice and Red Onion Soup

Wanting to use wild rice in as many ways as possible, we tried this recipe which combines our basic onion soup with wild rice. The onion soup is excellent on its own, but with the addition of the wild rice, it is elegant enough to be served as the first course of a festive dinner. Follow it with a "holiday bird" that has been simply roasted without a stuffing.

Serves 4 to 6

¾ cup raw wild rice
1 teaspoon salt
2 pounds red onions
3 tablespoons olive oil
1 tablespoon sugar
2 tablespoons unsalted butter
1 teaspoon crushed dried rosemary
½ teaspoon freshly ground black pepper
½ cup dry white wine
1 quart Chicken Stock (see page 109)
1 cup freshly grated Parmesan cheese

1. Wash the wild rice by placing it in a 1-quart saucepan filled with water. Stir the rice around in the water until the liquid darkens. Drain the rice through a sieve.

Rinse the saucepan and add 1½ cups of water and ½ teaspoon of the salt. Bring to a boil and add the rice. Turn the heat to low, cover the saucepan, and simmer for 30 to 35 minutes until the liquid has evaporated.

Check the rice several times while it is cooking and fluff it with a fork. Set aside, still covered, until it is time to add it to the soup.

2. Peel and slice the onions. They should be about ⅛-inch thick. Slice them on the bias to avoid rings.

3. In a 2-quart saucepan, heat the olive oil. Add the onions and the remaining ½ teaspoon of salt. Toss to coat the onions with the oil. Cover, and over low heat, "sweat" the onions for 20 minutes. During this time, the onions will become limp and give off their liquid.

4. Remove the cover and turn the heat to medium. Add the sugar, butter, rosemary, and black pepper. Toss to mix. Continue cooking uncovered for another 15 minutes or so until the onions are very lightly browned.

Begin warming your soup plates.

5. Increase the heat and add the wine. Bring to a full simmer and cook until the wine has almost evaporated. Stir to make sure that the onions do not burn.

6. Add the chicken stock, cover, and simmer for 10 minutes. Just before serving, add the wild rice and cook only long enough to heat the rice.

7. Serve the soup in heated soup plates, sprinkling each serving with 2 tablespoons of the Parmesan cheese.

PORTUGUESE KALE SOUP FROM PROVINCETOWN

This soup is not for puny appetites. In Provincetown, Massachusetts, it is generally consumed in the early morning hours after an evening of partying, and followed by a brisk walk on a chilly beach. If no beach is available, just rest afterward in front of a roaring fire. In any case, plan to serve the soup only when the weather is very cold. It makes a very good basis for an informal supper for close friends where large bowls can be eaten with gusto and without pretense. Serve the soup with Cornmeal Round Loaves with freshly grated Romano cheese and Pesto. Sprinkle the cheese liberally on the soup and add a dollop of pesto if you wish or spread the pesto on the bread.

Authentically, linquiça would be the sausage of choice, but we find our Hot Sausage makes a good substitute; you may also use hot Italian sausage.

Serves 6 to 8

½ pound dried chickpeas
2 pounds kale

2 quarts Chicken Stock (see page 109)
1 pound boiling potatoes
1 teaspoon salt
½ teaspoon freshly ground black pepper
5 whole cloves, freshly ground
5 whole allspice, freshly ground
2 large cloves garlic, minced
½ pound linquiça or Hot Sausage (see page 45)
1 tablespoon olive oil
2 cups dried, tubular pasta, such as macaroni or penne
1½ cups freshly grated Romano cheese
1½ cups Pesto (optional; see page 309)

1. Several hours before you are ready to begin the soup, rinse the chickpeas. Pick out any that are not perfect. Place the chickpeas in a 1½-quart saucepan. Add water to cover by 1 inch. Cover the saucepan and bring the water to a boil.

Remove from the heat and let the chickpeas stand, covered, for 1 hour or so. This is done in lieu of an overnight soaking.

2. Carefully wash the kale. Set aside to drain.

3. Over medium heat, bring the chicken stock to a simmer in a 1-gallon capacity stock pot or saucepan. While the chicken stock is heating, peel the potatoes and cut them into ¾-inch cubes.

4. Drain the chickpeas and add them with the cubed potatoes to the simmering stock. Sprinkle with the salt, black pepper, cloves, and allspice. Add the garlic. Stir, cover, and bring the ingredients back to a simmer. Cook for about ½ hour until the potatoes and chickpeas are tender, but not mushy.

5. While the potatoes and chickpeas are cooking, fry the sausage. In a skillet, heat the olive oil. Prick the sausages in three or four places and add them to the heated oil. Fry over medium heat, turning, until they have

browned all over. Remove from the skillet and slice the sausages into pieces ⅓-inch thick.

6. When the potatoes and peas are tender, add the kale, tearing or cutting the leaves into pieces 2 to 3 inches in diameter. Cut the stems into pieces about 1 inch long. Leave the water that may be clinging to the leaves. Add the sausage. Stir, cover, and simmer for at least an hour so all the flavors can intermingle.

7. About ½ hour before you are ready to serve the soup, cook the pasta in a separate pot until just *al dente*. Drain and add the pasta to the soup 10 minutes before serving, just to heat through. Warm your soup bowls or plates at the same time.

8. Serve piping hot in large, heated soup bowls or plates, being very generous with portions. Pass the cheese and pesto separately for guests to serve themselves.

TOMATO AND CHEESE FONDUE

On very cold evenings, we like to serve this fondue as the main dish at a very informal supper. It is easy to make and can be prepared several hours ahead up to the point where the cheese is added, which must be done at the last minute.

Serves 4 to 6

2 Baguettes (see page 17)
3 medium onions
2 large cloves garlic
3 tablespoons olive oil
1 cup dry white wine or vermouth
1 teaspoon wild thyme
1 teaspoon freshly ground dried hot red pepper
3 cups drained, canned tomatoes
1 pound aged Colby cheese, grated coarse

1. Preheat the oven to 375° F.

2. Cut the bread into slices 1 inch thick. Cut each slice into 1-inch cubes, but do not remove the crust. Arrange the cubes of bread on a large baking sheet and toast them on a rack in the middle of the oven until they are dry and golden brown. Turn them several times so the cubes are evenly browned. Be careful that the bread does not burn. Set the bread aside, still on the baking sheet, until the fondue is almost ready to be served.

3. Peel and chop the onions coarsely. Peel and mince the garlic. Heat the olive oil in a heavy 2-quart saucepan, preferably one that you can bring to the table and set over a flame. Add the onions and garlic to the saucepan and sauté over medium-low heat until the onions are translucent and begin to take on color.

4. Add the wine, wild thyme, and red pepper and turn the heat to medium high. Cook, stirring with a wooden spoon, until the wine has been reduced to ½ cup. Coarsely chop the tomatoes and add them to the saucepan.

5. When the ingredients come to a simmer, reduce the heat to medium-low and add the cheese, ½ cup at a time, stirring constantly. Cook just until the cheese has melted.

6. Serve immediately, transferring the fondue to a fondue pot or a chafing dish. Keep the warming flame turned very low as the fondue will require very little additional heat because of both its thickness and the tomatoes, which will remain hot for some time.

7. Reheat the bread cubes briefly in the oven and serve them in a basket lined with a cloth napkin. Pass the bread around the table, with each guest taking a handful. Using long fondue forks, let the guests dip the cubes of bread directly into the fondue to serve themselves.

Note: It is doubtful, but if there should be some leftover fondue, it is very good the next day, spread over toasted, thick slices of bread and reheated in a 350° F oven until very hot.

A MESS OF GREENS

When we lived in Charleston for a brief spell, we learned that one never asks for "greens" by the pound, but buys them by the "mess." Traditionally, the greens should be cooked with some leftover ham, ham fat, bacon, or drippings, but we like pancetta.

Serves 4 to 6

2 pounds greens such as kale, collard, or turnip
3 ounces pancetta (Italian bacon, see page 54)
1 tablespoon olive oil
1 small onion, chopped fine
3 tablespoons wine vinegar
½ cup water
½ teaspoon salt
¼ teaspoon freshly ground black pepper
½ teaspoon or more freshly ground dried, hot red pepper (optional)

1. Thoroughly wash the greens. Set aside to drain, but do not dry them.

2. Cut the pancetta into ¼-inch dice. Heat the olive oil in a 1-gallon pot. Add the pancetta and, with the heat on low, sauté until the dice are well browned. Add the onion and sauté briefly.

3. Mix the wine vinegar with the water and add to the pot. Stir to deglaze and loosen any bits of pancetta or onion clinging to the bottom of the pot.

4. Tear or cut the greens into pieces 2 to 3 inches in diameter. If the stems are long, cut them into 1-inch pieces. Add the greens to the pot, leaving any remaining water on the leaves. Add the salt and black pepper and toss the ingredients thoroughly.

5. Cook, covered, over medium-low heat for 25 minutes. The greens will greatly reduce in volume. Toss several times while they are cooking. When ready to serve, toss with the hot red pepper if you are using it.

BRAISED ESCAROLE

This recipe for escarole differs only slightly from A Mess of Greens, but the adjustment of seasonings and a longer braising time work better for this vegetable. The recipe also adapts very well for any of the Chinese cabbages. Serve the escarole with one of the polenta recipes and Hot Sausages (see the recipe index).

Serves 4 to 6

1½ to 2 pounds escarole (or Chinese cabbage)
3 ounces pancetta (Italian bacon, see page 54)
2 tablespoons olive oil
1 medium onion, chopped coarsely
4 large cloves garlic, minced
¼ teaspoon freshly ground black pepper
2 tablespoons lemon juice
⅓ cup canned, coarsely chopped Colorado peppers, or a good quality
    of mildly hot peppers packed in brine
2 tablespoons liquid from the peppers
1 teaspoon unsalted butter

1. Wash the escarole and set it aside to drain.

2. Cut the pancetta into ¼-inch dice. Heat the olive oil in a heavy 3-quart saucepan. Add the diced pancetta and sauté over low heat until it has lightly browned.

3. Add the onions and garlic to the saucepan when the pancetta has browned. Sauté the vegetables until they wilt, but do not let them brown.

4. Tear or cut the leaves of escarole into pieces 2 to 3 inches long. Add them to the saucepan. It may be necessary to add them gradually, letting them cook down before adding the next batch. The water clinging to the leaves will be sufficient liquid for braising.

5. When all of the escarole has been added, sprinkle with the black pepper and lemon juice and stir in the chopped peppers and the 2 tablespoons of liquid from the peppers. (Do not seed the peppers.) The pancetta will supply adequate salt, so no extra is necessary.

6. Cut a piece of waxed paper to fit inside the casserole and rub it with the butter. Place the paper, buttered side down, directly on the vegetables. Cover the saucepan with a tight-fitting lid. Braise the escarole for 45 minutes over medium-low heat. Stir occasionally. The buttered waxed paper, by sealing in the moisture, will give the escarole a flavor otherwise impossible to achieve.

A GRATIN OF SWISS CHARD RIBS

Use a round, ovenproof dish (about 10 inches in diameter) for the gratin and cut the ribs so that they may be arranged in a circular fashion, like the spokes of a wheel. Save the chard leaves for Baked Flounder on a Bed of Swiss Chard Greens (see page 123).

Serves 4 to 6

2 pounds Swiss chard
2 cups water

½ cup dry white wine
1 large, imported bay leaf
4 large cloves garlic, peeled and crushed
Juice of ½ lemon
1 teaspoon salt
½ teaspoon freshly ground white pepper
¼ cup chopped parsley for garnish

Mornay Sauce:
2 cups milk, heated
3 tablespoons unsalted butter, plus an additional 3 tablespoons
1 heaping tablespoon flour
½ cup heavy cream, at room temperature
1 cup freshly grated Parmesan cheese
⅛ teaspoon freshly grated nutmeg
Salt and white pepper, to taste

1. Wash and drain the Swiss chard. To remove the ribs, place each piece face down on your work surface and, with a small knife, cut out the rib. Trim the ends of the ribs if necessary, and cut to fit your gratin dish.

2. Prepare your braising liquid by bringing the 2 cups of water to a boil in a saucepan large enough to comfortably hold the ribs. When the water is boiling, add the white wine, bay leaf, garlic, lemon juice, salt, and white pepper. (The lemon juice is not only for flavor, but is an aid against the discoloration of the ribs.) Bring the liquid to a simmer and add the chard ribs.

Cover and braise for 15 minutes. The liquid should be absorbed within this time and the ribs should still be crisp. If not, remove the cover and toss the ribs over a higher heat until the liquid has almost evaporated. Remove the bay leaf and garlic.

3. While the ribs are braising, begin the preparation of the Mornay Sauce. In a small saucepan, heat the milk. In another, 1-quart saucepan, melt 3 tablespoons of the butter over medium-low heat. Add the flour and whisk until the butter and flour begin to bubble.

Gradually add the milk, whisking constantly, until the mixture is smooth. Lower the heat and let the sauce simmer until it has been reduced by one-quarter. Whisk occasionally during this time, about 20 minutes. The sauce should be lightly thickened.

4. Preheat the oven to 425° F.

5. Rub the inside of your gratin dish with another tablespoon of the butter. Arrange the braised ribs in the gratin dish.

6. When the sauce has reduced, add the heavy cream. Bring back to a simmer and add ¾ cup of the Parmesan cheese and the nutmeg. Whisk until the cheese has melted. Taste for salt and pepper, using very little if any.

7. Spread the Mornay Sauce over the ribs so that the surface is covered. Sprinkle the gratin with the remaining ¼ cup of Parmesan cheese. Cut the remaining 2 tablespoons of butter into ¼-inch bits and scatter them over the surface.

8. Bake on the middle rack of the preheated oven for 30 minutes until the gratin is bubbling and the surface has lightly browned. Garnish with the chopped parsley.

MARTHA ROTH'S BRAISED CABBAGE WITH NOODLES

We think this cabbage recipe is exceptional. Not only that, it is easy to prepare. Care should be taken in seasoning; Martha's original recipe uses 1 tablespoon of salt and 4 tablespoons of sugar but we have cut down on these. You may prefer the larger amount, so taste the dish and determine for yourself before serving.

A meat dish may accompany the cabbage, but we often make it our main course, followed by a tossed salad with bread.

Serves 4 as a main dish, or 6 as a side dish

2½- to 3-pound fall or winter cabbage
¼ cup corn oil
1 recipe Pasta Dough, either Basic Egg (see page 305), Whole-Wheat
     or Buckwheat (see page 308)
2 tablespoons sugar
1 teaspoon salt, plus 1 tablespoon (for cooking the pasta)
½ teaspoon freshly ground black pepper

1. Wash and drain the cabbage, discarding any tough outer leaves. Quarter the cabbage lengthwise, remove the core, and shred the cabbage fine.

2. In a heavy saucepan with a 1-gallon capacity, heat the corn oil. Add the shredded cabbage and stir just to coat it with the oil.

Cover and braise over low heat for about 45 minutes until the cabbage is soft and has turned a light brown. Stir often during this time as the cabbage must not burn.

3. While the cabbage is braising, prepare the pasta dough. Roll out the dough as in the basic recipe, but cut it by hand into ½-inch squares. This is quickly done with a good pair of kitchen shears. Do not cut larger squares as the dough expands when it is cooked. Spread the noodles on a cloth towel until ready to cook. Meanwhile, in a large pot, bring 4 quarts of water to a boil. Also begin warming a serving platter.

4. When the cabbage has browned, add the sugar, stir, and cook uncovered another 15 minutes. The cabbage will turn a deeper brown with the addition of sugar. Add 1 teaspoon of the salt and the black pepper. Stir and taste for seasoning and adjust if necessary.

5. When the water is boiling and the cabbage is ready, add 1 tablespoon salt to the water, bring back to a boil, and add the noodles. Cook just until *al dente*, which should take 2 to 3 minutes if the pasta hasn't dried too long. Drain immediately and toss with the cabbage.

6. Transfer the cabbage and noodles to a heated platter and serve without delay.

A GRATIN OF WINTER CABBAGE

And yet another recipe using two of our economical stand-bys—cabbage and yogurt—which we combine to make a nourishing main course in frigid weather.

Serves 4 to 6

2 ounces pancetta (Italian bacon, see page 54)
2 tablespoons olive oil
2-pound head winter cabbage
2 medium onions
1 teaspoon crumbled fresh or dried rosemary
½ teaspoon freshly ground black pepper
1 recipe Basic Egg Pasta Dough (see page 305)
2 cups Yogurt (see page 67), at room temperature
½ cup heavy cream, at room temperature
2 cups coarsely grated Italian Fontina cheese (6 ounces)
1 tablespoon salt (for cooking the pasta)
1 teaspoon unsalted butter
¼ cup freshly grated Romano cheese
¼ cup finely chopped parsley

1. Cut the pancetta into ¼-inch dice. Heat the olive oil in a heavy 3-quart casserole and add the pancetta. Sauté over low heat until the pancetta gives up its fat and begins to brown.

2. Meanwhile, discard the outer leaves from the cabbage, then quarter and core it. Coarsely shred the cabbage either by hand or in a food processor. Peel and chop the onion coarse.

3. Add the cabbage and onions to the pancetta along with the rosemary and black pepper. It may be necessary to add the cabbage gradually as it cooks down, so that it will fit into the pot. Stir to mix.

Cover the casserole and braise the ingredients over medium-low heat for 45 minutes. The vegetables should be wilted, but not browned. Stir to prevent sticking.

4. While the vegetables are braising, prepare the pasta dough and roll it out. With a pair of kitchen shears, cut the dough into strips ½ inch wide and then into ½-inch squares. Spread the squares on a cloth towel and reserve them.

5. After the vegetables have braised for 45 minutes, bring 4 quarts of water to a boil in a large pot and preheat the oven to 400°F.

6. Using a wooden spoon, stir the yogurt (see page 68) into the casserole with the braised vegetables, followed by the heavy cream. Bring to a simmer. Add the Fontina cheese to the casserole, stirring constantly.

When the cheese is incorporated into the mixture, turn the heat to low as you cook the pasta.

7. Add 1 tablespoon of salt to the boiling water and when the water returns to a boil, add the pasta squares. Cook just until *al dente* (tender but still firm), which should take 2 to 3 minutes if the pasta has not dried too long. Drain the pasta and place it in a 14-inch oval gratin dish that has been rubbed with the teaspoon of butter.

8. Immediately add the mixture from the casserole and toss it thoroughly with the pasta. Smooth the surface and sprinkle it with the Romano cheese. Place the gratin dish on the middle rack of the oven and bake for about 20 minutes until the ingredients are bubbling and beginning to brown. Sprinkle with the chopped parsley and serve immediately.

MICHIHILI IN MASQUERADE

Michihili is one of the varieties of Chinese celery cabbage that we grow in the fall. It is the variety with cylindrical heads most often seen in supermarkets, 18 inches tall and about 4 inches thick at maturity. Hard freezes will kill the cabbages so we devised this recipe to use the immature heads. The Michihili are masquerading as a gratin of Belgium endive or of leeks and should be served in the same manner. If you prefer, use Belgian endive or leeks and you will still have an estimable dish to be served as the first course at a lavish dinner or the main course at a simpler meal.

Serves 4

8 young Michihili cabbages, about 10 inches tall by 1½ inches in
     diameter (about 4 ounces)
2 cups Chicken Stock (see page 109)
½ cup dry white wine
4 tablespoons unsalted butter, plus 1 teaspoon
1 heaping tablespoon flour
1 cup of the reserved braising liquid
½ cup heavy cream, at room temperature
⅛ teaspoon freshly grated nutmeg
¼ teaspoon freshly ground white pepper
¾ cup freshly grated Parmesan cheese
¼ cup finely chopped parsley

1. Prepare the cabbages by removing any blemished outer leaves and carefully cutting out the small cores, keeping the heads intact. Rinse the cabbages and drain them.

2. In a large, oval casserole in which the cabbages will fit lengthwise, bring the chicken stock and white wine to a simmer over medium heat. Remove the casserole from the

heat, add the cabbages, and arrange them closely against each other. It may be necessary to make two layers.

Cut a piece of wax paper to fit inside the casserole. Grease one side of the paper with 1 tablespoon of the butter. Place the paper, buttered side down, directly on the cabbages. Cover the casserole tightly and braise the cabbages over medium-low heat for 20 minutes or until tender when pierced with a small knife.

3. Butter a 14-inch oval gratin dish with the teaspoon of butter. When the cabbages are tender, remove them with a slotted spatula to the gratin dish, reserving the braising liquid. Arrange them lengthwise in one or two layers. The cabbages will be greatly diminished in size.

4. Preheat the oven to 375° F.

5. Prepare the sauce by melting the remaining 3 tablespoons of butter in a 1½-quart saucepan over medium-low heat. Whisk in the flour and cook until the *roux* begins to take on a little color. Add 1 cup of the reserved braising liquid, whisking constantly, until the sauce begins to thicken. Add the heavy cream, the nutmeg, and white pepper. Continue to whisk until the sauce is smooth, then add ½ cup of the Parmesan cheese. Incorporate it into the sauce, but simmer only briefly as the sauce should not be too thick.

6. Spoon the sauce over the cabbages so that they are completely covered. Sprinkle the surface with the remaining ¼ cup of Parmesan cheese. Bake on a rack in the upper third of the oven for 20 minutes until the gratin is bubbling and the surface has lightly browned.

7. Sprinkle the gratin with the chopped parsley and serve immediately, giving each guest 2 of the cabbages with some of the sauce.

SAUTÉ OF CHINESE CABBAGE AND MUSHROOMS

This vegetable sauté is highly seasoned so that the accompanying meat (pork or chicken are recommended) or fish should be simply prepared.

Serves 4 to 6

2-pound head Chinese cabbage
1 pound fresh mushrooms
¼ cup olive oil
4 cloves garlic, minced
½ cup coarsely chopped canned Colorado peppers
    or mildly hot peppers, packed in brine
½ teaspoon salt
1 teaspoon freshly ground dried hot red pepper
1 tablespoon red wine vinegar

1. Remove any blemished outer leaves from the cabbage. Wash and drain the cabbage. Cut it in half lengthwise and remove the core. Do not shred the cabbage, but cut it into pieces no larger than 2 inches in diameter.

2. To clean the mushrooms, first cut off the ends of the stems. Then wipe the mushrooms with damp paper towels and cut them into thin slices.

3. Heat the oil in a 12-inch skillet. Add the mushrooms and sauté over high heat until they give up their liquid and begin to brown.

4. Add the garlic to the skillet and toss just to mix. Add the cabbage, Colorado peppers, salt, and hot red pepper.

Sauté over high heat, tossing often, for 10 minutes. The cabbage should retain its green color and crispness. Just before serving add the tablespoon of red wine vinegar, toss and cook for a moment so the vinegar will lose its "edge."

A WINTER SAUTÉ OF PEPPERS AND TOMATOES

With this recipe, we begin to enjoy the rewards of our summer work—the frozen and canned peppers, the canned tomatoes—all prepared simply to approximate the fresh. Serve this sauté with Hot Sausages (see page 45) and Basic Polenta (see page 349).

Serves 4 to 6

> 2 medium onions
> 4 large cloves garlic
> 2 tablespoons olive oil
> 6 fresh green bell peppers (or if frozen, about 1 quart)
> ½ teaspoon salt
> ½ teaspoon freshly ground black pepper
> 2 cups drained canned tomatoes
> 3 or 4 canned Colorado peppers or mildly hot peppers, packed in brine
> 1 teaspoon dried oregano
> 1 teaspoon freshly ground dried hot red pepper (optional)

1. Peel and chop the onions and garlic coarsely. Heat the olive oil in a heavy skillet and add the onions and garlic. Sauté over medium-low heat until the onions have wilted.

2. Prepare the bell peppers. If you are using fresh peppers, core, seed, and quarter them. If you are using frozen, separate the frozen pieces and defrost slightly on paper towels.

3. When the onions have wilted, arrange the peppers skin side up on top of the onions and garlic. Sprinkle with the salt and black pepper. Do not mix.

Cover the skillet and cook over medium-low heat for 15 minutes. The cooking time is the same for fresh or frozen.

4. Chop the tomatoes coarse. Chop coarse, but do not seed, the Colorado peppers.

5. When the vegetables in the skillet have cooked for 15 minutes, remove the cover and add the tomatoes, Colorado peppers, and oregano. Toss with wooden spoons, just to mix.

Sauté, uncovered and without any additional mixing, for another 15 minutes. The liquid should almost evaporate. If the liquid is not evaporating, turn up the heat the last few minutes. Serve immediately. If you are serving polenta, surround the polenta with the sauté on a heated serving platter.

Note: if you want more "bite" to the sauté, sprinkle on 1 teaspoon of dried hot red pepper just before serving.

A WINTER CASSEROLE FROM A SUMMER GARDEN

This dish brings back memories of our summer garden as we begin to open the canned tomatoes and Colorado peppers, and defrost our bell peppers, and use our dried herbs. The casserole is very hearty, so we make it our main course, served with big chunks of the Braided Loaves with Cheese and Pepper (see page 33).

Serves 4 to 6

4 ounces pancetta (Italian bacon, see page 54)
2 tablespoons olive oil
2 medium onions
4 large cloves garlic
4 large green bell peppers, fresh or frozen
2 pounds boiling potatoes
5 canned Colorado peppers, or mildly hot peppers packed in brine
2 cups drained canned tomatoes
1 cup reserved liquid from the drained tomatoes
½ teaspoon salt
¼ teaspoon freshly ground black pepper
1 teaspoon crumbled dried rosemary
1 cup freshly grated Romano or Parmesan cheese

1. Cut the pancetta into ¼-inch dice. Heat the olive oil in a 2-quart casserole, preferably one that you can bring to the table. Add the pancetta and sauté over low heat until the dice have rendered their fat and are lightly browned.

2. Peel the onions and cut them in half lengthwise and then crosswise into slices ¼-inch thick. Mince the garlic. Add the onions and garlic to the casserole with the pancetta. Stir and sauté over medium-low heat until the onions begin to take on color.

3. If you are using fresh green bell peppers, core, seed, and cut them into quarters. If you are using frozen bell peppers, defrost them on paper towels and cut the peppers into quarters, if they have not been cut.

Add the bell peppers to the casserole and cover. Cook over medium-low heat for 15 minutes. Do not stir.

4. Meanwhile, peel the potatoes and cut them into 2-inch cubes. If the potatoes are very small, you may leave them whole. Remove the stems from the Colorado peppers and chop coarsely, but do not seed them. Chop the drained tomatoes coarsely, if they are large.

5. Add the potatoes to the casserole and cover them with the chopped Colorado peppers and tomatoes. Add the cup of liquid reserved from the drained tomatoes. Sprinkle the ingredients with the salt, black pepper, and rosemary. Stir gently, just to mix.

6. Cover the casserole tightly and bring the ingredients to a simmer over medium heat. Cook for about 45 minutes or just until the potatoes are tender. Check occasionally during this time to be sure the ingredients are not sticking to the casserole, but avoid stirring so that the vegetables retain their shapes.

Begin to warm the soup plates.

7. As the casserole will contain a large amount of liquid, serve it in individual, heated soup plates with a fork and soup spoon alongside. Give each guest a selection of the vegetables and sprinkle each serving with several tablespoons of the grated cheese.

BAKED OCTOBER BEANS

There is no doubt about this dish being healthy and hearty. If we enjoy October beans in the summer in salads, we enjoy them equally well in cold months, baked in the oven and served with Brown Rice, Alfalfa Sprouts, and possibly Hot Sausages (see the recipe index).

We use beans that we have frozen from our summer crop, but you may use either fresh or dried. If you are using unshelled fresh beans, you will need about 2 pounds before shelling. If you are using dried beans, you will need 2 cups. Rinse the dried beans and discard any that are not perfect. Place the beans in a saucepan and add water to cover the beans by 1 inch. Cover the saucepan and bring to a boil. Immediately remove the saucepan from the heat and let it sit, covered, for 1 hour before preparing the recipe. Drain the beans at this time. Frozen, shelled beans need only be partially defrosted; fresh beans, merely shelled and rinsed. Then the baking time for the beans will be the same whether frozen, fresh, or dried.

Serves 4 to 6

2 ounces pancetta (Italian bacon, see page 54)
2 tablespoons olive oil
4 large cloves garlic, minced
1 quart October beans (see above)
1 cup drained, coarsely chopped canned tomatoes
½ to 1 teaspoon freshly ground dried hot red pepper, to taste
1 cup or more of the liquid from the drained tomatoes
2 imported bay leaves

1. Preheat the oven to 375° F.

2. Cut the pancetta into ¼- inch dice. Heat the olive oil in a heavy, 2-quart casserole and add the pancetta. Sauté over low heat just until the pancetta begins to brown. Add the minced garlic and sauté for only a moment. Do not let it burn.

3. Remove the casserole from the heat and add the October beans, drained tomatoes, and hot red pepper. Salt is not necessary because of the pancetta. Stir just to mix.

Add the liquid from the drained tomatoes. The liquid should be level with the ingredients in the casserole; if you do not have enough tomato liquid, supplement it with water. Add the bay leaves.

4. Cover the casserole and bring the ingredients to a simmer over medium heat before placing the casserole in the oven. Make sure that the cover fits very tightly. If it doesn't, place aluminum foil over the casserole and then the cover.

Bake on the middle rack of the oven for about 1 hour. The time can vary depending upon your taste. We like our beans still firm, but you may bake the beans longer. Check the beans every 20 minutes or so, but do not stir. Remove the bay leaves before serving.

5. You may serve directly from the casserole or arrange the beans in the middle of a heated serving platter, surrounding them with brown rice, sprinkled with 1 cup alfalfa sprouts. And, if you are really hearty, add hot sausages.

HOPPIN' JOHN

In the South serving Hoppin' John on New Year's Day is considered a tradition, but sometimes it seems more like a superstition. Folks who are otherwise rational all year long *must* have their Hoppin' John, thereby insuring their good luck for the coming year. We confess to this practice and even make ours in a large enough quantity to share with others who are foolish enough not to have made their own. Of course, you can eat Hoppin' John any time of the year.

This is a family recipe which has undergone several changes. Using brown rice rather than white makes for a tastier dish, and with the scarcity of good country ham, we use pancetta (Italian bacon). Use ham if you can find it, or even slab bacon, but be very careful about salt. Although we don't include it in our ingredients, you may wish to add some.

Serves 8

1 tablespoon olive oil
4 ounces pancetta (Italian bacon), cut into ¼-inch dice
1 medium onion, chopped coarsely
2 cups dried black-eyed peas (about ¾ pound)
1½ cups raw brown rice
1½ teaspoons freshly ground dried hot red pepper

1. Place the olive oil in a heavy, 3-quart saucepan or casserole over low heat. Add the pancetta and sauté until it begins to give up its fat and starts to brown. Add the chopped onion. Stir and cook just until the onion has wilted.

2. Pick over the black-eyed peas, discarding any that are not perfect. Rinse the peas in a sieve under cold running water.

3. Place the rinsed peas in the saucepan with the pancetta and onion and add just enough water to cover (about 2½ cups). Stir to mix, cover, and bring the ingredients to a boil over medium-high heat.

Immediately remove the saucepan from the heat and let it stand, covered, for 45 minutes to 1 hour.

4. Add the raw brown rice to the saucepan along with an additional 3½ cups of water and the hot red pepper. To help prevent the rice from becoming mushy, carefully stir the mixture using the back of a fork.

Cover and simmer over medium-low heat for 35 to 45 minutes. Stir the Hoppin' John occasionally to make sure it is not sticking to the bottom of the saucepan, but stir as little as possible.

Taste after 35 minutes and if the beans are tender and the rice is cooked (we like the rice *al dente*), serve immediately.

Note: Use only 2 tablespoons of diced pancetta in the greens if you serve them with the Hoppin' John.

DISPOSING OF A 12-POUND HALLOWEEN PUMPKIN

We would never buy a 12-pound pumpkin for cooking purposes, but our cats insist on one for Halloween. Once it is placed at our door, they spend hours perching on it and posing around it. By Thanksgiving, after it has been scarred with claw marks, chewed a bit, and generally is looking rather sad, we must decide whether to compost it or eat it. If we choose the latter, we are able to use the entire pumpkin, composting only the shell. However, cooking the pumpkin poses its own problems. We find the following method the best for preserving the flavor and texture.

16 cups pumpkin purée and 2 cups seeds

1. Preheat the oven to 450°F.

2. Cut and remove the stem from the pumpkin. Carefully cut the pumpkin in half. Remove the seeds and fiber, reserving the seeds for roasting.

3. If your oven is very large, you will be able to bake both halves at the same time. If not, bake one half at a time. Line a heavy baking sheet with sides with aluminum foil. Place the halves (or half) on the foil cut side down. Cover lightly with another piece of foil and bake on the middle rack of the oven for about 1 hour. The pumpkin is cooked when the outer shell is easily pierced with a fork.

4. Remove the baking sheet from the oven and, while the pumpkin is still hot, peel back and discard (or compost) the shell. Most of it will come off easily, but use a knife if necessary. When the pumpkin is cool enough to handle,

PUMPKIN CAKE

With 16 cups of pumpkin purée on our hands, we decided to try our Carrot Cake (see page 393) using pumpkin purée instead. It worked perfectly and even with the large amount of spices in each cake, they are distinguishable as carrot or pumpkin in taste. Follow the recipe for Carrot Cake exactly except for the measuring of the pumpkin purée. As the purée has more liquid than grated carrots, measure 2½ to 3 cups of purée into a sieve and let the liquid drain from the purée for 15 minutes or so. Then measure again for 2 very thick cups of pumpkin purée. Proceed with the recipe for Carrot Cake.

cut it into chunks and purée it in a food processor, blender, or food mill. Refrigerate or freeze the purée in containers until ready to use.

ROASTING FRESH PUMPKIN SEEDS

2 cups seeds
1 tablespoon corn oil
½ teaspoon coarse salt

1. When removing the seeds and fiber from a pumpkin, try to remove the seeds separately, leaving behind as much of the fiber as you can. Place the seeds into a bowl of water right away, for if they dry with any fiber attached, it will be almost impossible to remove it.

2. Drain the seeds in a sieve and rinse them with cool water, rubbing off any remaining fiber. Dry the seeds briefly on paper towels.

3. Preheat the oven to 350°F.

4. After drying the seeds, spread them on a baking sheet that has been oiled with corn oil. Toss the seeds to coat them. Roast in the oven for 20 minutes, tossing them every 7 or 8 minutes until they are golden.

5. Remove the seeds from the oven and sprinkle them with the coarse salt. Toss again.

When cool, store them in an airtight container.

PUMPKIN SOUP

This soup has the richness of a cream-base soup, but uses Yogurt instead. We like the addition of aged Colby cheese for a sharper flavor, but a milder cheese, such as Monterey Jack, may be used.

Serves 4 to 6

2 medium onions
3 cloves garlic
3 tablespoons unsalted butter
4 cups pumpkin purée (see page 376)
½ teaspoon salt
½ teaspoon freshly ground white pepper
½ teaspoon crumbled dried winter savory
2 cups Yogurt (see page 67)
¼ pound aged Colby cheese, grated coarsely
¼ cup chopped fresh parsley for garnish

1. Chop the onions fine and mince the garlic. Melt the butter in a 2-quart saucepan and add the onions and garlic. Sauté over medium heat until the onions have wilted.

2. Add the pumpkin purée, salt, white pepper, and winter savory. Whisk to blend and bring to a simmer. Add the yogurt (see page 68) and, once again, whisk and bring to a simmer.

3. Simmer for 15 minutes, whisking occasionally. Just before serving, add the cheese. Cook just long enough for the cheese to melt and the soup to bubble. Serve garnished with the chopped parsley.

WHAT TO BUY OR ORDER NOW

We order almost nothing in the way of staples this month, unless we have forgotten something or run out of an item. Of course, there is always a good chance we will be tempted by all of the holiday catalogs offering irresistible foods. In fact, by the end of the month we will probably find that United Parcel has delivered a dozen little delectables to us.

AND IN OUR GARDEN

Cleaning is our garden pleasure for November, and it is a pleasure as we want our soil to rest comfortably during the winter. Once cleaned, we cover the soil with leaves. The leaves are free for the asking from the city so we order three or more large truck loads. If we happen to be passing by a very tidy neighborhood and see trucks picking up the leaves, we ask that those leaves be delivered to us. Parks and cemeteries are also good spots to scout trucks. The extra leaves will decompose and be used next spring for mulch. Field mice tend to winter in the heaps and neighborhood cats are often spotted sitting on top, either attentively or with smug satisfaction.

With the garden orderly, we clean and store all garden equipment that will not be used until spring. Smith & Hawken, in their informative catalog, have a section devoted to the care of garden tools. Their tools are like works of art and should be treated as such.

And, in the house, we tally the performance of the year's crops so that in January, when we order seeds, we will have a general idea how our next garden will look.

DECEMBER

DESSERTS AND HOLIDAY
GIFT IDEAS

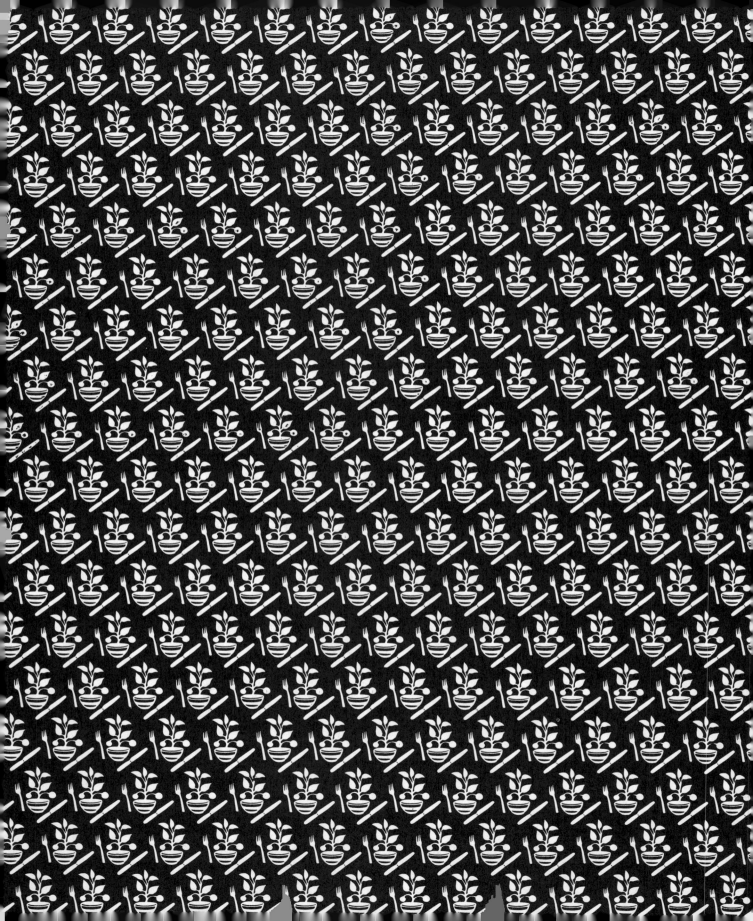

Desserts and Holiday Gift Ideas

December, and the year's end, brings to mind sweets, both to serve as desserts and to give as gifts at holiday time. Although our meals usually end simply with a selection of cheeses and seasonal fresh fruits served either plain or with a sweetened yogurt, occasionally we bake up a suitably rich and irresistible confection. Most often it is a truly Southern Pecan or Buttermilk Pie, or a creamy Cheesecake made from our own Cottage Cheese, or either of these two favorites—Belle Sherrill's Jam Cake and our own Carrot Cake.

Not only do our sweets make perfect gifts, but so do many of our bread and canned food recipes. At holiday time we bake large quantities of all of our breads to give either singly or, for a very special gift, packed a half dozen or more in a half-bushel harvest basket. Single loaves can be given just tied with a brightly colored ribbon, in a bread basket, or on a wooden bread rack. Several of our mail-order sources sell these racks in threes, each being a different size.

We select canned food gifts to suit the tastes of our friends, and will sometimes combine them with other freshly prepared foods arranged in a basket, to create a theme. For an Italian basket, we include a freshly made pasta, a jar of Tomato Sauce, a pint of Pesto, a string of Hot Sausage, a dozen Bread Sticks, maybe a few heads of garlic, and a string of dried hot red peppers. Another grouping might be all pickled: Aunt Robin's Pickled Shrimp, Dill Pickles, Pickled Eggs, and Pickled Beets. Preserves and jams are given with either cookies or Cornmeal Muffins and some freshly made Cottage Cheese. Any of the seasoned and shaped cheeses make suitable gifts accompanied by any of our breads. For a sizzling gift, arrange a pot of Liptauer Cheese and Cornmeal Crackers in a basket lined with yellow tissue paper.

For those who appreciate them, we like to give our dried herbs, either for hanging or stripped from their stems and placed in little tins or wooden boxes. These herbs can also be combined for bath bouquets and tied in small cheesecloth bundles. When tossed into a steaming bath, they scent the whole house.

If you do not have your own dried herbs, they may be mail ordered from Aphrodisia (see the mail-order listings). They also have their own blend of bath herbs, sold by the weight or in little tins and jars. Their blend is lovely and contains, among other herbs, bay leaves, mint, lavender, and southernwood. From our own dried herbs, we select and balance southernwood, bay leaves, mints, lemon balm, lemon thyme, rosemary, sweet woodruff, and tarragon.

COTTAGE CHEESE CHEESECAKE

We developed this very fine cheesecake using our own recipe for Cottage Cheese. We do not recommend that you make it with commercial cottage cheese, as what makes this recipe such a delight is the flavor and creamy texture of pure, homemade cheese. Use a good, dry cookie — not graham crackers — for the crumbs.

We begin the preparation of the cottage cheese the evening before and the next morning finish the cheese and proceed with the cake early in the day. It must have a cooling period of at least 3 hours before slicing.

Serves 8 to 10

4 cups homemade Cottage Cheese (see page 88)
2 tablespoons unsalted butter
¼ cup very fine dry cookie crumbs, preferably from Almond Toast
    (see page 387)
1¼ tablespoons grated lemon rind (1 lemon)
4 tablespoons lemon juice
2 tablespoons dark rum
1 cup sugar
4 eggs, at room temperature
½ cup heavy cream, at room temperature

1. In the evening before you plan to prepare the cheesecake, begin making the cottage cheese (through Step 2), using 1 gallon of milk and 1 cup of buttermilk.

2. The next morning complete the cottage cheese, following Steps 3 through 5. Drain the curds very well and let the cottage cheese cool to room temperature. You will have 4 cups of cheese.

3. Meanwhile, prepare your cake pan. Rub the bottom and sides of an 8 × 2½ inch spring-form cake pan with the 2 tablespoons of butter. Sprinkle the cookie crumbs evenly over the bottom and sides of the pan. Place the prepared pan in the refrigerator until you are ready to fill it.

4. Using the smallest holes on a hand grater, grate the rind from the lemon, being careful not to grate into the white membranous tissue as it is bitter. Squeeze the juice from the lemon. Set the grated rind and juice aside.

5. Preheat the oven to 325° F.

6. In a large mixing bowl, cream the drained cottage cheese with the back of a wooden spoon. Add the rum and sugar and beat them in thoroughly. Blend in the eggs one at a time.

Do not beat the mixture once the eggs have been added, otherwise they will cause the cake to puff as it bakes. When the mixture is smooth, blend in the heavy cream, and finally the grated lemon rind and lemon juice. This entire step may be done using an electric mixer on medium speed, but again, be careful not to overbeat the eggs.

7. Pour the batter into your prepared cake pan, smoothing the surface with a spatula.

8. Bake the cheesecake on the middle level of the oven for 1½ hours. The top will be a pale golden brown and light to the touch.

9. Remove the cake pan from the oven and place it on a rack to cool. During this time the cake will sink somewhat in the pan. When the cake has cooled for 3 hours, release the spring on the side of the pan and carefully remove the ring. Do not remove the bottom of the pan, but when serving, place it on an attractive cake platter for presentation. The cheesecake may be served after the cooling period, but if you prefer, it may be chilled for several hours or overnight in the refrigerator.

If fresh berries are available, surround the platter with them or spoon Strawberry Preserves (see page 133) over the cake, decorating the sides with the whole berries from the jar.

FRESH FRUIT WITH A YOGURT AND CORIANDER SAUCE

This is a delightfully refreshing dessert that can follow even the heaviest of meals. The presentation is determined by the fruits you choose, which should be of the highest quality. A general selection would consist of one or several of the following: mangoes, pineapples, pears, grapes, figs, strawberries, raspberries, peaches, plums, or any fruit that is not too highly acidic.

Do not assemble the ingredients more than an hour before serving.

Serves 4

6 cups fruit (see above)
2 teaspoons coriander seeds
2 cups Sweetened Yogurt (see below)
4 tablespoons finely chopped crystallized ginger

1. Depending upon which you have chosen, rinse, peel, hull, or pit the fruits.

If you are serving this dessert in stemmed goblets, cut the fruit into bite-size pieces. For a platter arrangement, the fruit may be left larger.

2. Toast the coriander seeds in a small skillet over low heat for 5 minutes to bring out the flavor. Grind the seeds.

3. If you are using stemmed goblets, arrange the fruit in them and top each serving with ½ cup of the sweetened yogurt. Sprinkle each with 1 tablespoon of the ginger and ½ teaspoon of the coriander.

For a platter presentation, arrange the fruit in individual groupings or in an alternating pattern, circling the platter. Place the sweetened yogurt in a small serving bowl. Sprinkle the ginger around the inside rim of the bowl and dust the surface of the yogurt with the coriander seed. Center the bowl in the middle of the serving platter and let the guests serve themselves.

Additional Serving Suggestions: When in season, garnish the dessert with sprigs of fresh mint. Also, if you are serving mangoes, heighten their flavor with a touch of freshly squeezed lemon juice and thin slices of lemon as garnish. And, freshly made cookies are always a perfect accompaniment.

SWEETENED YOGURT

Makes about 2 cups for 4 servings

4 cups Yogurt (see page 67)
4 tablespoons light, natural honey, or to taste

1. Line a sieve with cheesecloth and place it over a bowl. Add the yogurt and let it drain, refrigerated, for about 3 hours until the whey has filtered into the bowl below. With homemade yogurt you will have approximately 2 cups of thickened yogurt and 1⅓ cups of whey.

2. With a rubber spatula, scrape the thickened yogurt into a small bowl and whisk in the honey until the sauce is smooth.

3. The yogurt may be served right away or covered and refrigerated for several days. If more whey should separate from the yogurt, just whisk the sauce to smooth it.

COEUR À LA CRÈME

No commercial heavy cream or cream cheese is needed in this recipe—just delicious homemade Cottage Cheese. Do not use purchased cottage cheese, as you will corrupt the honesty of this delicate dessert.
Serves 4 to 6

1 recipe homemade whole-milk Cottage Cheese (see page 88)
3 tablespoons raspberry brandy or 2 tablespoons dark rum
½ pint Strawberry Preserves (see page 133) or 1 pint fresh strawberries
2 tablespoons powdered sugar, if you are using fresh strawberries

1. Prepare the cottage cheese through Step 5. After most of the whey has drained from the curds, bring the corners of the cheesecloth together and tie them with twine. Hang the bundle of cottage cheese, still over a bowl, in some convenient spot for 1 hour so that more whey will drain from the curds. Press on the cheesecloth occasionally to facilitate the draining.

2. Prepare the traditional heart-shaped molds for coeur à la crème.

If you are using the large mold, line it with a piece of cheesecloth large enough so that the excess fabric can be folded over the top of the mold after the cheese has been added.

If the individual molds are being used, prepare them in the same manner. If you wish to serve 6 rather than 4, the portions will be smaller, but still adequate.

3. When most of the whey has drained from the curds, scrape the curds into a small bowl and cream them with the back of a wooden spoon. Add either the raspberry brandy or the rum and blend it into the cheese.

4. Spoon the mixture into the mold or molds, small amounts at a time, making sure that there are no spaces in the cheese. Pack down the cheese as you add it and pull the cheese-cloth so that there are no folds in the fabric. When all of the cheese has been added, smooth the surface. Fold the excess fabric over the top of the cheese and press down upon it to firm the cheese. No weight is necessary. Place the mold or molds on a plate. Cover with plastic wrap and refrigerate the cheese overnight.

5. When you are ready to serve the coeur à la crème, open up the folded cheesecloth, place your dessert plate face down upon the mold, and invert the cheese onto the plate. Remove the cheesecloth. If you are using the smaller molds, invert each one onto a small plate and carefully transfer to the dessert plate.

6. The choice of preserves or fresh berries will depend upon the availability of fresh berries. If you are using strawberry preserves, simply arrange the berries with their liquid around the cheese. For individual cheeses, place a portion of the berries and some of the syrup on top of each heart.

If you are using fresh berries, rinse them very quickly and then remove the hulls. Pat dry. Place the berries in a small bowl and add the powdered sugar. Mix gently until the sugar dissolves. Arrange the fresh berries as you would the preserves.

Note: For a special presentation with the large cheese, unmold it onto a stemmed cake plate. Surround the heart with the berries. Place the cake plate upon another plate on which Almond Toast (see page 387) is arranged.

PIGNOLIA COOKIES

Over the years macaroon-based, slightly chewy Pignolia Cookies seem to have disappeared and in their place has emerged a poor flour-base substitute, short on pignolia nuts and heavy with extracts to make up for the lack of flavor. The reason, of course, for their disappearance is price, as these cookies are expensive to prepare, but the cost will be forgotten immediately upon sampling them. We use slivered almonds ordered from Sunnyland Farms (see the mail order listing) and keep them refrigerated until we need them. If you prefer to start with unskinned, whole almonds, cover them with boiling water to loosen the skins. As soon as you can handle them, take the almonds from the hot water one at a time, and pinch an end. The skin will slip off easily. Sliver each almond as it is skinned.

Makes about 40 cookies

2½ cups (½ pound) slivered almonds (see above)
1½ cups sugar
3 egg whites, at room temperature
1¼ pounds (5 cups) pignolia (pine) nuts

1. Preheat the oven to 225° F. Spread the slivered almonds on a baking sheet and toast them on the middle rack of the oven for 20 minutes. Toss them occasionally. The toasting will bring out the flavor of the nuts. Do not let them brown, but only color slightly. Remove the almonds from the oven and let them cool.

2. In a food processor fitted with the metal blade, grind the almonds to a paste. You may also use the Varco Grinder by Moulinex or a blender, but grind the almonds in small batches.

3. Place the almond paste in a mixing bowl, and using the back of a wooden spoon, work in 1 cup of the sugar until the mixture is smooth. Set aside.

4. By hand or with an electric mixer, beat the egg whites into a meringue. Once they begin to hold their shape, gradually beat in the remaining ½ cup of sugar. Continue to beat the whites until they are stiff, but not dry.

With a spatula, gradually fold the meringue into the almond paste, creating your macaroon base.

5. Turn the oven temperature to 350° F. Line two large aluminum baking sheets with kitchen parchment or aluminum foil. Do not use black steel baking sheets as the cookies will burn on the bottom.

6. Spread the pignolia nuts on a large platter. With a small metal spoon, scoop up a rounded teaspoon of the macaroon mixture. Using another metal spoon, gently push the mixture from the first spoon onto the pignolia nuts. Using both spoons, toss until you have a rounded cookie that is well coated with the pignolia nuts. Finally, place the cookie from the spoons onto one of the lined baking sheets.

Continue with more cookies, placing

them 2 inches apart on the baking sheet until the sheet is filled. The cookies will flatten out a little as they bake. If your oven is not large enough to hold the two sheets on a single rack, bake the sheets of cookies separately, forming the second when the first is almost baked.

7. Bake the cookies on the middle rack of the oven for 20 minutes. They should be a light golden brown. Remove the cookies from the parchment or foil to a wire rack to cool. (It may be necessary to peel the parchment or foil from the cookies.) When the cookies have completely cooled, store them in an airtight container. They will keep for at least a week.

ALMOND TOAST

Almond Toast is baked until it is quite dry, and will keep for several weeks, making it a perfect holiday gift that can be prepared in advance. As the toast is so dry, we prefer to use slivered almonds rather than whole almonds. If your almonds are whole and unskinned, cover them with boiling water to loosen the skins. Take each almond from the water before it cools and pinch an end. The skin will slip off easily. Sliver each almond as it is skinned.

Makes about 30 toasts

> 2½ cups (½ pound) slivered almonds (see above)
> 2 cups all-purpose, unbleached flour
> 1½ teaspoons baking powder
> ¼ pound unsalted butter
> 1 cup sugar
> 1 teaspoon vanilla extract
> 2 eggs, at room temperature

1. Preheat the oven to 225° F.

2. Spread the slivered almonds on a baking sheet and toast them on the middle rack of the oven for 20 minutes. Toss them occasionally. The toasting will bring out the flavor of the almonds. Do not let them brown, but only color slightly. Set aside.

3. Turn the oven temperature up to 400°F.

4. Sift the flour and baking powder together. Set aside.

5. Prepare the batter. You may do this in a mixing bowl, using a wooden spoon, or in an electric mixer. Cream the butter. When the butter is smooth, blend in the sugar. When the mixture is creamy and light, add the vanilla and then the eggs, one at a time.

Gradually add the flour and baking powder, beating the batter until it is smooth. Stir the almonds into the batter by hand, mixing them in thoroughly.

6. Line a large aluminum baking sheet (approximately 14×17 inches) with either kitchen parchment or aluminum foil.

Spoon the batter onto the lined baking sheet, creating 2 lengthwise strips, 12 × 2½ inches. Leave at least 3 inches of space between the strips. Smooth their surfaces, using the back of a spoon or a spatula. If the strips stand taller than 1½ inches, flatten them.

7. Bake the strips on the middle rack of the oven for 15 minutes. They will color lightly during this time, but will still be soft to the touch. With a wide spatula, remove the strips to a rack to cool for about 10 minutes.

8. Lower the oven temperature to 300°F.

9. Using a serrated knife, cut the cooled strips crosswise into ¾-inch toast. Remove the liner from the baking sheet and place the toast back on the sheet. Leave an inch or so of space between the toasts.

Bake for another 25 to 30 minutes, turning the toast every 10 minutes so that they are golden brown on all sides. Place the toast back on the rack to cool and dry completely before serving or storing. Store in an airtight container.

PECAN PIE

We felt something so completely Southern as Pecan Pie could use a little Southern whiskey, so we have laced our pie with bourbon. This pie is so inordinately rich that it should serve a dozen people, but it probably won't. At most, figure on 8 servings.

Serves 6 to 8

3 eggs, at room temperature
1 cup light brown sugar
1 cup dark corn syrup
2 tablespoons bourbon
1½ cups broken pecan pieces (do not chop)
1 Basic Pie Shell (see next page), partially baked and cooled
½ cup pecan halves

1. Preheat the oven to 350°F.

2. In a mixing bowl, beat the eggs until they are light. Whisk in the sugar, corn syrup, and bourbon. When the mixture is smooth, fold in the pecan pieces.

3. Spread the mixture evenly in the prepared pie shell. Arrange the pecan halves on top so that the surface of the pie is covered.

4. Bake the pie on the middle level of the oven for 45 minutes or until a knife inserted into the center of the pie comes out clean.

5. Cool the pie on a rack before removing it from the pie plate or before cutting it. Serve at room temperature.

BASIC PIE SHELL

You may use a regular brand of all-purpose, unbleached flour for this pie shell or you may vary the flours. Our favorite is to combine ¾ cup of a regular brand and ¾ cup of the unbleached white flour from Walnut Acres (see the mail-order listings). Not all of the bran is removed from this flour so the pie shell has a delicate golden color, plus superior flavor. You may also use whole-wheat flour as half of the flour mixture.

Makes one 9-inch pie shell

1½ cups flour (see above)
2 tablespoons sugar
½ teaspoon salt
½ cup cold, unsalted butter (if mixing in a food processor, use
      frozen butter)
3 to 4 tablespoons iced water

1. Prepare the pastry dough either on your work surface (preferably marble) or in a food processor. We feel one method works as quickly and well as the other.

2. *If making the dough by hand*, measure out the flour onto your work surface and sprinkle it with the sugar and salt. Cut the *cold* butter into ¼-inch cubes and add to the flour mixture.

Using only one hand, rub the butter and flour together between your fingers until the mixture resembles coarse meal. Work as rapidly as possible so that the butter does not soften. It is useful to keep a metal scraper in the other hand to gather up the dough as you work, cutting in the butter as you do so.

Pour 3 tablespoons of the iced water over the surface and mix the dough quickly to incorporate the water. If the dough seems to crumble, add the remaining 1 tablespoon of water.

Gather the dough into a ball and flatten it into a thick pancake, 6 inches in diameter.

Wrap the dough in a sheet of waxed paper and then in a piece of plastic wrap. Refrigerate for 1 hour before rolling it out. The dough will not look smooth at this point, but it will after refrigeration.

If you wish to make the pastry dough in a food processor, add the flour, sugar, salt, *frozen* butter (cut into ¼-inch slices), and 3 tablespoons of the water to the work bowl, which has been fitted with the metal blade. Process with several On/Off motions for a few seconds to mix and then continue to process until the dough forms a ball. The entire processing time will be only 10 to 12 seconds.

Flatten the ball of dough into a thick pancake, 6 inches in diameter. Wrap in waxed paper, then in plastic wrap and refrigerate for 1 hour before rolling out the dough.

3. Try to roll out the pastry dough after an hour's refrigeration. If it becomes too cold, it will be difficult to roll out. If it is very chilled, let the dough warm at room temperature for 10 minutes or so before attempting to roll it out.

4. Lightly flour your work surface and proceed to roll out the dough, giving it a quarter turn after each roll. Always roll from the center of the dough to the outside, never back and forth. Continue to roll the dough until you have a circle approximately ⅛-inch thick and 14 inches in diameter. If the dough sticks to your work surface as you roll, gently lift it up and lightly flour the work surface.

5. Fold the circle of dough in half and carefully place it in an ungreased 9-inch pie plate so that when it is unfolded, it will be evenly centered on the plate. Unfold the dough and press it down into the bottom of the plate, the sides, and up over the edge.

With a pair of kitchen shears, trim away the excess dough, leaving ½ inch of dough extending from the rim of the plate. Fold this ½ inch of dough under the rest of the dough so that the pie shell extends just to the rim of the plate. Crimp the edge of the dough between your thumb and index finger to form a pattern.

6. Our pie recipes call for partially baked pie shells. *To partially bake the shell*, preheat the oven to 400°F. Prick the bottom of the pie shell with a fork in a dozen or so places. Loosely fit a piece of aluminum foil that has been lightly buttered (to prevent it from sticking) onto the shell. Place several handfuls of dried beans or aluminum pellets on the foil. This will keep the shell from puffing up as it bakes.

Bake on the middle level of the oven for 10 minutes. Remove the foil and beans or pellets and bake for another 2 to 3 minutes until the pie shell is very lightly colored. Let the pie shell cool before adding the filling.

If you wish to make a fully baked pie shell, proceed as above, but let the shell bake for 10 minutes instead of 2 or 3 after the foil and beans or pellets have been removed. The shell should be lightly browned. Again, let the shell cool before filling it.

TATTY'S BUTTERMILK PIE

Like the Pecan Pie, this very sweet Southern favorite should serve more guests than it actually does. It is just so delicious everyone usually wants more than a slim piece.

Serves 6

½ cup unsalted butter, at room temperature
1½ cups sugar
3 eggs, at room temperature
3 tablespoons flour
1 cup Buttermilk (see page 96)
2 tablespoons dark rum
1 teaspoon grated lemon rind
1 Basic Pie Shell (see page 389), partially baked and cooled

1. Preheat the oven to 350°F.

2. In a mixing bowl, cream the butter and sugar

together using the back of a wooden spoon. Add the eggs, one at a time, incorporating each into the creamed butter and sugar before adding the next. When the mixture is smooth, blend in the flour. Add the buttermilk, rum, and lemon rind. Mix thoroughly.

3. Pour the filling into the prepared pie shell and bake on the middle level of the oven for 45

to 50 minutes. The center of the pie filling should feel firm when pressed. A knife inserted into the center does not give an indication, as the pie will become more solid as it cools.

4. Allow the pie to cool on a rack before removing it from the pie plate or before cutting it. Serve at room temperature.

BELLE SHERRILL'S JAM CAKE

Grandmother Belle and Grandfather Jesse Sherrill had eight children as well as many other relatives, so the original recipe made an enormous cake. We have cut down on the amounts without sacrificing the quality of the cake. Even so, it is still a large, rich cake and should be served in thin slices. It will keep for weeks in the refrigerator or can be frozen. If possible, grind the spices freshly. The Moulinex grinder (see the mail-order listing page) accomplishes this and there is a notable difference in freshness. Serve it with lightly whipped cream that has been sweetened with powdered sugar.

Serves 20 or more

> 5 eggs
> 1½ cups Monnuka raisins
> 3 cups all-purpose, unbleached flour
> 1 teaspoon ground cinnamon
> 1 teaspoon ground nutmeg
> 1 teaspoon ground cloves
> 1 teaspoon ground mace
> ¾ pound unsalted butter, at room temperature
> 1½ cups sugar
> 1½ teaspoons baking soda
> 4 teaspoons Buttermilk (see page 96)
> 1½ cups homemade Strawberry Jam (see page 135) or 2 jars of a
>   good-quality purchased jam (blackberry is excellent), each 12
>   ounces

1. In a small bowl, beat the eggs. Add the raisins and let them plump for ½ hour or so.

2. Into another small bowl, sift the flour with the cinnamon, nutmeg, cloves, and mace.

3. With a wooden spoon, cream the butter and sugar in a large mixing bowl. You may do this in the bowl of an electric mixer. Add the egg and raisin mixture alternately with the sifted flour and spices to the creamed butter and sugar. The batter will be very thick, so unless your mixer is powerful, you may have to do this by hand.

4. When the ingredients are well blended, mix together the baking soda and buttermilk in a small bowl and add them to the batter. Stir in the jam and mix thoroughly. The batter will be manageable at this point.

5. Spoon the batter into an ungreased 9½ × 3½-inch tube pan. Smooth the surface of the batter.

6. Do *not* preheat the oven. Place the cake on the middle rack of the oven and, at the same time, set the oven at 350°F. Bake for 1½ hours or so, until a cake tester inserted into the cake comes out clean.

If after 1 hour the surface of the cake seems to be browning too quickly, lightly cover it with a piece of foil.

7. Remove the cake from the oven and let it cool for 10 minutes in the pan. To remove from the tube pan, run a small knife around the outside edges of the cake and around the tube. Place a cake rack on top of the tube pan and invert the cake onto the rack.

If it does not lift off easily, very carefully run your small knife around the bottom of the tube pan to remove it. If the cake has not been damaged in removing it from the tube pan, consider it right side up. If it has been damaged, invert it again onto another rack and consider that the top of the cake. Let the cake cool completely before attempting to slice it.

QUICK CRANBERRY RELISH

Our relish retains the texture and tartness of the cranberries as the cooking time is minimal. The ginger and citrus in the Tomato Marmalade combine perfectly with the cranberries. If you do not have your home-canned marmalade, use any purchased marmalade of a good quality. Besides being delicious with a holiday bird, this relish goes well spread on the Jam and Carrot Cake in this chapter, or the Pumpkin Cake (see page 377).

Makes about 4 cups

> **3 cups fresh cranberries (12 ounces)**
> **1 cup Tomato Marmalade (see page 141) or a good purchased brand**
> **1 cup water**
> **1 cup raisins, preferably Monnuka**

1. Rinse the cranberries under cold water, discarding any stems or berries that are soft. Drain.

2. Over medium-high heat, bring the marmalade and water to a boil in a 1½-quart covered saucepan. Add the raisins. Return to a

boil and cook for a minute or so until the raisins begin to plump.

3. Add the cranberries and continue to boil, uncovered, for 7 minutes. Stir occasionally with a wooden spoon. The berries should all pop during this time. If not, pop them against the side of the saucepan with the wooden spoon.

4. Cool the relish and transfer it to glass containers and refrigerate. If you are planning to give the relish as gifts, use decorative jars or pots. It will keep in the refrigerator for 1 month.

CARROT CAKE

This Carrot Cake is so rich it needs no icing.
Serves 20 or more

> 1 cup raisins, preferably Monnuka
> 1 cup light, natural honey
> 1 cup corn oil
> 3 eggs
> 1 pound (2 cups) finely grated carrots, tightly packed
> 3 cups all-purpose, unbleached flour
> 1 teaspoon ground cinnamon
> 1 teaspoon ground cloves
> 1 teaspoon freshly grated nutmeg
> 2 teaspoons baking powder
> ½ teaspoon baking soda
> 1 cup coarsely chopped pecans

1. Place the raisins in a large mixing bowl. Add the honey and oil. Mix and let stand for ½ hour so the raisins will plump.

2. Beat the eggs well and add them along with the carrots to the raisin mixture. Mix thoroughly.

3. Preheat the oven to 350°F.

4. In a separate bowl, sift together the flour, cinnamon, cloves, nutmeg, baking powder, and baking soda. One cup at a time, add the sifted dry ingredients to the carrot and raisin mixture, blending well with each addition. Make sure the raisins are distributed evenly. When all the dry ingredients have been well incorporated, fold in the pecans.

5. Spoon the batter into an ungreased 9 x 3½-inch tube pan. Smooth the surface of the batter.

6. Bake on the middle rack of the oven for 1¼ hours or until a cake tester inserted into the middle of the cake comes out clean. Remove from the oven and let cool for 10 minutes before removing from the tube pan.

7. To remove from the tube pan, run a small knife around the edges of the pan and around the tube. Place a cake rack or plate on top of the tube pan and invert so the cake falls onto the rack or plate. To turn the cake right side up, place another rack on the cake and again invert. Let the cake cool completely before cutting into thin slices.

A CHESTNUT HORS D'OEUVRE

As an alternative to roasted chestnuts during the holiday season, serve these spicy morsels. They keep well for 4 or 5 days in a tightly covered container, and therefore make an unexpected and pleasureful gift for those who are ardent about chestnuts. We gather our Chinese chestnuts in September and store them, unshelled, in the refrigerator for use throughout the winter. If you are purchasing your chestnuts, we would advise that you prepare them right away as sometimes the shipped chestnuts do not keep well.

Makes about 3 cups

> ¾ pound fresh, unshelled chestnuts
> 2 tablespoons corn oil
> ½ teaspoon coarse salt (kosher or freshly ground sea salt)
> 1 teaspoon freshly ground dried hot red pepper (or less, according to taste)

1. With a small, sharp knife, make a tiny, lengthwise slit on the shell of each chestnut, being careful not to damage the nut itself. Place the chestnuts in a 2½-quart saucepan and cover them with water.

Cover the saucepan and bring the water to a boil over medium-high heat. Lower the heat and simmer the chestnuts for only 12 minutes.

2. Remove the saucepan from the heat. Allow them to cool slightly and as soon as you are able to handle them, remove the chestnuts one at a time and peel them either with your fingers or the small knife, removing the shell and skin attached to each nut. The chestnuts will be easy to peel as long as they remain somewhat hot in the water.

Work as quickly as you can, but if the water should cool and the chestnuts become difficult to peel, return them to the stove and bring the water back to a simmer for just a few seconds. Be careful that you do not overcook the chestnuts, as they must remain whole and crunchy.

3. When all of the chestnuts have been peeled, place the corn oil in a 10-inch skillet over medium-high heat. Add the chestnuts and sprinkle them with the salt and hot red pepper. With two wooden spoons, toss the chestnuts constantly for 3 to 5 minutes until they be-

come golden brown. (We like them even a little charred, so often we will increase the heat to high for a minute or so.)

4. With a slotted spatula, remove the chestnuts to paper towels to drain. They may be served immediately while they are still hot or later at room temperature. Do not store them until they have completely cooled.

AND IN OUR GARDEN

We find it impossible to stay out of the garden. So, even in December when nothing is growing, there are still tasks we find to do: more tidying, reshaping our beds, and always, burying the compost material from the house. We also start saving the leakproof, plastic trays in which supermarket vegetables are often packaged. These trays can be used to hold Jiffy-7 Peat Pellets when we begin to seed them in February.

DOG BISCUITS

Even if we had a sign in front of our house stating "No More Cats Need Apply" our fearless family of felines probably would continue to increase. The number we have now makes it impossible for us to have dogs, so we must go visiting in order to share their companionship. At holiday time we always come with a gift we know they will enjoy.

These healthy, "all-natural" dog biscuits are truly fun to give to our dog friends, who respond with much surprise and delight. Their owners also are elated and try to snitch a few for themselves as they smell so good. However, they are disappointed, as the biscuits, although wonderful for a dog's, are very hard for human teeth. We like to give them as inexpensive holiday gifts, arranged in a decorative box with tissue or in little baskets. The dog biscuit cutter may be included as well as our recipe. Several dog biscuit cutters are sold, but we made our own by cutting down a coffee tin with a pair of metal clippers. We first removed the bottom of the tin and cut the tin down to a 1-inch-high circle. With a pair of pliers, we shaped the circle into the form of a dog biscuit. Actually, you do not need a cutter, as the dough is so dense it may be cut freehand with a knife.

Makes about sixteen, 3½-inch-long biscuits

2 cups whole-wheat flour
½ cup yellow cornmeal
1 teaspoon finely minced garlic
¼ cup freshly grated Romano cheese
1 egg
¼ cup plus 1 teaspoon corn oil
½ cup whey

1. Preheat the oven to 350°F.

2. In a mixing bowl, blend the whole-wheat

flour, cornmeal, garlic, and cheese together.

3. In another small bowl, beat the egg with ¼ cup of the corn oil and the whey. Pour the mixture into the dry ingredients and stir with a fork until well blended. With your hands, scoop out the dough onto your unfloured work surface and knead just enough to form a ball.

4. Roll the dough to a thickness of about ⅓ inch. The dough will not be very cooperative, so press it with your hands, if necessary. Cut the biscuits with a cutter or a small knife.

As the biscuits are cut, place them on an aluminum baking sheet that has been oiled with the remaining 1 teaspoon of corn oil. Gather up the scraps of dough and roll and cut the biscuits until all of the dough has been used. Since the work surface is not floured, you may need to use a spatula to remove the biscuits. If the biscuits should break when you do this, just press them back into shape.

5. When all of the biscuits have been cut, bake them on the middle rack of the oven for 30 minutes.

WHAT TO BUY OR ORDER NOW

We do very little mail ordering during December so we are using this space to recommend three magazines for the gardener and cook. Even if you have no garden, all these magazines should be of interest, as all contain food sections and excellent articles that will increase your knowledge of what you are eating. Order your subscriptions early in December so that your first issues, with luck, will arrive with the new year.

Blair & Ketchum's Country Journal, Subscription Center, P.O. Box 2405, Boulder, Colorado 80321. One year subscription (12 issues): $15.
Horticulture, Subscription Department, 125 Garden Street, Marion, Ohio 43306. One year subscription (12 issues): $14.
Organic Gardening, Organic Park, Emmaus, Pennsylvania 18099. One year subscription (12 issues): $10.

6. Remove the baked biscuits from the baking sheet and place them on a wire rack to cool completely. The biscuits will keep for weeks, if stored in an airtight container.

Mail-Order
Sources
and Index

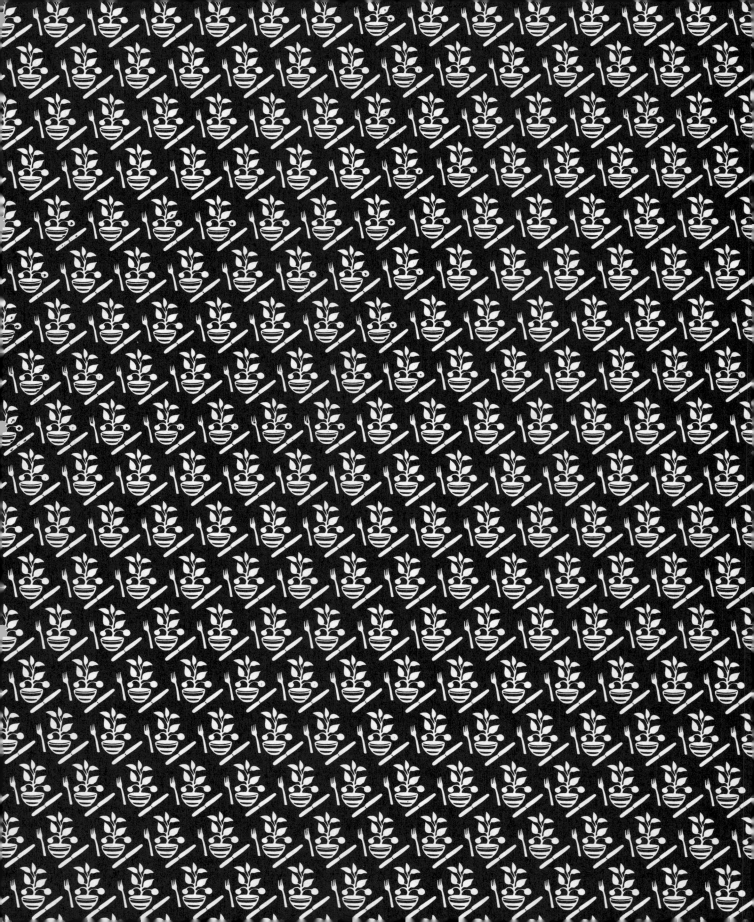

MAIL-ORDER SOURCES

We have a special fondness for all of our mail-order sources, some of whom we have ordered from for over 15 years. They are all very reliable and swift to handle orders. So swift that sometimes we will receive a telephone order within three days. We also want to thank the United Parcel Service and our local post office for facilitating the arrivals of our precious packages.

We have by no means listed all of the items available from our sources, but only the items that are of particular interest to us or are needed for our recipes.

FOODS

Aphrodisia
28 Carmine Street
New York, New York 10014
(212) 989-6440

Catalog: $2.50

This is our favorite source for herbs and spices such as wild thyme, black caraway seeds, mustard seeds, peppercorns, dried whole chili peppers, and chia seeds. They also have fresh ginger root, crystallized ginger, mustards, French wine vinegars, chutneys, pignolia nuts, and Indian, Chinese, and Indonesian food specialties.

Casa Moneo
210 West 14th Street
New York, New York 10014
(212) 929-1644

Catalog: $2.00

Dozens of peppers, mild to fiery, canned and dried, can be ordered from here. This shop carries a full line of specialty items for Spanish and Mexican cooking.

Cheese Junction
One West Ridgewood Avenue
Ridgewood, New Jersey 07450
(201) 445-9210

Free Catalog

Most of our cheeses are ordered from here. The prices are reasonable with discounts for bulk orders. The cheeses are cut to order, wrapped first in plastic wrap and then in heavy paper. Each package of cheese is labeled with its name, weight, and price. We recommend especially the Canada Black Diamond Cheddar, aged Colby, Explorateur, Brie, Italian Fontina, Swiss Gruyère, feta, and string cheese.

J. A. Demonchaux Company
827 North Kansas
Topeka, Kansas 66608
(913) 235-8502

Free Catalog

This is the place for French specialties: mustards, olive oil, wine vinegar, coarse and fine sea salt, flageolet beans (canned and dried), couscous, and fine honeys.

Manganaro Foods
488 Ninth Avenue
New York, New York 10018
(212) LO 3-5331

Free Catalog

The foods we order from this friendly store are so delicious that we begin eating as we unpack: all Italian cheeses, pancetta, roasted peppers, ripe and green olives by the pound, Genoa (Genova) tuna packed in olive oil, Bertolli olive oil (our favorite cooking oil), canned tomatoes, wine vinegars, 500 different dried pasta products, and some kitchen equipment.

Maytag Dairy Farms
Rural Route 1, Box 806
Newton, Iowa 50208
(515) 792-1133

Free Catalog

The colorful catalog describes how their fine blue cheese is made. The cheese is available in 1-, 4-, and 8-ounce wedges and 2- and 4-pound wheels.

Moose Lake Wild Rice Company
Box 325
Deer River, Minnesota 56636
(218) 246-8143

Free Brochure

This company generally has the lowest prices

and the choicest long-grain wild rice.

H. Roth and Son
1577 First Avenue
New York, New York 10028
(212) RE 4-1111

Free Catalog

This store was a favorite of ours for shopping when we lived in New York. Their mail-order department is just as reliable. We order: herbs, teas and spices (especially their paprika), fresh ginger root, nuts, dried fruits, sesame tahini; buckwheat, chickpea, rye, and semolina flours. They offer specialties for Hungarian, Brazilian, Chinese, Indonesian, and Dutch cooking.

Sunnyland Farms
Albany, Georgia 31703
(912) 883-3085

Free Catalog

This company offers the finest pecans, available in the shell, shelled and sorted according to size. There are special rates for bulk orders. We order the extra-fancy large pecan pieces for Pesto. Sunnyland Farms has dozens of other excellent nuts, both raw and roasted.

The Vermont Country Store
Weston, Vermont 05161
(802) 824-6932

Free Catalog

We order their delicious 3-pound wheel of Vermont Cheddar cheese, old-fashioned Common and Seafood crackers, honey, mustards, and stone-ground whole grains. Their cheesecloth, sold by the yard, is the finest in the world. The catalog contains hundreds of old-time items. The English Dinkie Knives are little gems.

Walnut Acres
Penns Creek, Pennsylvania 17862
(717) 837-3874

Free Catalog

Everything from Walnut Acres is of the freshest and highest quality. Many of the vegetables, fruits, and grains are grown on their farm. We recommend their grits (yellow corn), flours, yeast, yellow cornmeal, baking powder, brown rice, dried beans, sesame tahini, seeds for sprouting, dried pastas, dried fruits (the enormous prunes and Monnuka raisins are unequaled for excellence), and Wildflower honey. They have sprouting equipment and the Varco Grinder made by Moulinex.

Williams-Sonoma
Mail Order Department
P. O. Box 3792
San Francisco, California 94119
(415) 652-1515

$1 for 4 seasonal catalogs

Better known for their equipment, Williams-Sonoma has some very fine food items: huge shallots from France, garlic braids, superb vinegars including raspberry; French olive, walnut, hazelnut, and almond oils, semolina flour, Maldon sea salt from England, and 10-pound bars of baking chocolate.

EQUIPMENT

Brookstone
5 Vose Farm Road
Peterborough, New Hampshire 03458
(603) 924-7181

Free Catalog

Along with gift items, this company sells kitchen equipment: teak trivets that can be used as bread racks, earthen bakeware, the Moulinex food mill, black steel baking sheets, loaf pans and deep-dish pizza pans, plate warmers, and Madeleine tins in 2 sizes.

W. Atlee Burpee Company
300 Park Avenue
Warminster, Pennsylvania 18991
(215) 674-4900

Free Catalog; Harvest Catalog

In addition to the garden catalog, Burpee publishes their *Harvest Catalog* with a full line of canning and preserving equipment, including French canning jars. This catalog also has garden equipment with wooden harvest and berry baskets.

The Country Loft
South Shore Park
Hingham, Massachusetts 02043
(617) 749-7766

Free Catalog

The Loft is our favorite source for inexpensive tins, baskets, bread racks, and jars. These are used to hold homemade gifts during the holidays. Not inexpensive, their reproduction of a Shaker Spice Keeper is an extremely handsome item.

The Crate and Barrel
195 Northfield Road
Northfield, Illinois 60093
(312) 446-2100

Free Catalog

This company, with stores in the Chicago and Boston areas, offers many intriguing items not found in other catalogs: unusual baskets and trays, bottles, tins, and handpainted earthenware plates from France. In addition, they have wine vinegars, French jams, beautiful copper cookware, Calphalon cookware, and baking stones.

Garden Way
Charlotte, Vermont 05445
(802) 425-2121

Free Catalog

Garden Way has an extensive selection of items for canning, freezing, and preserving, including the steam canner, graniteware blancher (the Everything Pot), aluminum funnel, and the helpful Tomato Core-It. Another section of the catalog pertains to gardening with a full line of tools. Other items they sell include sprouting lids with screens, wooden half-bushel and bushel harvest baskets, and wonderful dried fruits.

Kitchen Bazaar
4455 Connecticut Avenue N.W.
Washington, D.C. 20008
(202) 363-4625

Free Catalog

Kitchen Bazaar, with retail stores in the Washington area, has a full selection of cooking equipment and there are often excellent sales on Le Creuset and Copco cookware and expensive appliances. Their equipment includes all major brands.

H. Roth and Son
1577 First Avenue
New York, New York 10028
(212) RE 4-1111

Free Catalog

In addition to all the food items, H. Roth and Son features many useful pieces of kitchen equipment: scales, grinders, sausage equipment, graters, cutters, tins, and baking sheets for every purpose.

The Sausage Maker
177 Military Road
Buffalo, New York 14207
(716) 876-5521

Free Catalog

Rytek Kutas has everything for sausage-making, including his own book. The lively and fascinating catalog is filled with information. Mr. Kutas has the natural hog casings we prefer, plus bungs, rounds, casings with knitting, and stockinettes for hams. Equipment includes professional knives, sausage stuffers, and meat grinders.

Williams-Sonoma
Mail Order Department
P. O. Box 3792
San Francisco, California 94119
(415) 652-1515

$1 for 4 seasonal catalogs

Williams-Sonoma always has the latest equipment and information on it. Their selection of cookware is as complete as one could hope for. Several items we recommend for our recipes are the pasta equipment, semolina flour, the Pizza Brick for pizza and breads, or the baking tiles, all the baking pans and sheets, the garlic press by Zyliss of Switzerland, and the Pop-Up Sponges for cleaning. There are seven retail stores across the country, with one to be opened in New York.

GARDENING SUPPLIES

HERBS

Hemlock Hill Herb Farm
Hemlock Hill Road
Litchfield, Connecticut 06759
(203) 567-5031

Catalog: $.50

The owner of this herb farm, Dorothy Childs Hogner, is the author of numerous books on growing herbs and gardening. The service and herb plants are first rate.

The Sandy Mush Herb Nursery
Route 2, Surrett Cove Road
Leicester, North Carolina 28748
(704) 683-2014

Catalog: $1, refundable with order

The beautiful catalog is filled with lovely drawings and information about herbs. It contains illustrated plans for herb gardens, recipes and a lengthy listing of available herbs. They ship small Sweet Bay trees.

Taylor's Herb Gardens
1535 Lone Oak Road
Vista, California 92083
(714) 727-3485

Free Catalog

The plants are of an excellent quality and carefully packaged for travel. The listing is extensive and the catalog contains a guide for companion planting. Taylor's also has Bay trees.

SEEDS, PLANTS, AND SUPPLIES

As many of the seed companies sell the same varieties, we are listing only varieties we grow that are exclusive with a particular company or are of special interest to us. All of the catalogs are filled with valuable information for the gardener and the cook.

W. Atlee Burpee Company
300 Park Avenue
Warminster, Pennsylvania 18991
(215) 674-4900

Free Catalog; Seed Catalog

Seeds and plants, bush fava beans, Burpee Hybrid Chinese cabbage, Supersteak Hybrid VFN tomatoes, Burpee's Sugar Sweet corn, Green Ice loosehead lettuce, Royal Oak Leaf loosehead lettuce, Bell Boy Hybrid sweet pepper, gardening and canning equipment.

Comstock, Ferre & Company
263 Main Street
Wethersfield, Connecticut 06109
(203) 529-3319

Free Catalog

Seeds only, varieties are notated with recommendations for areas to be grown, Chinese cabbages, Corn Salad (mache), Turnip broccoli (rapa), finocchio (fennel), gardening supplies, herbs, and accessories for potpourri.

J. A. Demonchaux Company
827 North Kansas
Topeka, Kansas 66608
(913) 235-8502

Free Catalog

Unusual seeds from France, Corn Salad (mache), flageolet beans, Chicory Witloof

(French endive), cardoon, sorrel, shallots, Baby Nantes carrots, Long Black radishes, rocket (roquette).

Gurney's Seed & Nursery Company
Yankton, South Dakota 57079
(605) 665-1671

Free Catalog

Seeds and plants, Lady Finger potato tubers, Jerusalem artichoke tubers, rhubarb plants, jicama, elephant garlic, garden and canning supplies.

Hastings
434 Marietta Street N.W.
P. O. Box 4274
Atlanta, Georgia 30302
(404) 524-8861

Free Catalog

Specialists in items for the Southern garden, okra, corn, "greens," field peas, nut and fruit trees, seeds and equipment for sprouts, gardening and canning supplies, planting guide.

Horticultural Enterprises
P. O. Box 340082
Dallas, Texas 75234
No phone number could be found

Free Brochure

Seeds for peppers, jicama, some unusual herbs and tomatoes. Bright yellow brochure with drawings and descriptions of the peppers: Colorado, Pasilla, Anaheim, jalapeño, and cayenne.

Johnny's Selected Seeds
Albion, Maine 04910
(207) 437-4301

Free Catalog

Specialists in seeds for the northern garden. Detailed catalog with photographs of the farm.

They feature a Seed Swap. Large selection of beans, including adzuki and mung, scorzonera (Black salsify), farm seed, including grain amaranth. Equipment and supplies.

George W. Park Seed Company
P. O. Box 31
Greenwood, South Carolina 29647
(803) 374-3341

Free Catalog

Large and complete selection of seeds and plants, seeds for sprouting, vegetable spaghetti, top-quality fruit. For a tall curly-leaved parsley, order Paramount. Gardening equipment and supplies.

R. H. Shumway
P. O. Box 777   628 Cedar Street
Rockford, Illinois 61105
(815) 964-7243

Free Catalog

Full selection of seeds and plants. A large catalog that is well illustrated with photographs and drawings. Elephant garlic, Luffa sponge seeds, decorative corn and popcorn, gardening and canning supplies, wholesale catalog for bulk buyers.

Smith & Hawken
68 Homer
Palo Alto, California 94301
(415) 324-1587

Free Catalog

Beautifully crafted garden tools. The tools shown on the cover look more like sculptures than tools, they are so exquisite. The catalog is a delight throughout, with detailed line drawings and excellent information about tools and their care.

Stokes Seeds
737 Main Street Box 548
Buffalo, New York 14240
(416) 688-4300

Free Catalog

Full selection of seeds with a special selection of Chinese vegetables, dozens of varieties of cucumbers, large section with garden supplies, and some canning equipment.

Thompson & Morgan
P. O. Box 100
Farmingdale, New Jersey 07727
(201) 929-0028

Free Catalog

This firm, based in England, sells worldwide and features varieties not to be found elsewhere: special shallots and onions, Shiitake mushrooms, Romanesco broccoli, Chinese and Oriental vegetables, seeds and equipment for sprouts.

Vermont Bean Seed Company
Garden Lane
Bomoseen, Vermont 05732
(802) 265-4212

Free Catalog

Charming catalog, listing every bean imaginable, many exclusives: Thomas' Famous White Dutch Runner, beans for shelling and drying, Jacob's Cattle beans, chickpeas, flageolet, Vermont cranberry, peas, corn, squash, seeds for sprouting, and garden supplies.

Wayside Gardens
Hodges, South Carolina 29695
(803) 374-3387

Catalog: $2, refundable with order

Noted mainly for extraordinary ornamental trees and shrubs, the lavish catalog has fine herb plants and fruits. The Sequoia strawberries are unequaled for sweetness.

White Flower Farm
Litchfield, Connecticut 06759
(203) 567-0801

Catalog: The Garden Book plus 3 issues of "Notes," $5, refundable with order.

The detailed *Garden Book*, featuring exceptional flowers, bulbs, and shrubs, is filled with general garden information, herb plants, Fraises des Bois "Charles V" strawberries, baskets, and tools.

INDEX